IN THE RED

Another day at the 'coalface'.

In the Red

by

J.T. Kingsley

The Pentland Press Limited
Edinburgh · Cambridge · Durham · USA

First published in 2000 by
The Pentland Press Ltd.
1 Hutton Close
South Church
Bishop Auckland
Durham

British Library Cataloguing in Publication Data.
A catalogue record for this book is available
from the British Library.

ISBN 1 85821 754 7

Typeset by George Wishart & Associates, Whitley Bay.
Printed and bound by Bookcraft (Bath) Ltd.

Contents

Illustrations

Foreword

I AM HONOURED to have been asked by Terry to write this Foreword to *In the Red*. Having read the draft for his massive story, I am totally amazed at the depth and accuracy of his recall. If nothing else, I am most grateful for his updating of my mind with facts and figures of some forty years ago that are normally now only a blurred memory to me.

Terry was and is a pilot's pilot – always at the sharp end and with a brain to match his piloting abilities throughout his career.

Terry and I first met in the late 1950s at Royal Air Force Benson with the Overseas Ferry Wing. Terry's description of his tour with that unit is not only excellent, but brings a little-known RAF activity to the reader, including the fact that RAF pilots delivered all but one (and that by Hugh Merewether of Hawkers) of the initial order of 160 Hunters to the Indian Air Force.

As for the Red Arrows, Terry was a totally dedicated and responsible member of the team with the big picture and the Air Force at heart. Of course, his flying was superb. I feel privileged to be part of that 'Band of Brothers' and to have been associated with Terry now for so long, always at 'full throttle' and never less than 101 per cent!

Ray Hanna

Introduction/Author's Note

I AM SOMETIMES ASKED how my wife put up with all of this, and I usually reply that she is a good Air Force wife. The risks may not have been quantified nor the rewards identified, but raising the children and seeking out a balance was her choice.

She could be accused of living in my shadow, but there is no argument if you share the rewards and she feels fulfilled in the massive part of the deal, that of raising a family and providing a stable home life.

She knew that I would always make it home, unless my body parts could not be assembled in one room, and I guess, but do not know, that her vision was that I would succeed. It was my job to take the bullet and I did, and that means shouldering responsibility, a dirty word in today's society.

I have no wish to skirt the obvious stresses and strains that 'risk' in all its forms brings. I never denigrated the massive job of running a home and raising children with absent fathers, a point the strident women's libbers might bridle about. She is insistent that her part of the equation was her choice, and thank you very much, but I do not wish to be a soldier or Chief Executive anywhere. She does not feel diminished in any way, and retirement after what we have done is a welcome circumstance.

Do it again, yes. Same again is a useless introspection, because you cannot unlearn life's teachings. However I would get going earlier, with better braking for the hazards and be on the gas earlier on the exits.

Acknowledgements

SUCH A JOURNEY through aviation could only be completed with the help and guidance of the many masters of aeronautics that I have been lucky to meet. They know who they are, and most of their knowledge kept me alive.

From the earliest days, Mac, Muzika, Ken A, the Pembrey Air Force, THE BOSS, Les B, Jak T, Ray H, Doc W, Shirley H, definitely not Pete S, but Mickey S, Wally E, Dinger B, Ralph C, Roy B, Pete E, Frank H, Ian D, Bill L, John Mitch, Don M and Dave N.

Raunno, Paddy and Tony and the BLMH gang, for all the roadcraft.

Chapter I

THE FIRST DAYS OF January 1955 were cold and seasonable. My parents waved an emotional goodbye from Nottingham station, and until they were lost to sight, the impact of what was happening did not strike me.

Years of waiting, marking time for just this moment and I had accepted, not prepared for the occasion. Then, what did I know, could possibly know, straight from school where I had endured the slings and arrows of staff and schoolmates alike. What was it they said, 'Oh yes, you want to fly' as if such a long-held goal was a sign of infirmity. Well here we were, with the plan unfolding, not quite as expected, for I had wasted most of the summer awaiting the answer from the Fleet Air Arm.

The Aircrew selection for the Navy had been fierce, and I felt proud to be in at the finish, sort of justification that my chosen profession was going to be a good choice for me. When I contemplated the competition, the son of a South African Navy Captain, who had many hours of flying under his belt, there seemed to be little chance that the over 100 candidates, slimmed down to just him and I, would result in the offer of a commission for me. And so it was to be, but that delay stopped a seventeen-year-old from becoming among the youngest ever commissioned in the RAF, post war.

The war environment was ever with us, I knew every fighter pilot and every aircraft that had been our recent history, and the grinding Korean conflict was still much in my mind. Not that my family was military, far from it, my father was graded unfit by virtue of ulcers, and a distant relative had served in the Great War.

Nottingham High School was a severe educational establishment – cadets yes, but no streaming into Sandhurst or any of the military colleges. They were hot on duty, but my single-mindedness always seemed to make the staff uncomfortable. It was as if a military career did not need the polish and succour that this very ancient establishment was able to give. So be it, I had studied the subjects required for pilot entry and become something of an all-rounder at sports. Little career guidance was given or offered, and I often felt the uncertainty of decisions made alone.

The last sixth months had passed in a series of odd jobs and a passion for Rugby with the Old Nottinghamians and the Notts Colts. The odd jobs had provided their share of excitement when I, as driver for my father's managing director, had reversed his car into a Lincolnshire canal. His bad directions had necessitated the attempted turn around, but I had to accept that without a doubt it was my fault. The canal banks were steep, and a trunk full of water made any attempts to salvage the situation impossible.

Boots the Chemists provided easier employment and allowed me to play rugby mid-week. Here, the learn from your experience mode took an abrupt turn. The manager knew of my career aspirations and used me wherever he found the need. Work-to-rule strikes were just things one read about and yet I found myself right in the middle of a labour dispute. In order to force overtime most of the workers slowed down after noon, so that two or three hours overtime would be declared in order to catch up with the backlog. My stocking tasks, entirely physical, were just a fitness opportunity for me. I ran, doubled the loads, planned my routes and in general played havoc with their overtime gauge. When nobody was in evidence but me, management quietly told me how it was and could I please slow down. However, at a later stage some work to rule was going on and like Mr Magoo I was asked to operate the binding machine. The operator had stopped work and left for union consultation.

It was not that complicated a machine to operate, and I found it an interesting challenge. The silence was deafening and I looked up to see my workmates in a threatening half-circle around me. Peace was negotiated, I was sent elsewhere and I reviewed the learning bricks that resulted from this incident.

You cannot operate in a vacuum, and 2 per cent of the information is rarely enough to formulate an opinion. Many courses were offered in the summer holidays, and I flew as many times as I could at the RAF summer camps. One such trip was with another cadet in an Auster. This small aircraft had two seats up front and an observer's seat sideways in the back. I managed to grab the front seat, for this other unfortunate was unknown to me. He climbed in the back and we immediately started to taxi out for take-off. Nothing was said and I detected the scent of fear from the back. It was a cold day, and our air experience options were limited. After about forty-five minutes we returned and landed. We were hurried from the aircraft, and the pilot taxied away. The other cadet, his face now contorted in pain, limped away to the hangars.

In looking at his leg I noticed that his foot was covered in oil and he managed to get out that his foot was frozen. He had somehow stepped off the floorboard in the Auster and put his foot through the aircraft fabric. Fearing reprisals, he had endured the whole flight with his foot in the airstream soaking up the engine oil as it flowed back from the engine.

With my hopes on the Fleet Air Arm, I was accepted for the Royal Marine Commando course on the south coast of England. An enthralling course which culminated in a seaborne assault on the Isle of Wight. We had been eager students, and an actual cliff assault from the sea was going to be challenging. There were numerous landing craft assigned to the exercise and we set off in rough seas. I had never tested my sea legs before and I quickly learned that keeping your lunch down took priority over being a trained killer. It was apparent that the worsening seas were of serious concern to the supervisors, but press on or turn back soon became irrelevant as we struggled to make landfall, any landfall. The seriousness of the situation was conveyed in true British military style, and at the top of the waves we could see that the assault force was being scattered by the wind and currents. We made the beach, climbed the cliff albeit in the wrong place, and learned that several cadets had drowned.

Of my nine lives I would later apportion that incident a 'half'.

The other half came all too soon when we were taken for a trip to the Air/Sea Rescue boat. After the trip, we were given the afternoon off. It was a warm day and we returned to the beach opposite where the ASR launch was moored. The Solent is notorious for its currents, but seventeen years of (in)experience is sufficient for any task.

We set out to swim the estimated 4-500 yds to the launch. Some competitive hormones surfaced and the race to the boat was on. Judging distances at sea is difficult and the bunch of swimmers soon realised that this was going to be a long swim. The ever-watchful military appeared in a helicopter and through a loud hailer enquired if we were OK. Discretion only comes with scar tissue, and nobody was scared enough to accept the help offered. The helicopter could not have known that the launch was about to depart and we were unable to stop it from turning and sailing away. We had now been in the water about one and a half hours, and we turned to begin the swim back to the beach.

Assisting anyone was out of the question as we faced an every-man-for-himself situation. With leaden legs I struggled from the water unable to see any other swimmers but the two who had remained in close company with me. We were some three miles down the shore from our start point, and the long walk back collected the others who could now join us in blistering our feet on the sands from skin made soggy from five hours in the water.

At a previous camp I had begun an association with the venerable Anson, a communications aircraft known affectionately as the Cloth-Bomber by virtue of its fabric-covered wings and original designation. It was to feature much in my later flying career, but this time it implanted the seeds of introspection that I believe were very much part of my survival mechanism, very necessary for those times. Seven cadets were ushered into the Anson for another dose of air experience. I never made the co-pilot's seat this time, but by loosening the seat belt I could kneel on the main spar and have a reasonable view between the front two occupants.

There was some other flying in progress, and we took off on the grass runway and entered a climb which removed the horizon from my view. It did not prevent me catching a brief flash of silver as we were hit from below by another aircraft. I have little recall of the next moments, but do not remember them being fearful as I really had no concept of what was supposed to happen next. We fluttered to the ground and landed after a fashion, stopping where we finished up. Vehicles arrived and before we were loaded the scenario unfolded thus: a Chipmunk taking off on another runway had hit us from below, damaging the wheels and one propeller. He had made a forced landing and only pride was injured. I would later learn that

Auntie Air Force took a dim view of such incidents, and expected that the pilots were given a front-row seat at a Court of Inquiry.

We were bussed to the holding camp to be documented and inducted into Her Majesty's Royal Air Force. The military way is order and procedure, and what followed was just that. A long Nissen hut was our accommodation, and one coal-burning stove was the only heating. It was seasonally cold, such that the windows were iced over each morning. The corporal in charge of our hut was marginally articulate, but rules were rules and our coal allowance was the few meagre lumps of black rock masquerading as coal. It rapidly became evident that supplementary heat was required. With every item of newly issued uniform arrayed on your body, you were still going to freeze.

A quick scout of the camp proved beyond all doubt that our problem was not new for the area. Anything remotely capable of combustion was guarded or locked away. A particularly redundant piece of furniture seemed to be the towel rail attached to the back of each locker. After due deliberation it was agreed that we would all contribute our towel rails, the all-or-nothing argument. Warmth was instantaneous, and it seemed a ready solution to our corporate problem.

The corporal did not see it that way, and severe threats were made. It was obvious that he somehow was going to be personally involved in this gross breach of Queen's Regulations. And so he was, for our coal ration was being used for currency on the camp, he believing that we were too new or green to be able to cause him any grief.

Kirton in Lindsey was the basic training facility buried deep in Lincolnshire. Discipline in the name of the drill sergeants was powerful and immediate. These gentleman ran Basic Training with an iron will and more than a soupçon of anecdotes and British Army humour. In these days of political correctness, any comparison brings a wry smile to my face.

Our first meeting was covered thus. 'Gentleman,' he said, for we were officer cadets and entitled to use that form of address, 'you will call me sir at all times, and I will address you as sir also. However, the difference is that you will mean it.'

The three months passed in exercises, drill and more drill, lectures in military matters and the demands of the officer corps. Friendships were beginning to form and the strengths and weaknesses of all were quickly made evident. The quiet piano player, sensitive and non-sporting, was an early casualty.

Several fell by the wayside as a result of injury, possibly to rejoin later. Cadet leaders were selected, and leadership qualities became understood mainly by what they obviously were not. Some bullied, some stood their ground. I found myself often too far out front, and watching your back is vital in so competitive an environment. Home was missed, not in the accepted way, but that it had always provided a place to rest and regroup.

We were rarely allowed out to the delights of Scunthorpe, and the twenty-eight shillings a week was mainly used in the Naafi, to supplement the awful diet. About this time military feeding was under scrutiny, and massive changes were eventually made. The Orderly Officer was tasked with circulating during each meal and enquiring if there were any complaints. The presence of two wasps in my main course drew the comment that it was a supplement to my meat ration.

Kirton was a grass airfield and used for gliding. On a fine spring day we were marched outside to view some of this activity. Several aerobatics were demonstrated, and on one of them the glider crashed into the hangar, the sudden deceleration being fatal. I had little experience of death, and had no ritual expression on which to call. Here began my acceptance of the Royal Air Force attitude to this all too common occurrence. It was unsettling, and stayed with me for some time; only later did I grasp and understand the RAF way.

Gazing out over the airfield during lectures was an inevitability and this was the first myxamatosis infection of the UK rabbit population. We often were forced to end the misery of some of the unfortunate animals, usually with the ceremonial bayonet that was part of the daily uniform. I found it disturbing that I was more perturbed by their suffering than I was over the demise of the glider pilot. The pilots' creed of death being acceptable provided that you had not screwed up and caused your own and maybe others' untimely end, was grasped and well understood. Many examples of this attitude were experienced later on, and I certainly found that the competitive pursuit of excellence needed this balance valve.

There were usually three courses in residence at any one time, and end-of-course high jinx often resulted in raiding. The barrack block was kept in a high state of spit and polish, toilets cleaned with tooth brushes, window brasses shining and the floors buffed continually. We did this by positioning felt pads by the doors, so that everyone skated around on the pads all the time. The evenings before an inspection were hives of activity. Jobs were scheduled so that everyone had a community task as well as his personal kit. The junior course would normally be the target and in the early hours the raiders would sneak in. Soap powder on the floors, oil in the white ablutions area and gas cream on the brasses. Gas cream was a corrosive agent that destroyed brass almost as you looked at it. I never queried what it would do to a human as a reagent for war gases.

As a consequence of these raids sentries were set up at times thought likely for an attack. One's bed space was totally your responsibility. Failure to pass inspection brought the wrath of the staff on all in that block.

Making the bed and arranging the locker was a tiresome job, and so I took to gluing shirts and towels to cardboard, so that the corners were just so. I even slept on the floor to save time and energy in the frantic morning rush around. Some tried to lacquer boots to obtain the ultimate shine, but the first smash of boots on concrete during drill had some interesting results. Being bawled out by the DI was an unforgettable experience.

Before one major inspection we were painting everything in sight, including the grass which had a distinctly brown tinge around the block. Some two hours before the inspecting officer was to arrive, our DI noticed that the window over the stairs, at least fifteen feet in height, was grimy. We did not have access to a ladder long enough for the job, but he was insistent that we clean that window.

Barking orders he secured rope and manpower for the work. 'Mr T, you will be lowered from the bathroom window on the knotted rope and clean that window right now.' Mr T was not particularly agile and more afraid of falling to his death. He made little attempt to fend off the window as his momentum took him straight through it. Laughter is impossible to contain at such times, and the DI swore for at least ten minutes, an 'Oscar' winning performance. Replacement was out of the question in the time remaining, and we therefore removed all the glass in the hope that it would pass unnoticed. It did, with that quote about fooling some people some of the time etc., clearly in mind.

The end of course exams were due and I was feeling the strain of the endless days and so few hours sleep. I ascertained that drill and military studies were going to be my weak points. The academic stuff was really a follow-on from school and cadet lectures. Here I made a major mistake, and my assessment of the requirement was way off beam. Suffice it to say that I passed all but some of the academic papers. It was like surfacing midway through drowning. I felt inordinately tired, half accepting that I was not capable of continuing and that maybe I just did not have it.

The Review Board was severe and I expected no mercy. My call home to my folks was like a dream. How could I have failed? Did they not know that I had waited years to do this? After an interminable wait I was called back in and sternly told that I was to be recoursed, starting in a few days. Goodbye to your old course, hello the new. Not quite that simple as some of the friendships had the makings of that bond so necessary in a military environment. I could not know that paths cross and recross in the Service.

The few days between courses were lost as I was admitted to hospital with a severe infection, boils, blanket rash, the effects I suppose of poor diet, little sleep and hyperactivity.

The new course was a different status for me, for knowing the ropes, changed the way course members dealt with me and I with them. The schoolboy was growing up and fast, and I clearly understood what for now was required of me.

Each course completed a tented camp at one of several locations. This one was at Donna Nook on the wilds of the Lincolnshire coast. The more physical tests were run here and learning how a military encampment functions was the intention. The DIs ran all the sections from cookhouse to guard duties, the students provided the labour. The kitchen was positioned in a former Lifeboat House, now a shell. Cooking was accomplished by petrol burners being placed under sheets of metal. The cookhouse detail had to rise very early to deal with these difficult and dangerous machines. They had to be filled outside and lugged into the dark corner of the boathouse, blackened from previous courses. Here they were pumped up by the attached pump and pressure gauge. Opening the valve allowed fuel to spray onto a ceramic ring which when lit provided an impressive amount of heat. The valve was usually in need of cleaning and a thin wire was used for the purpose.

The major players in this skit were Mr Hoskins and the DI whose name I forget, for it is overpowered by his caricature, and yours truly. He was ex-indian Army, ramrod straight creases like razors. He sported a waxed moustache that was extremely mobile when he screamed his orders and his thinning hair was oiled to his scalp. He appeared whilst we were trying to get enough burners going to start breakfast. Mr Hoskins was brushed aside as he told us that he was an expert on these things, learned it in India you see. Pump Mr Hoskins, put some effort into it whilst I clean these jets. I watched in horror as Mr Hoskins pumped well into the red area on the gauge. The Indian expert could not see the gauge, nor was he surprised by the fuel vapour, to be expected as he freed up the jets. I backed away as he demanded a match, and was blown the rest of the way by the resulting explosion.

What a movie scenario, his face was black, but his moustache was gone as was his hair almost to the back of his head. He started swearing and as before did not repeat himself for some considerable time. He vented his anger on Mr Hoskins as people came running to the source of all this noise and consternation. Their laughter propelled him into greater efforts of profanity as Mr Hoskins was drilled at the double up and down the beach with his rifle. Only the arrival of the other DI who fell about almost in tears defused the situation.

It is strange how men relate to men, and the incidents that form the rights of passage. He felt a little humanised by this incident, but still was not comfortable with his new position.

One evening when we were preparing for a morning trip he appeared in the barrack block. I had obtained two sabres and helmets from the sports store, and was teaching basic swordsmanship to those who had requested it. I had had the good fortune to be taught by an Olympic champion, and felt at ease with the sport. He picked up one of the sabres and professed to be somewhat of a dab hand at the sport. He looked around for an opponent and chose me at the urging of the assembled crowd. Our little huddle pressed me to murder him and the scent of the mob was in the air.

The clothing was extremely rudimentary, the helmets being more suited to foils than sabres which are flexible at the end. In the cleared area we fought and it was obvious that he was only game not skilled. It is possible by flexing the sabre in a chopping motion to curl the tip over the helmet and impact it in the back of the head and neck. In this way small lumps of flesh can be removed quite effectively.

He fought on and the plan seemed to be unfolding as expected. Bleeding profusely, we saw another side to this man. Passage was completed, and as one he became a compatriot. We ended the bout and shook hands warmly. Thereafter he became a father confessor, and appeared genuinely saddened when we parted at the end of the course.

The final test was to complete an assault course and cross-country run, and get all your team over the final wall. All had to be over to be counted. Teamwork not individualism was the order of the day. I knew that I had passed and all that remained was to discover whether I was bound for Canada and the Empire training scheme, or to Hullavington in Wilts for pilot training.

Arrival at the Flying Training School (No 4 FTS) was a march into the unknown. We were newly commissioned as APOs, acting pilot officers, well outfitted by the London tailors who haunted Kirton to be ready to seduce the unwary into parting with their Uniform Allowance. Time of arrival was set for Saturday, so that all the formalities and briefings could be completed before work commenced on Monday morning. Course leaders had been selected by the staff so that there was, as it were, some chain of command. We had the good fortune to have Bill J, who was an ex-Hong Kong policeman, and Jerry B. Jerry was just doing his National Service, a two-year stint. Few qualified for pilot training under the National Service entry, unless you possessed university qualifications. Jerry was a lawyer and very useful he turned out to be in our battles with the establishment.

Even the grapevine had not passed on that new arrivals were given an accepted hazing by the senior course. Ours was fairly innocuous as I recall it, being told to report all over the camp for never-ending tasks. One's willingness to be ill-lead and ill-advised has a limit, and it was interesting to see how far innocents could be pushed in the name of fearful discipline. Our old hands soon smelled a rat and the game was over.

No 2 Mess was the home of junior courses, it being a more salubrious Nissen hut than previously seen. Amenities were good and the food more akin to an officers' mess. Washing facilities were centralised and the buildings were raised off the floor. Rooms were compact but entirely satisfactory for one's needs. The following morning we were told to assemble for a briefing and marched to the airfield to watch a practice Battle of Britain fly-past by the instructional staff. August was always the time for such activity, and the massed Piston Provost formation took off across the airfield. They ignored the runways for this unusual departure, and roared away to form up for their display. Such a formation is called a Balbo, after an Italian airman of that name, and it is not an activity likely to be practiced more than once a year by instructors at an FTS. They flew by in various formations and eventually turned for a massed landing, again across the airfield. There were other aircraft movements going on around the perimeter, and one aircraft appeared to be running up its engine prior to take-off. It turned into wind just as the Balbo lined up for landing. With perfect timing, it commenced its take-off under the first of the landers. What seemed like a huge explosion was the next frame of this view. Pieces of aircraft, wheels bouncing and people running from a red cloud of dust and the noise of the rest of the Balbo hitting full power. The airfield was red marl, a kind of dusty sandstone, and the first aircraft hitting it put up the cloud. When the dust settled, two planes had been destroyed, several had repairable damage and there were no casualties. All in all a remarkable intro to my flying career.

Several weeks of lectures were completed so that the groundwork would always be in advance of the airwork. The days and weeks were full, and for me it was an extension of school, the only disciplined system that I had known. Close friendships were difficult, but left in the embryonic stage. It seemed that getting too close was likely to be an unnecessary burden. The reasoning for this was made apparent when a mid-air collision at night killed four pilots.

Nevertheless, bonds were formed amidst the very important weeding out process that was going on. Our flight instructors were mostly ex-wartime, with a hard-to-grasp attitude to life. They were not too communicative in the early days, just focused on guiding/driving you towards the first hurdle, first solo.

I loved the challenge and could not get enough of my instructor's humour and easy-going ways. I never identified the complete requirement as my analytical skills were very basic. I soloed at the relief landing ground (Keevil) on a fine sunny day, and some of the impact hit me as I trundled downwind for this oh-so-important first landing. He climbed back on board for the short trip home, and gave me the friendly thump that was to become his trade mark when things went well.

Some eight hours were taken in this first period, and my hours were the lowest. Here the schoolboy attitude took over and my progress thereafter slowed to a danger point. Mac's other student was a good friend and rival, and we felt comfortable as other students started to face review and suspension. Cementing the early lessons was the next phase, and I found myself again at Keevil, facing a few hours of circuit practice. Mac had climbed out to lay in the grass and watch me pound around this piece of Wiltshire. The runways are laid out in a triangle having all the sides extended, sort of like a wigwam. The instructions were to join the circuit pattern in concert with other aircraft, land, turn off and taxi around the triangle to await further t/o, and then, when cleared, repeat the process.

I approached for my first landing feeling that all was as close to the previous attempts as I could make it. Several aircraft were awaiting t/o just clear of this landing runway. I touched down and promptly veered off the asphalt heading towards the idling aircraft. They saw me coming, applied power, and tried to anticipate which way I was going. After numerous feints, we missed each other and I sheepishly taxied around for another go.

If Mac had been closer, he probably would have ended the day's session right there. However, circumstances would conspire to allow me to repeat the performance on the next circuit. At that point, one of the aircraft that I had chased contained the Squadron Commander and he ordered me back to my instructor. Analysis was required, and I believe that I stiffened up on the brakes and rudder at the moment of landing, initiating the swing all by myself. Mac was not pleased, and on arrival at base he ordered me onto the wing of the Provost, where I stood with my parachute banging at the back of my legs. He then applied full power and blew me arse over teakettle into the grass. It was a good mile and a half walk back around the field to the squadron.

The next few days were to become one of the turning points in my life, something that I describe as a mental high jump. Mac took me on one side and told me that my progress was not acceptable. He berated me about attitude and continued hard work, and tellingly made the point that Bob T, his other student, was a natural pilot. I would need to work extremely hard to come even close to his abilities. He knew of our friendly rivalry and hoped that I would gain incentive from this information. Emotion was at an all-time high, and I moved from schoolboy to the first stage of maturity right there. With feelings of determination to prove him wrong I left the briefing room.

I would use that avenue to motivate my students years later when I was an instructor. From that moment on I was able to understand the goal, keep up the pressure on myself and enjoy the whole thing that was aviation. There were incidents galore to brighten the days and the initial failures had long since left us. There would be more, but the daily goodbyes had ended. The students' crewroom was just down the passage from that of the instructors. Coffee facilities were very primitive, and a yell from the instructors for a student to fetch water and make coffee was an hourly occurrence.

Mac and Phil had selected me for most of these chores. They also liked to play 'Knuckles', a painful game involving placing a clenched fist against your opponents and in turn trying to strike the top of the other fist. If you struck and missed, striking passed to the other player. Mac's hands were huge, and a hit from him was with you for days. He missed one day and removed a large chunk of the table on which we were sitting.

They were extremely physical and it became a daily game to avoid too many bruises. Having been selected for coffee duty so often, I decided to up the stakes a little. I bought a tin of Andrews Liver Salts, known for its effects on the bowel and introduced it over that week into their coffee. By Friday all were complaining about the need to stay close to a toilet, and the laughter from our crew room gave me away. I ran for it but was held for punishment. The large wartime hangar had chain pulleys all around for lifting engines and I was tied and hoisted to the roof, to be left for several hours. This was my right of passage and the family of the flight line was happier for it.

We had an Iraqi student with us on the course, George, who had a good sense of humour. He was insatiably attracted to anything female, and was the centre of much leg-pulling because of it. He did have a fierce temper, and his eyes would change to red when he had been pushed beyond the limit.

Students somehow believed that their antics when flying solo were not observed. We would agree to meet at a certain location for a little combat, and use of the primitive four-channel radio was clearly out of the question. One day we planned our rendezvous, and purposely left George out of it. Not to be outdone he followed screaming into the radio, 'Kingsley where are you?' I immediately fled to Keevil so that I could be seen by staff members performing some accepted training manoeuvres. Questions were asked, answers phrased and the case was closed for lack of evidence.

Mac was a keen low flier, and on our dual sorties would sometimes chase hares and pheasants with the Provost. One such time he was speeding over the fields and he inverted the aircraft at very low altitude. Without warning he said to me, 'Say after me, Our Father.' I responded in the interrogative, 'Our Father,' and he promptly righted the aircraft and flew directly home. He rushed into the crew room and said, 'I got him to say the Lord's Prayer.' Needless to say, my leg was pulled unmercifully until somebody else claimed the spot.

Life in a Students' Mess was continual practical jokes, and as I came to understand, it prevented most APOs from taking themselves too seriously. Bill J was something of an athlete, he could be sucked into a long diatribe about his athletic exploits, realising too late that he was having his chain pulled.

We returned one night from the local pub, having experimented somewhat with the malt beverages. Bill being that much older had a developed taste for beer in all its forms. He had been primed in the pub to tell us how long and high he could jump. At the gates to the Mess, very impressive sculptured brickwork guarded the entrance. Unbeknown to Bill, Bob and I had discovered that beyond the wall, there was a serious drop into a large ornamental flower bed, which would not be seen from the road. We suggested that although he was a jumper of renown, he could not possibly clear the Mess wall. No problem, he said, and launched himself over the wall with ease, to be lost from sight. The alcohol had stimulated his sense of humour, and he lay in the flowers convulsed with laughter.

Cars were a major source of entertainment, most were pre-war examples; even the staff had trouble paying for a new car on the meagre salaries of the day. This lack of money and transport conspired to keep most students in the Mess and on base where prices were bearable. A mess bill is part of the learning experience of military living. To be unable to pay the monthly mess bill was unthinkable. It was grounds for dismissal. Young males need to learn how to hold their liquor, and in the controlled environment of the Mess much learning was done. Drinking and driving was rarely a problem even with the relaxed attitudes of the times. There was however a constant struggle going on to get a car, any car, as a mark of independence. One unfortunate, whose name escapes me, had purchased a 1933 Hillman. Never a shining example of British engineering, it was, however, transport. It had bald tyres, two windows missing and very dubious brakes. He proudly displayed his new possession to the rest of the course and announced his intention to take a trip into the local town. Only one brave soul chose to accompany him, and the rest of the course loaded up into other cars, to follow him to town. He wound the thing up to its maximum speed, and crested the hill for the long run down into town. The road was shining after a recent rain shower, and the tyres were not up to the task of keeping the vehicle pointing downhill. He began to oscillate and hit an oncoming vehicle a tremendous thump, which caused the Hillman to totally disintegrate. Pieces, just pieces, flew over the hedge and into the field. All the vehicles stopped and people ran to see what remained of the occupants. They were sitting amidst the wreckage, the largest item being the engine. The driver's career took a severe nudge when it was discovered that the new Triumph that he had hit belonged to his Squadron Commander who was returning from town having just collected it. The final ignominy was delivered by the police constable who demanded that they remove every piece of the car from the road and hedgerow.

After one of the rare early trips home, I had arranged to meet another student in Litchfield for the drive back to Hullavington. My parents drove me to the meeting point late on Sunday night, where he was to be in a new car. My father had reservations about a new driver, a new car, and four high-spirited trainee pilots. How right he was, for from the front suicide seat, given to me in deference to my driving experience, I realised that friendly behind the wheel was far from skilled. We set off at a blistering pace in the loaded Ford Popular. At warp eight we entered a long, gentle, sloping curve. The back end started to slip out in classic oversteer, and our hero overcorrected wildly. I tried to talk him through a gentle correction, putting much emphasis into my Italian body language. 'Twas to no avail, we slid on the wet surface, snapping from side to side. It was obvious that either the nose or the tail would finally contact the banked sides of the road, and then we were over, still doing sixty miles an hour on the roof up the road. In vivid slow motion, I can recall looking at these yellow pear drops rushing at my head. Pain drove me to more relevant action, as I tried to use my hands to keep me away from the roof. Then it was over, I kicked out the remains of the windscreen and crawled out concerned only that we should not be hit by another vehicle.

The crash had alerted some homeowners opposite, and I met them coming towards me with a flashlight. In that few moments the others had extricated themselves and were all OK. With the help of some other motorists, we righted the very bent Ford, and I managed to start it using full choke. It was drivable after a fashion, having very little power and no windscreen. The pear drops I had seen were sparks coming from the windscreen pillar as it wore down, and the pain was from glass being pounded into my head. I was covered in blood, and my new uniform raincoat was shredded from escaping through the broken glass. Matey insisted on driving, as not returning to camp was only excusable if you were dead. The first stop for fuel in the early hours of Monday morning was memorable. The garage attendant nearly died of fright at this wrecked vehicle and bloodied occupants.

The duty officer directed us all to Sick Quarters, where I had two pounds of glass picked from my scalp. Matey was given a sleeping pill, and we were all excused duties for the day. On Wednesday, our hero was given his 'chop ride'. This is the flight that decides whether or not you will be allowed to continue training. He failed! In an attempt to solve our collective transport problems, we agreed to buy a 1939 Austin Ambulance. Terms were drawn up, and rules accepted. It was a St John Ambulance vehicle, with a working siren, stretcher beds and one-way glass. It became quite famous over the next months, and was a source of hours of entertainment. It was possible to carry at least fifteen people, and therefore much in demand for outings and parties.

On one day trip in the narrow roads of Wilts, a motorcycle came around the corner and slid into the spare wheel housing on the side of the Austin. We leapt out to find him unconscious with a broken leg. One APO was an ex-medical student, and he straightened the leg as we rushed the rider to hospital. He recovered confused and with little memory of the accident. Phil was congratulated on his medical expertise, and we received guarded approval from the Station Commander.

Bath was the home for many girls' colleges, and therefore the weekend destination for those with money. One college party involved driving the Ambulance back from the occasion full of party goers. Bath is a very hilly city, and we were climbing this very steep hill slowly in view of the load on board. The Austin had a gearbox lacking synchromesh on first gear. It was extremely difficult to engage first gear at the best of times, and I knew that I had one chance to make the change, or face going backwards down the hill. As soon as I tried to make the change the Austin was off backwards. Pre-war brakes were only designed for forward motion and they certainly would not hold the load on this hill. With no rear vision, and a mass of bodies behind me, I tried to steer from memory into a laneway that I remembered. We were moving quite fast as we crashed through some bushes and a large flower bed to come to a stop in front of a large stately home. The lights came on and I could not prevent everyone from spilling out onto the lawn. A portly figure appeared at the door, straight from the movies – Colonel Blimp, complete with smoking jacket and shotgun. He bellowed at us to ask what the hell we thought we were doing. Then promptly asked, nay demanded that we come in to make ourselves known to him. His wife produced tea, although we were urged to join him in stronger stuff. He was a marvellous character, ex-Indian Army and we made our excuses to take our leave. I kept contact with him until he died a short time later.

Terry O had an Austin Seven, a tiny but superb vehicle. Our group of four would head for Bath whenever, Mike D would fall in love with the girl in the coffee shop, and we would arrange to meet at one a.m. outside the bank. On this occasion Terry had parked the car in the bombsite not far from the bank. I arrived first, to find a large truck with the back open and the ramp down. Midnight in Bath was like a morgue, and I wondered if I might push the Austin into the truck and hide it. It had a soft roll-back roof and I managed to insert my hand and flip open the door. Pushing the tiny Austin up the ramp was no problem, and I hid in the shadows to await their arrival. I must have been seen by the local constabulary, for I became aware that there was a figure crossing up the centre of the road looking for 'me'. When I moved from the shadows he jumped about three feet into the air, and was immediately embarrassed about it. Explanations were called for, and I flannelled enough to convince him. I walked away to go around the block and back to the car park. By the time I got around, the rest of the gang were frantically looking for the car. The noise brought the constable back on the scene, just as they found the Austin. It was impossible to slink away from this one, but a cup of tea at the local police station soon cleared things up, for they were well aware of the crazies at Hullavington.

My flying progressed satisfactorily, and the course started to develop a merit order. This is so much a part of RAF squadron life, where everyone gravitates towards the position he thinks he holds. It acts rather like a squash ladder at a sports club. You bury into the group, selecting a position that you think you merit. You can challenge those immediately above you, and be challenged from below. Large jumps are rarely made or tolerated, but there is always a shuffle when new blood is posted in. On a course the skills are learned at varying rates, and so the meritocracy alters almost weekly as fresh phases of the course are tackled. I loved the formation phase and it was easy to compare oneself to others as it was the one occasion when we flew as a three-ship formation and the other students' progress was observable. I struggled with the instrument flying, and everyone knew that I was having trouble with this aspect.

I tried to make up for these low marks by excelling at aerobatics and other skills. Mac tried everything to help me on the way, saying that it would come, eventually.

The Provost was a metal-skinned aircraft, and we were just beginning to see the arrival of 'g' meters. This instrument showed the acceleration force on you and was used to limit overstressing on the airframe. Up until then, the limit was what a pilot could stand without going unconscious, around 6g. I recall doing loops continuously and looking out at the wings to see how the surfaces were wrinkled under the stresses. Being short in stature, I could stand very high 'g' loads, and when I finally flew an aircraft fitted with a 'g' meter, I found that I was severely overstressing, well beyond the limits that we now had to watch on the instrument.

Low flying is the one aspect that draws all young pilots. The thrill of having your life in your own hands coupled with the sensation of speed is an adrenalin high. We moved into the navigation phase, which included low-level nav trips. One such trip went down to the Dirty Old Man of Cerne Abbas. This was a huge figure cut into the limestone of the hillside dating back to ancient times. It was the turning point on the low-level nav. Set in a valley, it could be difficult to see from certain approaches. I made my run in at 250 ft as briefed, and then settled down for a much lower pass over the figure. A turn in the valley was called for and I banked steeply to reverse my direction. At the instant I was steeply banked I could no longer see the ground beneath me. Only the exit was viewable, and that out through the top of the canopy. Being so close to the ground I had little alternative but to continue pulling and hope that my wheels did not hit the walls of the valley. Flying memories are made up of incidents from which you learn, and this was one of them.

On return to base there was too much activity, and my initial thoughts were that I had been observed. Bob had hit the high tension wires and plunged a large portion of the county into a power outage. He had chosen to do it on the Duke of Beaufort's estate during a garden party, hardly a time when it might pass unnoticed. He was trying to bring back the badly damaged aircraft and the fire trucks were waiting. Without one wheel, an aileron and parts of the engine cowling, he approached very low and threw it on the ground, stopping just in front of Mac's house on the edge of the airfield.

Survival, but he would not finish the course with us. All the instructors helped by concocting stories of the incident that were placed before the Board, as excuses. In reality he had been attempting a practice forced landing, an exercise that we practiced incessantly, and had extended his overshoot into some illicit low flying.

The next hurdle of sorts was the aerobatic competition. Four students were selected, and much practice was endured, pressured by your own instructor, to whom having a student in the competition was seen as a personal success.

Mac and I worked hard at my weak points, the major one being vertical rolls. The Provost has few lines on which to judge the horizontal, and therefore trying to find the vertical needs skill. If the control forces are not neutralised as one hits the vertical, attempting a roll almost invariably results in a kind of corkscrew manoeuvre. The plan is to finish still vertical, and then hammer stall out, or if speed permits complete a stall turn. On the morning of the competition I practiced my sequence with Mac observing. Most of it went OK, the vertical roll was marginal.

With everyone watching we circled the field awaiting our turn to perform. The event was flown so that each student flew with another instructor acting as safety pilot. The initial manoeuvres were flown well, much better than during practice, but now the dreaded vertical roll. I ran in, on speed, and pulled up into the vertical, checked forward to hold that angle and realised that I was beyond the vertical. A correction was required, and I pushed forward on the stick, hard. The aircraft reacted instantly, and flicked completing a perfect roll. Not phased one bit I stall turned out, and turned downwind for the spot landing piece. All was progressing fine, I had enough speed in hand, maybe a touch too much and I was aiming for the runway markers. Phil, believing that I was going to overshoot the zone, retracted the flaps, causing the Provost to sit down heavily just short of the markers. It transpired that we had been excluded because of the prohibited flick roll, which all believed was an intentional manoeuvre on my part.

The flight commander was a Polish fighter pilot from the War. He was long suffering and fatherly, but quite difficult to understand especially when he was excited. On one performance evaluation, he asked me to demonstrate bad weather low flying. This procedure requires first flap to be selected to lower the nose, so visibility is improved. For some reason I lowered full flap, and he asked why. My response was immediate: this is for very bad weather, I said.

The night-flying phase always had its moments, and our course produced two beauties. Normally the main runway was used such that after landing one would taxi onto the grass following the blue lights, and return to the take-off point for another circuit. There were four aircraft in the circuit area at one time, spaced out so that a flow pattern could be established.

A check on the routine calls needed in the pattern would identify the position of all aircraft. It became apparent that one aircraft was missing from the sequence, far more apparent to the watchers on the ground than it was to us in the circuit. We were ordered up to 2,000 ft whilst they tried to contact the missing callsign. A very weak transmission was heard, but not enough to establish his position. We were ordered to land with caution as the instructors prepared to get airborne to look for the 'lost' student. Once we were all down a vehicle drove around and found the 'lost' aircraft at the other end of the runway. What transpired was that he had taxied beyond the blue lights towards the other end of the runway and in the process had managed to place the small fixture that supplied power to the runway controller's caravan between his tyre and the oleo (undercarriage) leg. All he was able to do was taxi around in circles, which he did trying to extricate himself from his predicament. Knowing that he had blown it had kept him quiet for a long time, apart from the one transmission that we heard. He did not survive the course.

Number two incident was more comical in that Keith M, now a senior ATC expert in Australia, became lost on a night nav trip. He also lost most of his radio antenna, preventing him from receiving but not transmitting. He put out a 'Pan' call very sensibly, but then when he was unable to receive, started thinking out loud on the radio. He was quite pissed off that nobody would answer him and the language got richer by the minute. He eventually found a red light that he initially thought was base, only to find that it was the cinema in Malmesbury. At this point the staff knew where he was and a shepherd aircraft was able to make contact. The record of that night was played to him when he visited the ATC centre, much to his chagrin as most of the staff were female.

Motoring still featured heavily in day-to-day life, and I had the good fortune to drive one day with John W. He had a Riley 2^1/2, a superb car for its day. John was really a hero of mine, as well as an instructor. He had been on 74 Squadron during the War when Sailor Malan was the boss. This made anything he said doubly gospel. We were speeding round the lanes, John happy to demonstrate that power was everything. On the return from the pub, I journeyed back in another car behind Bill J. He flew past us up Box Hill in his excellent MG. We rounded the bend to see the car in a field beyond the hole in the stone wall that he had just made. There was no way that we could hide the incident and a passerby drove down the hill to the police station. We walked him up and down in vain attempts to sober him up. Jerry, ever the legal mind, was coaching everybody as to what happened. When the local bobby appeared on his bike, after cycling up the long hill, he must have sized up the scene pretty quickly. No harm was done, except to Bill's pride and the wall, which he agreed to pay for. A far cry from today's drinking and driving laws, but then there was little pressure to deal with it other than socially.

I made one more fateful trip home with Bas who was not on my course. We departed at high speed and only went about twenty miles before he rolled it into somebody's garden. These observed incidents convinced me that being in control of one's own motoring destiny was necessary for my health. One more trip, albeit to buy a car, was made back to Nottingham. The gentleman in question only had a learner's licence, which required him to be accompanied by a licenced driver at all times. He was collecting the car in Nottingham and could I drive back with him? The car was a Singer 1^1/2, a two-seat sports car circa 1935.

We met on Sunday evening, and set off back to camp. The Singer has a 'crunch' box for a gearbox, and a fine appreciation of such a device is required if forward motion is to be maintained.

We crashed our way through the gearbox all the way to Bicester, and on crossing a particularly rough bit of road, the car leapt forward, rapidly gaining speed as he sought to control it. I managed to flick off the ignition and we came to a halt. Inspecting the engine, we discovered that the throttle was normally spring loaded fully open, only the throttle mechanism balanced this tension. We had lost a piece of the linkage, allowing the throttle to go full open. Simple wire could not replace the missing piece, and some initiative was needed.

We removed the engine bonnet and placed it in the back of the car. The engine is placed far forward in a Singer such that there is room for tool kits on the front bulkhead. He donned his Sidcot suit, a cold-weather issue item made for use in unheated aircraft, and sat in the engine bay to operate the throttle. We communicated by shouts to synchronise the power requirements for each gear change. Progress was quickly made and I became alarmed by his choice of speed, for he completely obscured the left-hand side of the windscreen. We stayed on the side roads, which were windy and narrow and got by with only minor excursions off the highway. He yelled 'left, left', and bailed out of the engine bay. I was then confronted by a cricket net, posts and all, as the road had made a sharp turn left, unseen by me. He was well protected in his Sidcot, unhurt but thoroughly enjoying himself in the engine room. The standard garage encounter was entertainment as the attendant first showed amazement at what we were doing, and then concern as he tried to dissuade us from continuing. No way, we had to be back come hell or high water.

Although the pace of life could be stimulating, there were many periods, particularly weekends, when lack of money prevented us from leaving the confines of the camp. At times like these it is better to be unavailable. Window jumping consisted of jumping out of a second-floor window into a flower bed, extricating oneself and running back upstairs in the shortest possible time. One would think that there was little attraction in this exercise, but I guess active minds when idle are susceptible to group pressure. Before long the whole course was out there, and then the challenges flew from other courses and a real marathon was taking place. Only the noise and lack of people in the Mess drew attention to the game, and the senior staff put an end to it.

To more readily use our exuberance, station defence exercises were organised. They were an annual thing throughout the Air Force, and I believe the Hullavington one finally put an end to them. The total student population was used as an attacking force, all other personnel were to be defenders. The plan was to take the attackers some 25 miles away from base by truck, during which time the defence would organise itself to protect the major installations on the camp. The attackers had to make their way back and attempt to infiltrate the defended areas.

As the timing was known, for it was to be a night exercise, we stole a Land Rover from the civilian maintenance people who maintain military sites, known as Works and Bricks. They would not be involved in the exercise, and therefore immediately prior to the start would be returning early to their enclosure to leave the base area. We hoped the vehicle would not be missed, and now faced the problem of where to park it. A close look at the map narrowed down the possible places that the students could be dropped from the trucks, to a small area. We parked it in full sight, and returned by car to await the start of the exercise. At 1800 hrs we were loaded and driven to the drop-off point in closed trucks so that we would have to orientate ourselves when we were released. It was estimated that it would take us 6-8 hours to make our way back, but we were running as fast as possible to our parked vehicle, by chance only about 2 miles away. We climbed aboard and were back in camp before the gates were sealed. The Rover was hidden in the Students' Mess area, not an unlikely place to find one. We then waited until dark, with no real plan of action for the first bit had been too easy. We discussed good targets, and decided that the four of us could seriously disrupt the headquarters building. With most eyes looking outwards, we easily made it to the unlocked HQ. The Accountant Office's door opened readily to my bit of wire, and we looked around for something to take. The safe was sitting on a concrete platform by the window of the second floor. We could not lift it, but with improvised levers, propelled it towards the window. A ramp was made of shelves and books, and the safe shoved onto the window ledge.

It took little effort to boost it through the window, but the noise of the impact was astonishing. We beat a retreat with little idea of what to do next. The guards soon made chase, and I hid in an old air raid shelter. Most of us were caught and marched to the guard room cells. An RAF guard room is a pristine place with everything polished or painted. It was to become a war zone very quickly. The cell walls are removable and so for the exercise they were just barred cells with one window. All prisoners were stripped and herded into the cells.

We created as much commotion as possible, using the beds as battering rams against the bars. Rifles were pointed at us, and even the blanks they contained can be injurious. They came too close, and a rifle was grabbed. The order was given to hose us down with the ever-present fire hoses. In the pandemonium a hose nozzle was seized and a tug-of-war began through the bars. They were on a wet floor, we had leverage from the bars. The hose finally snapped or was released, and now we had some tools. Using the heavy tubing to pound against the window frame, in unison, quickly separated the window and bars from the wall and we were out in a flash. Stark naked, barefoot, we ran through the camp. Must have been an interesting view from the WAAF quarters. Several stand-offs occurred, with naked men facing a ring of rifles. Peace broke out when we were herded into a bare hangar and guarded in the centre. What a night, it must have been for I never took part in a similar exercise again. I do not recall any repercussions, although the safe remained embedded in the floor for some time.

A new course was expected and we were now in a position to plan their arrival prank. Having several older members, we persuaded the Medical Officer to let us use Station Sick Quarters for the plot. A message was left for the arriving course that they were to report to Station Sick Quarters immediately on arrival. Here one of our aged students dressed as the MO, advised them that there was an outbreak of lice on the camp – pubic lice. Medical staff were on hand to administer the lotion, or they could do it themselves. Cubicles were available, and the lotion, a mix of Gentian Violet and other staining substances, was offered along with plenty of swabs. They retired to generously douse themselves in the mixture, and we removed all the clothing that was left outside the cubicles.

To see two naked people sharing one raincoat and trying to walk back to the Mess was a joke in itself, especially as it was a long walk and past the WAAF quarters. They knew that they had been had, worst of all had done it to themselves. Scrubbing the genital area can be painful but futile in this case, as the dye has to wear off naturally.

In the pursuit of initiative so favoured by the MOD as a

prerequisite for pilots, we were given endless tasks to identify resolve and free thinking. Security in those far-off days generally related to special military installations and the Atomic Energy Commission. Our task was to plan entry into a secure establishment. The scope of the exercise was left to the individual, an unbelievable mistake. When there are few limitations, it is amazing what can transpire.

Marconi had a radar factory not far from the base, and it was believed to be secure. We approached by road to check out the gates area, and sure enough, they did check people in and out. We split up, and walked around the facility. A stream ran through the grounds and under the wall by a wired-off tunnel. It would have been possible to enter that way, but someone soaking wet was sure to attract attention inside. A large tree grew by the outer wall and view of it was obscured by some work buildings. I was over quickly, and hidden from view. We carried cigarette tins wrapped in paper with the inscription that this was an exercise bomb. I had a clipboard to make my youth look official, and I wandered around the facility completely unchecked. One bomb was placed under the fuel storage and another in the power generating building. The test laboratory was entered by mistake, but I brazened it out, walking through and placing a bomb as I exited.

On the roof were several radar units with working antennas. They could be reached by climbing onto a flat roof area. Fortune favours the brave, for after a quick search I found a ladder in the work area where I had entered. With the clipboard and ladder I was untouchable and soon on the roof taking notes. This area was in full view of the offices and I placed all the remaining bombs. I retraced my steps and left over the wall.

No others of my group were seen and so I presented myself at the main gate and asked to see the security officer. Low-key British security was just that, but the Special Branch officer at Marconi was more than perturbed. They denied that such a penetration was possible, and at first refused to accompany me to find the bombs. A call to Hullavington validated the exercise and me, and then we retraced to collect the bombs.

It had been relatively easy, and I did not comprehend the stir I had caused. Compliments flew and I was driven back to base. Here the Station Commander interviewed me and in true military fashion said well done for you have highlighted security deficiencies at Marconi, but how about a week's extra orderly officer duties for exceeding your authority and giving me all this extra work. Seemed like a deal, so I took it.

Friendships were cemented, Derek B, Dick F and Mike D. The lack of money saw us walking to Malmesbury to play darts at the Black Horse pub. Here the English country ritual of taking the chalk and scoring the game gave you the chance to play the winner. Dick and I played well together and fancied our chances in so small a village. The game was played in almost total silence, apart from the odd comment. The ancient farmworkers, bent from overwork, made short work of these two foreigners. We paid the price, which was a half pint of beer and took up the chalks for the next opportunity. Our continued appearance at the pub eventually gained us some measure of acceptance. Conversation was carried out in brief sentences, which never became discussion. When I returned to the pub some years later, I was welcomed as a long-lost son, with more animated conversation than we had ever encountered when we were there twice a week, strange but true.

The long-awaited arrival of the Jet Provost 1 occurred. This aircraft was the world's first jet ab initio trainer. It was anticipated that large savings could be made by training only on jet aircraft. I had given up my chance to be on this first course, mainly because of the delay involved. It was an ungainly aeroplane on long spindly undercarriage legs. Dignitaries from all over the world were always visiting and we were constantly being used for some function or another.

Mike D was a character like no other. Known as Nellie the Moocher for his moods and short-tempered attitudes, he had distinguished himself at basic training by his answer to the Inspecting Officer, the C-in-C. We were on parade undergoing inspection and Mike was asked how he was finding the RAF so far. Being in a particularly truculent mood he said, 'Sor right'. The C-in-C moved on, but Mike was left in no doubt that that was not the right answer.

At the Summer Ball, our first, Mike decided that he, after all was not going to come down to join the festivities. We were at the bar as a group, in high spirits. Mike arrived and glaring at me demanded to know how many Scotches I had drunk. Eight I said and he ordered nine, which he immediately consumed. We watched in silence, but he became his funny self and carried on as if nothing was amiss. Having now caught up, as it were, drinks were imbibed at the usual rate. When the need overtook him, he got up to go to the mens' room. We followed, certain that he would fall down sometime soon. He faced the door of the Gents and straight-armed it to open it with a flourish. His timing was off as the door was opened by the C-in-C, causing Mike to fall flat on the floor. The C-in-C stepped over the body and we hoped that Mike had gone unrecognised.

Some hours later the effects of alcohol were evident and we were in the urinal keeping careful tabs on Mr Mike D. The urinal was one of the long ones without any intervening dividers. Mike, feeling weary, rested his arm on the non-existent wall and slid sideways to the floor, to come to a soggy stop at the feet of the C-in-C.

His career may have suffered as a result of these and other escapades, but he won handsomely in the end. When postings to fighter squadrons were in short supply, he was banished to RAF Hawkinge as officer in charge of gliding. What a miserable job for a twenty-year-old. It was, however, the home of the WAAF officer training unit. I think he was the only eligible bachelor on the unit – so much for punishment postings.

In the final days of Hullavington, we went to a jazz evening at the drill hall in Bath. There Mr Acker Bilk and the Paramount Jazz Band were about to launch themselves onto the music world. Having grown up in the jazz clubs of post-war Nottingham, I had always fancied myself at picking successful acts. They were excellent, and my prophecies of a bright future for the band were drowned out by the usual, 'yeah right' and 'swadup'.

Pass Out was a formal affair, followed by a series of course parties both on and off the base. The site selected for our off-base evening was the Vine Hotel, which still stands, an old country inn, just off the low-level route back to base.

The mess party was very informal, and Dickie E could not be persuaded to delay his departure until morning. He tottered off to return a short while later, minus his car. This fine old vehicle was embedded in a tree, and an alteration to Dickie's face is a perpetual reminder of that evening.

Between the basic and advanced stages, we were allowed leave and as we could not all use the ambulance, the need for transport convinced me, unwisely, to buy an old Morris 15. The chassis had sagged, indicating a break somewhere. The price was right, and I set off home happy to be mobile and independent. Most of my school friends were away at university, but I was able to re-establish contact with some of them. Roland F was trying to be a dentist, and would shortly join me in the Air Force to practice his new-found skills. Emotionally and socially they were difficult days, the old framework of relationships had altered. The common bonds were no longer common. It was as if all required a question. The question was: 'I have to go, are you coming? If not it has been nice knowing you.' And so we all fanned out to make our way in the world, realising that only some of the past can be carried into the future.

In a well-ordered society, emotional security comes from knowing exactly where you fit in. Changing this structure can be very disconcerting for some people. One of the UAS course was a high-brow fellow with a degree in welding or something similar. The UAS entry was a university course of students previously trained at a University Air Squadron. As such they enjoyed accelerated promotion and a shorter course. When he was away for a weekend, his course mates dismantled his room, even to removing the floor. As the building was raised, he returned on Sunday to step into a black hole that had been his room. Somewhat angered he sought out his course mates to demand an answer. They expressed surprise at this visitor, and demanded to know who he was. They ignored his protestations and all professed not to know him. They said that that room was condemned and had always been empty. He did not have the strength of character to surmount this testing moment and was almost reduced to tears by the frustration. He did not survive the course.

Middleton St George was a north country base outside of Darlington. The advanced training was carried out on the Vampire, a twin-boom jet by the makers of the Mosquito. It had been designed at the end of the War, and entered service shortly after the War ended. There were two major versions in use for training, the original single-seater and the much newer two-seater, the T11. The airframe was mostly of wood construction, and versions were to be

29

found all over the world. The arrival nightmare took place all over again, for as we were walking around the unit to complete our paperwork, a Vamp could be seen overhead trailing smoke. It circled and on the second pass dived steeply into the ground.

Ken D was in a single-seater, from which a bailout was most difficult and unlikely to be successful at that altitude. The two-seat T11s were in the process of being equipped with the Martin Baker ejection seat. Accidents were a fact of life, in fact in the early 1950s, fatalities were running at one a day.

We met our instructors and launched into this new phase of training. Because we were through the initial filtering process, relationships with the staff were somewhat warmer. They knew that we would lose a few in the early stages, and after that it became a common goal to get people through the course.

My instructor was an ex-fighter pilot, with a love of good motor cars. He was a little distant as I struggled to cope with speed of the Vamp, particularly on landing. Our very first flight sort of set the tone, for as we set off down the runway with him talking me through the procedure, the engine exploded with a loud bang. We were just at the point of lift-off, and he calmly asked for me to close the LP cock, obviously struggling to slow the Vamp down. The tyres went with a pop, and we slowed to a halt just short of the end of the runway. The engine had split, firing dinner-plate sized pieces forward out through the air intakes.

My next trip was with the Squadron Commander, I guess as a sop in case I was disheartened. He had trouble raising the gear, but finally it retracted. He then decided to return in view of the initial problem. Little was said to me during this time as his concentration was on the Vamp. Needless to say, the gear would not extend and we circled to try everything and use up the fuel. A wheels-up landing is not a common occurrence, but in the Vamp it is not usually a death-defying experience. We skidded down the runway without a problem.

After these false starts I was taken aside in a fatherly way and told not to worry. I was relatively unmoved but the delay had meant that I was now well behind on the progress board.

First solo removed a lot of insecurity, but it at least meant that you could continue to the next hurdle. As before, instrument flying was my Achilles, and Mac's belief that it would come was wearing thin.

The ambulance and the Morris featured a lot in our lives, for coffee at the Green Tree or days at Redcar on the coast seemed to be the norm. Traffic to the coast was always busy at weekends, but use of the siren on the ambulance seemed to clear the way beautifully. As ever, overuse attracted the attention of the police and we were politely asked to remove it. A bugle was substituted and fear replaced respect in those ahead of us, but the result was the same, we had clear passage to the coast. It was often wise to hide the ambulance once we arrived at Redcar.

On one such outing we were jockeying back from the coast in two vehicles, the Morris and the ambulance. Just as we passed the airfield boundary the clutch on the Morris let go. Being an oil unit, there was nothing I could do but try and attract the attention of the ambulance in front. To no avail and so we set out to walk across the airfield to the Mess. The ambulance returned when we did not arrive, but drove by on to the parked Morris. By the time they had turned around, we had run back to the boundary fence and the road. We lay down in the road and formed barriers to prevent the ambulance from getting through. Dave G, seeing the throng, accelerated to such a speed that we fled onto the grass verge. Nellie the Moocher, overacting as usual, was the last to flee and therefore furthest away from the Austin when Dave G finally stopped. We all ran to the open back doors and sat on the stretchers as Dave kept the vehicle in motion. Mike was now running as fast as he could and just caught hold of the large doors. He put one foot on the low step but could not make the final stride into the Austin. He was now hopping world championship distances, with less and less chance of making it into the back. He was almost too far away for us to reach him, and yelling at Dave to slow down was a bad move. He braked hard unable to see what was happening, and Nellie flew through the stretcher area to bury himself through the small window that connects the driver's cab with the back. He was out cold but coming to as we unloaded him into Sick Quarters. So much for bravado.

The St John Ambulance sign on the sides of the vehicle had been altered to show a hand dripping with blood. This was supposed to represent a drop for each member of the course who was terminated. The artwork was good and to be the cause of another incident.

Returning from the coffee shop in the evening could be timed to coincide with the Middleton bus. The bus stop was on the corner by the fish and chip shop. Patrons of that delightful establishment would queue for the bus armed with a bag of cod and chips. The ambulance could be cornered at fearful speeds, as the overhang on the rear wheels would strike the ground and prevent it from overturning. At ten past ten, we would slide round the comer, looking well out of control, and the queue would disintegrate into a melee of bodies and fish and chips.

The agreement was that the vehicle was to be fuelled at all times and under no circumstances was the spare fuel can to be left empty. We motored back from Darlington, six of us in all. Reaching the outskirts of Middleton One Row, the Austin stopped, out of fuel. A quick look in the back showed that the spare can was empty also. We prepared to walk back to camp, and realised that we had stopped outside a pub set well back from the road. In the north, an ambulance always brings out the inquisitive, and so it was as a troop of patrons spilled out onto the road. They furtively edged around the Austin, and we in a flash decided to play to the audience. Bob lay on the stretcher and was covered by the blanket. We carefully carried the stretcher out making noises as to the seriousness of his condition. He was given a cigarette, and made no attempt to inhale. The cigarette was removed and I placed my ear to his chest. Looking very serious I laid the blanket over his face. The locals, ever respectful of death, lowered their heads and removed their caps. We were now out of ideas and so carefully returned the stretcher into the ambulance. One observant local noticed the altered insignia on the side of the ambulance, and commented in a broad north country accent, that there was a hand dripping with blood on the side. He was hushed into silence as we turned and walked away. Once around the corner, we ran, hoping to be unobserved. After a few minutes we returned to peer round the corner and see if they had left. Bob was trapped in the vehicle, and we did not wish him to give the game away. He was released without incident and we fled to find some petrol.

The locals must have returned looking for the corpse, for the following day Dave and I, as owners of the ambulance, were called to the Chief Instructor's office. He had received a call from the *Daily Mirror*, a widely circulated national newspaper, regarding a corpse that never was. Not knowing what had transpired, he played for time and eventually found us. We were bound to silence and avoided the calls that came for us, for a local garage had identified us as the owners. After work ceased the next day, a rush of students found us and said that there was a gorgeous blonde in the bar looking for the ambulance guys. She was made to feel quite at home, but nobody let on that we indeed were the wanted men. It was an intelligent ploy by the *Mirror* but she left knowing that the true story was being withheld from her. The next day a full half page article appeared entitled, 'The Corpse that never was'. The unit was used to high jinx, but the message was relayed from above: no more, or else.

Middleton is infamous for its Window. So the story goes that a student was practicing single-engined work in a Meteor. This aircraft commands a healthy respect when flying on one of its two engines. It was probably the most difficult of all the twin jets, and so made a superb training aircraft. It had however been the last resting place of many pilots. In this case, a single-engined overshoot was attempted and somewhere along the way, he lost control and veered off the runway. The Mess was a sturdy structure and even a Meteor at full power on one engine failed to knock it down. The pilot hit the corner of the second floor, just below the roof. He went into his own room and was terminated by the large coping stone falling onto him. The damage was repaired, but stands as a memorial to the necessary skills of flight under asymmetric conditions. It now forms part of the terminal hotel building at Teesside.

With the Korean pressure now receding, FTS's were being amalgamated. The Vampire training was to move to Worksop, in the lee of the industrial Midlands. The weather factor was probably worse than anywhere else that could have been selected. We arrived in dismal weather to find an RAF station that had altered little since the War. It was arranged in Nissen hut sites, spread around a large airfield. One central road connected all the facilities. Our squadron building was around the far side of the airfield, set in the woods.

As an austerity measure, RAF ground crew were replaced by civilian contract workers. The local labour pool was mostly miners, laid off or unable to further work in the Notts coalfields. They knew little of aircraft, but could be delightful with their dour manner and dry humour.

The next months were seemingly interwoven unendingly with the weather. It restricted our flying and our everyday life. Tougher living always seems to bring out a camaraderie, a common attitude to difficulties, that the miserable conditions would have otherwise brought. Nissen huts became centres of entertainment.

One of our diminished number was a printer by trade, used, it seemed, to living in a state of chaos and marginal cleanliness. He was a National Service entrant, and therefore paid even less than we were. He used to do his own laundry to save money, and to pass the weekends, was rebuilding an early Morris in his room. It became a joke to try and discern what was laundry and what was oily rags. He built a clothes line outside to hang up his washing, a regular weekend affair. Each room had a coal stove and coal bin as the only heat source. It was fairly common to actually climb on the roof and feed coal down the pipe, to ensure that the fire burnt for as long as possible. We fed turf down Keith M's chimney and watched to see his reaction to his blackened clothes hanging on the line.

There were many model aircraft builders, but with a difference: Saturday was combat day. The sky was filled with gyrating models bent on ramming other aircraft and surviving to be declared the victor. It was wise to be able to take cover, for these tiny models travelling at high speed could be lethal, especially when the nose of some of them was filled with lead. Damage to the outer shell of the huts was easily concealed, but windows were another matter.

I had the misfortune to be appointed inventory holder, as that very necessary secondary duty that all junior officers are required to perform. Inventories and JTK never did get along, but this intro was a fascinating look into entrenched RAF thinking. Secondary duties made and dismantled many a young officer's career. Really it was a cheap labour scam. Flying was a big enough job in itself and there were professionals recruited to perform these tasks, but not enough.

Worksop was so widely spread out that the main transportation was bicycles. The bike inventory was a nightmare, as so many were 'borrowed' and pedalled to a new location. The weekend spot was by the bus stop, a mile away on the main road. Returning revellers would search the hedgerow for a machine and in general few were lost. The RAF system was that you could be issued with a bike, and a log card was made up and duly signed. If you lost your bike, you had to pay for it. Of course the bike serial numbers were so abused that they were unusable. This meant that handing a bike in to retrieve your log card was a simple matter of finding a bike, any bike. When I took over the inventory from the previous holder, we spent days driving around the base collecting bikes. The two senior NCOs did a number on me, and I believed that the 179 bikes were actually on the unit.

My assistant ran the issue on a day-to-day basis, and all was fine until it came time for me to hand over to a new unfortunate. We obtained the truck and searched the base for bikes. No matter how we cooked it there were some nine bikes missing. No problem, says my wily assistant, well schooled in the ways of the military mind. He then proceeded to saw nine bikes in half. No attempt was made to disguise the work. No sir, stores needs to see enough to prove that these are the remnants of bikes, and bingo, we had proof of the now missing eighteen bikes. Needless to say, aircrew were eventually dropped from these duties, but I banged into the problem several times more before I was able to avoid them.

The ambulance had been consigned to vehicle heaven, or maybe it was left at Middleton; the new attraction was a lovely London taxi. Ron W's father was the operator of a fleet, and we therefore were able to obtain a 1939 version as a course vehicle.

It had the authentic baggage area where the front passenger seat usually is, and the rear was glassed off with a landau roof that folded back in summer. We decorated the back as a party area with Chianti bottles and the baggage area received a large metal beer barrel (88 pints). To pressurize the barrel we installed a foot pump on the wide running board. It was a simple matter to step out onto the board and apply a few pumps, but very disconcerting for other traffic. We discovered that one could crouch down behind the beer barrel and see through a hole out to the front of the car. Nellie managed to thoroughly disturb some slow-moving traffic that we were in, when he, as the driver, left the seat and asked the car alongside if we were at this spot on the map. The taxi moved steadily along with Nellie standing on the running board and the hidden man steering and using the hand throttle.

The winter was awful, with heavy fog and low visibility. Flying dropped to an all-time low. There were several accidents, and the black armband never seemed to be off my greatcoat for the funerals. The aerobatic ace on Meteors got cement poisoning when he smacked into the concrete at high speed. He flew the same aircraft for his display work and likely overstressed it continually. This accident re-occurred in like conditions many times in my career.

Towards the end of the course, when I was still having trouble with instrument flying, we were up doing formation practice. I loved this activity and was comfortable with it. It was also necessary to make up for my instrument deficiency. It was a standard Midlands day with a thick haze below 12,000 feet. A tail chase is a follow the leader exercise, led by an instructor with two students in the middle and another instructor at the end. We twisted and turned, learning judgment in power and control movement. The leader pulled up in a loop and I as number three in the chase followed the sports star ahead. The descent over the top of the loop led into the thick haze. He was slow pulling up and even slower to follow over the top. It became difficult for me to keep them both in sight. He continued to descend at very high speed and disappeared into the haze. Having split my attention, I half followed until the instructor behind called for me to climb out of the haze.

At that moment there was a flash and I knew instantly what it was. All manner of conflicting arguments rush through your head, but you know that he has gone in at high speed. Bailout is almost impossible at those speeds. He had impacted the village of Harby, down the main street, at a fairly low angle, close enough to believe that he was almost at the point of recovery. Harby had been voted one of the prettiest villages in England. The accident and the civilian casualties put a pall over the course.

I mention the sports star for it features much in RAF thinking. Such is the importance of sport, that many stars were eased through pilot training when maybe they should not have been. He was definitely struggling with his flying, but it is believed that the airbrake in the Vampire could deform the structure at very high speed. If so, recovery could be delayed or even prevented. They were aging aircraft and this learning curve was to impact upon me later.

Chapter II

ABOUT THIS TIME the fixture in the RAF was looking bleak, and I was having much navel gazing to assess my future. Girlfriends, driving too fast and flying with a vengeance all seemed to necessitate a rethink of my future. Life could be most enjoyable, but I kept returning to the belief that this could not be all that there was. The sight of my instructors sitting night after night at the bar, forever railing against the system, brought on a sense of foreboding that I found unsettling. I was not really a drinker. I had passed through the learning phase, drunk my share, and then been shunted to one side as I selected Coke or other soft drinks as my tipple. This may seem a minor point, but you were a social outcast if you did not drink like a man. People would say, 'I am not buying you a Coke, have a beer like everyone else.' Once on this route, you are under continual pressure to forget soft drinks. I even created a mystique over Coke, by asking for a spoon with which to stir the beverage. I liked it flat, but initially everyone believed that I was adding something to make it bubble up so much. I always stayed till the end of parties, and found less and less need for alcohol. That is not to say that I did not have a drink, but it was what I wanted when I wanted.

It will be easy to see that by making certain stands on aspects of life, I was drifting away from the main stream. I needed to understand the philosophical reasons, the What, the Why and the How.

I was journeying to Nottingham most nights, going to jazz clubs or returning with my girlfriend to the Mess. This meant four round trips, if I was to return her back home. I had a series of vehicles, none of which lasted too long. One such ancient marvel was a Triumph Dolomite circa 1934. It ran after a fashion, but to keep the rear doors closed I had jammed a pair of flying gloves where the lock should have been.

It was a particularly foggy period, with visibilities less than 50 yards for over a week. I left for a Nottingham pick-up, intending to return later that night. Vis dropped to a few yards and the electric fuel pump decided that now was a good time to quit. I was unable to get the car off the road by virtue of high grass verges. The bonnet was opened so that the required thump could be given to the pump. I heard traffic grinding towards me and thought that I should turn on the headlights to at least try and illuminate the car. Reaching in from the left-hand side whilst still peering for the traffic I could hear, I accidentally turned the lights off. At that moment a truck loomed out of the night and I stepped back to avoid the crash. That step put me flat on my back in a water-filled ditch.

I scrambled up to peer through the grass as the truck thumped into the back of the Triumph. What followed was screeching of brakes and the tinkling of broken glass, as the vehicles following the truck all drove into each other. Do you run or bluster?

When they saw this soaking wet figure now weighing hundreds of pounds in a sodden duffel coat, the lynch mob mood was in the air. I explained about the pump failure and my inability to get off the road and they were more interested in settling their accounts. Damage was all minor and they drove on leaving me, which was ideal, as the shunt had somehow freed the pump and I resumed the trip to Nottingham.

The Triumph was replaced with a memorable Riley Nine. It had originally been a saloon, but the fabric roof had been cut off and replaced with a custom-built soft top. The crash box was a learning affair particularly as the gear selector mechanism had a second gate remote from the gearbox. It was possible, if you were too rushed, to select first gear in the gearbox and third gear in the remote box. The previous owner had been doing the rebuild in his front room until an ultimatum from his wife, 'either it goes or I go', had forced him to sell it.

Dropping off my girlfriend, I had removed the side covers to permit easier exit. These I placed on the top of the roof. Mental focus was not on the car when I left, and thus they were lost, which made for very draughty driving from then on. Fitted at the rear were Ridemaster springs which allowed you to compensate for loads or alter the road holding. With six new tyres many an hour was spent behind the squadron experimenting with cornering speeds and technique. This sense of pushing it to the limit started to pervade everything I did. In the search for some revelation about what all this was about, living on the edge was the route chosen.

Two things happened which deflected me enough to survive this period. I tried to have a discussion with my father, to see if he had an attitude to life that I might borrow. He had never been very verbal and I do not ever recall any deep conversations. Such was the case again, for he considered that looking for some meaning to life was ridiculous. Maybe I did not explain myself adequately, but I realised that I was truly now on my own, formulating my own philosophies and standards. My mother was always there, but as a listener and comfort.

The second happening was at a Mess function where the fatherly figure of the Flight Commander, Mick M, spoke to my girlfriend about his concerns for me. He had seen enough students face this point, and he said that I would be dead if someone did not take me in hand. There's pressure for you, but she gave a new twist on life, a responsibility that I slowly accepted.

There was no dramatic revelation, just a view that it was worth continuing to see what was around the corner. Curiosity and the belief that not knowing is bad enough, but that not knowing that you do not know is the ultimate crime, became my rules for living.

Suez came and went, its impact on me was that a flying job was most unlikely after finishing the course. I even tried to join a number of foreign air forces and all but the Canadian required citizenship. Our political masters were pontificating about the new era of missiles where pilots would no longer be needed. Britain introduced fuel rationing and fuel coupons became the new currency. Being now emotionally tied to my girlfriend, I needed transport. The new minicar age was with us, and West German technology responded with a whole slew of remarkable vehicles. The Heinkel, Messerschmidt of aircraft fame, along with BMW and Goggomobil all produced cheap transportation.

My Heinkel would seat three/four, using a 198cc engine that had its origins in a ground power unit made for German jet fighters. At 45 m.p.h. it would do over 65 m.p.g. When money was very tight I managed to coax 102 m.p.g. on a cross-country trip. The front-opening door and futuristic shape always attracted attention, for you were very much like goldfish in a bowl. It had aircraft-type construction using tubular roll cages and these were to save my skin some months later. The Goggo was a miniature car, much smaller than the famed Mini Minor of the sixties. It had a 360 cc engine and its diminutive weight allowed for a spirited performance.

The Course was coming to the end and memorable parties were organised with the staff in Clumber Park and on the Trent river at Gunthorpe. My folks produced the food, and the convoy pitched camp on the river bank. We started cooking round a camp fire when an irate farmer appeared. This was his land and only a right of way existed. Fatherly Mick M took him on one side and in no time he and his wife returned with better cooking equipment. They joined us for a camp fire session and we were entreated to leave the borrowed pans under a bush where he would pick them up. People drifted off and the diehards were left to return en masse. The taxi certainly could not transport fourteen people back to Worksop, but we might make it to my house to borrow Dad's car. With twelve inside and two on the roof covered by a blanket to avoid the eyes of the law, we struggled to my home. Waking my folks up at 4 a.m. to borrow the car is not an everyday occurrence, but I promised to return it by midday Sunday. Several of the girls of the group accompanied me home on Sunday to thank my mother for the food. She was most impressed.

On one of my last trips as a student, I was preparing to start the Vamp 5. A look down the flight line showed several other aircraft in preparation. As I turned away there was a gigantic explosion, I could not run with this aircraft strapped to my back, and then the pieces started to fall; large slabs of tarmac and a powerful smell of kerosene.

The dispersal area had tarmacadam applied over the wartime concrete. The civilian refuellers were none too careful in their refuelling practices. Fuel over the period had pooled beneath the tarmac and ignited when the Vamp flamed a start. An enormous area was exploded, with some damage to aircraft, but nobody was hurt.

Passout Parade was going to be an unforgettable affair. We had tried marching at a practice parade outside a hangar. Our Fuehrer had led us off the concrete area into the drainage mud. Apart from a major cleaning bill, it was a sight never to be repeated. They decided that as we were only going to be eight passing out, that we would do the whole thing in the Mess. The Mess floor was painted, I think with red lead, for it never dried. Continued movement resulted in increasing your height as your shoes picked up layer after layer of the paint.

It was found that there was not enough room to manoeuvre in the ante-room and so we assembled in the bar to march through the curtain into the ante-room. There was much hilarity as we suggested a Conga, but composure was regained for the serious matter of wings presentation. The presenting officer was an old VC, who lived locally. He was a tremendous old fellow, but the pre-ceremony drinks had unsteadied him somewhat. The Course photo shows not one pair of coveted Royal Air Force wings pinned on straight.

We were now posted to Worksop to await further posting, which meant that you became the available labour pool. Jerry, get your Queen's Regulations out and tell them that they cannot do this to us. We eventually were tasked with building an assault course, amongst other things. Tools were provided, and every morning, like the seven dwarfs, it was off to work we go. Mike fought it then decided that he would dig the biggest damn hole the RAF had ever seen. He would accept no help, and slowly he disappeared from sight as the days went by. We never finished the assault course, but Mike's hole could be seen from the air long after Worksop was returned to farmland.

The story now was that flying jobs were going to be few and far between. Therefore only the top few would likely get a squadron post. There was, as before, a sort of pecking order. I had finished Hullavington seventh, Worksop as fourth held up by my poor instrument flying. The next phase, Operational Conversion Unit, would be the make or break for all of us.

Pembrey lies in south Wales, close to Pendine Sands of motoring history. Many early speed records were attempted there. Pembrey had its own beach many miles long and was a very happy camp. The staff were all ex-fighter pilots who, in the main, were keen for you to be the best. The first check flight there was the dreaded instrument ride. Failure usually resulted in immediate posting to less arduous duties. Removal of your wings was possible, for it was necessary to complete at least six months productive flying before the Ministry of Defence considered you to have irretrievably earned them.

I approached the trip with the cold realisation that it was up to me, and me alone. There was little friendliness between the staff and students prior to this trip, it was all business. I landed in a state of euphoria having done an impeccable ride. My instructor must have sensed my state, and I had to tell him that I had never flown that way before. He echoed Mac's belief that it would come – I could not believe it.

The first phase of the course was completed on the Vampire again. Weapons and tactics were now paramount. It was assumed that you could fly; all that remained was to learn how to do something with your aircraft. We started into battle formation, flown as a four ship, two instructors and two students. At 45,000 ft we were learning battle breaks. This manoeuvre is called for when an enemy aircraft has appeared behind the formation, and is in a position to threaten. In the Vamp it calls for max power, max roll until the nose of the Vamp is below the horizon, and then max rate turn to throw the attacker off his aim. All four aircraft turn in unison, and so contact is necessary between all members of the formation and maybe trying to locate the attacker as well.

The Vamp has small rudders that free stream and light pedal pressure can initiate a yaw, or sideways motion. Most aircraft are not as sensitive to this control input, being more directionally stable.

A break was called and the learnt response carried out meticulously. I was careful to counter any yawing tendencies, and pulled the max g load required. The bang on my head from the canopy opening mechanism, stunned me momentarily. I was in a rapidly rotating spin and arching into the vertical. Spinning is a prohibited manoeuvre in the Vamp, as the small rudder area can make recovery difficult. I worked out that I was spinning to the left, and the reassuring voice of my instructor informed me that that was the case. I applied recovery controls, being very careful not to apply too much forward elevator. The necessary pause, and the Vamp snapped out of the spin. I was down to 12,000 ft and with a smashed flying helmet, ready to go home. No such luck, join up and we will commence a tailchase. I knew that I had not initiated the spin and was therefore cautious in handling the controls. The rearmost instructor kept urging me to keep up, and I was not given time to dwell on the incident.

RAF Worksop, Vampire FB5.

On landing, it was assumed that it was my fault in that I had applied the rudder as I tensed up. The aircraft was the Station Commander's personal plane, and I was treated to some harsh words. After questioning, it was prudent to check the aircraft and lo and behold, they found that the cables going to the elevator were badly out of tolerance. Apologies do not feature much in military discipline and such was the case here.

The next day I was returning from another flight when I saw the Chief Instructor walking back across the concrete. He was ashen-faced and deathly pale. I thought that he was sick and walked towards him in case. He eventually was aware of me and turned to place a fatherly hand on my shoulder. 'Go to my office,' he said, 'and I will meet you there, for you were right.'

It transpired that he was doing the air test on the CO's aircraft and had entered a spin at 48,000 ft in similar conditions to me. The recovery was attempted and as he was at least six feet six in height, he was able to apply far more elevator than I, with his long arms. This minor difference in physical dimensions almost caused his demise. Too much elevator caused the aircraft to bunt or go negative on recovery, and immediately flick into an inverted spin.

Recognition of an inverted spin is usually the problem, but here he knew what had happened. Recovery from the inverted spin was tried and on recovery it flicked into a normal erect spin. He was unsure how many reversals were completed, but he was well below bail-out height before he managed to level out. He warmed to my predicament, and we were to meet again later in my career.

The aircraft was declared 'rogue', and the test pilots called to evaluate it. The imbalance in the control cables had distorted the airframe, and the rogue designation is usually given to aircraft that demonstrate unusual flight characteristics, such that they have a special red log book. Within the week it was to kill the test pilot who was tasked with evaluating it. My bone dome (helmet) was retained as an example of the protection it gave.

Llanelly was a quiet town, with little to attract active pilots. We therefore made our entertainment on the beach almost nightly. Car races were run and the challenge made to drive across the river estuary to the Pendine side. John E had a Buick Straight Eight, an enormous monster by UK standards. He waited until the tide was out and he flashed across the river and sands. He stayed there a little too long, and was confined to a small dry island in the estuary. He raced around the confines of the island and wound up the Buick to high speed. Suddenly straightening when he had enough speed, he charged through the waters as we cheered and watched. It disappeared in a large cloud of spray and reappeared sideways with much wheelspin. He made it to the bank and we rushed to see the damage. The radiator was finished and the fan blades highly polished. The engine must have swallowed a lot of sand but it ran satisfactorily after the radiator was replaced.

Returning from the beach one afternoon, I was driving around the perimeter track and entered the corner a little fast. The three-wheel Heinkel cornered well to the left, the side of the driver, but to the right could easily become a two-wheel affair. In my efforts to keep it on three wheels I dropped off the hard surface and rolled it. It took off the mirrors and turn indicators, and a paint job was needed. This imprudence cost money and as I was travelling home regularly to visit my wife-to-be, I felt the irritation of no money.

A short time later, when returning in the rain from the Post Office, I slid across the road and into the ditch on entering the camp. I ran back to the Mess and asked for able-bodied assistance to throw the damn thing into the river. They flooded out of the TV room to view my incident. When we returned to the car it was surrounded by amazed Welshmen, who had never seen such a vehicle. I had struck the bridge over the stream and climbed out through the sunroof. Whilst I urged them to tip it into the stream, they easily pulled it back onto the road. Repair number two was less costly, the roll cage construction prevented major damage.

The Vamp stage was completed by all and the assessments were keenly noted. My goal of finishing at the top was not helped by only average shooting scores.

The next phase was carried out on the Hunter Mk 1. The Hunter had been rushed into service on super priority production to meet the MiG threat. It replaced the F-86 Sabre, a US aircraft on loan to the service. It was inferior to the Sabre in some respects, but later models redressed the balance. The Mk 1 was only in front-line service for a short time and relegated to the OCUs.

It is worth taking a moment to look at design philosophy of the times. The Hunter is a superb looking aircraft, just retiring from service in the Swiss Air Force in 1995. The designer faced formidable problems in trying to cram the large engines of the day into a small airframe, along with sufficient fuel for the job – air defence. It was a transonic aircraft with an exceptional rate of climb. Power controls were needed and they had a learning curve also. The fuel load was 289 gals, sufficient for about forty-five minutes flying. This meant that everything happened fast if you were to accomplish anything,

The Mk 1 had three weaknesses. The brakes were meant to be anti-skid, or Maxaret. Only a few of the OCU Hunters were so equipped. Landing at these new higher speeds, some 35 kts faster than the Vamp, could easily burst a tyre with the attendant risk of running off the runway. The fuel system had manual balancing and it required constant attention. A slight imbalance needed a pump to be turned off which almost invariably meant that you were busy doing something else when the fuel became balanced. This led to a need to swap pumps and the see-saw began. If you ran a side dry, the engine would stop, a pretty good incentive for apportioning the fuel system much of your time. The final sort-the-men-from-the-boys feature was the power control system. This was a time of no simulators or dual-control Hunters. We were checked out blindfold, sitting on an ordinary wooden chair against a photo of the cockpit.

To engage the power controls required you, after engine start, to hold up the elevator switch with one hand and beat the elevator for and aft to engage the Pawl locking mechanism. Three thousand psi was opposing you in this task, but the locks usually went in after the regulation curses. You then had to repeat the procedure for the ailerons. It was possible to reduce the pressure by lowering the flaps whilst you tried to engage. Now to the real point of the explanation. The switches were electric controlling hydraulic circuits. All manner of failures could result in partial locks and other dreadfuls. Any time you sensed a problem, you hit those switches down and off. This meant that you would be in manual, with very stiff controls, but a get-you-home situation.

Some selection process was used to allocate aircraft for the first solo flight. I did not know whether to be thrilled at being given a non-Maxaret aircraft. All solos took place at the same time, and instructors stayed to watch all the landings.

The acceleration was adrenalin producing, and the Hunter wobble from overcontrol was evident in us all. One instructor used to do a Hunter solo demonstration on a bar stool, so common were the reactions. After getting the feel of the beast, we wandered back to the circuit with high pulse rates. All the landings were safe, and nobody burst a tyre. The second trip was to expand the flight envelope and involved a high-speed run at 1,500 ft down the Bristol Channel; 525 kts was a rush and I raised the nose to complete my run, when there was a thump and the hyd light glowed red. Just thinking about the drills took me to 16,000 ft where the stiff manual control forces made themselves known. A manual landing is not a major problem, unless it is gusty. I landed OK, and little was said, as if to prepare you for these everyday occurrences.

We entered the tactics phase, and as this is mostly formation, I was enjoying it immensely. We briefed for a four-ship take-off in two pairs. I was number four following the instructor lead at number three.

We lined up and the first pair rolled down the runway. Brake release and off we go in pursuit. Lift-off gear up and I am aware that all is not well ahead. We pass number two who is now going very slowly, and I am struggling to stay in contact with my leader. I look back to see the Hunter explode on the rail line. Little was said but we are diverted to Chivenor, the other Hunter school across the channel. Bill J and I had come through the training together, and we were both survivors of the original course. I doubted that he had escaped but it was always possible. Not concentrating on the landing at Chivenor very nearly put me in the undershoot. I was mad at myself for not being able to detach and focus, and I swore never again to allow myself the opportunity to become emotionally distracted. Dream about flying, do not fly about dreaming.

Bill had had the dreaded partial lock situation. He had power on part of the aileron range and in trying to avoid his leader, he had throttled back and probably used two hands to try and resolve his predicament with the ailerons. He stalled onto the rail line and ejected far too low. The crash vehicles damaged themselves on the railway, delaying our return till late afternoon. We were all in the Mess when the tannoy ordered everyone back to the flight line. All the students were put back in the air, so that introspection was avoided, a risk that I doubt would be taken today.

Whist the Heinkel was undergoing repair, I desperately needed to go home. I was offered the use of a 750 Triumph, a large motorcycle by any standards. I had used a 125 Velocette at Worksop to eke out the fuel coupons, but had no experience of a big bike. I set off on sports afternoon, a time set aside for anything but sports, and climbed into the mountains. Power delivery was like a light switch, on or off and I realised that the over 200-mile trip was going to be risky.

With a rare submission to common sense, I turned back. The owner was pleased to see his machine back in one piece, for he had been ribbed that he would never see me or the bike again. Years later we would meet at Benson and he would suffer a Vamp accident not far from Pembrey. The cause is still a mystery.

Pembrey was due to close after our course; this fate can be most disconcerting when almost every base you land at closes down. We wound down towards the final selection process and by now knew that there would be one, maybe two, postings to front-line fighter squadrons. In the end Mac's students won out. Bob, of power line fame, was second, and I got first choice of the two available squadrons. The instructors all tried to bias you towards their old outfits, but the consensus was 66(F) Squadron. This was a squadron with a long history, now based in the north of England at Acklington. The first tour is a make or break situation, it colours opinions that follow you around for a very long time. You arrive with the basic tools of a fighter pilot, but need to demonstrate a rapid learning ability and that indefinable esprit.

I arrived at Acklington knowing little of the people there. One friendly face was Derek B, who had been ahead of me all through training. In fact we were acquainted from Kirton days. This long friendship still exists and is counted as one of life's richer experiences.

The mood at 66 was sombre and not conducive to conviviality at all. They seemed to be little more than a bunch of individuals going about some ill-defined duties. I should explain that squadron training was a chore for someone. Leadership has to come from the top and 66 was in the process of yet another squadron commander change. Morale was non-existent, and Derek was even cautious about talking to me, in case it broke some unwritten rule. The attitude was make the coffee, keep the place swept and tidy, and do not bother us. 66 Squadron flew the Hunter Mk 6, a more powerful version and also heavier. I expected to be led into the new version in a controlled manner, similar to the training environment that had been the norm for the last two years. The squadron was broken into groups who protected their space and attitudes closely. It was oppressive and a great letdown. I guess as a hold-over from the War, nobody wanted to get too close, in case you did not make the grade.

After a long time of being ignored, I was briefed for a flight by the abrasive naval officer, who was doing an exchange tour with the RAF. He was short, curt and just civil. The short flight passed without event and drew no comment from anyone. I was aware that the runway was marginal for the Hunter 6, certainly for early flights. The second trip was again briefed by the 'Fishead', as naval aviators are known. He demanded a speed of 128 kts on finals and would brook no argument that this was necessary. Naval aviators were known for their slow approaches, a requirement for carrier landings. The Hunter with the unmodified wing did not perform that well at very slow speeds. With the worry of the short runway in my mind and the need to follow his dictates, this was going to be a tense trip. I returned to the circuit at exactly the briefed landing weight and turned finals for landing. There was a gusty cross wind that should have modified my approach, but he had sneeringly demanded 128 kts and I would try and oblige. Now flying to a couple of knots is almost impossible, it just becomes a target.

I aimed for the very end of the runway, to waste as little as possible. Runway behind you is of little use. At less than 50 ft the aircraft caught a gust and the wing dropped. With my slow speed I was on the way to a stall and maybe a rotation into a spin. Aileron would not work at that speed and I applied rudder in a desperate effort to pick up the wing. The Hunter hit hard and I knew that it was damaged. I had put the main wheels on the concrete and the tail had struck the grass. A tail strike put an aircraft out of service for a long time, and our daily serviceability could scarcely do with another Hunter unavailable. It was put down to inexperience and shuffled in the changeover to yet another boss. Nevertheless, I had slid to the bottom of the pile and would face staying there for most of this tour.

Flying was very limited as we had so few aircraft on the line each day. Flying with me seemed like leper duty and absolutely no information flowed from the old hands to the new. Quite the reverse, for you might learn something and be better at it than them. A cold, stern-faced decision was made to learn in spite of them and as ever in those situations I overdid it and stood my ground when maybe I should not have.

Socially there were several who were uncomfortable with the atmosphere, and they tried to lessen the burden. My mild drinking habits did not help, and I became more of a loner. Betti and I had planned to get married, which at that time was frowned upon. You were treated as unmarried until the age of twenty-five, and received none of the benefits. The more that these barriers were placed before me, the more I determined to beat the system. I ignored the protocol and gave the now fragmented squadron as little as they gave me.

Chris B bailed out after an engine failure, and the new boss was a total disaster. We put a stick on a plaque on the wall, entitled the Big Stick from Group. He was incapable of any meaningful decisions –

every morning he would call Group HQ for orders that he himself should have made. Hence the big stick.

Combat was the lifeblood of a fighter pilot and skills at this aerial dogfighting are hard learnt. There are techniques that can be passed on, but on 66 Squadron nothing was taught. You would go up in a pair, enter a predetermined scenario and generally be derided as the old hand appeared on your tail. This derision further stiffened my resolve in that I would never again be caught. Easier said than done, but on one fateful trip, the leader known for his put-downs, lead me off for a sortie. We started the manoeuvring and I set up the best turning mode that I could. He was able to make very little headway against this accurate turn. Pulling high g is tiring and there was a lot of grunting going on in my cockpit. We stayed with no advantage until the fuel ran out and a return to base was necessary. He did not know that I would have dived into cloud rather than lose that fight.

Gradually I improved my combat skills, using all the legal and illegal manoeuvres to avoid ever getting caught. Several other things conspired to take the spotlight off me. There was yet another change of boss, the winter exercise, the arrival of more pilots and the rivalry between 66 Squadron and the night-fighter squadron, number 29 Squadron. With one day-fighter squadron and one night-fighter squadron on a unit, friendly rivalry is to be expected, if not encouraged.

For a period, this rivalry had very unfriendly overtones. They were using the NF 14 Meteor, an aircraft at the end of its useful life. Our succession of new bosses and appalling record and spirit, meant that we were not held in very high regard Their boss, later to be a very very senior officer, was imperious and unbending. It had all the makings of an unfortunate conflict.

In the bar one night, the usual chant about 29's abilities reached a high spot when their boss tried to order 66 to leave. Such behaviour is not normal, although he was within his rights to do so. You may perceive that you have won, when in fact you can rarely climb back from such action – 29 therefore felt the scorn of having a boss that was seen as a clown.

On a lighter note, the poor old Meteor came in for a lot of ribbing. One night, when asked by the GCI (Ground Controlled Intercept) to climb to 45,000 ft and turn onto a northerly heading, the pilot was heard to reply, 'Which do you want?' Certainly he could do one or the other, but the Meteor just did not have the performance to do both.

The winter exercise came and put a stop to inter-squadron antics, as did the arrival of two former 66 Squadron pilots, Colin C and Glyn O. These two reprobates tore through the unit and turned it upside down. They were returning as part of a scheme to keep former pilots current on the Hunter. They had little regard for stuffy formality, and their careers were safe from all but gross errors during the exercise. I managed to fly with them a number of times, and they were ready to help and advise. They were actually instructors taking time off from their primary duties, and it showed.

I witnessed several major foul-ups – one involved two aircraft going off the runway as the leader had problems and failed to advise his number two, and so they both went off. Another involved a visiting pilot from the MOD who was cadging trips. He tried to take off in manual, a no-no, and he aborted successfully. He then taxied back up the runway causing the next pair to abort. Two more aircraft were scrambled from our dispersal area and they met him coming the other way on the narrow taxiway. He had now locked up six squadron aircraft and we had failed to get more than one airborne.

The rumblings were within me that success on a fighter squadron such as 66, was having a loud voice and a good PR campaign. It often had little to do with ability. To compound matters, the dreaded secondary duties were being dished out. I had to be I/C Boxing, which demanded that you manage this sport, mostly in the evenings. It destroyed any home life and meant staying on base to take care of things.

The inventory reared its ugly head again, and I was given control of the Squadron Clothing and Equipment Inventory. This mammoth task was usually run by two officers and two senior NCOs. The paperwork was staffed by two permanent airman. I did not know, could not know, what all the items were. Therefore on accepting the inventory I had to believe that this was a left-handed grommet snatcher, whereas it looked just like that one over there. I had all the squadron aircraft on the schedule, including all the ground equipment. What an archaic system, bound to failure, but of course there was always going to be somebody to hang for it. The winter was cold and the ground crew had to work outside in freezing conditions. I sought proper winter clothing for them, and my persistence finally led me to the Stores where cold weather clothing of Korean war vintage was held. I demanded and cajoled to get it released to me. The troops were impressed when I arrived with the truckload of clothing. What a coup, but it was short lived, when the kapok-filled clothing became soaked in our English winters. Totally useless and in fact dangerous as the troops chilled in their heavy soggy garments.

I had married quietly and treated the system with just enough reverence to quiet any indignation. We moved to a cottage high on the Pennines, about twelve miles from base. Whilst I was committed to burning a future for myself in the RAF, I knew that it could not be alone. Without caring, behaviour can develop unchecked. I needed the burden of someone depending upon me. At twenty years of age with a ready-made daughter of seven, it was going to be a daunting task. We had driven up from Nottingham where I had traded the Heinkel for a 1939 Vauxhall.

The trip from Pembrey to trade in the Heinkel was momentous. I left my friends and headed into the rainy night rather than wait till morning. Through the steep valleys and coalfields of south Wales, on a misty corner in blinding rain, I was confronted by a vehicle well over on my side of the road. Avoiding action was successful, but there was no way that I could prevent it from ploughing ahead off the road. We flew over the hedge and I waited for the bang. I knew that I was dead, for the drop-offs were notorious in this area. We hit quite gently and then began tumbling. The round shape of the Heinkel allowed it to tumble unchecked. Then we were stopped, engine running for I must have pushed it into neutral, lights on and wipers going. I never even got out, just drove straight ahead until I came to a stream. Left or right made no difference, and so I turned and saw a dim light in the distance. Over a small cattle bridge and into a farmyard where somebody was mucking out. He must have thought that I was a Martian and stood transfixed as I drove out into a lane and finally the main road I had gone off and tumbled down the only stretch of grass hillside for many miles. Strike three left me believing that although i was not lucky, I was always lucky when it mattered most, when your life was at risk. The Heinkel was scratched and all the external bits were missing, but they still traded for that Vauxhall.

Incidents were commonplace, but one stands out as a classic of communication and attitude. I had gone into the hangar to sit in an aircraft and utilise my time practicing checks and drills. The Hunter selected after checking with the hangar supervisor, was just one of the squadron aircraft. On climbing in I found a new switch panel not known to me. Marked in yellow and black, which in RAF language means for emergency use, there were two buttons. I looked around and tried to find some indication of their purpose. With power off the aircraft, I risked a quick poke at one button. The cockpit lit up momentarily and went black again. Pressing both lights illuminated all the warning lights and the fuel system visual indicators. The implications of these switches was large and I therefore retreated to the crew room to ask if anyone knew about them. The response was the usual: you must think we are stupid or something.

Several of the old hands trouped out to critique this junior pilot nonsense, and they by chance went to another aircraft. By the time I arrived they were crowded around the front of the Hunter. The Chiefy was on his way over to see what the commotion was about when both drop tanks hit the floor and split – 200 gals of Avtur makes quite a mess. As it was a very senior finger that had pushed the button, some mystical reason was sought for the accident. Then of course it was seen as a set-up, for had I not pushed the button also. What a mess, with few friends made.

The switches had been installed and somehow they had forgotten to tell the pilots. The two aircraft were the only ones modified. Those dreaded hydraulic power switches again and the mod was to supply electrical power from a standby source to enable selection of manual in times of emergency. Too late to save Bill, but maybe it would save a few others. As a side effect, it powered the drop tank release mechanism, which as fate would have it was live at the time, for some unknown reason.

We left Nottingham with all our possessions in the car and had not gone far when a bang from the transmission pronounced problems. We returned to discover that we had dropped a gear tooth into the gear box. Lack of money and time dictated that we attempt the long drive in the hope that it would not fail completely.

We drove very slowly, but arrived without further problems. The tooth must have ground itself up for, apart from the whining noise, it never troubled us again.

Weather in the border country, particularly on the lee of the high ground, could be brutal. After a heavy snowfall, I set out in darkness to cycle the twelve miles to camp. The roads were not cleared and in the hollows I often left the road surface and stalled into the ditches. The journey took over three hours, but such was the demand of 'be there at all costs', that I would have crawled if it had been the only way. I was met with a casual response. No possibility of flying today, so go home. Another three hours of numbing effort and I was home.

This became a pattern for me in that they always knew that I would make it home, no matter what the conditions were. Lowly goals, but high endeavour.

About this time I flew a memorable trip with Les B, one of the friendlier old hands. He was a Geordie, strong of tongue with an accent that was unique. They have been on the border lands between Scotland and England for centuries. Bounded by the Roman wall of Hadrian, I am not sure if it was there to keep them in, or the Scots out.

We often flew this low-level strike mission into the Scottish Highlands, to attack a reservoir pumping station. Timing had to be very accurate to catch the small, railed vehicle as it transitted from each pumping station on the rim of the reservoir.

We navigated under the clouds, hemmed in by the mountains. Battle formation in such conditions requires that as number two, you remain in a cone behind the leader, looking through him always into the ground. This ensures that you are always above him, and it allows you to search forward for obstacles and rearwards for attackers. He anticipates that you will respond as planned, and therefore radio transmission is kept to a minimum and concerns only unplanned items. We were forced lower and lower by the clouds. I positioned myself close in case penetration of cloud was necessary. Without that move I would be forced to take evading action and break away, should we enter cloud.

I saw a cloud penetration was likely and zipped in to close formation as we hit it. A few seconds and we were again in clear air. Back to battle position and then back in again as other clouds loomed. We were in and out so many times that I tried to finesse the distance between myself and the leader. Just hold position and boom, you were out again. We entered with me holding steady, but the cloud was very thick, and we did not pop out. One second, two seconds, three and no clear air. This half light between formation flying and now switching to instruments can be difficult. I realised that I would have to separate and climb out of the valley. When I settled to look at the instruments, we were descending rapidly. A hard pull into a climb, full power and into a very ragged recovery on instruments. I was aware of some light as I bottomed my descent and I must have been very close to the rocks before the aircraft actually began to climb. Strike three and a half for this is airmanship that you have to experience and maybe survive.

As an extension of that point, we had a young aggressive pilot who was selected to go on the Instrument Rating Course. This taught how to become an examiner, and was accepted as being one of the best courses in the Air Force. Brian S returned from the course with a glowing report. The day was the worst for a day-fighter, with clouds from 300 ft to 30,000 ft. Practice interceptions (PIs), our daily bread and butter, were therefore restricted to the clear air above. Brian was attacked, and maybe like me he had made the commitment not to be caught, for he rolled into the cloud tops at high speed. The Hunter had been designed without an airbrake, intending use of the flaps instead. Tests had shown that the flaps caused large trim changes and could in certain circumstances blank the elevator. An airbrake was added in production, but was not as effective as it might have been. Flaps were sometimes used in combat to enhance the turning performance. It was a trade-off, but careful use did give you an option.

In Brian's case, he was very close to transonic speed. With the steep dive and the flaps selected, his ability to pull out was severely restricted. Compounding this was the solid cloud all the way down to the ground. He punched a neat hole into the mountain bogs and once again put the leadership of 66 Squadron under scrutiny.

Every so often each day-fighter squadron was sent to Horsham St Faith near Norwich for the 'unmentionable'. This exercise placed one on armed alert to cover the Eastern approaches. Russian airliners were fond of straying over East Anglia, and we were required to escort them back to the prescribed route. This month-long exercise was an Easter present from Fighter HQ.

The daily routine was to position two armed aircraft on the readiness area at the end of the runway (ORP). Wired directly to the radar units, we were updated as to weather and targets continually. Duty time, strapped into your aircraft, was one hour. You would then be replaced to return at a later rotation. As it was Easter few Air Force units were working. The master airfields were of course open but the choice for alternates was limited. As pilots grew in experience they earned different instrument ratings. The initial was a White card, followed by a Green after a certain number of flying hours. The ultimate was a Master Green, but this was not possible on your first tour.

As we flew as pairs all the time, poor weather required that the leader had to have a Green card or better. On this day Derek and I were banished to the wet and miserable end of the runway. The weather was below limits in fog. No flying was expected and therefore we could be utilised to free up more senior people for other duties. It was usual to pass the time reading, or dismantling the gunsight. Such was the case here, for when the scramble bell went, my heart stopped for two reasons. Firstly they could not be getting us airborne in this weather, and secondly what should I do with all these bits in my hand. The telebrief crackled to life and gave us the data. Only in perceived real situations would they risk two aircraft in these weather conditions. It was well below limits for take-off and a landing was remote. The rules clearly stated that even if aircraft were put at risk, they were to be launched.

A formation instrument take-off is interesting, as was the thought that we may be required to initiate an international incident. Derek devoted himself to following the Ground Control Intercept (GCI) instructions. I was on other frequencies getting updates on our alternates. For we would need to know how much fuel to hold back for our landing somewhere. The pursuit rapidly became soft as the unidentified target was tracked as an errant airliner now returning to its proper route. With both now on the same frequency, we went to the recovery cell who were supposed to direct you to the required alternate for landing. As the weather picture was fully revealed to us, it showed that the only real alternate was in southern France.

There was nothing in UK any better than Horsham which we had just left.

Mike C came on frequency from his position as duty supervisor at Horsham. He was the best flight commander at 66, and very calm in relaying our options. We committed to returning to base and trying a radar approach (GCA). These would be tried until the fuel ran out, and then a bail-out would be the last resort. Last resorts were not discussed of course, for we had to succeed.

A Ground Controlled Approach requires the lead aircraft to follow precise instructions, and is literally talked onto the ground. We would carry out this procedure as a formation, for it was easier and less time-consuming. It did however, require the leader to be spot on, if both aircraft were to land together.

Derek was a new Green card and I knew the burden that he was carrying. Neither of us had ever attained a landing in such conditions, and the adjustments at the last minute before touchdown could force one aircraft to be unable to land.

The first GCA was flown in thick fog with Mike listening on frequency. He knew, as we did, that a landing was unlikely the first time around. It is possible when conditions are right to burn a hole in the fog. The heat and swirling motion of two aircraft is capable of leaving a hole and mixing the air mass enough to improve visibility. Such was the case here. We saw only a darkening and then the impression of lights as we were forced into an overshoot. Round again for another attempt, we could at least concentrate on this one venue as there was nowhere else to distract us. I saw ground through Derek's aircraft as I stayed in tight for any landing. Lights were seen well below minimums and we jockeyed for position and the landing. Altogether an adrenalin let-down, with no real problems in the end.

Horsham was to be another turning point for me in that I emerged from another test. By chance, Derek and I were airborne for the daily dose of PIs. I had the Hunter with the drop tanks on and Derek was in the shorter range version. We completed our sortie and flew into the circuit as a pair. Derek landed off the pairs approach, and I continued, leaving the circuit to use up the extra fuel. I was about twenty miles away at 5,000 ft, when the Fire Warning Light illuminated.

A fire on any aircraft is a major emergency and in a single-engined aircraft events unfold in such a way that each decision limits one's options.

I carried out the drill of closing the throttle and waiting, at the same time as converting all my speed to height. The latter action does several things: it slows the aircraft so that the fire extinguisher, if activated, is used effectively; it gives the best gliding options if the engine fails or is shut down.

At now 7,000 ft I had some time to review my choices. If I shut down the engine, which was the next thing called for in fire drill, then a bail-out was inevitable as there was no airfield within gliding distance. The waiting period was to establish if in fact it was a fire or a hot gas leak. With the latter it was possible that the light would go out and power could be reapplied until the light came back on again. In this way, with limited power you might be able to return to an airfield for landing.

My wait was interminable, and well beyond the required thirty seconds. Still it glowed and I considered the ejection. The drill now demanded a shutdown, and as a consequence the loss of the Hunter. My logic said that if I fired the fire extinguisher bottle, it might put out the fire. This was contrary to all the instructions, but I thought relevant to my situation. At idle power, I fired the bottle and the fire light extinguished immediately. Power had to be applied as I was getting low. Sufficient power was available before the light came on again, and this identified how much you dare use. After checking that the light would go out again, Horsham was contacted and told that I was returning with a fire. I gently approached the circuit for I was faced with an overweight landing that strangely concerned me more than the fire. The next few moments were ones that I would rather forget, for my airmanship was lamentable. A voice that was not mine said that I was going to burn off fuel before landing. It was stupid, for the aircraft needed to be on the ground pronto. Air Traffic, in the name of the duty pilot, quickly overruled that idea, and I turned for my landing. As I touched down, the Hunter had a total electrical failure. Inspection of the rear of the aircraft showed a massive hot gas leak which had burnt through the main electrical cable. I was only seconds away from an uncontrollable fire. Now came the inquisition, for although I had saved the Queen's property, orders were that I should have abandoned it.

I was congratulated for saving it, and summarily threatened for disobeying orders. In my mind I had stood the test and survived. This occurrence is a test for anyone, and it certainly affected my attitude to real emergencies, which is just as well for there were to be many. One of my flight commanders at Pembrey had said that if faced with a like emergency, point it out to sea, put full power on, and bail out. To prove any complicity or pilot error they would have to dig it up.

The new boss arrived and immediately things began to change. He was sent with extraordinary powers to turn 66 Squadron around. The manner in which he did it reminds one of Douglas Bader when he became CO of the thoroughly demoralised Canadian Squadron. He was brusque, abrasive and ruthless. Anyone who did not wish to be on his squadron had better apply for a posting right now. He visited the troops to discover the terrible morale and lack of leadership. One of the junior corporals was called Mr 66, and he had the backing of most of the groundcrew. He was promoted on the spot, and the disgruntled senior NCOs were fired. He then visited the Engineering Stores and demanded all the equipment that was limiting our flying through lack of spares. Needless to say he did not get it, and so he returned to the squadron and for dramatic effect, called the Group Commander. In Bader-like tones, he declared the squadron to be non-operational. He then joined us for a coffee. The phone jumped off the wall, as he knew it would and a few words were uttered. Within hours, trucks were to be seen driving across the airfield with our spares.

The next task was to settle the pilots and we were all ordered into the air. Many were not current, or even rated. The weather was far from ideal, but he needed to make us sit up and believe. Any idea of a home life vanished. He said, 'My children go to bed at six p.m, the squadron will not cease work until then.'

Many of the old hands were unwilling to accept this, and a spate of postings followed. He cleaned house and obviously had the backing to do it. He said that the squadron would be the premier squadron in one year, and he did it. We won the Dacre Trophy at the next opportunity. His stern unbending manner was counterbalanced by one of the flight commanders, Mike C. Mike was the best shot, and his low-level ability was uncanny. I tried to emulate him, and discover how he did those things. He was unable to articulate his skills and in the idiom of the day would say, 'I don't know horse, just what is it you want to know?' I followed him on many a low-level sortie and his navigation was superb, and at speeds well above the norm. He was able to adjust his speed to be spot on time, and when searching for a well-hidden target, would always find it. He was a natural.

British political aspirations took a turn for the worse in 1958, with the collapse of some of the Arab quasi-states. Hussein's line of succession was adjusted, and Lebanon slipped into anarchy. Such was the importance of the Middle East, that the Cyprus base was bolstered by the addition of two fighter squadrons. We were placed on alert on Thursday and all other tasks were cancelled. We worked through the night doing air tests and compass swings to rally the majority of the fleet for the long trip to Cyprus. All the peacetime rules were relaxed and I left to travel by transport aircraft.

Having spent a full day fruitlessly running from one aircraft to another, I finally returned to Acklington at sundown to await further orders. Another flight was laid on for the next day and I would try again. On the way home, I passed by the village hall. A bring and buy sale was wrapping up, and I wandered in to see the results. Outside was parked a lovely Alvis Firebird which had been donated by a local resident. Nobody had offered to buy it, and I jumped in to ask what was required to purchase. A few minutes later I was the proud owner of a 1934 Alvis. Twenty-five pounds changed hands and I did not see the car again for three months until my return from Cyprus.

When I finally made it to the Akrotiri base, the rest of the Squadron were already set up in the dispersal areas, ready for conflict. They needed able bodies, and in my winter flying clothing I was quickly sitting in a Hunter on alert in the hot sun. The aircraft were not equipped with hot-weather cooling units, and the temperate ones soon failed under the strain, leaving us without any cockpit air-conditioning. We had no time to acclimatise, and fatigue rapidly became a factor. Temperatures were so high that the metal of the seat harness blistered ones shoulders. I sweated so much on one sortie that the fluorescein sea marker, a green dye in my life jacket, leaked out and dyed me a brilliant green.

I had not received my vaccinations prior to departure, and so the medics came to us whilst we sat in the aircraft. He gave me my jabs, standing on the aircraft ladder. Two days later, my smallpox vaccination was in the small blister stage. Awaiting a turnaround, one of the overworked groundcrew was assisting me in strapping in, a usual procedure. The ladder slipped and he grabbed to save himself from falling. A large grimy thumb impacted my smallpox blister and I knew that I was in trouble. The arm swelled dramatically and I was in hospital barely conscious shortly thereafter.

When I returned, the war had honed up a pace, the US Sixth Fleet was cruising just south of Cyprus, watching developments. Relations were strained between the UK and the US, as US foreign policy sought to limit colonialism and increase its power in the area. As the Brits and the French struggled with their altered diplomacy, the US searched for a new status. In NATO, or in any area where operations were on a war footing, 'bouncing' other aircraft was the high point of a fighter pilot's day. This involved getting into an attacking position and then carrying out an attack profile during which cine film would be taken. This film was the lifeblood of a fighter squadron, for it proved beyond doubt that you could have downed a target.

Several encounters were made with the Sixth Fleet, whose aircraft were generally superior to ours. At extreme altitude we were patrolling south of Cyprus. Ahead appeared some unknown aircraft. We were ideally placed for an attack and were in process of taking film when we were spotted. They were Crusaders, a USN supersonic fighter. In unison, they lit their afterburners and started to accelerate away from us, all but number four, whose A/B failed to light. This put him in a precarious position, and without support he was attacked by all our formation in turn. Film of this kind was never obtained by a UK squadron, as we were never exposed to USN aircraft. The other members of his group were now well above us, circling to get down and assist their number four. This put them at a disadvantage yet again, for they could not turn with a Hunter. A minor dogfight ensued, and they disengaged leaving us jubilant.

When the film was developed, it showed clearly that we had won the day. Radar warned that there were several aircraft inbound, and we scrambled to meet the threat. What followed was the Akrotiri war. Almost hourly, there were runs by the USN at very high speed over the field, and very serious dogfights right over the runway. The troops thought this was fantastic, and even the base hospital used to bring out its patients to watch.

The other squadron, 208, was having a difficult time. It remains the classic case of attempted elitism that I know of in the Air Force. The new boss had been in charge of pilot postings in his previous job. When he was given command of 208 Squadron, he selected the best people from Fighter Command to form his outfit. What he in actual fact got was numerous chiefs and no Indians. The squadron fractured and the lack of cohesion was very visible.

During the 'War', they were holding alert state, ready for immediate scramble. The USN came in very fast, and so all four aircraft were scrambled. As is the procedure, red-flagged pins are inserted into the Hunters, to inactivate the firing circuits. These are removed immediately prior to take-off by armourers stationed at the end of the runway. If they are not removed, the undercarriage will not retract. With USN aircraft streaking over the field, 208 rushed into the air. The call to 66 Squadron was quickly understood by us all; 208 were now frantically hiding in the lake marsh area at very low altitude, for they were sitting ducks with the pins still in and the gear locked down. We got as many aircraft into the air as possible, and engaged the variety of USN types that were overhead. Almost everyone on the station was outside watching, and I have film of a FJ3 chasing a Hunter chasing a Demon chasing a Hunter chasing a Crusader.

We made several runs on the US carriers, which involved diving from a great height, aiming at the carrier, such that you were pointing your shock wave directly at it. We hoped that the sonic boom really rattled them inside the metal can that was their home. Daft Jim made a pass at a carrier and as he approached he saw an aircraft pushed over the side. Thoroughly scared, he scuttled off hoping against hope that it was just a coincidence, for it did happen that disabled aircraft were pushed over the side in an emergency.

We bounced a flight of Royal Navy Sea Hawks, who promptly dropped their tanks and turned aggressively to defend themselves. On consideration we decided to leave them alone, if that was the way they felt about it.

With the build-up of forces, space became a priority. We moved to Nicosia, the civil airfield in the centre of the island. Here living conditions were very cramped for a time, with crews living in the squash court. I was sharing a chalet with an RAF Regiment officer, whose work schedule rarely coincided with mine.

The Turkish/Greek troubles were heating up, so much so that we only employed Turkish workers on the base. The Greeks had blown up a fuel truck at Akrotiri, and a Canberra had been damaged. We rarely left the base area, and we were armed or escorted if we did. British forces landed in Amman to find themselves nose to nose with the Arab League. The Hunters that landed were trapped as the fuel truck was made unusable in a strange incident.

British heavy transport aircraft were few and far between. The Beverly was the only type capable of carrying heavy vehicles. When they tried to load a fuel truck, necessary for the support of the Amman landing, they found that it was too high. Letting down the tyres was also ineffective. This forced the removal of the fuel tank which would be carried separately. When it was unloaded in Ammin, they dropped it and cracked it. Please could you stop the war until we have repaired our truck.

The US landed on the beach of Beirut, but all in all operations were conducted with virtually no co-operation. The Israelis demanded, quite rightly, that overflights of their country cease, for all the British force had to overfly Israel, and we did. The US F3s landed at Nicosia and displayed their Sidewinder missiles. These were the first that we had seen close up, but there was little or no collaboration.

We were alerted early one morning and called to the squadron area for a briefing. Survival kits were handed out, including gold coins and the venerable 'goolie chits'. These and the silk maps were supposed to give some measure of comfort in some very hostile territory. Whether a chit would actually be accepted by the natives was in doubt, but we did have the Smith and Wesson option. The mission included arming the Hunters with long-range tanks and guns only, for the target was at extreme range. I later learned that it was a one-way mission with no hope of making the return flight. No doubts were raised, and I have no fear that, had the order been given, all fourteen aircraft would have left without a qualm.

The last Indian Hunter delivery.

Life at Nicosia had its moments in a series of incidents, some hilarious, some not so. We held readiness state on the ORP at the end of the runway, and so could observe all the landings. An argument arose over the quickest way to arrive in the circuit and land. Fighter aircraft are most vulnerable when they are slowed down, particularly with their wheels down. Thus to take minimum time decelerating for the landing calls for a technique. Some slowed as they arrived overhead and completed a very tight turn to land, believing that this was minimum time. Others arrived very fast, pulling into a high g turn, which slowed the fighter enough for landing. The watchers on the end of the runway timed each try. Every squadron has its 'golden balls' – someone who by loudness of voice or opportunistic presence, generates a status that is not entirely supported by ability. In this case, 'Mighty Voice' told everybody that he had the solution for the quickest arrival. He arrived at some humongous speed and broke into a high g turn downwind. The g load must have been on the limit, but unfortunately it proved too high for the undercarriage locks. The wheels came down and the aircraft began a series of rapid rolls disappearing out of sight. We waited for the flash, but none came. Very sheepishly a Hunter crept into the circuit and landed. As a tribute to the strength of the aeroplane, nothing was damaged but pride.

I had the misfortune to be Orderly Officer at the height of the build-up of forces. Many arrived from UK completely unprepared for duty in a war zone, thus Orderly Officer could be a hard night's work with many surprises.

I took the O/O's vehicle and driver and commenced my rounds. Certain areas had extra guards who were supposed to patrol continuously. I got out of the Land Rover some way from where the sentry was supposed to be. He stopped the Land Rover correctly and identified the driver. When I appeared out of the dark, he was so startled that he jumped and stuck his bayonet through the canvas side of the Rover.

We continued to the aircraft dispersal area. Here, sodium lights were pointed at the aircraft so that nobody could approach them unseen. The sentry, however, had stationed himself inside the lit area. This meant that he was looking into the lights and could not possibly see any threats outside them. He could make out some movement, but felt safe inside. We waited for the routine challenge, but he seemed to think that we should come to him. Eventually, he just ignored us and went off to patrol another area. I had to brief him that he was useless inside the lit area, however fearful he might feel in the dark outside.

We proceeded to one of the weapons sites. This was fenced and locked, with the sentry outside. He challenged me and asked that I place my ID on the ground. Step back ten paces he ordered. I complied, and he then tried to find my ID card. Unable to find it, he was forced onto his knees and eventually laid down his rifle to feel for it. Anger at indiscipline is often unnecessary, my laughter made the point.

The final episode in the night's entertainment occurred when we arrived at the bomb dump. This was away from the airfield, fenced and guarded separately. As we approached, the guard tower shone its light on the vehicle and we were ordered to dismount. The loudhailer called out the guard detail and there was a burst of activity from within. The senior NCO left the guard tower to descend by the makeshift ladder, all military, moving at the double. He hit the top step and descended like a skater on one leg, removing every rung of the ladder and landing in a pile of firewood of his own making. The guard detail could not help themselves, and after an attempt to retrieve the situation with barked orders, he too saw the funny side.

My second stint at O/O duty was seriously unfunny. I was awoken in the early hours to be told that one of a swimming party, recently returned from Kyrenia on the north coast, had left his sten gun on the beach. He had delayed reporting the loss for several hours, and therefore the chance of recovering it was slim. I organised an armed party to return the forty or so miles to Kyrenia to search for the lost weapon. Luck was with this individual, for had we not found it, he would have been severely punished. Had we waited until daylight, there is little doubt that it would have been found by the locals.

The chalet that we shared had a small verandah and railing. My room-mate returned from an exercise and crashed out for a few hours sleep. He was so tired that he just deposited his kit and equipment all over the room. He says that he awoke late, and left hurriedly, without clearing up. What followed is a little like a Monty Python skit. I was walking back from the Mess when the fire bell went, and the guard detail skidded by in hot pursuit. I was held at the corner and prevented from approaching my chalet. There was smoke and minor signs of fire, but I could make out a body hanging over the rail of our verandah. When all the shouting died down, the plot unfolded thus. The Turkish batman had entered our room and tried to tidy up. He saw on the bed a cylinder with a small piece of paper attached. He promptly tidied up this irritant and believed that he was then attacked, as there was an explosion that ignited the curtains. He dived through the open window very inexpertly, breaking his shoulder in the process. He made it as far as the railing where he passed out. The explosion was the pyrotechnic flare that he had ignited by removing the pull strip. Trying to sort out what really happened was an arduous task and it was some time before every one was certain that it was not an EOKA attack.

The boss was now in full song, with an operational outfit that befitted his image of a good fighter squadron. His imperious manner made him very difficult to approach. He brooked no arguments, and was careful to do the early morning trips so that his weapons scores were obtained in the cool calm air of early morning. When someone came close, he was quick to re-establish his superiority with another ideal sortie. He did lead me through a session of formation aeros and was complimentary. This was not usual, but meant a great deal to me, as he had lead an impressive formation team on 43 Squadron.

I was elected to try and humanise him, a difficult task as he was not known for his sense of humour. He would come into the operations room and alter the flying programme to suit his needs. I took to casual criticism of his planning in such a way that it would be hard to take offence. One day he threw the chalks at me and said, 'If you're so damn clever, you do it.' For such a junior pilot to do the schedule was unheard of, but the boss had spoken and so I ran it for the rest of the day.

A major failing was that he was a terrible driver. When we were able to leave the base, he would always drive. I asked if he had learned to drive in France as he spent most of the time on the wrong side of the road. Whether he detected an attempt to mellow him, I do not know, but he did make the effort to join in the inter-squadron sports.

Once during an inter-squadron game of water polo, he got carried away and savaged the 208 Squadron boss enough to be sent off. His driving skills, or lack of, caused Jim B, also known as Daft Jim, to be ejected from the Rover as we dashed for an alert scramble. The boss decided to drive Jim and I to our aircraft, being the quickest way to the parking area. He made as if to drive up the loading ramp of a parked transport aircraft. At the last minute he jerked away and Jim flew out of the poorly locked door. We were moving fast, and Jim rolled across the concrete, saved in the main by his flying clothing. He abraded his face somewhat and we sympathetically named him 'Ugly daft Jim'.

To be seen doing nothing was a crime, and the boss took issue with Mike T, the squadron PAI (Pilot Attack Instructor). Mike's job was to review the cine film and assess the squadron's shooting skills. He had a dark room to project the film and keep records. This was ideal for sleeping and keeping out of the way. He was caught napping by the boss, who promptly removed his chair. But Mike had the ability to sleep anywhere, and so could be found fast asleep standing up in the dark room. The key to the room was then held by the Ops Officer, and Mike was banned unless film work was called for. He could be seen thereafter, asleep by the 'chatty' outside, hiding from the sun. The chatty was a large earthenware pot in which drinking water was held, keeping the water remarkably cool by evaporation through its porous walls. Mike was later to survive a horrible crash in the Oman. He was badly burned, but recovered to regain his considerable skills as a pianist. His hands were completely rebuilt by the RAF Burns Unit, who had gained their techniques during the Second World War.

We were scheduled for an air-to-ground weapons training period. This was new to many of us as the Hunter was new to this role of air to mud. Most of the equipment originated in the Second World War, and much had been left in Egypt, our supposed adversary. The range was at Larnaca, the site of the new main airport of Cyprus.

Another of TK's learning experiences took place there. I was ordered to the range for a live-firing sortie. This training enables you to refine your technique and learn the art of air to mud. I made the requisite entry into the pattern, and began my non-firing passes. When approved by the range safety officer, I was cleared for a hot firing pass at the canvas targets. As I turned in and checked the armament switches the two drop tanks left the aircraft. These switches are multi-purpose and if wrongly selected can lead to wing ordnance leaving the aircraft. I checked the switch position and confirmed that they were in the correct position. The tanks, partially full of jet fuel, had demolished a Turkish church just outside the range. The church was derelict and abandoned, but nevertheless still a church. Ordered home, I rethought every action to be clear for the inquisition that would surely follow.

The experts checked the aircraft and readily declared me the culprit – 'finger trouble' they said. The switches could not be in 'guns' and 'bombs/tanks' at the same time. Case closed, but for me my integrity was now in question. The weight of engineering evidence was too much to question, but I knew that I had not placed the switches in anything but 'guns'.

The next day the tanks left a Hunter being prepared for a range sortie by the armourers. The boss, sensing a real problem, ordered a proper inquiry. What was revealed was that the switches remained at the position they were in when the power was turned off. They could be selected to guns with the power off, but would still be electrically in the 'bombs/tanks' position, if that was the position selected when power was last applied to the aircraft. No apology was expected this time, but my integrity was now unquestioned. It did confirm my ability to analyse and give me the confidence to doubt the system whenever I believed that its logic was faulty.

At the height of the military build-up, the parking area was severely congested with nearly fifty aircraft. Our line operations were conducted from a tent on the edge of the concrete, and the explosion caused everyone to rush outside to verify the cause. We all knew what that sound was, it was an ejection seat firing. The seat was still in the air, but there was no sign of a body. Miraculously, the falling seat missed all the aircraft, and we ran over to the Hunter. There was a writhing body on the ground at the base of the ladder, and he indicated that someone was in the cockpit, where we found an airman on the cockpit floor, gibbering in a state of shock. They had been lowering an ejection seat back into the fighter, one standing on the ladder, the other in the cockpit. As the seat was lowered, they initiated the firing sequence. The fellah on the ladder bailed off, knowing that one-and-a-quarter seconds later the seat would fire. The armourer in the aircraft was leaning forward, with his back to the instrument panel. He needed to hold onto the seat for support and as the seat rose up the rail it would decapitate him. Somehow he managed to make himself impossibly small and recoil all at the same time, such that the seat missed him as it left the aircraft. He was shuddering and smoking three cigarettes all at the same time, but our attempts to recreate the sequence proved impossible. There was no way the seat could be lowered in or extracted without it impacting heavily on him.

When all the amazement had subsided, we turned round to see the line ops tent blazing merrily away. It was gone in seconds, taking with it most of the squadron records. The engineers were very happy to recall the aircraft statistics by memory, which showed that all the outstanding maintenance had been completed.

We covered the landings in Amman and were constantly on the lookout for Egyptian aircraft. I was airborne one day and vectored to a target which proved to be a fleeing IL28, an outdated Russian bomber. He was diving for home territory and he made the fence before I could get him.

John D and I were scrambled after a target coming up from the south. We knew that Egyptian aircraft regularly sneaked in between Cyprus and Israel, bound for Syria. They were obviously more scared of the Israelis than they were of us. Our concern was a sneak attack, thus the rapid response. We climbed as fast as possible to 40,000, but could not find the target. In those days, height-finding radar was the weak link. Slowly we descended, searching at each level. Finally at 8,000, we identified an IL14M, a Russian-made transport. He was flying north heading for Cyprus, or the gap. I sat on his wing to gather some specifics for the now very interested controller at the radar station. It was a shiny new aircraft, with an amazing series of insignia on the tail – big stars, half moons, obviously a VIP transport. I could see clearly into the cockpit, and there appeared to be nobody on the aircraft. I pushed in closer and both pilot seats were unoccupied. By now, the controller was getting excited. All controllers had a numbered callsign, and we had been controlled by a lowly number like 28. A new controller would come on the air, announce his callsign and request the same data all over again. Slowly the more senior numbers came up, until finally it was 01 himself. This was the sector commander who could smell an international incident brewing. John D sat back and finally came in to verify my assessment of the situation. The IL14 was slowing almost imperceptibly, and it was flying at the stalling speed of the Hunter. We had gear and flaps down and were very vulnerable in that condition. Fuel was becoming a serious concern, but Control would not release us. In a few minutes we would not have enough fuel to be able to return to Nicosia. I looked at the IL14 and nearly spun in laughing as I made out a pair of very bushy black eyebrows peering over the edge of the cockpit windowsill. The crew must have been lying on the floor, operating the autopilot.

The aircraft closed into Cypriot airspace and we were unable to get any instructions on dealing with it. I realised that the system was just not able to respond and knew that we needed much clearer rules of engagement, something that the US had enormous trouble with much later in Vietnam. The following day the incident was reported in the world press as piracy in the air, and needless to say all our cine film was removed pronto. The IL14M was a gift to Nasser from Kruschev.

Returning to Nicosia after a normal training sortie, it was discovered that there was a strong crosswind. For some reason I was placed in echelon port (left side of the pair) for a pairs landing, not that unusual, but not something that I had practised, and in a very strong crosswind. As we settled into the latter half of the approach, there was a strong smell of burning, followed by pain in my left foot. Smoke could be seen in the footwell area, but the landing was only seconds away. I tried to move my foot out of the way, but the realities of a formation landing took most of my attention. When we finished the landing run, my boot was burning nicely.

The canopy jettison handle extends down the left side of the footwell and the wires at the end of it, worn bare by numerous boots, had ignited the boot polish in the welt of my boot and welded my nylon sock to my little toe. If you want sympathy it is in the dictionary between shit and syphilis, or if you cannot take a joke, you should not have joined, were the extent of the responses offered.

One of my last trips in Cyprus was a dusk strike with Mike C. He fascinated me with his low-level abilities, most of all with his skill at making gate times almost to the second. Our task was to hit a camouflaged army position at dusk. This strike required us to carry out a round-Cyprus navigation exercise, and then attack the Army at a specified time.

We left as a four ship formation, with me flying number two to Mike. The Hunter had no navigation aids to speak of, so fine map-reading was needed. Even holding the map was a skill in itself. Many held the map in the left hand, the throttle hand, thus freeing the right hand for aircraft control. This meant that the map was down in the cockpit and to read it one's eyes had to be diverted from the task of keeping you out of the scenery. If you used the right hand and balanced the folded map as it were on top of the stick, it obscured the instruments but did give you throttle and stick control. It also was in the sight line for flying and viewing the ground and the map.

Mike had planned the strike at high speed, well above the usual 420 kts. At an altitude of 200 ft, speeds above 420 kts take almost all your mental energy just to stay in formation, avoid the obstacles and be in contact with the route. We edged up to 540 kts, and at the last turning point went to almost 600 kts. Staying in formation is now difficult as there is little excess power available for adjustments. He called the pull-up and we climbed into a wing over to pick out the targets for the shallow dive attack. I stayed in close and gave myself the required separation so that I could perform the attack profile. When I finally focused on the barren rock face that was the target area, I was unable to pick out any vehicles. Nothing to aim at so I took no film.

We landed in darkness, which comes very quickly in Cypriot latitudes. When the film was developed, Mike had his aiming cross fixed on a vehicle hidden in a cave. He also had struck at less than five seconds from the selected time. Making those speed adjustments to be spot on time, requires many hours of practice I was to find.

We completed a desert survival course in El Adem and were treated to the delights of desert snails. These sandy beasts were chewed to extract the moisture, but not eaten as digestion took too much precious fluid. A trial was carried out to see what altitudes trained pilots were capable of keeping in desert conditions. The usual briefed height was 250 ft, but fatigue and terrain would force errors in all but the most capable. A barograph was fitted, and a route prescribed such that 250 ft was to be judged and flown meticulously. The results were interesting in that the average pilot would be close to 250 ft in judgment, but he would be unable to complete the sortie without excursions as high as 400 ft. The very accomplished low-level pilot would be under 200 ft all the time. This seemingly small variation was a life saver, as the risk of being shot down increased with every foot you increased your altitude.

I returned from Cyprus in haste, after the boss received a signal that my wife had miscarried following the sudden death of her father. Release from a war zone is not usual in Her Majesty's fleet of foot, but the tension in the area was easing and I guess that it was seen as a morale booster to allow one of the squadron home.

Derek B was still looking after things at Acklington, which was still the squadron base. He was shortly to depart for Cyprus, leaving me with the make-work projects that remained. We had a few aircraft, but no ground crew to speak of to service them. The US marine captain posted in on an exchange tour took a while to come to terms with these very temporary conditions. He mellowed into an excellent squadron member when the aircraft returned and life settled to some level of normality.

Derek had looked after the Alvis for me and we set about using it for everyday purposes. The fuel tank was discovered to be rusting on the inside, causing the glass fuel filter to fill with debris almost hourly. Taking off the glass, discarding the fuel and rust was becoming expensive. We therefore decided to drain the tank and remove as much of the rusty bits as possible. The slab tank on the car was of unknown capacity, as the gauge had long since expired. I used a dipstick to ensure that there was always fuel available, and it appeared that we needed to drain two or three inches of fuel. A few fuel cans were gathered for the task and were quickly filled.

The flow did not diminish and every receptacle was grabbed to hold fuel. The few gallons we had guessed at, became fifteen then twenty. Old cars, we learned had very large fuel tanks.

Betti had moved in with my parents during my absence, and so we needed to find new accommodation. The northern coast is not filled with rental units, and some of the offerings were decidedly grungy. House-hunting needs to be completed in a light-hearted manner, if the constraints of Air Force living are not to overwhelm you. By now, Derek and his wife Sheila had pooled resources with us, and so we set out to find acceptable digs. My wife, like many women, has a keen sense of smell. Odours that men seem to accept were quickly identified and catalogued by her. Such was the case with a small dark cottage that we inspected. It was damp smelling and musty, but her nose detected other unacceptable aromas that mystified us. In an effort to lighten the now foreboding view she had of the place, Derek sat at a giant sideboard unit, a piece of furniture so large that the house must surely have been built around it, and using a drawer as a keyboard and the knobs as organ stops, proceeded to play the organ. I guess you had to be there, but the laughter is forever in our collective memories as we extracted ourselves from this eerie building.

Smell kept us from that place, but could not save us from the castle on the cliffs. The flat had no running water on our floor, but Betti in true Air Force style made it comfortable and marginally satisfactory for our needs. We had the use of two gas stoves, and that meant that cooking could be cheap on a communal basis. In exchange for using their bath tub, we cooked large meals on our up-market kitchen arrangement.

A treasure hunt/rally was run several times on the base and Derek and I began our rallying career quite unknowingly then. He was the proud owner of his father's old Wolesley, which, in an age of vehicles of suspect engineering, was quite a possession.

The inventory problems that plagued me returned with a vengeance when I tried to complete a check of my inventory after my return from Cyprus. The inventory had been moved without the holder's presence, into new storage. This is a definite no-no, and I refused to accept any responsibility for possible losses. The check revealed many losses, not least of which were the life jackets, or Mae Wests as they were called. These items had the new Sarbe emergency radios and were very valuable. When they were found to be missing a Board was convened to examine the circumstances. Squadron Leader John P was given the task of allocating responsibility, and although he might have had some sympathy for my predicament, we were dealing with the basic dishonesty of the Air Force system. Somebody had to be responsible, so you set up a system that catches the poor unfortunate at the bottom of the ladder. I was supposed to monitor the inventory day and night. I had no staff to speak of, and this was in addition to my daily flight duties, which at that time were twelve to fourteen hours a day. The normal system is to get recipients to sign for any item on a log card. The Mae Wests were in use day and night by ourselves and the Station Flight aircraft. Some equipment had not been written off correctly following aircraft accidents, but the rest was not capable of being found. I was invited to pay for the missing equipment, a large sum well beyond my ability to find. I reasoned that so many mistakes had been made that to make me the catcher was illegal. The dcwnside of sticking to your guns is the discomfort you give to those above you. All would prefer if the problem just went away and you with it. When the alternatives of a full inquiry were considered, ranks closed, the issue fell through the cracks, but your name is remembered.

Shortly thereafter, the Squadron ended its stint in Cyprus and returned to Acklington. We were tasked with delivering the special equipment to squadrons about to take our place in Cyprus. This entailed flying into East Anglia, having the equipment removed and then flying back. All the aircraft were rotated this way over a few days, and the trip was a break from routine. We flew down in formation at fairly low altitude, and there occurred an incident that remains with you forever.

With the usual restricted visibilities that occur in UK in summer, purely from haze and industrial pollution, we needed to keep a sharp lookout for other aircraft. Out of the murk appeared another formation of aircraft. We were at the same altitude on opposite headings. That electric moment when nothing is said, for it all happened far too fast, and our whole formation communicated by telepathy. We had just been saved by luck and happenstance. It was a formation of Piston Provosts, training aircraft, and so four had passed through four, like the interlocking fingers of both hands.

The Hunter Simulator and Emergencies Course (HSE) was a relatively new adventure, but brought about by the large number of Hunter squadrons. Chivenor in Devon was the site where all the drills and emergencies could be practiced. There occurred two incidents that are indelibly imprinted in my memory. Firstly we were standing out on the windy airfield being briefed on parachute drills. A pilot chute is smaller than the army version and therefore landings occur at higher speeds. Preparing for this can save you from serious injury. Our hero was instructed to pull his chute and deal rapidly with the problem of being dragged over the ground. Immediately it was pulled he took off at 30 m.p.h. rapidly turning green in the process. The wind speed made observing from the Rover almost impossible and he was semi-conscious when they finally got him stopped. Not a good start, but it certainly increased your attention span.

Phase two was the sea drills, whereby we were taken into the Bristol Channel and turfed over the side to clamber into our dinghies. We wore immersion suits which leaked, but the plan was to retrieve you by helicopter and deposit you back on the Air-Sea Rescue launch quickly. There were eight people in the water and it was very rough with driving rain, most uncomfortable.

The helio hovered over us and the first lift took place. He was lowered onto the launch which was pitching badly, so badly that it broke his leg, so he was airlifted away to the distant shore, leaving seven of us to survive. The launch tried to retrieve us but it was too dangerous in the mounting seas. By the time the helio returned, I was thoroughly frozen, having lost the use of my hands and feet. The first lifts were taken to the ambulances on shore, but it was going to take too long by this method, and so the risks of being deposited on the launch were again taken. I was the last to be picked up, and could not help the helio rescuer. He came down and hooked onto me and we were lifted as far as the helio exhaust where movement ceased as I was still tied to the dinghy. The connector was impossible to free, and I was being torn apart by the cable and a dinghy full of water. He took out his knife and swung at the dinghy strap, to no avail. I had visions of having my legs chopped off in the name of safety training. We then pulled the strap between us, using my useless hands and attempted to saw the strap. It worked and we fled back to the hospital as I lay like a beached whale on the floor of the helio. How quickly the situation had gone out of control, with serious implications for all those involved.

The news was bad, politics had cut the Air Force overnight and many of the proud Hunter squadrons disappeared forever. 66(F) Squadron was cut in half and a few flying jobs were tossed on the floor. I was seemingly lucky enough to get a flying job, any being better than none. It all fell apart very quickly for me and my departure was an embarrassment that I would love to expunge from my memories. Being a quiet drinker, the Squadron decided to set me up at the farewell dinner. They were successful, and I only recall that the loss of control I found very unsettling.

Chapter III

THE JOB IN QUESTION was as a communications pilot at Andover in Wilts. Any new flying job is seen as a challenge, and even though the equipment was the ancient cloth bomber, the Anson, it was still a new role and all the experience that goes with it.

I viewed aircraft with doors as something to be avoided, but there were enough fighter pilots on the staff to make my quips acceptable. The boss was another case altogether. An ex-flying boat man, he had a distinct dislike for exuberance and anything that was light-hearted. Aviation survives on its humour; without it, military aviation would be a morose, risky business. He was without doubt the most vain man I have ever had the misfortune to meet, and he had any or all my career aspirations in his hand. I did not have sufficient flying hours to quality for the necessary rating as a comm pilot, I had never flown a twin-engined aircraft, and my piston experience was limited to basic training. To resolve this I was dispatched to Aston Down, to be checked out on the Anson by the Command test pilot.

I enjoyed the introduction to this form of flying, but it was not without its moments. As the only activity on this lonely outpost, he looked at the weather one Monday morning and authorised me to go and practice approaches at some local airfields. I dutifully got airborne and flew to Lyneham for some approach work. They were most surprised when I popped up on frequency, for the weather was zero/zero. Where have you come from, they queried, as most of UK was blanketed in fog. I beat a hurried retreat to Aston Down, for at least it was reasonable weather there when I left.

A check around the frequencies showed that the nearest useable airfield was beyond the range of the Anson, and only local conditions at Aston Down were responsible for it being as it was at take-off. When I called the tower at Aston, there was a significant elevation in the pitch of my instructor's voice. The fog bank was creeping out of the valley and the airfield was going to be zero/zero in very short order. He had found some flares and the calm in his instructions was synthetic. I made out the main road that ran along the northern edge of the field and ducked under the cloud deck to feel my way back to the airfield. Aston had no approach aids and so I was on my own to sort out the mess. Cars were using their headlights and I could even make out the use of windscreen wipers; yes, I was that low. Some landmarks were identified and I prepared for a landing.

The Anson is far from an ideal aircraft for low flying, the view is too restricted, and at the extremely low altitude I could not turn too steeply. I guessed the turn onto the runway and missed by a scant few yards, passing between the runway and the control tower. The southern edge of the field was enveloped in fog and I turned from almost memory, to retrace my steps back to the road. If I missed the road this time, I would be in serious trouble. I crossed the road at a less than ideal angle and flew away from the field for a reversal and another attempt at landing. Instructions and flares were evidently being fired in a stream from the tower, but I recall little other than the determination to save my own skin (there was no parachute in the Anson). This turn was a make or break, and I decided to land anywhere on the field if I missed the runway. Over the telegraph wires in a turn earlier than the first attempt, and there was black runway. An awkward alignment and I was down, saving my neck and my instructor's. I received an excellent report from that establishment; no doubt that incident had something to do with it.

The return to Andover was not a happy event – lack of accommodation had forced us to buy a mobile home (caravan). The job deteriorated almost in concert, and I was left to accumulate enough hours to be able to be rated for the position of comm pilot. I flew as often as ordered and used the Chipmunks to get rid of some of my frustrations. These two-seat trainers were used by the HQ staff for continuation training and also for some comm work which I was able to do.

For a short time the squadron had the use of two Vamps at RAF Wroughton. Before the boss managed to rid himself of these embarrassments, I had a memorable trip as safety pilot with one of the HQ staff. These flights are used to allow pilots on desk jobs to keep their hand in. He landed the Vamp on an icy runway after an ill-constructed approach and was sideways as we skidded off the end. Wroughton sits high above Swindon and a long downhill slide looked distinctly possible. With much luck and minimal judgment he drifted the aircraft across the grass and snow in a prolonged slide, kept the power applied and we surfed back onto the perimeter track.

Several things conspired to upset the uneasy peace between myself and the boss. I would add that I was not the only target of his mental ineptitude, just the most public one. After a reasonable time, I was tasked to fly with the flight commander to see if some dispensation could be made with regard to the 200 hrs twin time supposedly needed.

We left for a passenger flight to northern England, which I did under supervision from the flight commander. The weather was lousy and a good test for my captaincy skills. After dropping off the pax, we were returning and hoping to carry out some further training en route. It turned out to be unnecessary, for with a loud crack the right engine failed. Drills were performed and the Anson stabilized on one engine. Flight on one engine is not a problem unless the failure occurs at a critical moment. In the cruise mode we had time and altitude on our side. He allowed me to continue and we made for Shawbury as the nearest useable airfield. After a short time I was having trouble maintaining speed and having more problem with control than should have been the case. He took over and simultaneously we discovered that the failed engine was drooping in its wing mounts. In short order, it was hanging almost vertically and bits of the cowling soon departed. We recalled that an Anson had actually had an engine fall off and still managed to fly.

We began to think that it would be better if it did fall off for the drag of this useless piece of ironmongery was becoming severe. We were close enough to Shawbury to be able to make a safe landing, and I hoped that this trip would convince the powers that be that I was worthy of special treatment.

The flight commander approached the boss and suggested that I be allowed to fly as a comm pilot. Whilst he was considering this, the other pieces fell to the floor. Andover is a grass airfield surrounded by houses. In a single-engined aircraft an engine failure on take-off was almost certain to be fatal. The cardinal rule for small piston aircraft is that when an engine fails on take-off, you land straight ahead.

I considered all the options and worked out that the Chipmunk could be operated in such a way that you would have some chance of survival if you were allowed the turn-back option. Turn-backs were a feature for jet aircraft, but too many people had tried to turn back to the airfield that they had just departed from, and stalled in with fatal results. Most jets had ejection seats and therefore when the situation became insoluble, you could leave.

My strategy was to climb at a high airspeed (70 kts), so that a turn-back could be completed onto the large triangular grass field. The flight commander and I tried it out under all normal circumstances and it worked. I wrote a paper and it was passed to the boss for action. He rarely flew the Chipmunk, and therefore guardedly gave his assent. Now I could practice openly, and on such a day was authorised to carry out the manoeuvre. Take-off, climb at 70 kts, reasonable altitude, chop the throttle and commence a turn-back. Lovely, straight back down the runway really moving under the brisk 10-15 kt wind, a tail-wind of course. Commence the overshoot, power on and away we go. Bang and the prop stops dead. I knew the cause from an earlier incident – a broken crankshaft. Analysis was not what was required – I needed to save my skin from the absolute worst scenario you could devise. Downwind, much further up the runway than on a normal take-off and I needed a successful turn-back. I tried to combine a steep turn with a stall turn using as much rudder as I dared. The airspeed bled away and the nose dropped; making the crash survivable was all that I now considered. The windsock appeared in front of me and I levelled the wings and pulled. We hit hard on three wheels and stopped almost instantly. I got out and mentally crossed another life off, for the aircraft was covered in oil and we had gone barely 20 ft from the impact point in very soft ground. Himself arrived in a state of apoplexy, and there was little that I could say.

As a Roman dismissal, with a wave of his hand, I was ordered to be in charge of the Link trainer. This venerable piece of history was run by a senior NCO as a full-time job. What the major really meant was for me to have the key when the SNCO went on leave, or so I thought.

Piston Provost, Hullavington, 1955.

An Air-Officer-Commanding (AOC) inspection was on the cards for Monday morning. I realised that as the SNCO was on leave that I had better check the shiny Link trainer room. This room always sparkled, so much so that everyone slid on large pieces of felt when moving around that room, to keep the floor spotless. The fire extinguishers stood on painted spaces alongside the buckets of sand, all very correct.

It was as expected, ready for inspection. I left for the squadron, to return later as an escort for the AOC. He arrived at the site and I opened the door for him. It was as though a bomb had gone off. The soda-acid fire extinguishers had operated, spraying everything in sight. Two very chastened airmen tried to explain the circumstances, but the AOC departed leaving me to sort out the mess. They had tried to move a fire extinguisher that was freshly painted, by pulling it along the ground, and in true domino fashion, one had fallen knocking over another. They had run to the door to throw it outside but slipped on the polished wet floor. My boss did not see the funny side and I was given some extra days as Orderly Officer. People would approach me on the base and ask what he had done to me today. This kind of ridicule is very destructive, and whatever status he assumed he had, was reduced steadily by this kind of action.

The final straw happened quite innocently. He decided to resolve the rating question himself by giving me a check ride. He was not an instructor and therefore was in the grey area of responsibility and qualification. I had no warning or, more importantly, any kind of briefing. Go to the aircraft and I will be there in a moment were his orders.

In absolute silence I started the engines and taxied out for take-off. Because engine failure practice close to the ground has killed more people than actual engine failures, flying orders prohibited simulating an engine failure below 4,000 ft. In addition, when an engine is pulled back to idle in the air, a very loud horn set just behind the pilot's head goes off.

My hero said nothing as we retracted the gear after take-off, but further conversation became impossible as he pulled back one throttle and simulated an engine failure. A windmilling propeller has more drag than a feathered item and so I chose to feather the prop and try a low-level circuit on one engine, landing back at Andover. The 'feathering drill' in an Anson is slightly different to other aircraft, and when he unfeathered the prop, I thought that I had done it incorrectly. He was shouting and gesticulating, but of course I could not hear a word. I therefore repeated the drill and wobbled round the circuit for a successful landing (on one engine). He was not very complimentary, but I was quite resolved in that the whole incident was unbriefed.

Take me to Aston Down was the command, and off we set. At 4,000 ft we levelled off and settled into the cruise. The fuel slides are on the co-pilot's side of the cockpit, and they are closed to induce an engine stoppage. You cannot see which slide has been closed, and so cannot guess which engine is going to stop. Any time now an engine was going to stop, for I had seen his sneakiness reaching down for the slide. Just before it stopped, he reached up and hit the magneto (mag) switches. The right engine stopped and the aircraft yawed. I stepped on the rudder to correct the swing and the aircraft yawed violently in the other direction as the left engine stopped. We were now flying a grand piano, for the Anson does not react very well without some propulsive force. Horns blowing, arms flailing, much noiseless cursing for he erupted into action to right his mistake. He had hit the mag switches on the right engine and cut the fuel in the left. Strangely I was quite calm, possibly because he was sweating so much.

He finally enquired of me what the flapless landing speed was. I looked at the fuel and empty passenger cabin and said that it was the same as the speed for flaps, for we were very lightly loaded. 'No,' he said, 'with so much fuel and full pax it should do xxx knots. You will land at that speed on the runway numbers.' I pointed out that we were light and such a landing was not possible. He made it an order, and so I touched the main wheels on the numbers, but could not prevent the aircraft from ballooning back into the air. At that point he took control and flew back to Andover.

Not a word was said until we landed, and he then told me to remain in the squadron until called. The rest of the gang clustered around asking what had transpired. There was disbelief that himself would have set up such a trip, but more importantly, what was he going to do now? We did not have long to wait, for I was called to his office and presented with a form 1082, an unsuitability report. My faith in the system was under severe pressure at this point. I could not believe that anyone could set out to destroy a career so blatantly and actually get away with it. I read the report which said nothing of the gross infractions he had committed, and read as though all in the chain agreed with his evaluation. I refused to sign it and requested an inquiry into the whole affair. Failing that, I would file a Redress of Grievance. This procedure is rarely used, for even if you win, you lose. Rocking the boat is unacceptable in most organisations, even if it is 100 per cent accurate.

He left to confer with the Station Commander, and so the issue was not going to be contained. Before he left, the flight commander eased in for a quick meeting. Voices were raised and there was an air of disbelief outside in the crew room. The meeting became very acrimonious and two very angry supervisors stomped off presumably to see the Station Commander, and we all discussed the possibilities.

I was summoned about two hours later to the Station Commander's office, to be faced with both the boss and the CO. With grave faces they informed me of the situation as they perceived it (rehearsed it). Please sign the 1082. The CO unfortunately was not a pilot, and therefore could only guess at the relevance of the evidence before him. No, I would not sign and I wished to redress the whole deplorable incident. I welcomed the inquiry that they said would surely follow and was dismissed feeling very unsure of myself. I just could not believe that the institution of the Royal Air Force could possibly allow this turn of events to continue unchecked.

Some months earlier I had volunteered to tow gliders at the World Gliding Championships to be held at Lasham in Hants. A special unit was to be formed and I was well qualified for the job. It got me away from him and vice versa. We had six Chipmunks under the command of Tony R, a former instructor of mine. It was a happy unit, and it was super to be viewed as a capable and able pilot. My wife spent several days with me and all in all it was rewarding. I flew the weather flight early in the morning in the specially equipped Chipmunk and with the senior meteorologist chance intervened yet again.

The weather was early morning fog with clear weather reported to the north. We took off and popped through the fog to top at about 300 ft. It was one of those textbook days when rare met conditions were clearly visible. The fog lifted into roll cloud, then puff balls and finally fair weather cumulus. The met man was ecstatic taking many photographs that later appeared in his book. The return was just as memorable. We let down in the clear to funnel back underneath to Odiham. The visibility worsened and we were unable to get over the power lines about 5 miles from base. Back out to try again up another road, but still no success. Finally, I was able to close to the outskirts of the airfield by the antenna towers. Another few yards and I would be over the runway, but the fog closed the door and I was forced to climb out of the situation. The fog bank was only a few hundred feet thick, but I was committed to the climb when the engine stopped. At such times the brain is capable of extremely rapid data assessment and decision making. I knew that I must be virtually over the centre of the airfield, but I had not been taking precise note of my heading. I lowered the nose to sustain a useable airspeed and entered a tight, descending spiral. My supposition was that I should be able to choose a heading on which to land immediately I broke out of the fog and thereby avoid flying into something solid. I looked down the core of my spiral and saw concrete – it had to be the west end of the runway, even though I knew that the same sort of concrete formed the parking area between the hangars. It was a question of spatial orientation and I guess I had the courage to accept that choice. A quick reference to the direction indicator (DI), and I rolled out the turn on an easterly heading, simultaneously picking up the runway. Luck, maybe but we stopped on the runway and my passenger congratulated me on the landing. I pulled the starter and fired the cartridge to start the engine, it started and we taxied back in. On telling him what had taken place I realised that he had been unaware of the engine stoppage.

What a good job, I thought, but the investigation revealed a series of errors. Chipmunks are prone to carb icing, so much so that they were all to be wired permanently in the carb heat position. This took away some power, but removed the icing risk. All Chipmunks were supposedly wired, but the pilot was still required to check. I had not done so on this aircraft. Copper wire is used so that you can break it if necessary. This one was locked with steel wire and would have frustrated any attempts to break it, not that I ever had the time to.

One of the pilots was an old Spitfire pilot of Polish extraction. He wore very thick glasses and had been banished to the RAF Gliding Unit. He could not see the ground from 2,000 ft, but loved to fly anything anytime. We put on a formation fly-by during a period when no gliding was possible, but knew that Lefty Kurylowicz would demand to join in. We departed before Lefty could join us, for formation flying when you can see as little as he could would be too exciting for my blood.

We were engaged in flying over the Lasham runway when Lefty came up on frequency and asked for our position. He found us as we made our way back to Odiham and came racing towards us to join the formation of three. He joined outside me and promptly stuck his wing into the fin of my aircraft. As he moved away from the impact he dragged out the wiring to the navigation light he had left embedded in my tail. The damage was covered up and nobody was any the wiser.

He is, however, legendary for his name-changing exploits. Wherever he went he was asked to spell his name, Kay Yew Argh Why... etc. This apparently bothered him and so he proceeded to Somerset House to change his name. What do you wish to change it to was always the question, for which he was unprepared. Brown was agreed upon, and so Lefty Brown rejoined the Air Force. When next he checked in somewhere, he was asked for his name. The thick Polish accent demanded the question, 'What was your name before?' Kurylowicz, he said; spell it, they said; KAY YEW ARGH WHY – and so back to Somerset House he went for another name change. Same scenario, what name would you like; same answer and so Smith was chosen. Lefty Smith now rejoined the Air Force. How long it took before the obvious happened is not known. Name please; Smith; what was your name before; Brown and before that, Kurylowicz. Could you please spell that; KAY YEW ARGH WHY. He returned to Somerset House once again and changed it back to Kurylowicz.

Tony R informed me that RAF Benson was looking for Hunter pilots for the Ferry Wing, to deliver Hunters to the Indian Air Force. He would put in a good word for me and I could expect to hear shortly.

I returned to Andover and got into my routine of flying an hour's aeros in the morning and an hour's low flying in the afternoon. Using the activity in the corner of a farmer's field as my target, I would sneak around the field and pull up for a diving attack on the 'clamp' that he was building. This was a large pile of vegetables for winter food stock, usually mangold wurzels, a sugar beet-like root crop weighing at least a couple of pounds. This constant dive bombing must have excited him for on one run he stuck his pitch fork into a wurzel and lobbed it in my direction. In very slow motion I saw this object arcing towards me. At very low level my options were limited and it struck the Chipmunk somewhere at the rear of the aircraft. How to cover this one up, was heavily on my mind.

I landed in the far corner of the airfield and told the tower that I was getting out to check something. There was a large muddy mark on the tail fin and only the slightest dent. I wiped the mud off and promptly made it very obvious. I taxied back hoping that himself was not around. He appeared at the aircraft as soon as I left it, and walked all around looking for evidence. The inquisition was not long in arriving. No, I could not explain the mark on the fin, but I had stopped to check the tail wheel. He knew, but proving it was another thing.

My appointed nav was a wartime Pathfinder nav who had been shot down about one year before the end of the War. He was an unforgettable character, a huge bear of a man constantly relating stories and totally overpowering any group that he was in.

The boss could not deal with Stew B, and he ran interference for me all the time. We monopolised the games room at lunch, until everyone came to watch our lunchtime activities. We played snooker, chess and darts simultaneously. Eventually there was money being wagered, the high point on an otherwise very dull place.

Being appointed Air Cadet Liaison Officer (ACLO) was the kiss of death. It meant that you were responsible for running the Cadet summer camps, in this case at Andover. Responsibility for mummy's little darlings was a no-win situation. They were out to break all the rules and you just had to be available 24 hrs a day to protect them from themselves. I had been an air cadet myself and knew the wrinkles. Keep them so tired that they have no energy for mischief.

I ran exercises and leadership training events from dawn till dusk, to limit my risk. We had a heavy flying programme and were using a Pembroke for some of this task. The Pembroke is a high-wing aircraft and so it is possible to be hit by the prop if you walk under the wing. Very careful briefings were constantly given to ensure that they entered and left the Pembroke by the prescribed route.

On my shift, I was supervising this activity when a party were about to disembark. The pilot had the engine right back to idle power, and the cadets started to leave the aircraft. One of life's dreamers turned the opposite way to the rest and walked through the prop. All the shouts did not deter him, but woke him up enough for him to turn around and walk back through it again. My heart stopped and all the red-coloured scenarios flashed through my mind. I can only surmise that the prop was turning so slowly that what he did was technically not that risky.

The Chipmunk days were coming to a close and my towing exploits sort of ended them. Bebe S was the RAF Glider Aerobatic champion. He liked me to tow him over the field for his practices. We took off for a routine tow, and I circled to arrive overhead at 3,000 ft. Just prior to the release point, the nose of the Chipmunk pitched forward and the negative 'g' stopped the engine. I struggled to pull the tow release, but the tension was too great. We were now heading towards the vertical and all my control inputs were to no avail. At some point the rope either broke or released, and I dived earthwards, recovered and landed.

The Station Commander's car was throwing up dust as he hammered towards me. He was livid, so much so that I never said anything. I did not know what had happened until Bebe later explained. He had decided to try an inverted release, but had not mentioned it to me. The Skylark 3B has a large wingspan, and so he barrelled as he inverted, lifting the tail of the Chipmunk at which point I was a passenger. A small boy managed a photo of the Chipmunk hanging from the nose of the inverted Glider.

These activities were now under a cloud, but we were allowed to depart for the Shoreham Air Display that weekend. We set off and climbed to about 3,000 feet for the trip. On levelling at three, I throttled back and the glider elasticated off the hook. We communicated by hand signals and he said he would make it to Shoreham. I landed and awaited his arrival. A message was passed that he was down at Ford, an old naval air base. It was in process of being converted into a prison, but I landed there and quickly departed with Bebe. As soon as I gently throttled back, the hook disengaged again. We were very close now and so I landed at Shoreham, this time with the tow rope attached. As I crossed the boundary there was a tug on the rope, but I thought it was just the drag of the rope in the long grass.

There was a commotion as I parked and it was connected with the tow rope still attached to the Chipmunk. The car park was across the landing runway. Traffic was allowed to cross when no aircraft were landing. One car had not seen the police directing traffic, he was probably staring at the sky. My tow hook had caught the bonnet of his MG and rolled it up in a ball as I dragged it across the field. He was incensed at this and ran over the field to retrieve it. So many laws were broken that he was heavily fined at the subsequent court case.

A call from Tony R brightened my spirits considerably, for he said a posting to the Ferry Squadron was on the way. The 1082 and the posting must have coincided, for I was told that I was to be removed to RAF Benson, the home of the Ferry Wing.

Fate yet again intervened in the shape of the dreaded inventory. As one of my secondary duties I had the inventory for an officers' barrack block. Not normally used, it was totally repainted and refurbished whilst I was away towing in the Championships. I began my handover inventory check to discover that the spare wool blanket always stored in the bottom drawer of each dresser, was missing. A total of over 100 blankets were missing, but from that earlier experience I knew that my responsibility ended when the inventory was moved without my presence.

I informed the Equipment Officer that he had a problem and left to continue my departure procedure. They were not about to let me escape without a fight and a tannoy broadcast called all inventory holders to perform checks where blankets were involved. It was quickly apparent that there was something more sinister here, as over 500 blankets were found to be missing. My release was cancelled and in a futile attempt to make me pay, I was asked to contribute for the losses on my inventory. This was bigger than both of us, was my position to the boss, and so I was quite ready for the inquiry that must follow. Holding up my release would not stand any test, thus I escaped late on Friday.

The boss had one final display of small-mindedness, by refusing to sign my log book. This I needed for the new job, but he said he would ship it later. The blankets were being stolen systematically by the batting staff, it would be discovered.

RAF Benson was a breath of fresh air; on the river south of Oxford it was happy and vibrant. I was welcomed guardedly, for the average age of ferry pilots was almost double mine.

The whole structure of aircraft delivery around the world required determination and initiative. You were often left to your own devices, unsupervised with a great deal of responsibility. There were special orders to allow you to obtain help from almost any military unit. We often dealt with our embassies abroad, and certain of our activities could be said to be 'fringe'. It was a new world to me, with a whole new series of challenges. All this had been the jealously guarded turf of the old hands, many of whom had continued on from the Second World War.

To start the acceptance, you were required to be trained by the Ferry Training Wing, using the Meteor twin jet. This was a hurdle in itself, for the Meteor has a special place among asymmetric trainers. It had a fearsome reputation following its introduction in the last few months of the War. The engines were mounted relatively far out on the wings. This made flight on one engine potentially difficult. It became a delicate balancing act to find a way to hold the fierce rudder loads needed to oppose the one operating engine. In some circumstances it was necessary to reduce power on the operating engine so that control could be maintained. It suffered from the 'phantom dive', a phenomena associated with the operation of the flaps and airbrakes, usually with the gear down and therefore in the landing circuit. In such circumstances any delay in resolution was usually fatal.

The RAF had a terrible accident rate in 1950/51, with almost one fatal per day, much of which was associated with the Meteor. The instrument rating scheme came into being during this period, and a new look was taken at training and specifically asymmetric instruction. Fighter Command developed a superb Instrument Course, and the Meteor really gave you confidence in that if you could pass an instrument ride in the Meteor 7, you had to have some ability.

The instruments were very basic, the major reference being an attitude indicator that suffered from a whole load of errors. On take-off it was necessary to compensate for acceleration error which showed a false climbing turn. Hence the often seen wreckage off the end of the runway. I quote the Russian adage about training difficulties: 'Do you not kill a lot of pilots, yes, but the ones who remain are very good'.

The instructors at the Training Wing were excellent, friends even to this day. They took the green eager material and turned it into aware, analytical ferry pilots. I loved the environment and knew that I had done well. Now I could move on and become the 'type hog' that I was focused on. The squadron flew so many types that the ability to move around from type to type was a learned one. It required a different manner of thinking, in that you needed to be able to take off, land, deal with emergencies, particularly those specific to that type, and fly the correct range techniques. I soon carried a card system that told me the essentials of each type, so that eight types in a week was possible.

Benson 1960, types galore.

Before departing the Ferry Training Wing, there was an interview with the Wing Commander. In the mail had arrived my log book, duly completed by himself. At the back of the book is an assessment page and the worst restriction to a flying career was printed there: below average; as a Comm pilot on an Anson was akin to child molestation. The fact that I had never been allowed to become a Comm pilot had been ignored. I had to produce the log book for the Wing Commander to sign and knew that it would colour his attitude. He turned out to be the same wing commander from the spinning incident at RAF Pembrey, welcomed me warmly and had been well briefed by Tony R and the Ferry Wing staff; I showed him the poison entry and he sat me down to discuss the matter.

From what he knew and the above average assessment he was about to give me, he recognised that an injustice had been done. The RAF selects its bosses carefully, but occasionally one slips through the net. He stood up and looked out of the window and said that if that offending page disappeared, he would not look for it. I duly tore it out, and felt that somehow the system had cleansed itself.

91

My first trip delivering a Hunter to the Indian Air Force was an epic in my mind. A brand new Mk 56 was collected at the factory, Dunsfold, having the total time of 1.5 hrs on the airframe. The Indians would not pay for extra tests and so we usually put 5 hrs on each aircraft to ensure that there were no 'Friday afternoon' mistakes. We left as a 'convoy', as the formation was called, and flew south to Orange in France. A quick stop to refuel and make an olfactory acquaintance with urine and Gauloise, and then on to Malta for the night. Our navigation equipment was limited to Distance Measuring Equipment (DME), usually capable of telling you that you were anything up to 180-200 miles from somewhere. The further east you went the more unusable became DME. Navigation therefore sorted out the average from the very good, and many rules of thumb were passed on from the old hands. One of the very experienced Master Pilots became my mentor and was not above testing your judgement and leadership on these long trips. Bob would slide slowly back as we flew battle formation – he wanted to see if you were watching all the formation, such that anoxia in one of the group would not go unnoticed.

Ray H was my flight commander, and in some way he recognised my overpowering interest in aviation for we were to meet again years later when he made the Red Arrows into the premier display team in the world, bar none. Malta radio was a reassuring voice after a long sea crossing, but presented some problems in that a runway blockage was very serious as there was nowhere else to land.

Food in the Mess was typical RAF outstation: tinned, packaged, war reserve stuff. Green eggs, triangular sausages and khaki vegetables, all to be avoided if possible. We usually headed for the 'Gut', a sleazy area that can be found in any port city. Full of dubious entertainment, it did house the Lighthouse Bar. Besides good food, the barman was a class act. The very long polished bar was his arena. He would pour multiple drinks at the same time and fire them down the bar to arrive unerringly in front of the correct customer.

The Royal Navy still had a large presence in Malta, which was struggling to find some identity. It faced an unhappy future, and politics almost destroyed it, a far cry from its George Cross days.

One piece of entertainment, it is recorded, was a night club favoured for its floor show. Such extremes are common now, but then were rare. A comely maiden was strapped to a rotating board affixed to the wall. A large, well-constructed gentleman, on roller skates, shorn of clothes, would whizz around the dance floor and at some speed seemingly impale himself on said maiden. What it lacked in artistic merit, it certainly made up for in physical risk. The set piece continued with calls for volunteers from the audience. One very drunk sailor was propelled by his mates onto the floor to be disrobed for the attempt. They spun him around unsteadily on his skates and fired him at the maiden. Well out of control he was at least going to get a near miss(?). However the wall opened into a doorway straight onto the street, and the matelot found himself stark naked on roller skates at the top of a steep hill. I guess you had to be there.

The next day was two legs to El Adem in Libya and then on to Nicosia. The standard-fit Hunters could not make it directly to Nicosia very often and so the easy secure route was chosen. Cyprus was still unsettled by internal politics and several of the EOKA killers could be seen in our hotel.

The next leg was the difficult one, north into Turkey on a circuitous flight plan to Diyabakir. This Turkish Air Force base was deep in a hole in the mountains and there was no approach aid for us to use. Compounding this was the language problem in that we had to request an English-speaking controller. This signal was to be sent early in the morning and the reply was expected along with the weather forecast. Usually there was no reply of any kind and the 'go' decision was based on the knowledge and interpretation of the convoy leader. We could make it back from Diyabakir, but only by cutting the corner over Syria. At this time Russia was rearming the Arab States, Syria in particular, and there was considerable traffic over the gap. The gap was about forty miles wide: the north/south border between Turkey and Iran with Russia to the north and Syria to the south.

At one stage there were about 2,000 flights a year over the gap, much to the consternation of Turkey and Iran. From Diyabakir to Teheran was the second leg of the day and again there were some problems that local knowledge could help you avoid.

The descent had to be done visually, into the bowl in the mountains that was Diyabakir. Contact was established as soon as possible to request the weather. This was why we requested an English-speaking controller. More times than not, the reply was, 'we have air firing'. The air-to-ground range was situated alongside the runway and the extent of his English was 'we have air firing'. The decision to let-down was crucial, for there was not enough fuel to climb back out and return to Cyprus. There were potential landing strips around, if you could find them; unmarked and unmanned, they served as emergency dispersal strips for the US Strategic Air Command (SAC). In typical cavalier fashion the Turks did conduct air-ground firing exercises right alongside the runway, so that identifying the side with metal fragments was a necessity.

The base was huge and in theory the RAF kept a small supply of spares there for emergencies. Their stores system was to take each pallet and park it somewhere in a maze of roads. You want a starter cartridge, fine, commandeer a vehicle, start at bottom left and drive up and down the lines until you see a British WD insignia on a box.

There was no guarantee that other parts were in the same area and so the need for spares could extend your day into a night stop at the Diyabakir 'Hilton'. This establishment was part of the wall of the walled city. Immensely thick, much of the city life took place in these walls. Your room was a cubicle without a door, on the main street/passageway on one level of the wall. Smokey oil lamps, braziers and other cooking contrivances all contributed to the smells and noise that continued without a halt, for there was little to indicate to the citizens whether it was night or day.

For us, planning and a sense of urgency usually kept you from this experience, but the leg to Teheran could be interesting also. At that time, Iran was a test case for US foreign policy. Bent on not emulating the conduct of the colonial powers, they had massive presence and the Yankee buck was everywhere. The Shah was being reinvented and heavy military spending obvious.

For us, unable to navigate by accepted means, the airport needed to be seen visually. If the weather was a problem, we had the Demervan let-down. This entailed flying to the distinctive mountain called the Demervan, turning onto a south-easterly heading and descending out over the southern desert. Once you hopefully were below cloud, a turn-back towards Teheran was initiated.

We parked on the military side and were picked up by the BOAC handlers for the drive into the city. On this, my first Indian trip, the descent was interrupted by a loud bang signalling a bird strike. The 'Shite Hawk' is a heavy vulture-like creature and he impacted the leading edge of my wing and vanished inside. A low speed-handling check was carried out to see if the damage materially affected my ability to land. Inspection on the ground showed that there was major damage all the way back to the main spar. I waved goodbye to my compatriots and settled down to organise the repair team via the British Embassy.

I was ordered home by airline and left for the airport. At the passport control, the lack of an entry permit was suddenly a major issue. My explanations went unheeded, slam, mind your fingers and I am inside a very businesslike cell. At twenty-two years of age, with little experience of these sort of situations, I could only believe that a British passport would overawe the natives. Two hours passed and I had nobody to complain to. The stern-faced attaché propelled me onto the BOAC aircraft that had been held for my arrival. This incident modified our procedures somewhat.

The daily routine at Benson was Met and Ops briefing at 0800 hrs, when trips were allocated. If you were not flying, the card school was the next stop. Flights were planned by using the Ferry Comm Squadron to take crews all over Europe to pick up their assigned aircraft type. A good day would entail an Anson flight to the Maintenance Unit at Shawbury, pick up a Vampire and ferry it to St Athan. Pick up a Meteor and ferry it to a fighter base. Await Valetta of Ferry Comm for the flight back to Benson.

At that time we were moving the Hunter, Swift, Meteor, Jet Provost, Piston Provost, Canberra, Javelin, Chipmunk, Anson, Venom and foreign marks of these types as well. The Sabre had all but vanished, but the Spitfire and Sea Fury, even a Mosquito, did very rarely turn up.

I left for Cranwell to collect a Vampire 9, the last one from that Training School. It had a pile of log books and looked very pristine. I should have guessed. The trip to St Athan was planned at 2,000 ft, a gentle run across England. Thick haze would make navigation interesting and I was barely out of shouting range when the DME failed and the radio became very weak. No matter, I needed neither for this short flight.

A loud rumble preceded the explosion just behind my head. The vibration was enough to make the instruments unreadable and I throttled back and put out a 'Mayday' call. Too low to bail out, I turned back for a disused airfield that I had seen in the murk. Unable to find it I prepared for a forced landing. My speed was now low in readiness for an off-airport landing and then the vibration stopped. Quickly putting on a little power, I increased speed and the vibration started again. Not engine, I said, just speed related. Nothing for it but to continue with my flight plan to St Athan.

Close in I was able to raise them on the radio and advise them of my predicament. The marshaller's face was a picture as he guided me in to park. When I climbed out I could see why. The Vamp has a fabric skin over its wooden airframe. This newly skinned aircraft had inflated and burst just behind my head. The flapping skin was the vibration that nearly caused me to force land.

Since the early 1950s, I had been driven to fly the Swift. This aircraft had been introduced to service at the same time as the Hunter, for the same role. The RAF needed a transonic fighter and it was seen as a risk to put all the defence eggs in one basket. And so it turned out that the Hunter was a success, whilst the Swift was a dismal failure as a day fighter.

56 Squadron was brought to its knees when the Swift Mk1 was introduced. The attrition rate was so high that it was withdrawn from service after a few months. It went on to have a stellar place as a fighter reconnaissance aeroplane. The 'Boiler' as it was known, was superb at low level, but a disaster at high altitude. It was strong, complicated and a test for any pilot.

Some of its unusual design features were: an afterburner for added thrust at take-off, an offset nose wheel and two-stage 3,000 psi brakes. To cope with the complications of the A/B were an array of lights that gave some measure of protection against zone fires. These lights sequenced at take-off, and the fire protection/detection depended on which zone had the problem. It was very intense for its day coupled with a fuel system that was largely automatic, so the wisdom was that only experienced pilots were selected to fly it in squadron service.

We were required to deliver the Swift and a few pilots were trained for this task. I tried everything to be allowed to be checked out and finally was sent back to Ferry Training for the conversion. The runway at Benson was sufficient, but full fuel was not usually carried. The Ferry Squadron had had its share of mishaps with this aircraft, including a take-off incident that had put the Swift in the bedroom of a cottage when the take-off was aborted.

First flight was just that, a first as there was no two-seater for dual instruction. Taxiing out was a softer ride than the Hunter and I lined up for take-off. Squeeze the brakes, then apply the switch to lock on the brakes at 3,000 psi. This allowed the A/B to be engaged against the brakes and a good check of the light sequence carried out. Release the switch and off we go, all OK, gear up and now watch those fuel transfer indicators. This transfer happened just a few seconds after you were airborne and a failure to transfer was an engine stoppage. It was something you paid attention to. At altitude the wing showed its poor characteristics, any turn caused a rumble and warned of an impending stall. The rate of turn was terrible. Back in the circuit the fighter was telling you that it was not a glider. It was always advisable to keep enough speed/height to make the runway, in case of an engine problem. Gear down selection required a rudder trim input, and was quite disconcerting to those used to centreline thrust aircraft.

The Jet Provost was now being delivered to the training schools and it was necessary to be checked out. I did my familiarisation on the way to the factory. When I went to start the engine I could not turn out the fuel booster pump light. Maybe I had forgotten it. I searched everywhere for the switch, even to the circuit breakers as used on the Meteor. I dare not start without that pump, and so I asked the factory engineer if he could start it. With a puzzled look he climbed in and placed the LP fuel cock on; this put out the light. He was still puzzled when I took off.

The Indian trips continued in a routine of 10-12 days en route, with a couple of days enjoyed in Delhi winding down. After each trip we were entitled to up to three days off. Very few people took this time off, such was the attraction of the card schools. Cards for me was a vital part of my finances. If I did well, I could journey home to Andover where my family were still incarcerated. The move to the Benson caravan site was a welcome one. With so much time away from home it was more than a pleasure for Betti to be able to join in when I was away. Such was the squadron esprit that wives were not left out when husbands were away.

Our caravan became the No 2 Mess, for we were able to supply 'eggybake' at all hours of the night. This immensely varied lifestyle was much to our liking, the social life was a riot, and the local pubs were a home from home. One such establishment was the Chicken in the Basket, run by the ex-CO of 85 Squadron. He was notorious in the service and no less as a civilian. Parties could extend over the whole weekend if Binks had anything to do with it. The drinking laws were such that at closing time after lunch, he would draw down the blinds, walk over to the parked police car and say, 'Private party, OK.'

The long-range trips had more chance of being memorable, and so they were. I almost always returned with a severe case of the 'runs'. Dysentery is not funny when you are committed to sitting in an aircraft for a living. They got to know me well at the tropical diseases hospital, for we would often divert there on the way back from the London airport. I was very careful about eating and I finally tied it down to Teheran. Blacky had a diet all his own, eggs and beer – one to cement him, the other to loosen. The sight of a seven-egg omelette for breakfast is enough to restrict anyone's diet. He was known to have eaten twenty-seven eggs in a day.

After a protracted stay in Teheran, the hotel fare was beginning to pall. Blacky went into the kitchen to see what he could produce. Irish stew with choice steak, fresh from the US of A, was an immediate hit with the patrons. Whilst helping in the kitchen, I noticed the soup pot bubbling away in the corner. Soup had been my staple diet here and it was always served so hot that I believed it to be very safe. The flies were using it as a refreshment centre. Thereafter, Teheran was not a problem for me. I was so ill on one trip that we made a run for it to Sharjah in the Gulf. This was an RAF base, but still primitive. Some relief was gained but I thought that I could hold out till Delhi. Sharjah to Karachi was an interesting run along the coast of Iran. In the summer we went to Karachi in Pakistan, very much as civilians, for India and Pakistan were very close to open conflict most of the time. In the winter we were forced south to Jamnagar in India. From there it was a short run to Delhi and maybe the end of the trip. I say maybe, because sometimes we had to go on to another IAF airfield. We arrived in Jamnagar ready for a quick turn around and off to the capital. Not to be, the worst fate we could consider was a night stop in Jamnagar. I was dehydrated and barely conscious. A visit to the base sick quarters was most depressing. They still had a few Second World War packets of aspirin, but otherwise the shelves were bare.

We were taken to the tourist hotel, formerly the Maharajah's palace, a red fort in all its glory. It was as though they had just left and the locals moved in. The lakes and fountains were being used for washing animals and children, and the gardens seemed to be supporting multitudes of people. Up the stairs, still thickly carpeted, with families living on many of the levels, cooking fires and all. The tourist area was massive and clean. All I wanted was rest and clean water. Large four-poster beds with mosquito netting in enormous tiled rooms were the scene. The rest of the convoy left to find food, while I stayed close to the toilet, and what a toilet. In a room the size of a squash court was a single toilet against one wall. Tiled from floor to ceiling, it contained a bath tub the size of a small boat. At least twenty feet long, it had steps to get into it and a large handle outside the tub that operated the plug. I gather it was for the harem, but it did cause me to reflect on those times as I spent most of the night on the 'loo'.

The following day came the realisation that I could die here. I struggled to cope with the Hunter, but oxygen gave me new life. Our young leader, who had been uncaring when he returned from the IAF mess, had been eaten alive by the mosquitoes. He insisted on a fly-by the red fort, but I had little interest in that. In Delhi it was no formalities please, just get me to the hospital at the British High Commission. Dysentery kept me there long after the others were home.

Delhi seemed to garner more than its fair share of incidents. The Ashoka Hotel was the focus of several. It was the meeting place of many of the airline crews and we generally congregated around the pool in the morning. Delhi was a 'dry' state, and so it was always bring your own liquor.

We were sitting by the pool when Robbie sat briefly on the glass table. It shattered and he sat down heavily on the floor in a pile of glass fragments. Being in a swimsuit, he was bleeding from many small cuts. We went with him to the hotel doctor, where Robbie, on removing his suit was told in a strong Peter Sellers accent, 'Oh my god, sir, private parts, I cannot do it.' We trooped over to the High Commission doctor and asked him to remove the glass – same reaction. Back to the hotel for a strong dose of embarrassment for the locals when we laid him out poolside and a stewardess proceeded to remove the glass from a very hairy rear end in full view of everyone, with her eyebrow tweezers.

The front door was guarded by a tall, impressive Sikh. The revolving door was massive and also impressive. We were waiting for a taxi when an elderly lady in a sari stepped onto the pavement. The next rotation of the doors grabbed the tail of her sari and spun her around like a top. She did not fall, but was caught by the Sikh, left in her bra and pants.

Motoring in Delhi was always interesting due to the poor quality of the vehicles. We came back to the hotel ramp one night in a collection of badly designed British parts that was a Morris built under licence in India. Poor fuel and the driver's complete lack of understanding brought the car to a stop at the base of the ramp. He raced the engine and slipped the clutch, but it would not climb the ramp. We watched in amazement and waited to see what he was going to do. Finally I reached over and pulled the column gear lever back into first gear. He was absolutely stunned, for it was obvious that he was unaware of the existence of other gears. He thanked us profusely and departed with a huge smile as though we had given him a new car.

Occasionally the Ashoka was full and we were put in alternate accommodation. The Janpath was downtown and an unknown quantity at that time. We were an unusually large convoy, eight in all and we agreed to meet for breakfast the following morning. Placed at a bare table we asked for eggs, bacon, toast, coffee, the works, just bring it. The waiter departed and slowly items began to appear – plates, utensils but no food. Aha, here comes the eggs, a whole plate full. Ten minutes go by; the eggs are one congealed mass and inedible. He then appears with a plate of bacon and takes away the eggs. Same story, bacon gets cold and we tell him to try and bring it altogether. This is obviously a real problem and so I follow him to the kitchen. He went straight out of the front door of the hotel and dodged the traffic on the four-lane highway to reach the other side. The cooking facilities were across the road. We gave up, ate the toast and left.

The IAF was modelled on the RAF and therefore we were aware of its idiosyncrasies. Bob H was a SNCO and also one of the most experienced pilots on the squadron. He had flown under age in the Second World War, and being found out later on, was discharged and reinducted simultaneously. He was usually the convoy leader and therefore responsible for dealing with the IAF directorate. This unusual state of affairs offended the IAF protocol. There were several officers on the convoy and so there had to be some face-saving adjustment to make them comfortable dealing with Bob. They called him Captain H, and he always said, 'I am not a Captain but a Master Pilot.' Yes, yes, but they could not bring themselves to refer to him any other way.

The vote of confidence that promoted you to convoy leader was a responsibility I felt strongly. Thus you were sometimes constrained in what you would like to do by what you had to do.

We landed at Jamnagar amid the thousands of 'ants' extending the runway – manual labour was the only way when you lack heavy equipment. The runway was set 10-12 feet below the surrounding surface, so any excursions from the runway were going to be exciting. They were the scene for one of our fatal accidents when one of the pilots, inexperienced in the Hunter, was taking off in formation. He did not have a fighter background, and so these small pieces conspired against him. The formation started its take-off run and he fell back. A formation take-off is not something you just pick up, it takes practice. To fall back is not critical, but it can quickly become so. He was now out of sight of the other formation members who could not see that his tail chute had deployed. He was struggling to maintain formation, probably believing that he was just not coping very well. As the speed increased the drag of the chute increased. He realised too late and impacted the wall at the end of the runway. So much for runways built below ground level.

The system required you to have signed by all the relevant departments, your flight plan and weather briefing. I was informed, as the convoy leader, that we could not proceed to Delhi as there was no crane available. It was quite easy to reply that we did not need a crane and we would therefore continue to Delhi. They would not release us and it became a judgement call whether or not to ignore them and just proceed.

I decided to call Delhi to find out what the problem really was. Indian telephones were never high tech and what followed was another Peter Sellers skit. The line went to Bombay, then some other PBX in central India and then to Delhi – not connected as you might expect, but relayed by the two operators. My question to Delhi when all the connections were finally made was: why are we restricted because of a crane we do not require? Pass it on resulted in, 'He does not require a crane . . . He does not need a crane . . . you do not need a crane'. I tried to sort it out, but my interruptions just made it worse. Once the theme was lost, it was impossible. Delhi could just hear me, but the operators insisted on translating everything, I did not know whether to laugh or cry, but did enquire whether airline traffic was landing. It was, and so we informed them that we were going anyway.

Flying in UK was varied and enjoyable, and the friendly rivalry between Ferry Comm and ourselves continued unabated One flight to Rearsby in central England was a classic. The Anson was flown by a Cat A crew, supposedly VIP qualified. Rearsby is a grass field, shaped like the letter L. The weather was very poor, but they found the airfield and overflew it to get lined up for a landing. We touched down and immediately started to go sideways, so much so that I could see the mud flying up from the wheel as we now were in a violent skid. He had landed on the short arm of the letter L, an impossibly short distance. I could not see what we were heading for, but a few bumps and bangs told me that we were there. We all piled out, or tried to, only to find that we were perched on top of the sewage treatment plant. The gravel looked firm enough, but there were no takers to find out. It was possible to make the wall and then march off to tell the Rearsby people that we were all in one piece.

Valley is an airfield NW of Snowden, the highest mountain in Wales. Any flight in that area has its attendant problems of high ground. We were all playing cards in the back of the Valetta when we were told that the radios were out, probably because of icing. No problem, Frank K was a staff navigator so we would let down out to sea and then come back underneath to Valley. As soon as the nose of the Valetta dropped there were all the ferry pilots peering through the door watching this blind descent. Frank had a map alright, but there was no ground to see. We broke out to see a granite wall right ahead. The Captain hit full power and climbed very steeply. So much for VIP navigators. We had a saying about navs, 'In a survival situation they are OK, 'cos you can always eat them'. This nav/pilot thing has been around since before the War, but was the source of much amusement.

Ray H was scheduled to pick up a Javelin from the factory. It was a short trip and therefore a nav was not necessary. He said that he did not need 'talking ballast', and left leaving the nav to continue his card game. On take-off he had a double hydraulic failure, and went off the end of the runway crossing a sunken road in the process. The nose-wheel detached and came up through the floor and out through the canopy. If the nav had been there, it would certainly have been fatal.

The friendly rivalry between Ferry Comm and ourselves caused Ron an embarrassing moment. In the Anson, the main spar passes through the cabin area, and in it there is an inspection panel for the aileron cables. By using the fire gloves, it was possible to grasp the cables and prevent the pilot from moving the ailerons. We waited until Ron turned into the circuit for landing and then as he was about to turn finals for landing, grabbed the cables. He was forced into maintaining the turn and also telling Air Traffic something to cover up his screwed-up circuit and landing.

The new long-range Hunters were beginning to appear. They had 660 gals of external fuel, and made some special flights possible. We did much of the development work, including evolving the long-range techniques. It was found that the range barely altered at speeds between M.70 and M.85. However there was a large time difference and you nearly froze to death at the low power settings, which did not pass enough heat to the cabin. We flew direct to Malta, much to the annoyance of French Air Traffic, for we rarely spoke to them at all. It was not unusual to say goodbye to Benson and the next call would be Hello to Malta. We made Cyprus the first night, and Sharjah the second, arriving in Aden the next day. For a while we held the speed record for UK-Malta.

Derek B was in UK from Kenya to re-equip his squadron with the

Hunter. It so happened that I was scheduled to go to Nairobi to pick up a Vamp and return it to UK. We met in UK and renewed our friendship. The trip to Kenya was by Transport Command in a Comet. We routed through Kano and clouted the lip of the runway there, requiring a delay of a few days. On to Elizabethville in the Congo, and into Nairobi.

It was my first trip to East Africa, and so I did all my test flights in the Rift Valley and around Kilimanjaro and Mt Kenya. Fantastic scenery, but now to get this ancient Vamp home.

We flew to Mogadisu in Somalia and a short stroll by the sea renewed my fear of sharks. The beach is steeply shelving with large breakers. A large shoal of small fish appeared out of a breaker. By the time my brain had worked out that something must be chasing them, the shark had smacked down in the shallow water, just a few feet from me. My departure was rocket assisted.

The second leg was to Aden across some very inhospitable country. Slowly I began to lose sight of the other formation members as the canopy iced up. My heating system had failed, probably from lack of use in a tropical environment. In trying to clean a hole to see through I inadvertently squeezed the brakes which promptly locked on. It would be more than warm enough to burn off the ice in Aden, as long as I had enough fuel to wait. We descended with me looking out of a tiny hole in the ice, and they landed first. I could only try to free the locked wheels by touching them gently on the runway. If they were locked it would burst the tyres. I used up the remaining fuel flying as fast as I could to heat up the airframe. The touch and go was gentle but unsuccessful as all the tyres burst. Now for an uneven landing on burst tyres.

It was very hot in Aden and the only place that was air-conditioned was the bar. The change of temperature for me had been close to 100 degrees C – minus 56 in the aircraft to plus 45 degrees in Aden. Couple this with drinking 'jungle juice' undiluted and my body said enough. This juice is available in most tropical messes, being a concoction of salt, sugar and vitamins. Usually it is diluted and placed on the tables, but not this time. I drank a full glass before my taste buds sent reject messages to my head. It was like drinking hot lead, and it cleaned out my system from both ends instantly. We delayed whilst I recovered and they fixed the Vampire.

Several short legs up the Oman coast followed to Sharjah in the Gulf.

From here we had a decision to make. Teheran was really marginal, but Abadan was rarely used and prone to flooding. The airport was right at sea level and could be unusable very quickly. We set off for Abadan to be informed that it had flooded and we diverted to Teheran. This was now an extreme range trip in aircraft that we did not know thoroughly. We started the descent with the fuel gauges reading empty. The formation opened up and we left room to glide in if the engines stopped. The landing was an anti-climax, but I was a little drained as we were guided into the military parking.

We refuelled and I had to move to another parking spot. It would not start, great, now what. The batteries appeared weak, and so the large ground power unit, used to start Comets, was brought up. What amperage would you like? he asked. Not a question usually faced; I guessed at 700A. The start was again attempted, and this time the Vamp wound up to 200-300 rpm. Not enough to start, so I asked for 1000A. Again only 350 rpm, so I requested 1,300A, but he said that 1,350 was his limit and I knew that we were in deep trouble. Still no start and so I started to climb out. The Iranian mechanic was undoing panels before I realised it. The words choked in my mouth as I tried to prevent him from touching the high energy igniters. These multipliers of all those amp/volts were dangerous for hours after a start. There was a flash and he flew through the air like a rag doll. The impact on the concrete was a horrible sound. I knew that he was dead – from the fall if not from the electric shock. We walked, not ran to the body, for it was pointless. He sat up and shook his head looking at his fingers. His only mark was the polished skin of his fingertips where he had touched the igniter. I climbed back in to collect my stuff and placed my foot where the step should be. It did not feel right and on looking down my foot had gone through the side of the Vamp. Tropical beasties had reduced the wooden fuselage to powder. There was no way that this aircraft was going to make it to UK, and so I was again left on my own in Teheran.

The hotel owner was a friend of ours and he liked to take us around and show us off to his friends. Being alone now, he insisted that I join his group for the evening. I was a little unnerved by the sight of him slipping a small automatic into his trousers. We ate at a local establishment and were walking back to his hotel when there was a commotion on the street corner opposite which resulted in gunfire from at least two places. Teheran had several police forces who all seemed to have different responsibilities. The guys in white uniforms seemed to be the law and so Alex started shooting at the non-white uniformed group. It was unanimous from the rest of the group, as we dived into the front garden of the nearest house. Bullets were whistling around and shrubbery is not an effective shield. We climbed the wall and I felt a tug under my arm. The firing was still going on when we reached the next street and I found that I was bleeding from a wound under my arm. The bullet was obviously at very low velocity when it hit me, but the scar is nevertheless still there.

Back to UK for a round of deliveries including a brand new Hunter Mk 9. This aircraft was en route to St Athan to be fitted with more service equipment; as such it was devoid of the usual tanks and blisters. I ran along the south coast at 500 ft, pushing to see what a perfect Hunter would do. There are many errors related to pressure instruments and so any readings had to be suspect. A good Hunter at that altitude and temperature should indicate 620-630 kts. The Mach number was hovering around .97/.98. It reached 638 kts before I aborted and turned north for my destination. This seemed high and so I called the factory to discuss the readings. With this error and that error it was possible, so no speed record for me.

We lost a Vampire en route to St Athan flown by my old course mate who had lent me his motorcycle at Pembrey. The cause was unknown, but I was certainly more careful for a while.

Ejection seats were a possible source of drama, for at that time there were so many marks and variations. Returning one old Vampire to the Maintenance Unit, I found that the drogue gun was not armed. There was no cartridge in it, and really there was no way that I could tell. I designed a fix for this problem, just a matter of leaving the loading tool in the gun and marking it. Lots of complementary letters, but nothing was done.

We were taking a flight of Meteors to Singapore, a mixed formation of single and two-seaters. I had the Mk 7 two-seater which had less range than the others. Diyabakir in a Meteor is a potential problem if there is bad weather. We arrived overhead and could not see or communicate properly. The decision to turn back is not taken lightly, but it was the only real choice here. We now had to cut the corner over Syria and hope that they were asleep. We climbed to max altitude and I faced a rock and a hard place choice. All the others were pressurised and so extreme altitude was required for the best range. It was also the case for me but we were limited to 35,000 ft in an unpressurised aircraft. The oxygen system was not designed for flight at higher altitudes, even though for brief periods we often flew the Mk 7 over 40,000 ft. I was not going to make it lower down and so one risk overpowered the other. We coasted out of the Syrian airspace and I shut down one engine to further stretch my fuel. We drifted down towards Nicosia and when a landing was assured, I relit and landed uneventfully.

Dunsfold was a hive of activity producing aircraft for many air forces. The testing staff were friendly and informative. They had much to pass on and I was all ears. By virtue of being around such a lot, I managed to cadge a ride in a Sea Fury, a large radial-engined fighter that could be said to have evolved from the Hurricane. They were being prepared for a West German contract as tow aircraft – the end of an era.

I checked out in the Canberra by changing seats in mid channel en route to West Germany. Never got to fly it much but it was a significant aircraft to have in your log book.

We flew so much on airlines that we were required to log all airline flights as a kind of record of your workload. That much airline exposure in the late 1950s was bound to have its share of incidents. Air India had the Constellation or Super Conny as it was known. This large four-engined airliner was used on the European route, and was replaced by the Boeing 707, whose introduction to service was no less checkered than the Comet.

We landed at Cairo in the early hours and were parked very close to the tower. Too close it turned out, for I felt the bump as he knocked 6 ft off the wing. Air India often landed in Geneva en route to London and I was not impressed with the approach when we broke cloud out over the lake at ninety degrees to the runway. We had just been served a fine curry lunch, but the Captain whacked on eighty degrees of bank and pulled. Few stomachs were strong enough for this test, and the scene became indescribable. I was at the head of the stairs choking to get off when we finally came to a stop.

Occasionally they would route through a Communist country and we were told to be very careful at such stopovers. I was hyper-sensitive because of my other activities, but apart from demanding to stay on the aircraft whilst it was turned around, there was little that resulted from these excursions.

I had the misfortune to be travelling back on a Super Conny and faced a 27-hour trip. Dysentery was with me and I explained to the stew that I wished to sit right by the toilet. All went well until I had to go and no amount of knocking could bring out the lady inside. I spent the rest of the trip washing my clothes in the toilet and being passed sandwiches through the door by the cabin staff.

When the US started its support of the Shah of Iran, money, technical and military assistance flowed into the country. One of our contacts was an ex-ferry pilot now working for a US oil company in Iran. We were at a night club one evening where there was a Flamenco orchestra. A huge black US serviceman in uniform was a little the worse for drink. He was calling to the orchestra that he wanted to hear 'Temptation'. You take the bass, man, and you take the sax, now I want to hear 'Temptation'. The bouncers were trying hard to remove him but he just swatted them away like flies. We moved away only to meet him coming down the stairs muttering about no English speakers being there. I passed him but made the mistake of saying, 'That's what you think.' A large black arm grasped mine and shook it warmly. He just needed someone to talk to and so we passed the time with him. When he found out that we were visiting aircrew, he launched into a whole story about 'Gold'. He was the SNCO in charge of the gold shipment that came up from a Gulf port. He would split it with us if we could fly it out of the country. Needless to say we beat it out of there as fast as we could.

The US, insistent on not appearing to be a colonial power, had agreed to abide by Iranian law. The Brits and French were appalled, for it was impossible to meld the two attitudes. We had always taken law-breakers out of the country immediately, for justice at home. One night an Embassy officer hit a pedestrian with his car. He was incarcerated in the local jail and left to await trial. The Brits demanded that the US remove him from the country as soon as possible. No, they would stay with their agreement and leave him in an Iranian jail. He would be dead in two weeks, if not from malnutrition, from other unmentionables. So the RAF flew in a military party and at night went to the jail and demanded the prisoner. The armed party were sufficiently impressive for them to release the prisoner, who was then flown to Cyprus and handed over to the US authorities.

This was the time of the U-2 flights and Mr Gary Powers. Many of those flights originated in Iran including the one from which he did not return. It has always been stated that he departed from Pakistan, but from local knowledge I am assured that he left from Iran. You could often see the contrails high above us, eventually heading north, and knew that it was U-2 activity.

Apart from leaving the Vampire in Iran, there were several other incidents involving damaged aircraft. One Meteor convoy had been fitted with remould tyres. At every landing the tyres failed, causing damage to the flaps and brake lines. It finally arrived in India where it awaited more tyres and airframe bits. With little else to occupy us, we thought that we would start the work whilst waiting for the working party to fly in. No Meteor jacks were available, but we could possibly make Vampire jacks work. With more ingenuity than knowledge, we bodged the jack pads to make them do the job. Now to jack up the Meteor. The noise of the jack going through the main spar is a sound that I will never forget. I wanted to be a million miles away. The aircraft was beyond reasonable repair and they tried to give it to India who wanted untold money as import duty.

Chapter IV

MANY OF OUR TRIPS eastwards routed though Beirut. It was a more than pleasant place to nightstop in those far-off days.

We were staying at a hotel some distance from the city proper, and had gone down town for the evening. On returning to the hotel, we found it locked and bolted. We should have arranged for a key, but had not been informed that this was necessary. One of the group was Dickie F, an extrovert, who was a prankster extraordinaire. We got into the garden area, but no amount of noise was enough to attract their attention inside. Dickie saw that his room, on the second floor, was reachable by climbing up the stout drainpipe. To cope with tropical rains these are square and pinned to the wall with decorative fastenings. We watched as he shinned up the pipe and reached the guttering. He was forced to hang from the guttering and make his way a short distance to his window. He used his feet against the wall to help, and in doing so pulled the whole system adrift from the wall. It came in stages, with mutterings and exclamations from Dickie, as it creaked and groaned with every separation. We all knew what was coming and that he was in no real danger – the flower beds and ornamental trees were in for a pounding. As the whole lot detached, he let go and fell into a flower bed, but the noise of all this ironmongery crashing to the ground woke up the neighbourhood. Lebanon has police who guard property and who are paid by the local property owners. No matter what it really was, no amount of explanation could save us from a trip to the police station. They were polite but impassive and a minor embassy official freed us in the morning. I do not recall a bill for the damage, but then Dickie probably offered to pay.

There was a memorable trip to the Oman in a Piston Provost. We were not able to route through Egypt and the rest of the Middle East was a political minefield. A Twin Pioneer was the lead navigation aircraft for the formation. The route was through the Balearic Islands and down across the Sahara. The old French Foreign Legion forts were the stopping places at El Golea and Tamanrasset. Most of those stops were not even countries then, but lines on a map now separate one piece of desert from another identical bit. Once through the desert, we swung east across the top of the Belgian Congo and into Kenya, then the long haul up the coast to Masirah Island As the nav said, you look out of the window and focus on a feature. Read your book and half an hour later look again. The feature is still there, for at 90 kts we hardly seemed to be moving.

These Piston Provosts were special armed versions for Oman, having among other things, long-range fuel tanks. The fit was very temporary with one lever having two positions, one normal, the other long-range tanks. Ron R was bringing one of the Provosts back to Benson for the delivery flight. The engine noise was slightly unusual for Benson, and so people were watching. I was riding my bike back to the Mess for lunch and keeping an eye on him at the same time. The change in the engine note turned every head skywards. It cut and restarted a couple of times and Ron banked desperately, looking for an out. There was no simple resolution, for he was over the Married Quarter area. The crash bell went off as ATC were very quick off the mark. I was in front of the Fire Station as they came screaming out and ran over the wheel of my bike, thrown by me in an effort to get out of the way. The last I saw of Ron was as he was vertical and vanishing behind a building. I pedalled as fast as possible on my bent bike and realised that he had crashed into the field just in front of the Mess. As I arrived, people were clambering through the muddy ploughed field towards the aircraft that looked remarkably intact. The Station Commander was the first to reach him, followed by the medics. Ron had managed to fully stall the Provost into the field with such force that the wings came of forwards. They were detached and slightly in front of the fuselage. His major injury was a switch, the pole of which stuck in his forehead. Quite fetching it was, like Mr Munster with an on/off switch. He had been flying in long-range fuel position, switched to mains and forgotten where he was with the fuel sequence. He must have reverted to the other position in error and consequently run out of fuel.

The Accountant Officer was to accompany a Middle East ferry, and on landing in Nice, they visited the casino. He had one helluva night and succeeded in losing most of the Imprest, the cash that was necessary for certain flights overseas. No matter, he says, pick me up on your way back and I will stay and win it back. He did.

The Indian Hunter ferry was almost over and the RAF was faced with paying for a squadron that had been covered by the fees from India and other nations. I was able to be selected for the last delivery and we flew to Dunsfold for the PR that always goes with such events. The Indian Air Attaché was flown in the two-seater with one of the TPs (Bill Bedford) and the formation lead was a certain naval pilot of very high repute. The weather was not good and so we were forced above cloud for the photo opportunity. We flew with the photo Meteor along the south coast of England, and the required pictures were taken. Ray and I were getting concerned about recovering to Dunsfold, for the photos had taken far longer than briefed. We followed Very Senior Naval Person down through the murk, far from convinced that he knew where we were.

On arrival at Benson, I was greeted with the news of a posting to my next job. Not only would it prevent me from completing the last ferry, but it would also seem to be a ground job. Nobody had ever heard of it – called a Flyco Team, it was apparently a new venture in the reformation of 38 Group. This new group was tasked with supplying the Army with its aviation needs. The last effort, before 38 Group was previously disbanded, was the Arnhem landings in the Second World War. I tried desperately to hang on to my last trip, but the military mind is implacable.

Some time earlier, we had bought a superb MG L. This rare version was in pristine condition and the property of the Mess Manager. Over a fourteen-year period, he had worked on it and pampered it. His only reason for selling was that there was nothing left to do. An 1100cc six, with a four-seat coupé body, it was an exciting possession. It caused no end of heartaches when I tried to take over from the Manager's engineering expertise. I noticed a frayed brake cable at the front and as it was already at the limit of the adjustment, it was either cut and braze, or replace. The braze did not last very long and so I ordered a new cable. I told my long-suffering family that I would change the cable on Friday, and we would go out on Saturday. The cable ran through the bodywork and onto a lay-shaft that was the handbrake. Wings off; running board off; dash out and floor up, we are now deeper into motor mechanics than I have ever been. The project took three weeks, but I did finish it amid all the flak from family and friends.

At that time races round the Mess on a Saturday night were a favoured sport. Beer does not enhance ability, as the Accountant Officer, of Nice fame, found out when he skidded into his own garage at the back of the Mess, having failed to negotiate the corner. He was OK, but extracting his car was a spectacle.

The Gliding Club was now in full swing as flying wound down on the airfield. I offered my services as a tug pilot, and they accepted for weekend work. The airfield was now under serious construction for the arrival of a new Transport Wing and vehicular traffic was restricted on the airfield.

I took out the car to drive over to the gliding activity, taking great care to wait until the engine temperatures were at their required settings. The traffic flow was restricted around the airfield to a one-way system in view of the construction work. There were high banks of earth limiting my vision on the inside of the corner, and so the sight of a Triumph at high speed head on, was a shock. I tightened the turn to try and escape on the grass, for if I had tried to go outside, he would have broadsided me. He reacted from instinct to go to his right and so the collision was inevitable. An MG has a solid steering column that is usually fatal in head-on collisions, for it moves back into the chest area. I slid to one side, broke the gear lever mechanism with my aim, but the steering column went over my shoulder. We hit headlight to headlight, absorbing some of the force in the resultant spin. By far the worst injury was my head going through the windscreen, taking out the rear-view mirror en route, and then shredding my face as I came back through. I was quite able to get out and see that his injuries were minor, being restricted to his knee. My arm was my most serious concern for I believed that it was broken.

I was taken to the RAF hospital at Halton, where the Burns and Plastic Surgery Unit had a world-class reputation. Many Second World War aircrew were rebuilt there. They fixed me up temporarily, but the plastic work would be done when the swelling went down.

A Board of Inquiry was formed to fix the responsibility for the accident, and I was interviewed by a Ferry Comm nav who had been given the job. The question really boiled down to whether I was on duty. Gliding was official activity and I, technically, was performing a task for the club. I was going to pick up a Chipmunk parked at the gliding area. The nav agreed, and as a consequence wrote his report that way. Coincidentally, he was trying to extend his time in the service. This became very important when they disagreed with his findings and asked him to redo it. He was informed that he would not be allowed to extend in the RAF, and he responded by not therefore agreeing to redo the Inquiry. I was asked to pay one week's salary, for the 'self-inflicted' loss of my services. I declined.

Travelling to my new job was now difficult, as the car was kaput, however, I settled to the position of Flyco team leader as fast as possible and tried to find accommodation for the family.

The job entailed operating a new Land Rover with two RAF Regiment airmen as Gunner/Signaller and Driver. The Rover was equipped as a mobile Air Traffic and Fire vehicle to liaise with the front-line army units and organise their aviation needs. It was run by an old nav who had been involved in this sort of activity for ages. The squadrons assigned to army support were 230 and 225. One flew the Single Pioneer and the other a collection of helicopters. Britain had not embraced the idea of helios after Korea, as had the US, the main reason being cost. As an aside, helios then were high maintenance and not very reliable.

Nothing screams like an idea whose time has come, and so it was for army support, with short-range transport and helios, lots of helios. One task was to arrange an airhead, or point through which the Army could be supported. It could be a short landing strip for fixed-wing aircraft, a drop zone (DZ) for para-dropped supplies or an LZ for choppers. It rapidly became apparent that the aircrew would not fly into an LZ unless they were sure that the ground side knew what was what. This meant that they insisted that the Flyco team leader was qualified on the relevant aircraft. Lovely, for on our small unit there were two navs and two pilots. Flying, yes please, when do I start?

In short order, the two pilots were checking out on the Single Pioneer and later the Twin Pioneer plus the S-55 helicopter. Our boss had not really anticipated this turn of events, for we were away flying far too much for his needs. As a follow-on to this I put forward the idea that the local training area should have an array of landing fields for training purposes that would be pre-cleared with the farmers and the communities. I therefore asked for an Auster or Chipmunk to check out these fields, for if you could get either of those aircraft in and out, then it would be OK for operations day and night.

This became my project in that I would fly around the area, select some challenging fields and then take my team to get agreement from the farmers. Some fields were limited to day only, some to seasonal changes. At the end, a low-flying area map was produced with all the fields marked. The squadrons got to know me and rely on my judgement.

The other pilot, Pete S, was a plonker, and he soon fell by the wayside. Fine for me, as if there was any flying to do, I did it.

The Auster was used only by the Army Co-op people, and so ours were the only ones in the Air Force. It had a central throttle, civilian style, which meant that you had to fly left-handed. This may not sound too big a change, but old habits die hard, and it was quite a challenge at the start to have the same degree of control. I had checked out some time ago and reluctantly was given the task of checking out Pete S.

We did it at night in view of other commitments. Without the assistance of a runway, he was lost. On the first attempt at landing, he overshot and instinctively pushed forward on the stick and pulled back on the power. The correct hand motions for a normal aircraft, but this was an Auster. We sank over the edge of the field before I could wrestle the aircraft back into the air. I gave up – life is too short for teaching Pete S anything.

The Single Pioneer was an interesting aeroplane, Short Take-off and Landing (STOL) and able to carry nine people out of impossibly short strips. I have seen less than 20 kts on the ASI, although it is debatable as to whether the aircraft is under control. The control column was very long, pivoted through the floor to give you enough leverage to manhandle the manual controls. Slotted, slatted and Fowler flapped, it really did not stall, just started descending. It had an electric tailplane trim to assist with the massive trim changes associated with high-lift devices. There were no dual aircraft, and so your first flight was made with the instructor standing behind you. It had a very high accident rate in service, possibly due to the tight conditions under which it was operated, but more likely because of the C of G errors that were made. It was usual for there to be landing accidents under windy or gusty conditions. Flying into a very short strip, over trees where the wind could change rapidly, was a set piece for an aircraft that was marginally under control at very slow speed. After the Pioneer had been in service for some time and many pilots had been censured for some incident or other, it was discovered that the centre of gravity charts were inaccurate, and that the aircraft was restricted to a 900-lb load right where the pilot sat. Changes were made but you can guess that no apologies were given, nor careers adjusted.

The Twin Pioneer came later, and was about as strange an aircraft as you can get. Designed to carry sixteen armed troops for less than one hour, its flying characteristics were bizarre. It could be pulled off the ground at a speed less than its real stalling speed. My old friend Tony R was the training pilot, and to see him more or less standing up on the take-off roll and then heaving back to sit down and haul the aircraft off the ground, was an unforgettable sight. It had two engines obviously, but after failure of one, the other just took you to the site of the accident. One Twin Pin flew slowly into the ground after encountering heavy icing. The Board of Inquiry asked why, after meeting icing in a cold front weather system, did you not turn around and fly to warmer air. His reply was that he did just that, but that the front was moving faster than he was.

One day we were visited by the Army Group brass and a demo and inspection of the aircraft was organised. The General tapped the Twin Pin with his swagger stick and asked Tony R how far this could carry his troops. Tony was not impressed, and facetiously said, 'Over that hill, sir'. Marvellous, he said, we must have lots of them. After a short time in use it was discovered that the floor loading was 12 lb per sq ft. Any freshly polished private is certainly heavier than that with his feet together, and so it was suggested that the floor be covered with wood, to spread the load. Some wag ordered lime, being a very heavy wood, knowing that it would severely limit the ability of the Twin Pin to carry anything. When the bottom of the totem pole saw 2,000 ft of wood, he said you cannot have 2,000 ft of wood, it must be cubic feet. I was Orderly Officer when the trucks started arriving and now they had another problem on their hands: how to protect all this wood from the criminal element. As it was a Saturday, they called in all the stores people to measure each one inch thick plank and nail on the ends of these planks the exact length. The military mind is amazing. I pointed out that by removing each piece of wood with the length inscribed, you could saw off a piece, write a new measurement and replace.

I volunteered my services to the Group Communications Flight, run by Gordon S. This enabled me to fly the Anson and the Devon and retain my twin rating. When a Meteor was diverted in with a mechanical problem it took some days to fix. I offered to return it to its home base, for there were no current Meteor pilots at Odiham. There was much discussion, but I was finally released to fly it.

Gordon featured strongly in that period of our lives. He helped out by loaning us his car, but more importantly by introducing me to the sport of shooting. He was a consummate poacher, gun collector and the original 'greenie'. He collected everything and wasted nothing. I had been a .22 competition shot at school, but never had any interest in shooting small game. Gordon's interest was purely shooting for the pot. All RAF airfields were the shooting preserve of the Station Commander. He usually passed that right to a club, but some did not. We, with a young family, were hard pressed to survive on a military salary – supplementing the food bill was an opportunity too good to miss. I used his equipment initially, a silenced .22, and found that pheasant, partridge and rabbit were welcome additions to the diet. He was a mine of information, catching pheasants with raisins pierced with horsehair, or keeping partridge on the ground with a kite. They seemed to fear hawks enough to believe that a kite was a hawk.

Odiham was surrounded by prime-stocked shooting estates, much of which made its way onto the airfield. I was so successful that I started taking the .22 away with me onto the Army training areas (PTAs). The helicopter squadrons would be stationed in the PTA and forced to live off 'Compo'. This packaged food was adequate but very uninteresting after a few days. To supplement this fare with fresh game made living rough acceptable. We even entertained the army units, who were more than curious as to where all this fresh food came from. It is a strange fact, but smooth-bore shooters have nothing but disdain for other types of shooting. They believe in the mystique of the countryman and his twelve bore, and I suppose royalty has helped to sustain this mystique.

The PTAs were large areas set aside for exercise purposes, some had been appropriated during the War and never returned. The old village buildings still remained and were useful for all sorts of training scenarios. It was possible to rise early from my encampment, usually set away from other units, catch a few trout with a 'thunderflash' set in the water, collect whatever game was around, and deliver it to the squadron cooks who were only to pleased to have real food to prepare. We would then depart for the exercise and return to a feast in the evening.

A game warden once called on the squadron to be on the lookout for an injured deer that had been struck by a car. He thought that we might see it from the air. I asked if we could keep it if we found it, and he said that in that case it would be OK. We searched and found a badly injured deer, which I dispatched from the air. We now had a valid reason for the superb dinner that the cooks prepared. The army brass were somewhat bemused for they were not allowed to keep deer on their smooth-bore shoots. For the next few years, the .22 and the silencer kept the family in food, although the cry of 'not pheasant again' was all too common.

I managed to be checked out on the S-55 helicopter, quite a feat, as it was forbidden for helicopter conversions to be done anywhere but the heli wing at another unit. All that was required was a solo trip around the airfield, just to say that I had done it. The heli units then knew that I had an insight into their problems and could be trusted to organise a night strip that was safe.

I flew a great deal of time with the heli squadrons and as a consequence, was around for the incidents. We began to do a lot of work with SAS-type exercises, and it was here that I gained some admiration for the work of the Special Air Service.

A secure camp had been constructed, the enemy were the SAS. We were using the helios to transport 6-8 troops immediately to any sightings. An SAS observation point about a mile away was seen from the camp. Whenever vehicles approached, the SAS observer scuttled down the tree and disappeared, so it was decided to try and sneak up on him by helio. We left and flew away, hoping to return unseen. He was visible as we approached at speed, a quick stop was attempted and then a landing as close to the target as possible. The tail rotor hit a small tree as we manoeuvred for the landing – without a tail rotor a helicopter does not fly too well. It was at an awkward stage of flight, and the S-55 spun around very fast. It screwed itself into the ground, but did not tip over. The SAS man had long gone.

The heavy-lift ability of the RAF was activated by the introduction of the Belvedere. This large twin-rotor helicopter was designed by Bristol and it was advanced and unique for its time. Its destination was the Navy, where its design was altered to allow it to carry torpedoes. The Navy finally rejected it and it was forced onto the RAF. As it was, it was totally unsuitable for Army co-op needs, but politics usually wins out and in this case a special unit was formed to nurture this beast into service. The boss was John D, a character and possibly the most knowledgeable and capable helicopter pilot in the Air Force. He fought a long war with the Ministry over this aircraft and his records must make fine reading. I flew many sorties on its way to acceptance and some were very memorable.

Early on, it was decreed that a demo would be flown for the War College. The Belvedere would enter, stage left, carrying a Rover and trailer attached as an underslung load. This load is carried at the end of a long cable fastened to the centre of the fuselage of the aircraft. Much to John D's disagreement, it was not policy to practice 'engine off' landings in the Belvedere. The twin engine system was supposed to monitor torque and in the event of a malfunction, either engine could supply power to sustain the aircraft. The aircraft approached, and slowed so that the Rover could be landed in front of the grandstand. As he slowed, the load must have bent the tubular fuselage enough to send messages to the torque sensing system. An engine stopped and Ron S dropped the Rover and trailer and prepared for a crash landing. He should have had adequate power from the operating engine, but the flexing caused that engine to fail also. In an unpracticed manoeuvre, he put it down after a fashion, crowd front. The Rover and trailer were still entertaining the crowd, as they bounced and disintegrated. The Belvedere was still fitted with tiny wheels mandated by the Navy, and in soft ground they dug in and the front rotor hit the grass. No casualties, but an object lesson in how not to do it. The resulting correspondence between the RAF and the Army was concerned with who was going to pay for the Rover and trailer. The Army said you dropped it, the RAF said that the demo was at your request.

John D was fighting to get some autonomy with the introduction of this aircraft, which still technically was owned by the Ministry of Supply.

I was aboard the Belvedere for the Farnborough Air Show in 1960, when a massed assault was planned. The airfield was attacked by fighter aircraft and the helios followed with the ground troops. We approached the far end of the airfield in concert with the rest of the heli assault. Just prior to touchdown, when all the troops in the back were ready for a rapid disembarkation, the elastic broke at the rear of the aircraft. We reared up, and the tail struck the ground as the Belvedere rolled marginally in control. The troops were not strapped in, and they came hurtling forward as we pitched onto the front wheels. Rifles in a confined space can be lethal and there were many minor injuries, but they scrambled out, pleased to be clear of the incident.

This pre-production version of the Belvedere had a 'bungy cord' control system feel, whereby these elastic cords were stretched across the rear horizontal surfaces to give some feel in the rolling plane. I was dumbfounded to find that the engineers had installed two such cords. When one failed, as it did to us, the immediate response is a roll initiation. Why they had not used one cord so that failure only resulted in loss of feel, I never did discover. The incident had gone unnoticed by the Air Show crowds, for there was so much dust arising from all the activity and we were a long way away from the cameras.

I was involved in some slung load trials that provided some insight into the problems of dealing with front-line army units. We flew to a Royal Engineers unit to exercise with some heavy bridgework. They had guaranteed to have 5,000 lb of the metal tracks that formed the bridgework, ready for a slung load lift. We were carrying a strain gauge mounted on the floor of the Belvedere, and this was to observe the load variations in flight. We hooked up and using almost full power were unable to budge the pile of metal. We set down beside the tracks and asked to see the weighing slip for the load. The SNCO was most efficient, but there had to be a gross error. When it was finally resolved the load weighed 7,500 lb. We waited whilst they repacked it and then took off to see how it flew. There was much groaning and creaking from the aircraft and as we entered a turn the strain gauge read over 10,000 lb. Well over the limit, the Captain was forced to turn so that the centrifugal force did not multiply the weight of the load.

The evidence for the unsuitability of the Belvedere continued to mount as we exercised further. The blades were made of wood in the early models, and being parked out in the field overnight would warp them beyond limits. The front cockpit was separated from the load-carrying area such that the crew could not see directly what was happening. Wing mirrors were a help, but the loadmaster was forced to be on the intercomm all the time. The loading door was 9 ft from the ground, and troops running from cover to board were faced with a climb into the aircraft. It was seriously suggested that they carry an aluminium ladder. The noise in the front cockpit was way above any safety levels, as the gearbox was right by your head. I was deaf for days before special headgear was provided.

The squadron was eventually given a number, 66(F) Squadron no less – it was a pleasure to see some of the trophies and records with my name amongst them.

We travelled to West Germany for exercises and I took my team into the field to work with a famous army unit. We moved constantly, but one night there was a lull in the 'war'. We went to a local bar for a shower and a drink. On arrival, my hosts found several of their troops causing havoc in the bar. They were noisily inebriated, and objected when their officer ordered them out.

We went inside and the proprietor was glad to have us solve the problem. The noisemakers refused to quit, and the lieutenant went outside to sort it out. He had words with them and then took the ringleader around the corner for a more private discussion. A few moments later the ringleader flew backwards into the road out cold. His mates were unimpressed, and so the process was repeated. I was very impressed by this judicial system, even more so in the morning, when at 5 a.m. I was wakened by the sound of heavy feet. The whole troop, lead by the lieutenant were running up the road doing physical training. You can drink lads, but you had better be fit and capable in the morning.

We separated our camp from thereon, but were forced to take precautions in view of enemy para activity. We holed up in a barn with an earth floor, one door and one window. I wired the place and backed the Rover in as far as it would go. We felt reasonably safe and therefore got out the safari beds and sleeping bags. Amidst all the farm equipment the three beds were placed anywhere. Being a very light sleeper, I heard the enemy walking around the barn. He avoided all the traps and I knew that he was not a casual visitor. To extricate oneself from the tight sleeping bag is a job in itself, especially if you need to avoid any noise and upsetting the flimsy safari bed. I reached over to waken my driver and touched him on the face. I said, 'Wake up, we have visitors', and was aware of him moving about slowly. I was easing the bag down my body when the alarm bells went off in my head. Something was not right with my driver's movements. The sense of his speed and muscle movement caused me to roll off the bed making all kinds of noise. We put on the light to see a large survival knife stuck through the top of my bed, where my head would have been. He had awoken to believe that one of the many rats in the barn was running over his face. My arm movements made it seem like a rat was moving around, for it was the illuminated watch face that he was seeing. He did not remember where my bed was and so had tried to kill the rat. Chalk up another life right there, but it would have been an interesting court case, for who would have believed him?

There followed a period of working with the SAS, developing techniques for their special needs. Low-altitude insertions were a need for them, and they could not understand my incredulousness when they asked to be dropped at the slowest possible speed without a parachute into a forest of small pine trees. It took a while to convey the impossibility of flying that low at night over trees, and that any error would likely be fatal. Several exercises were laid on specifically for them. In almost every case, no matter what the numerical superiority, they always won. I had such a healthy regard for their abilities that as we were camped as a helicopter squadron in the Salisbury PTA, I walked the perimeter before slipping off to bed fully clothed. I had all my survival equipment in my jacket and expected a raid that night. The squadron were not used to being raided for it was almost law that you did not keep your pilots up all night and expect them to fly all day. Also, thunderflashes around aircraft were a hazard.

About 1 a.m. they attacked the camp; I tried to put on my jacket but the zipper was jammed. The other jacket was available and so I rolled out of my tent to see numerous scuffles taking place. I tackled one of the attackers and was still scuffling when I realised that I was the only one without his hands in the air. We were forced to lay face down whilst they stole all the transport. My Rover was seriously theft-proof and they ignored it. The main cable supplying power was wrapped around a tree. I managed to extract my survival knife and throw it at the cable. Luck and good judgement cut the cable and shorted out the lighting. Everyone took off as fast as they could but the camp was illuminated quickly by all the vehicle lights. One of the pilots blundered into the portable toilet area and fell, knocking one over. He was left behind by the raiders, who bundled the rest of us into the trucks.

I reached down the side of the truck and undid the lashing. A Rover was travelling behind and its lights made jumping off unseen impossible. The guards were positioned by the tailboard and so they could not observe what I was doing. The moment the lights were off our truck I slipped over the side followed by almost everyone. I ran a short distance and fell to ground as the pursuit began. All the runners were caught, but though they stepped on my jacket, they missed me. They needed the trucks for a raid on the vital bridge, which they successfully captured later that night.

I was on Salisbury Plain without the maps and flares from my other jacket and so I set out to find a phone. Walking in pitch black, when you believe that there are patrols out there, is a slow, tedious business. Cows and electric fences took their toll and I finally found a phone too late to influence anything.

The Campaign for Nuclear Disarmament (CND) were active at this time. Easter was a favourite time to demonstrate, which meant that many military personnel lost their Easter break. The US airbases were favoured targets and also the UK's responsibility to defend. I thus found myself flying and co-ordinating a small part of the defence effort. We had several helios with 6-8 troops aboard, so that when a break through the cordon was broadcast, we flew to the area and dropped reinforcements. The cordon was formed by some very pissed-off personnel, dressed in full uniform. It was hot and there was little sympathy for these people, the antithesis of a disciplined military way of life. The cordon was inside the fence, and the great unwashed were on the outside. Several breakthroughs were made and the orders were to 'return' them to the outside. I walked up the line to see an unconscious figure lying on the ground. He had a large shiner and the NCO standing to attention close by was indifferent to the body. What happened? I asked. 'He fell over and hit his head, sir' he replied. 'I think he should be returned to the other side of the fence,' I said. The reaction was instantaneous, they picked him up and threw him over the fence. There were no more incidents in that area.

My other flying had been curtailed by the workload, but Bill A and I did agree to fly the Auster back from a very large exercise in Germany. These European Exercises were potentially very costly and after ten days in the field, it was easy to see why. The sight of a tank being denied access to a barn by the German farmer was intriguing. No amount of shouting could prevent the tank from backing into the closed area. When the tank crashed through into the cider press in the basement, it left the gun just a few inches off the floor. It was easy to see why the civilian population hated these exercises with a passion. Tanks reversing direction on the town soccer pitch, left deep ruts that were irreparable. Non-co-operation usually resulted in minor nudges to the brickwork, or the firing of a 105mm in confined spaces. The damage budget was used up in the first few days of the exercise.

We checked the weather for the flight home and were briefed on some line squalls coming through the area. The Met man said winds gusting up to 55 kts. In a classic case of only hearing what you want to hear, I said, 'You mean that the winds will be up there when the squalls go through.' We set off to Koxyde on the Belgian coast. It was rough and bumpy. Arriving at the airbase we were told that the wind was 50 gusting 60 kts. As the Auster lands at less than 50 kts, this was going to be interesting. We flew down the runway trying to find a way to land. It was too turbulent to get very close to the ground, as it were, low flying. We could go backwards quite easily, but getting down that last few feet to the ground was difficult. Bill had a bright idea. He took off the doors and put them in the back. He then stood on the step, ready to jump to the ground and pull the Auster onto the runway. I slowed as much as I dared and tried to descend the last few feet. He jumped out and hung onto the strut, I cut the power and we fell onto the runway. Now how do we taxi in for fuel. They sent out about a dozen people, and we manhandled the Auster into a sheltered area.

We decided to go the long way around over the channel, a 17-mile crossing as opposed to a 100 miles of water. To taxi to the runway was impossible and so we took off across the parking area, being airborne in a few feet. The 17-mile crossing took 55 minutes, and the white cliffs of Dover seemed to be moving away from us. The cross-channel ferries were faster than we were. An Army Air Corps Beaver went the long sea route and crashed in the water. There were no survivors in those sea conditions.

The normal night strip for the Pioneers was a 250-yd runway with lights every 50 yds. Two at each end marked the limits and the width. I would join in the night flying in the Chipmunk, which whilst it might stop in 250 yds, would not get airborne in 250 yds. Take-offs were therefore a challenge, but an indication of the lengths I would go to, to keep flying. I was returning with the Auster one day, when the throttle linkage broke. The power setting was high and so whilst I could not alter it, I would need to cut the ignition for a landing. I thought about the landing and decided that a normal approach to be high, so that there was no chance of not making the runway, was the best plan. I followed the plan and cut the switches when I was over the concrete. The Auster fell like a stone, for with no airflow over the tail from the prop, its stalling speed had increased. The arrival was heavy and a lesson I shall not forget.

One of the major users of the airborne support was the Royal Engineers. They held a display for the brass and we supplied the necessary airlift. Our part went off fine, but their display was a disaster. They were demonstrating a mine clearing device which basically was a rocket fastened to a long hose filled with explosive. In one of its forms, it was loaded onto a tank. With so much explosive in one small area, they decided to fire the rocket remotely. The rocket left with a roar, leaving the hose behind. The firing sequence having been activated, the explosion took place on top of the tank. It lifted the turret off with a mighty clang and deposited it some distance away. For an encore, they brought in a bridgelayer. This massive bridge work is also carried on top of a tank, and lowered hydraulically to bridge a gap. Explosive cords release the bridge when it is close to the ground. This set-piece was done under simulated battle conditions, so that vehicles were waiting to race across as soon as it was in place. The drop was quite severe and the two-piece bridge separated and fell into the gap. The first vehicle drove straight into the bridge and smacked into the broken half. He could not reverse out as the aluminium was too slippy. Very impressive it was.

The CO of Odiham was an ex-fighter pilot who took an interest in the careers of his staff. He wanted me to switch to helicopters, but with so many friends lost, I was not interested in such a career move. I believed that there were about eight things that would kill you in a helio, all of which you could do nothing about. For a fixed-wing aircraft there was almost always something you could do. He sent me to MOD for a careers interview. They were efficient and blunt. If I spent as much time with my primary duties as I did flying around scrounging trips in other people's aircraft, I would be doing myself a favour. On my return to Odiham, the CO told me that I would be going to Singapore on Javelins, a delta night-fighter.

My posting came in and I guess that I should not have been surprised that it had nothing to do with Singapore. CFS, the Central Flying School, was a six-month course to teach you how to be an instructor. Instructors were not held in high regard, probably because they were always performing checks on flying standards and they were seen to be non-operational. This ongoing argument between operational flying and non-operational flying had been around since Major Smith-Barry first managed the CFS idea. Many CFS staff pilots had little operational experience. To be seen as a dyed-in-the-wool trainer was not a compliment. All this was unfortunate, but a true reflection of the ebb and flow of power in a multi-talented service. I accepted the challenge of the CFS course, but knew that my future was now entwined with instructing for a long time. Two tours, a minimum of five years would be involved in this discipline.

The course was intense and fast paced. I had flown the JP before, but that was of little use to me. The lesson plans were given by a staff instructor, practiced as a mutual exercise with another student and then given back to your staff tutor. Much emphasis was placed on briefings and blackboard technique. Being able to do it is one thing, to explain it is another. The ground school work I loved, it interested me and was an extension of my hobby, aeroplanes.

213 CSE was a very experienced bunch of aviators. They did not take kindly to bullshit, and would not be treated like basic students. The briefing patterns were expected to be word perfect. A quick trip along the corridor would allow you to see that the briefing patterns differed from instructor to instructor. If I was going to be word perfect, it had to be in the vernacular that I used and was comfortable with. I wrote up my briefing on the blackboard, which was an amalgam of the other staff briefings that were on view down the corridor. My instructor rejected it out of hand and said that it was not what he had given. I argued that we should be allowed to differ from them as they differed from themselves. My stand was echoed by other students and rapidly became an issue. A full-blown meeting was called and those far senior to me made it clear that they had better smarten up or there would be mass resignations from this course. We resumed flying and the trouble went away, but not very far.

There were some great characters on the staff. Tony D wore an immense flying suit miles too big for him. Stores insisted that this was his size, and so he wore it just to piss off the senior directing staff. Al P eventually made a name for himself by beating up all the fighter bases and flying under the London bridges on his last trip in the service. He was making a statement about something or other, and only Douglas Bader's intervention saved him. I was selected for the Aerobatic competition at the end of the course and worked hard at some negative 'g' manoeuvres. The headaches and redeye come with that kind of stress. I even asked the Doc what damage it was causing. He said maybe you can afford to lose that many brain cells. I vowed not to get involved in heavy negative 'g' aeros after the competition. I had severe haemorrhoids finally, and the competition was therefore extremely painful, but I received my B2 rating which is the initial rating obtained. Our departure was recorded for ever, as the staff informed us that we were required to give the Mess a gift on our dinner night. With the treatment we had received there was much discussion as to whether we would do this. It was agreed that a gift was a choice and we would not therefore be coerced into it. Because of that the course photograph is not in evidence on the walls of CFS, giving us all the notoriety that they were trying to avoid.

No 4 FTS at Syerston was an ab initio training school not far from my home town of Nottingham. Moving there was a little less painful as we could stay with in-laws until the long awaited married quarter became available. The RAF viewed anyone under twenty-five as unmarried and therefore not eligible for a quarter. It was therefore a red-letter day in the Kingsley household when I was promoted and eligible for a quarter. There was a significant change in our standard of living. I had borrowed from my in-laws to purchase an Austin van. At that time they were free of tax, IF they remained without windows. I reasoned that most of the time it was just my wife and I in the car and therefore the children could survive without windows for the small percentage of time we were all in the car. It also enabled me to shoot out of the van unseen, and there was much game to be had on the Syerston airfield.

The boss was an avid smooth-bore shooter, and he was curious as to why my van was driving slowly around the airfield perimeter, much of the time. I did not enlighten him and it became a joke as he was the only one who did not know what I was doing. When he was finally told, he would try and follow me and catch me at it, so to speak.

I flew as much as possible, for after the B1 rating, you needed 400 hrs of instructional time to be considered for an A2. Each unit would select its instructors very carefully to go to CFS for the long and involved test. It was seen as a reflection on the unit, if the failure rate was high. In order to get those magic hours quicker than the rest, I managed to fly with the other squadron when they were doing night flying. Derek was on that squadron, and this little short circuit continued until they discovered how much flying I was doing. The limit was 600 hrs per year and 60 hrs per month. By the time I had accumulated the necessary hours, Derek was on the Standards Unit, preparing people for their test rides. This unit was staffed by the best collection of pilot/instructors I have ever come across. Derek B, who would serve with me on the Red Arrows in a few years time, Wally E, who ended up as a Civil Aviation Authority (CAA) examiner, Ralph C, who was a natural instructor and would be my Chief Pilot many years hence in Canada, and Dickie F, who had been through training with me and who would end up as Chief Test Pilot for Atlas Aircraft in his home country of South Africa. I vaulted to the front of the queue and took my A2 successfully. Once you have that rating, it can also become a handicap. A2s are carefully used, and you could be stuck in Training Command for the rest of your days, which was a long way from my dreams of the future.

Instructing is like any other discipline in that you need to experience all its component parts to be confident and at ease. Sending your first student solo is a milestone. The RAF gives, or gave its teaching staff lots of room for individuality. You had a message to impart and you could alter the plan to suit the individual student. The aircrew selection system was supposed to weed out those who would not make the grade It was far too expensive to waste time and money on non-productive raw material. However, the candidates were selected by a government department called Science 3. They were known to check the selection process by sending material that had failed to reach 'the' standard. In this way they could at least prove that their criteria was correct, the proviso being, of course, that the training schools caught and discharged this sub-standard material. You were never sure, therefore, if you had a poor student, or if this was a test case.

There was a wide difference in abilities at various stages of the course, but this usually disappeared at the end. When a new Group Commander was posted in, he determined to save money and wastage by reducing the 'scrub' rate to 15 per cent, from its long-time figure of 30 per cent. This number had its roots deep in RAF thinking in that 30 per cent of everything was rejected. His comment was that there were no bad students, only bad instructors. The long-term effect of this inanity was that the service suffered a terrible accident rate when these people made it to operational units.

Of course, he was long gone by then, and it was somebody else's turf that had the problem.

My particular exposure to this edict was that as a new A2, I was given a difficult student. He was a sports person, and as we already know, the service would make special efforts for such candidates. He was a South African and in all respects a good prospect, except that he had no ability for flying. He had been put up for suspension several times already, but with this new edict fresh in the senior staff's mind, I was told to get him through.

Instead of being my usual abrupt self and telling them that he was unable to pass the course, I decided to do my utmost to sneak this fellah through and really beat the system. What followed was one of the most intense and demanding periods of my life. I taught him by rote, every moment of each flight. We would sit and go through every stick movement and he learned the instrument pictures by heart. He was programmed. I would seek out the testing officer's routine, and know that they would not stray far from a lesson plan. I would write it on the blackboard and insist that Van B was word perfect. At sixty hours he was at the thirty-hour standard, by one hundred, close to the sixty-hour ability, and ready for the check flight with another pilot. This wastage of flying hours was an implicit part of the reduction in the failure rate.

Whilst there were many who knew that it was a farce, they did not speak up sufficiently loudly to make a difference. I taught him instrument flying by numbers, and we would sit on the ground with a broomstick simulating the movements. By the progress he was making, I might have him ready for his final handling check at 160 hours, instead of 120. The plot was uncovered when the CFS 'trappers' came to our unit as they often did to ensure that the mythical 'standard' was being maintained. By accident they chose to fly with my student, and we now had to deal with an unknown routine.

The CFS examiner who did the flight was the same one who had given me my A2. We had known of each other for a long time and he was a no-nonsense instructor held in high esteem by the system. It was all up to Van B now, and I waited with a feeling of resignation that we were unlikely to pull this one off. When he landed he was smiling and we all trooped into the briefing room for the debrief.

The trip debrief was short and pointed out the major errors. Van B was dismissed, and he then called in my boss and the two flight commanders. He was angry, first at me and then at the supervisors. I protested that I had been ordered to get him through, and he commented, 'How on earth did you conceal his lack of ability from everyone?' It became a test case for the wastage that goes with these half-baked ideas. Pete W was unyielding, and it was no surprise that he made few friends and got little support in his quest to end this 15 per cent stupidity.

Derek B was on the unit aerobatic team, the Vipers, led by Wally E. I had to wait for a slot on the team, for it was an opportunity that I could not miss. Flying was a happy environment at Syerston, and there were many days that were memorable. Complicated practical jokes were the rage, especially between certain staff members. Brian N and Ray P would almost daily play tricks on each other. Brian ordered a ton of coal to be delivered to Ray's house, and please leave it in the driveway. Ray responded by advertising Brian's car for sale at a ridiculously low price, guaranteed to keep the phones ringing all night.

The squadron leader in charge of operations was proud of his exploits as a Spitfire pilot. He was jealous of this self-generated status, and was always trading barbs with another Spitfire pilot. Brian and Ray made up an application form for former Spitfire pilots to apply for a job flying a Spitfire for a TV series. The form requested details of experience and was routed through an office so that they could get at the replies before they left the unit. The replies were read out at a dinner night, to much embarrassment for the two who were legends in their own minds.

Pyromaniacs have always featured in RAF life. Tony B of Benson fame is reputed to have burnt down the Mess when a fire-breathing act of his went wrong. A training school seems committed to breeding new ones. For a period it was necessary to check everything in the morning, for a light switch would set off a display and plugging in the kettle would invariably cause an explosion. Even chalk was drilled out to explode when dragged across the blackboard.

Being subject to student flying brings its own share of incidents. I was sitting in with an Iraqi student doing the end-of-course aerobatic competition. He was an unknown to me, but his routine looked sound enough. Somewhere along the way, he got completely out of synch with his plan. We were limited to 1,500 ft above the ground and he looped and bottomed correctly at 1,500 ft. He then rolled the aircraft upside down and attempted to pull through. In the manner in which he tried it, it was impossible, besides breaking the rules. I took over, and tried to roll out, but he was still trying to complete the pull through. The judges said that we disappeared from view upside down well below 1,500 ft.

I was duty pilot one day when snow squalls were in the area. Student flying was in progress and I received a note warning of a line of squalls coming through. I informed the OC Flying and started a selective recall. A general recall can get quickly out of control as everyone rushes back to the circuit. The squadron commanders were now aware and they appeared in the control tower. When the Station Commander came up we had a full house and I stayed at the back having given over authority to the OC Flying. A full recall was initiated and I watched the weather, a series of squalls now less than twenty miles away. There was a staff-led formation recovering and so the students were OK as long as they were able to remain with their instructor. We tried to get them down first but they were unable to see the airfield and so went away to the nearest alternate, which was threatened by similar squalls. Several aircraft recovered satisfactorily, but the formation and three students were still at large. The formation did not get in at the alternate and was ordered back to Syerston. They were getting orders thick and fast from this high-powered gathering, and there were just too many people in the tower. One squall went through and a small gap opened up, such that you could see blue sky above. The three aircraft came overhead and started a slow descent to the airfield. The OC Flying could see that it was going to be a close call if they did not get down pronto. He could not say anything on the radio, for they were following the rules and their learnt techniques and descending oh so slowly. His frustration got the better of him and he went outside on the balcony and screamed at them to hurry up. I had to laugh even though it was getting very serious. Whilst we waited for a conclusion, I cut out some imitation medals in Day-glo paper and left them on the CO's desk. They were West Raynham Stars, for stop/go/come back decisions of the highest order. Some years before, the Day Fighter Leaders School was at West Raynham. It was the most operational unit in the Air Force, which translates into the pushiest risk takers around. They were caught out by weather and lost four or five aircraft – too little fuel reserve, and a return decision too late. When the directing staff at Syerston cooled down, they were able to see the humour, but through clenched teeth.

I was airborne during another recall situation, this time with a student. The weather was not good but I could see the ground from 23,000 ft. I dived straight down and flew back under the weather, whilst others were queueing up for instrument approaches or being diverted to other airfields. They could hardly refuse to let me land when I appeared downwind, for it was another aircraft safely recovered.

The Aerobatic Team was now going full swing under the leadership of John P no less, who had been the officer in charge of my inquiry at Acklington. It was different flying, and a start to the head-on opposition stuff that was developing in display flying.

I had traded my van in for another one with a slightly bigger engine. It was also modified to do at least twenty miles an hour more than the standard one. Derek and I had started rallying using his MGB, not really a suitable vehicle for such events and I hoped to be able to use the van. It was fast and nimble, but the brakes were not capable of stopping it. We did very well in the usual night club rallies, winning the Command Championship the first time out. Ordnance Survey maps were used for these events, and it is possible to navigate head down in very poor visibility. The Maple Leaf Rally took place in the Pennines at night in fog. I said that we could do it if he could trust my map-reading in less than fifty yards visibility. He drove magnificently, relaying road data to me as I called the twists and turns, climbs and descents, viewing the map through a magnifying glass.

There was much social pressure to get a car, for there was some stigma attached to the van. Much against my better judgement, I acquiesced and bought an MG 1100, which impoverished me in six months. I was sitting in a car park waiting for the family, when I was hit mildly from behind. I got out just as a large car drove forward releasing the bumper of my MG. He had compressed the rear of the car, but there was hardly a mark to show for it. Some time later we were driving to Derek and Sheila for the weekend, in heavy rain. The car started to handle very strangely and I stopped, thinking that it had to be tyres. When I checked the trunk, it was full of water. I reached the drain plug and speeded the drainage. A short time later, we had the same scenario, trunk again full of water. When we reached our destination, Derek and I went looking for the cause. It was that the rear quarter of the car had been bent in that impact in the car park. There were no paint indications, just that water from the roof now entered the drain channels and went into the trunk instead of by-passing as it was supposed to.

An abortive attempt to jack up the rear and bend it back, showed me that it had to go. It did and we were without a car for another year. The early pattern of things going awry was still with me; I seemed to be on an assault course all the time, whilst my associates were travelling light and enjoying the scenery. There was one important rider to the above in that when the chips were really down, I was lucky.

Chapter V

THE POSITION OF Station Flight Safety Officer was up for grabs. It was a Flight Lieutenant post, but at that time I guarded my seniority as a Flying Officer very carefully. I was a page one Flying Officer, which meant that you had reached the exalted position of being on page one in the Air Force List. Whilst you had no authority, you did have the recognition of being a professional pilot. I used to park my van outside the mess next to the CO's slot. The slot was marked Senior Flying Officer and after a lot of mutterings they accepted it.

I took the job as FSO and departed on the Rolls Viper engine course. The JP was having problems with engine stalls, and so whilst this was a necessary course for me, it was also a 'go and find out what is going on' mission.

Some way through the course at Bristol, I discovered by accident that the design specification for the Viper engine included the statement that the engine could stall below 90 kts in unaccelerated flight. Certain manoeuvres, like flapless take-offs, stall turns, even spinning could cause the engine to stall. It was generally much better than that, but the isolated incidents had spooked Training Command. All the graphical data and specifications were obtained, signed in the original order by the Ministry of Supply.

I rushed back to Syerston, ready for the first Flight Safety meeting, a committee of senior staff and one lowly Flying Officer, me. They asked for a report on the stalling problem, and I replied that the Release to Service had accepted a 90 kt point for clearance. They refused to believe me until all the evidence was displayed. It got very heated between the Engineering staff and the training squadrons. The CO was more than upset that nobody knew. He called Command and the cat was out of the bag. Bristol/Rolls were eventually forced to pay back many millions over this contract, which made headline news.

My new boss was an old Flight Lieutenant, newly promoted from Cranwell, John L. He appeared in the Mess and indicated that he was an avid sportsman. Table tennis was a number one sport for me and at the urging of the squadron I played John at the game. It was an excellent intro for him, not so for me, for I was soundly beaten. This set off a sports rivalry that exists even to this day, and we went to great lengths to devise any sporting activity that was competitive. He was not a golfer, but picked up the skills at once. We could be seen on the soccer pitch of an evening playing fast golf. This entailed hitting the ball through the soccer net at both ends of the field, but it was the first one to do it. He took the quarter next door and our families became extensions of the sporting competitiveness. We all joined in on whatever was the flavour of the month.

Training Command had been suffering a series of wheels-up landings, often by very competent people. There seemed to be no pattern, other than all the unfortunates declared that the indicator lights, 'three greens', were checked and were green prior to landing. Pilot error is the usual answer, and some careers took a nudge over these incidents. One Trevor E, at Syerston, an instructor since the War, who was so methodical that he could put you in a coma just talking to him, landed wheels up. He swore that he checked the indications and that they were green just prior to touchdown. The Engineering Officer set about looking for a clue. They jacked up a JP and plugged in a hydraulic rig. Gear up, gear down, up down interminably. Nothing was found. He was just leaving the hangar, putting out the lights, when he heard the sound of the gear cycling. He was alert enough to know that this was the first time anyone on the ground had discovered even the slightest indication that there was a problem.

What transpired was that the hydraulic system had a filter in it that was insufficient for the job. Under certain circumstances, the dirt in the hydraulic fluid could prevent the valves from closing properly. It allowed the gear to retract when the pressure bled through the gear selector. Need I say that those whose careers had been blemished were never pardoned, but that Trevor was saved from a nervous breakdown.

My departure was again less than satisfactory. We had a series of displays booked, culminating in the usual Battle of Britain air days.

My slot on the Vipers was not going to be filled quickly, and a deal was done to allow me to return from my new post at Church Fenton. This was unheard of and the cause of some ill-feeling. I was posted as Deputy Chief Ground Instructor, instructing in airmanship and instruments. I should have looked further into the attitudes of my new Station Commander, for he slowly made it impossible for me to complete the display season. His view was that I had a job to do, and it was at Church Fenton, period.

My new boss was one Les F, a legend in the service although unknown to me. He had been Sword of Honour at the Royal Air Force College, Cranwell, a position from which nobody has made Chief of the Air Staff. I think that it identifies the super intelligent, too clever for the service. He was for ever at war with some piece of pomposity and delighted in correcting Station Routine Orders and sending them back to the Station Adjutant with spelling, punctuation and other ambiguities highlighted.

He was forced to sit through interminable meetings by which the CO ran the unit. He would obstruct the CO's imperious moves with points of order and strict adherence to the rules of procedure. It became a fight that almost all on the unit were aware of and Les had really kissed away his career. He was an inveterate womaniser who needed the company of women. All very correct, but in the CO's view of the world, not correct at all. His view of the service had not matured beyond 1936.

Les was at one more of these departmental meetings, looking bored, but cutting pieces from Station Routine Orders (SROs), and pasting them onto sheets. They were discussing the rusting motor vehicles parked on the station parade square. The Station Warrant Officer was informing the meeting of his efforts to contact the owners, long since left, to come and remove their cars. This discussion had taken place for the last six months, and Les had recorded the time and effort involved in talking about it, instead of moving the damned things. When 'any questions' was invoked, he stood up and went laboriously through the record, itemising the committee time, printing effort and total lack of results. He said that he could not afford such time-wasting exercises and left. The CO took issue with this conduct and ordered him to report to his office at 9 a.m. Les knew what was coming and so he deflated the inquisition by 'grovelling'. I am so sorry, I do not know what came over me, etc., etc. When the CO could stand it no more, he was dismissed just to get him out of the office. As he left he said to the Adjutant, 'Silly twit, grovelling always is too embarrassing for him, but if that is what it takes, I will just give it to him.'

Les was ex-married, and had a suite in the Mess which he improved so that he could entertain. The CO had an inspection and demanded that Les return his suite to a more standard appearance. The rules and procedures were weapons for Les and he never did change anything. He was a good friend and a terrible waste of talent in a service that feared free spirits. Many of the wartime leaders could not settle to the coming bullshit and had been similarly herded out.

He was a major player during an incident that is burnt deeply into my psyche. We all have views of our integrity, particularly in a service that was not averse to asking you to put your integrity and your life on the line. I believed that I would not flinch if it became my place to stand up and be counted.

We were at a mess meeting, which is a democratic institution where the CO is respected but theoretically has the same status as every other mess member. It is run by a committee, chaired by a senior staff member, in this case Chris S who also worked in Ground School. He was obviously uncomfortable bringing up this matter, but asked the Mess to vote on sending a sum of money (large) to Command HQ, to pay for some picture frames of portraits of former Commanders-in-Chief. He mentioned that the money had already been sent, and really we were just regularising things. I should explain that just prior to this piece of business, we had voted our usual contribution for the local children's charity Christmas party. Les stood up and protested this irregular procedure, knowing that the CO had authorised it. A vote was called, and not surprisingly not passed. The CO seated at the front stood up and talked about a personal favour to him, and anyway the money had already gone. Another vote, not allowed by the rules, was demanded by the CO. He stood at the front and watched each person raise his hand. Under his gaze, hands were slowly raised. I half raised mine before yanking it back down. But too late, I had compromised my integrity, whether he had seen it or not. It now is the ultimate bad dream for me and forever in my mind when integrity is in question. Les of course had the last play of the day. He stood and said that we ought to get things in balance here, for if we were going to vote this horrendous amount of money on such trivia, we ought to rethink our contribution to the children's charity. He proposed a sum in excess of the portrait frames and it was seconded by many, myself included. Chris tried to inject that we did not have that money, and Les said, 'We found it for the frames, we can absorb it for the children.'

After one other piece of unacceptable behaviour, he was again called to task with a 9 a.m. interview. He crawled in on his hands and knees, to be immediately thrown out. Success comes in many forms.

I was able to fly with both of the training squadrons and so keep all my ratings current. This certainly helped one's credibility when they knew that you were speaking from experience during lectures. Ground instructing requires that you attend the School of Instructional Technique and receive at least a B2 rating. I managed an A2, probably because of my history at Syerston.

The course was expected to be dull, but the whole experience was marvellous. You had to give a series of lectures, 2, 5, 15 and 40 minutes long. The early subject choice was yours, the last two, theirs. The first lecture was by an NCO from an Electronics School, titled Doppler. He wrote 'Doppler' on the blackboard and took out a whistle. Blowing it, he ran from the room. The sound went away, and exactly two minutes later he reappeared. That was 'Doppler', the change in frequency aptly demonstrated as he went away.

John D's five-minute effort was even better: he wrote E T C on the board in large scruffy letters. Extra Terrestrial Crepitation told us about crapping in space. He used the acronyms from the US space program, which he said were codes for solutions to the crepitation problem. 'THOR' translated into Thunderbox Orbital Rocket, 'ATLAS' into Astronauts Toilet Lavatory and Shower'. He had a whole range of translations and said that the Russians were obviously doing research, for one of their cosmonauts had been heard singing on the 'toilet'. He ended by drawing a standard toilet bowl turned on its side. The similarities in design between that and a ram jet were clear, a large inlet and small outlet. Indeed, it could be demonstrated that this design would self sustain, and therefore it could be boosted into orbit and parked there for a long series of visits by astronauts.

I returned to the Aden Armoury that was the Ground School building. Chris and Les had offices alongside each other, but because of the design of the former armoury, they were both an unusual distance from their doors, which they always left open. They were blessed with abnormally loud voices and carried on conversations, mostly repartee, that kept the whole place in stitches.

Once, prior to an inspection, Les was driving the students nuts cleaning up the place. He had purloined a lawn mower to trim the grass on the path between the armoury and the airfield. One poor unfortunate was doing almost as ordered. He had cut a swathe down the airfield side of the path, evidently not what was required by Les. When the boss saw what he had done, he screamed at him, accusing him of having 'porridge for brains'. This tirade seriously upset his sense of direction, and he had wandered even further into the airfield grass. To square it all off needed about an acre of further mowing. He was still doing it when the CO started the inspection.

There was a student fatal, which was a rare occurrence at that time. Somehow, I finished up doing the identification. Not a pleasant task, but a reminder of the pitfalls in aviation – dream about flying, don't fly about dreaming.

I had reason to think that one through one night recovering back to Church Fenton. I had made all the weather checks, and knew that I had to be back before the weather closed in. I left with less than full fuel to save time, even though it made no difference in the end, it is carried mentally as negative. The weather was deteriorating fast as I started my approach. The alternates were also going down fast, and so it became stick with Plan A. The runway lights were not up fully bright and just at dusk that was a decider. I missed. There was no other flying in progress, but the duty pilot was on the ball. He knew that I was really trapped into staying at Church Fenton, rather than heading for an alternate that likely would be just as bad when I got there. The second approach needed to be as low as I dared, survival not rules. The radar was not really designed for such a low approach, but it was all there was.

At normal limits there was nothing. I was ready for an ejection, in case I hit a tree or something that was not runway. At the very last moment, lights, an ugly arrival, but I was down. All the soul searching and analysis only develops your attitudes for the next time. Decisions come down to nanoseconds and if you survive the first time, you have a bias that may help you to survive the second.

The Royal Air Force Aerobatic team, the Red Arrows was now going strong. Ray H, of Benson days was firmly entrenched there. After he retired from the RAF in 1960, I had kept in contact with him in New Zealand. His business venture there was not enough to keep this superb pilot out of the air. He returned to UK and ended up at CFS, eventually on the Arrows. Ever keen to join this elite bunch, I took all my leave and free time to visit and be checked out on the Gnat.

Flying aircraft at other units is frowned upon, but I was relentless and I guess my Station Commander was not informed. The checkout was a return to fast jet flying, and a relief; for deep within you is the fear that skills that you once had may have gone away.

The Gnat is a story in itself as is the formation of an RAF display team on the back of one man, Lee J. The 1965 team initiated the return to a permanent display team, rather than a skilled part-time operation that had been the Red Pelicans. I flew in the back with Ray and Bill L, and could not get enough of the atmosphere that was team life. The selection process is closely held, and the team has much influence on the choice of new members. I would rate the ability to get on with people to be of equal importance to sheer stick and rudder ability.

Flying Training Command issued a request for applications for the team. The qualifications required were, A2 instructor, above average, fighter background and some formation aeros experience. I knew that it was coming and was ready with my application. The CO turned it down flat, saying that I was needed at C Fenton. He was not within his rights to do that, but a Redress of Grievance you might win, only to be a pariah for the rest of any career. I was a convert to the Les school of thinking from then on.

To run interference for us, a new Wing Commander Flying was posted in. Ron N was known to me and was an old associate of Les. He also had run into the CO back aways. He introduced himself formally to Les and I, and when we were alone said bluntly, 'I am pleased to have you on my staff, but none of your damn crusades,

OK?' He became a confidant and friend later, when he left the service, probably driven mad by the CO. Les departed for the RAF Selection Centre and I became CGI, tasked with the last courses at C Fenton including the last Vampire Course.

By this time I was teaching High Speed Flight, Weapons and Military Studies. I expected a posting back to a flying job, even though I had only completed eighteen months of my ground tour. I had learned that pilots are not capable of knowing when they are fatigued. This ground tour had been very necessary for me, to recover from the draining tour at Syerston. I would never have admitted it, but I was a basket case at the end. I suppose that 'they' also knew that a full tour (30 months) on the ground is ideal for getting you motivated. And so it was to be, posted to Valley as High Speed Flight Instructor.

Before I left I took time off to visit the Arrows once more. I flew with Pete E on a flight from CFS to Fairford. The weather was low cloud, but Fairford was lower than L Rissington (CFS). We took off and descended off the runway into the valley. Good stuff; and now for a normal arrival. A beat-up was the norm and Pete was a master. The Gnat was such a tiny aircraft that extremely low flying was possible. We arrived up the entrance road and banking slightly went through the back entrance 'gate'. By now all the Arrows were out to witness the arrival. There was a volleyball court outside the crewroom, sans net. We went through the poles before turning in for a landing. I do not think that we had been above 100 ft the whole trip. I flew the manager's aircraft on one overseas trip, but if I could not get an application in, they could not respond.

The VW was loaded and I set off for Valley. It was a testing journey through the Welsh mountains. Enjoyable, but if I was going to survive numerous drives, I needed tyres, rather than the cardboard things that came standard on the VW. It was the only time that I made the choice of throwing away the standard tyres, even though they were hardly used. It was an excellent decision, and probably saved my skin many times.

Valley was the fast jet portion of the Wings course. Two aircraft were used, the veteran Hunter and the relatively new Gnat. I was operational on both, and so it did not take long to be used in a multitude of roles. My teaching duties allowed me plenty of free time, only ever two lectures a day and I was on a short tour so that I was not given any secondary duties. The two Gnat squadrons were helpful, not knowing that I was also flying with the Hunter outfit. I was getting more flying than almost any instructor on the base. The CGI and the rest of the staff were superb and Valley turned out to be a pleasant short tour. The coast is beautiful, with rocky beaches at your door.

The Mess was a lively place, and so when we settled into our quarter, it was only a short walk home. The Saudi princes were going through training, four in all, I recall. They had a pecking order of seniority which pervaded everything they did. The senior one had a Ferrari and so on down to a Ford. One of the instructors had a Jaguar E-type. Naturally there was some pushing and shoving as to which was the fastest. On a return from Bangor, a fast but winding road, they ended up in competition. The E-type left the road through a stone wall and was reduced to its component parts. The two occupants were very lucky since speeds were in excess of 120 m.p.h. The Prince reputedly bought him a replacement E-type.

The School was called one day by the harbour police over in Ireland. They had a number of vehicles which they believed were the property of the 'Princes'. They had tried to rent a car after a boat trip across the Irish Sea, been refused, and so bought vehicles for their weekend trip. There was too much red tape involved in bringing them back to UK, so they left them there.

Mountain flying in the Gnat and the Hunter was a time to hone skills and investigate just how far you wish to push it. Limit flying is an RAF creed, and so you can get very close to some of the absolutes of aviation. Once you have those skills, it is an interesting argument as to whether you can retain them without continuous practice.

We had a royal visit and somehow I managed to fly the Hunter demonstration for the Duke of Edinburgh. It was a practice forced landing (PFL), during which time the other instructor with me transmitted over the radio the teaching technique of a PFL. It is very easy to mess up a PFL, especially in front of a large crowd. The Duke visited Ground School, and I was rather put off by the fact that he was wearing make-up. I have met him several times but somehow that is the only impression that stayed with me.

As one of the most significant aircraft that I have flown, I think a closer look at the Gnat would be of interest. It originally flew as the Folland Midge with a Viper engine, designed to meet the NATO requirement for a light fighter. The French and Italians both produced prototypes, but the unified approach did not work, all three nations going their own route. The Italian competitor was the G 91, later used by the Frecce Tricolori. The RAF needed a fast jet trainer and the Hunter 7 was now in production. In some political deal, Folland, later Hawker Siddley, was chosen for the advanced training role, although the Hunter T7 was also used, a duality that did not make a great deal of sense. The Gnat was sold to India, Finland and Yugoslavia. The Indians had over 400 of them and in their war with Pakistan, they called it the Sabre Slayer. In the fighter version it had full span ailerons which drooped to act as flaps. The undercarriage is mounted on the C of G. When it is selected down, there is a large trim change, similarly the reverse is true when it is selected up. The fighter version had to live with this design feature, but the RAF felt that it was too much of a problem for advanced training. There was, therefore, significant alteration in this area. Weight is saved by the U/C acting as airbrakes. The trim change is

Swift FR5, 1960 – 'The Boiler'.

minimal in this case, as the U/C only comes down about one third of the way. Fully loaded it weighed in at less than 9,000 lb. With an engine of over 4,500 lb thrust the power weight ratio was excellent. Its diminutive size, 28 ft wing span, and superb field of vision made it a thoroughbred. It departed from mainstream thinking in many areas, and the tailplane/trim system was unique. The trainer version had slipper tanks which gave enough time for an instructional sortie of 75 minutes. However, it could be said to be limited by minuscule standard fuel capacity. It was supersonic in a dive, faster than the Hunter, with good supersonic manoeuvrability. For formation flying it had very light stick forces. Indeed during flight test, the testing body at Boscombe said that it would be impossible for formation flying in the training role. These ultra-light forces required a rethink for those who were musclebound. The roll rate was extremely high at 400 degrees/second in the Red Arrows versions. This was achieved by taking out the aileron limiter so that 14 degrees of aileron was available all the time, rather than below 200 kts as was the norm for the trainer. This fused limiter was the source of much entertainment for the Red Arrows. Mr Petter, who also designed the Canberra, had a stick-to-tail ratio problem with the Gnat. The stick was so short that the normal leverage and travel were limited. He solved it by allowing you to trim the stick back into the middle as it were, and start again. This meant that you could potentially have an emergency where the stick was at the limit of its rearward travel and you needed more to keep the nose up, or vice versa with the stick on the forward stop and you needed more to keep the nose down. There were several 'get you home' devices, including a manual reversion system that was far safer than the Hunters.

The RAF spends a great deal of time teaching and practicing emergencies. Meteor memories were fading in that they started using the emergency systems so much, that they started failing. Cables that had been designed for use once or twice, were in daily use. Thus the Gnat had a poor safety record, and many were lost. We witnessed a double bail-out close to the airfield, after which the Gnat flew around for several minutes before aiming at the beach which was packed with holidaymakers. It landed in shallow water, a short step from dry land, and was used as a ground trainer after retrieval. The Orpheus engine was thirsty at low level, but at altitude it was very economical. The wing was the Gnat's greatest success. A loop was possible in less than 2,500 ft, and if a mistake was made you could just pull into the buffet and gain altitude. It would spin, but only if you grossly mishandled the controls, or were at very slow speed.

I made one last try for a position on the team, but without due process, there was no real chance. We therefore committed to the number two choice of Fighter Recce. This time when the posting came through, it was as discussed with no surprises.

The staff at Valley and in Ground School were an extremely good bunch and I was sorry to be leaving, The Wing Commander Flying was amazed when he saw how much flying I had done, but with the best reports I was on my way. I was doing a fair bit of Hunter flying and to leave Betti with a car, I flew down to Chivenor in a Hunter, doing a check ride on the way. Many of the Valley students were going through the Chivenor course and so I had a slightly unique position.

I recognised that you are a marked man, a QFI and returning to flying from a ground job. Many of the staff were well known to me and I expected a hard time. Yarpy M was an old flight commander of mine from 66 Squadron days, but as CGI he was most helpful and not at all what I expected.

The first trip was in a T7 two-seater, more as a familiarisation ride. When we landed, I was asked when was my last trip in a Hunter. I said last week and it seemed to cause some consternation. The flight commander was somewhat ruffled, and treated it as though I was trying to play some sort of a game. I explained that trying to keep a low profile meant saying little. They had had the opportunity to ask, but I certainly had had little opportunity to do or say anything that was not capable of misinterpretation.

We entered the tactics phase and worked at battle formation. All was proceeding well until we almost inevitably banged into one of those hard-learned lessons that are worth standing up and being counted for.

Chivenor more or less ran its own show, and by circumstance I believe, had introduced the idea that during a full emergency you would switch to the emergency frequency. This was a no-no in my book, for if you were communicating satisfactorily on whatever frequency, to risk losing radio contact during the change was silly.

Air Traffic could change frequency far more easily than someone in the midst of an emergency. It was a minor point, but of course hard-headedness never lets it remain thus. I listened, but said that you can do what you like, however the mainstream of thinking says otherwise.

The argument was in full swing when during a night sortie, a student had an engine failure. He was being talked down by radar which allowed you to monitor your range versus height. They switched him to the emergency frequency and promptly lost contact. The time out of radio contact put him too far from the field to land. He bailed out satisfactorily and procedures were revised pretty damn fast.

Fighter recce in Germany where I was destined, was all low level and usually as a single aircraft. The results were yours and so it was very much a 'loner' job. The chance to go to an overseas squadron was a chance to improve your finances and buy a decent motor car. We were all in the planning stage when I received a call from Ray. He had been given the option to pick who he wanted for the very important 1968 Fiftieth Anniversary of the Royal Air Force. I was so far into my Germany planning that it was not an instant 'yes'. I had been trying for three years to get on the Red Arrows, and had mentally given up. I called home to discuss this turn of events. It was a very long call and probably the most significant choice I have ever made. As ever my wife left it to me as a career move only I could evaluate. So I did it and was told to be ready to move very soon.

The staff at Chivenor thought that I had gone nuts, trading the best fighter slot in the Air Force for the Aerobatic Team. Whilst it was held in high regard, it had not yet earned the status that became its destiny thereafter.

I jumped into the VW and drove home at high speed to collect my things and then on to Little Rissington and the Cotswolds. The year 1967 was an unusual one for the RA, really a holding position for the 1968 show year. I was the first to join for '68', and I was doing it mid-season. I flew with nearly everybody to learn the techniques and the pattern. On the transit trips, I flew with the Manager and could step in to become number ten when the moment called for it. I purposely looked at the solo discipline and also at the skills that Ray gave to display flying. The ability to be so accurate during manoeuvres and to be able to stay in front of the crowd no matter what the wind and weather was pure excitement.

The team possessed low-flying skills that you probably could learn nowhere else. I felt confident at low altitude, but knew that I would have to work at getting it down to these heights. Doug S arrived, also from Valley and so we both got into the training early.

Arthur G was finishing off his Red Arrows film and I flew him on many sorties beginning a firm friendship that took us around the world together on races and rallies. We wanted to get away from the standard shots from the side or rear of the formation. To do this entailed arriving head-on to integrate with the formation, such that you were looking through the nine aircraft at some backdrop. He had the uncanny ability to have his camera ready, pointing through the canopy, as we rolled upside down through the formation. His failure rate was negligible. All the rules were put aside, only common sense and your own abilities prevailed. It was, after all, viewed as science when in reality it was artistry.

The last phase of the year was with us: Jersey, Battle of Britain and into Farnborough. One aircraft had oxygen troubles and I was forced to remain with it whilst the rest flew to Biggin for Battle of Britain shows. Although the euphoria was strong, I still had doubts about my ability to perform. Each position has its worst moment in a display, maybe the roll rate, the rapid onset of a 'g' load, or the tailplane sensitivity at the top of a loop. You work at it, it seems insoluble, and then it is gone and you wonder what got you so wound up.

The vintage years were about to start with a close-knit team, that whilst it may not have been comprised of the best pilots, it made up for it in camaraderie and professionalism. The positions were selected by Ray and two new solo pilots were going to be needed. This is not a desirable situation, for to work up two new solos can be fraught. Roy was to lead, but as a moody perfectionist, he was often not easy to work with.

It was between Frank H and I, Frank of Syerston days. When Ray finally made the choice, Frank went flying and as if in confirmation of Ray's decision, hit the fin of a taxiing Gnat as he 'wired' the parking area. Wiring was the name given to very low flying, trailing smoke that lays on the ground like wire. The factory rep looked at the Gnat and declared it OK, for the cap had been bent and not the fin post. Ray then gave Frank that aircraft for the season as a consequence of his error.

Roy and I worked steadily at the pattern, no manoeuvres were practiced, just trying to consistently cross at datum, no matter what the conditions were. We had carte blanche to develop new solo manoeuvres, but until the pattern was stabilised, had little time to be imaginative. We worked at some new departures from the 'seven', and were able to pop out of the top or the bottom of the nine-ship, giving Ray more freedom, particularly in the bad weather show. The changes during a manoeuvre were getting very slick, such that almost all the 'movers' were hyper on landing if it had gone well.

We planned an arrival in 'Big Nine', which was a Vic (arrowhead) of nine aircraft. This large-wingspanned formation is unwieldy, but as we pulled up for the initial loop, Roy and I went from opposite sides to form the stem or shaft of the arrow, whilst eight and nine snapped in alongside us to complete the diamond. I needed Roy to hit his position spot on, so that neither of us overshot the centreline. Eight and nine delayed just enough to ensure that we were stable. There were large power adjustments and heavy use of aileron. When you got it just right, it was powerful emotive feeling, delicacy combined with brute force.

The solo acts were progressing, I did not like the opposition loop too much, for it went against my basic thinking. The idea was to enter the opposition loop so that the smoke circle looked round. If you pulled up fractionally too early, it was elliptical; too late and it became dangerous as you tended to fall in on each other. Over the top, you could only err one way, hence my initial dislike. Trying to pull down onto the other aircraft to make the loops concentric was difficult, and my 'out' was to rudder the Gnat sideways if I felt that all was not as it should be. The Blue Angels, US Navy Team, had a collision at the top of this manoeuvre. Strangely, the risk was never understood by the 'Wheels'.

Aviation offers its faithful small nuggets of information which can save your life and also adjust your thinking. We were trying to develop a new split, by arching away from the top of a loop whilst in a Diamond Nine formation. If we could extend our loop and 'walk' it away, we might be able to have enough separation at the bottom of the loop for the solos to have a useable time interval. The initial separation was made by Roy easing away at the top, where the speed is lowest. To gain more separation we were eventually pushing hard. The Gnat does not have much tailplane for inverted manoeuvres, and at some point I would start to fall in onto Roy, not a pleasant feeling, for the control limitations can start to intrude pretty damn fast. Running out of tail meant that I had to rudder the Gnat sideways, and learn the limit to that set of circumstances. It did of course provide the out to the 'opposition loop' that I needed to learn.

The 'Roulette' had always attracted attention from the press, and inevitably the 'Wheels' would wriggle under the pressure of responsibility. This manoeuvre required that both the solos appear from crowd rear and pass overhead at low altitude. They commanded a split at around 50 ft, such that they fly individual circles and pass head-on right in front of the President's tent, or crowd front: datum. The miss-distance was less than twenty feet, with a closing speed of 720 kts. The passage of the other aircraft could be felt as a bang, and a good one was a feeling like no other. The radius of the turns produced a circle that had a diameter of less than 800 yds. The other aircraft was not seen across the circle until about halfway around this high 'g' turn, and that was through the canopy.

In the course of the training and development of the manoeuvre, it would get lower and tighter, with miss distances that are pure adrenalin. In reality, it was an understanding of the small fine adjustments that made it a sensational display item. Practice confined us to strict format, from which minor adjustments were made. It is also worth remembering that Ray had developed three routines that allowed us to perform full, rolling and flat shows. We needed a cloud base of 3,500-4,500 ft for the looping display, around 2,000 ft for the rolling, and 500 ft and half a mile visibility for the flat show. At that time our competitors, the French and Italians, had only one show.

With those numbers, it can be seen that putting on some kind of a display in bad weather was all down to the skill of the leaders. To be close to the ground in a high 'g' turn, looking for your rapidly approaching opposite number in very poor visibility certainly

Kemble, during training.

A good one.

151

exercises the heart valve. I said that I would never die of heart failure for I had a heart valve the size of a dinner plate.

Whilst training at Valley during one of our detachments looking for fine weather, we were practicing at Mona, the relief landing field for the training school. The weather was poor, almost at the point where little can be achieved. Roy and I commenced a split and followed the pattern for the head-on pass. Some way around the turn I lost contact with the display line, and called on the radio to that effect. However I was still running in on a poorly executed pass, and I knew that the 'seven' were also heading for the same space that I was. With the poor visibility, it was too late to locate everybody, and so I went as low as possible believing that the only security was right on the deck, hiding behind the old buildings and then out onto the airfield, at which point we all crossed. Roy was above me, with the seven too close to identify. The experience was, I believe, significant.

They banned the Roulette for a time, but never recognised the true areas of risk inherent in this and other manoeuvres.

To display one of the Gnat's greatest characteristics involved an opposition roll at low altitude. The roll rate was 400 degrees/second, and we were required to retract the flaps from the normal setting of 10 degrees used in the rest of the display. Using the full 14 degrees of aileron at 400 kts, the RA were allowed just one revolution. The fin was close to its stalling angle and roll coupling was possible if more than one revolution was performed. This was in the early days of roll/yaw coupling knowledge and so it is not surprising that everyone had problems at some time or another with the aircraft seeming to do strange things.

Roy and I started practicing at 1,000 ft, trying to arrive at datum at precisely 400 kts. I had watched the other solo pilot's technique, but it was so quick that the subtleties were difficult to detect. If it went awry, the Gnat would exit the roll sliding sideways in a slight descent. We knew that 20 ft was lost in the roll anyway, but it was most unnerving to see so much yaw at low altitude. I went through a phase of being most unhappy with the manoeuvre, so much so that I would look for excuses not to do it.

Having taught high speed flight, I should have been able to analyse the problem. It all came together finally when I collected all

1968 – a magnificent year.

the pieces of the jigsaw. Any positive 'g', or increased angle of attack, would, on entry to the roll, translate instantly into yaw as the aircraft passed through 90 degrees of roll. The large fin would start its corrective action only to exacerbate the problem as you completed another 180 degrees of roll. This magnified corrective force was very visible as you tried to level the wings. The simple answer was to unload just prior to the roll, a slight push force would reduce the angle of attack, and the Gnat would rotate beautifully.

We worked at a new act away from Kemble, so that we could display it to the rest of the team when we felt ready. It was a complicated rolling manoeuvre started in close formation. Roy would invert his aircraft in place, then slowly roll out allowing me to follow him round this half roll. That left me inverted and Roy the right way up. A quick half roll by both of us, reversed our positions, and then Roy completed yet another slow roll back to normal flight. All this had to be done in 2,000 yds, a normal display line, and at

300 kts about 12-15 seconds. We started at 1,000 ft and slowly worked it down to less than 300 ft.

All the team were out to watch this event as we ran in for a test. It went well, but the response was very negative. Waste of time, etc., etc. Professional pilots would know what was at stake, but the difficulty would not be apparent to the general public.

We countered by inventing the opposition barrel roll, a manoeuvre that started with a wheels-down approach at ground level, pitching up into a roll and descending into ground cover with the wheels retracted. With changes in coloured smoke to amplify the effect, it was an instant winner. It had all the ingredients, looked dangerous, topped at 200 ft, full of impact and was carried out right in front of the crowd.

A normal day was to board the J2 as it circled the married quarters. This monument to British engineering was our transport to Kemble, some twenty miles away. It was thrashed at valve bounce all the way, with the poor unfortunate driving receiving all kinds of abuse for the quality of his roadcraft. Much of the attitude adjustment was occasioned on these trips, for sensitivities were illuminated, even identifying those who were perpetually late or who could not get up in the morning.

Roy's early morning dyspepsia was a source of entertainment and it became the norm to joke about his mood. Any problems from the four trips per day that we tried to fly, inevitably surfaced on the trip home. Nothing was left unsaid, and I believe that the basis of true comradeship was established here in that you became psychologically incapable of letting down your mates and the team. Everyone knew that you knew, and therefore so much of the trivia of life need not be discussed, you could focus on the stuff that could kill you.

The 'join-up loop' was a new manoeuvre that needed much refinement before it became an integral part of our display. It followed from a downward bomburst of the seven-ship formation, spreading out to pass over the crowd. Behind the crowd line, the solo pair would link up with the seven by as it were diving into the middle, and complete a reversal to reappear over the crowd from the rear. Thus you have seven aircraft rejoining from a fanned-out manoeuvre, plus two trying to drop in from above. With so many

Kodak Diamond.

Bomburst.

Malta and the 'split' out of the top.

aircraft to try and keep contact with, you invariably tried to find a little hole that kept you away from conflict.

One practice, I saw another Gnat flash past at very close range, an intruder in my bit of sky. The adrenalin is flowing freely and so the debriefing was a trifle high pitched. It turned out to be Derek B, who naturally was insistent that that bit of sky was his. The join-up was one of the most complicated manoeuvres to orchestrate, but as before, when we had all settled down, the sky full of aircraft was no longer a threatening scenario.

So much of the day-to-day life was humour that a set-up had to be expected. Once the equilibrium of the team was evident, anyone was fair game. Dickie D was given the responsibility for PR, an increasingly large task as our mail multiplied monthly. The 'Mange' (manager) would pass letters from all over the world to Dickie to deal with. One such letter was from Germany, or so it appeared, from an aviation enthusiast who had lived in Germany through the Second World War. He wrote in strangled German/English, the comedic

157

Biggin Hill Air Fair – MGBs to the rear.

language made up of half German, half English words. Dickie had lived in Germany on his last tour and should have been alert to the manner of the letters.

One letter contained a sepia photograph of a boy scout-like gathering. The photo had a hole in it, which the writer said was made by a bullet from a Spitfire. About this time we were let into the secret that the Mange was orchestrating this joke. Dickie, true to his career aspirations, was dutifully answering each and every letter. At the final year-end guest night, the correspondence was read out and everyone had been prepared so that Dickie was the only one not to know what was coming. When he considered the language, he could not understand why he had not seen through the joke.

The brochure was new for each year and every pilot was required to pass over a precis of his career to date. Any embellishment was an instant opportunity for a group inquisition as to the facts. Having had an unusual number of jobs, my resumé was a little long. The Manager was insistent that most of it was irrelevant anyway and so would I please cut it down. They had found a sensitive nerve and I had too much steam on to back away gracefully. Taking yourself too seriously was always pounced upon, this was my turn.

The Biggin Hill Air Fair was usually one of the early displays. However there had been a fault detected in the fin of the Gnat. The shims at the bottom of the fin post were incorrectly applied. This had led to a failure of the fin under severe stress. We were therefore grounded until all was checked and corrected. Ray had to fly a 'tin' one as his aircraft was not ready for the show. This was an ordinary school aircraft in metallic trim.

Biggin was very wet and miserable for our arrival having had lots of rain for days. We all landed safely, but Ray had brake trouble and sailed off the end into a very wet ploughed field. He was about 40 ft into the mud and sinking by the minute as we all dismounted and ran to his aid. Not being an active RAF airfield, the equipment was limited. With more bodies it was thought that we could push it out before it became a muddy monument. Some PSP (Pierced Steel Planking) was found and the slow job of returning the Gnat to solid ground began.

We were all in our new flying kit, but with trousers rolled up, about forty people eased the Gnat out of the field. It was washed down and after inspection and rectification of the brake problem, declared OK for the next day. This was the first time the BLMH had provided MGBs for us all as a publicity venue. They had been trucked to Biggin for our use. The arrival at the Bromley Court Hotel was a sight to be seen, new vehicles and a disgustingly muddy bunch of drivers.

With the lead-up to Biggin, the field incident, and rotten weather, I was hyper to do something. There were no takers when I said I was off for a drive in the new machinery. However there was a stream of 'Bs' leaving the hotel heading for London. Sitting at a traffic light in Soho, there were Red MGBs at all corners, and it was not too long before the populace realised something was afoot.

To have the transport problem solved on these long stays was a godsend. None were damaged, although at any given moment you could not get them all within a 200-mile circle of the operating base. Whilst operating from Manston, the lack of transport was very limiting. Ray had taken the team Mini up to London and in the middle of the night I was woken by the Air Force police with a frantic call from Ray. He had broken down on the A2, and needed a pick-up quickly if we were to make our departure for the continent within a few hours. He knew that as a non-drinker (nearly), I would be most readily available to get him out of his predicament. The Duty Officer would not authorise another vehicle to pick up Ray, and so I climbed over the MT section fence and borrowed a Mini, hoping to be back before it was missed. Talk your way out of that, but it was never necessary for we were gone before questions could be asked.

Memory recall is selective, as we all know, but flying scenarios seem to be part of a defence mechanism that are recalled with a shudder, for you just never want to be in that position again. Moving the nine aircraft around, particularly at low altitude, needs practice and a 'simpatico' that goes beyond training and SOPs (Standard Operating Procedures).

There are obviously times when arriving at the show site is restricted by local conditions. It may be OK for a flat show, but how do you get there all together? On one of my early sorties leading the back section, we were returning back to Kemble after a very limited show in the local area. Knowing the country was a help, but the vis was terrible with very low ceilings.

Ray started to turn the front five away from a mass of cloud sitting right on the ground. He went over a stone wall and was momentarily lost from sight. I just caught a glimpse of all of them tightening the turn. Over we go and the vis is just yards. Ray's section is now on the edge of my view and I must turn to follow, or this will get out of control very quickly. I cannot do a max rate turn, in deference to the three guys following me, but as low as I can as steady as I can, I must try and keep Ray in sight. You have to leave something for the aircraft following you, but not staying in contact will be almost as bad as demanding too much of your followers.

I believe the recall remains vivid, because you remember how close you were to the limit and that it is not a single factor that made it work. It would be lovely if you could isolate that factor, because you could bottle it and sell it.

To be working at the limit of your mental capacity, often means that you prejudge for ease, rather than slowing and starting from the

ARROWS
ON TOUR

Barnstorming through the Med with Hanna's flying circus

NARRATIVE BY ROBERT R. RODWELL: "FLIGHT" PHOTOGRAPHS BY TOM HAMILL

IT ALL BEGAN, as do so many things in British aviation, with a committee meeting in Whitehall, back in the dark months early in the year. Many applications for Red Arrows appearances were sifted. Foreign Office advice was that attendance at an air display in Bari in Southern Italy would be good for national prestige in an area showing a growing appreciation of British goods. So Bari was written into the season's early draft schedule. Later somebody, somewhere in the system, thought Malta would be a worthwhile addendum to the trip; the Maltese have had a lot of run-down shocks from the British Services in the past few years and deserved a show. So late in the day Malta was written in, too.

* * * *

Even later in the day insurrection in France burst its Left Bank bounds and threatened the tour. Only two days before departure, leader Ray Hanna and team manager Lew Willcox were energetically working on plans alternative to those previously arranged. An Austrian diplomatic clearance to permit the aircraft to route through Munich, then overfly Austria to Ravenna and points south was arranged as an alternative, but they still hoped to transit France. *Flight* arrived late at night at Little Rissington for an early departure from Kemble without knowing which way we'd be going.

We were hauled out from breakfast by several members already in their bright red, beflagged flying kit, and followed the team's crewbus to Kemble. Our luggage was whipped away immediately on arrival for Flt Lt Wynn David's Argosy from 114 Sqn, the support transport known in Arrows' argot as the

"Whistling Wheelbarrow" or the "Argy-bomber," to be away well before the team.

French airspace was closed to civil traffic, but we had clearance to route through Istres, the flight test centre near Marseilles. This route required slipper tanks, and was thus going to increase the groundcrew's work. The briefing in the pilots' crew room was short and to the point: the French wanted three small sections, of 4, 3 and 3, with 10min spacings, rather than the two sections of five in which the team normally transits. This was the first time the team had flown with tanks "for ages" somebody said, so there was a brief reminder on fuel transfer procedures. "Don't rely on any French navaids," the leader said. Three French military radars monitored our progress before we contacted Istres approach. "We should be overhead Istres with 1,260lb—enough to divert to Pisa." The situation about diversion airfields in France was very doubtful—"If you get any fuel transfer trouble before Paris descend to 30,000ft and it might clear, in which case go on. If not, come back here."

I flew with New Zealander Ian Dick (No 8) flying his first full season with the team. We lifted off at 1017, second in a section of four. At 1031 we crossed the coast near Bournemouth and settled down to a 38,000ft cruise at Mach 0.83. Left and right, distant, were our partners, bright red and minute.

Of a country with chaos reigning below we made a trouble-free transit. Raki, Rambert and Rhodia Blue radars all came up in turn, were intelligible, and there was a marked lack of other R/T. But we did see three Mirages proceeding on a near reciprocal course to ours, several thousand feet below

Bob Rodwell's epic article from the Med tour.

beginning again. En route to Chivenor for a show, Roy had a bird strike in his engine intake area. I moved in to carefully view the damage, and even looking back deep into the intake, could see little other than the bloody mark. He decided to continue, as all other indications were normal.

After we landed, it was quite a shock to look down the intake and see the fibreglass wall smashed with all the wires hanging out, so close to the compressor face.

We stopped in Cyprus for a few shows, and I was able to take my former boss for a trip in the back seat. Back-seat rides were up to the individual, and the solo pair had to think carefully about the extra weight, especially in the heat.

The show line was along the cliffs at Episcopi, and so departures for us were steep climbs up the cliffs and a roll at the top to stay close to the ground at the back of the crowd.

Routing to Malta on the way home we were looked at by aircraft of the US Sixth Fleet on our way in. We were flying as a five, a four and a pair. The extras were spares and included the Manager's aircraft. The front five were below us and the pair were above us. I saw the incoming F4 Phantom as it slid in behind the boss's group. I knew that there would be another F4 observing from way back. We turned in on the attacker and he dived away from now nine aeroplanes. The second F4 appeared, to be confronted by all the turning Gnats. Malta control were getting into the act, calling the incoming aircraft.

Just like the Second World War, for it developed into a real 'hooley'. We kept the formations together and Tommy, my expert mechanic in the rear seat, took film with a hand-held camera of the F4 as we got into a killing position.

The Malta show was a never-to-be-forgotten experience, for I had Bob R, from *Flight* magazine, in the rear with me. The display area was Valetta Harbour, right down on the water, necessitating steep climbs to clear the high buildings that surround the harbour. The Roulette was flown on the water, so that the crowds were looking down on the smoke patterns. Tommy had adjusted my stick force to the lower end of the range, and so it was now possible to fly with a stick force of slightly less than half a pound.

We had a series of shows in Europe around the Cologne area. The

Dumpel is forever remembered as a small gliding site on the top of a small mountain, more of a 'Bumpel'. We were taken up to the strip by transport and returned by helicopter or private aircraft to Cologne.

The return flight for Roy, Ray and I was done in a Wassmer, a small four-seater. We took off with a German who spoke no English. He slowly climbed into the cloud cover, and it was apparent that his skill level was very restricted. He kept looking at the map as though it meant something, even though we could not see the ground. We pointed down at the next hole in the cloud, but his attempts to descend were abysmal. We suggested to Ray that he lean on the stick and force the plane down below cloud. Ray finally asked if he could fly, and we slipped below cloud to see a river. Obviously the Rhine, but where? The pilot took over and landed at a small strip, running in to the tower to ask, we found out, the name of the place. He then took off and promptly headed in the wrong direction, till we herded him back towards Cologne. We were the last to arrive, one hour and twenty minutes for a fifteen-minute flight.

The show was superb, as Ray kept appearing from the valley floor and all our departures were disappearances into the depths. The festivities after the show were never to be forgotten. The RA never enforced a no-drinking rule, for we were required to be a public relations exercise almost twenty-four hours a day. You had, therefore, to know and understand your own limits, for there was only one test: the next morning you had to be able to perform to the satisfaction of the other eight team members. There was no tolerance there, and although I have seen some troubled constitutions, they made it without a whimper.

This system is akin to anarchy, the good anarchy, not the kind that is most described. Here nobody would think of doing anything that would impact adversely on others. Quite a burden, but an effective one in such circumstances.

One of the younger members was feeling some pain after a long night, and he faced a long, boring trip back to base. He said to his mechanic in the back seat, 'I will take it off, then you fly it home and I will land it.' 'No,' was the equally tortured reply, 'you take it off; you fly it home and you land it.'

The travelling circus was the best, most qualified and hard-

High speed taxi with wings.

working bunch of ground crew that ever existed. When back-seat selection for this sought-after position was made, they chose their pilots, not the other way around. With nine or ten aircraft on the road, there was room for one tradesman from each discipline. We would land and they would immediately start the turn-around. The transport aircraft would be 45 minutes behind, and it carried the rest of the support including the starters for the Gnats.

As long as we stayed together it worked, but if we were forced to split up, the logistics got exciting. I flew with Tommy all through my time on the RA, and he was always the engineering crutch that I needed. Flying your own aeroplane all the time has distinct advantages and also disadvantages. You have little to compare it to, and a flight in another member's aircraft always brought adverse comments. Too heavy, too light, too stiff or even its response at high 'g'. Tommy was the hydraulics specialist, and in the Gnat that was a critical area. I always felt that I had a tuned sports car, whereas some of the others had trucks.

In the never-ending round of repartee and comedy, there are bound to be moments of classic proportion. We were interviewed by a reporter from one of the German dailies, I think, *Der Stern*. He was the spitting image of the actor, Artie Johnson, who always played the German on the Rowan and Martin 'Laugh-In' on American television. The TV skit showed him in a Second World War German helmet saying the never-changing line 'very interesting'. We put the reporter in the Gnat with a steel helmet borrowed from an airport guard, and asked him to say 'very interesting'. Of course he did not get the joke, but in saying it over and over again, it caused hysterics for the watchers.

The burden on Ray was severe, for you cannot get to be that repetitively perfect without some sign of strain. We called it leader's disease, in that he would fall asleep at the end of the day, sometimes in inconvenient places, like the middle of dinner.

He roomed with the Manager on most of our trips, and was set up for a beauty. Dick S had discovered that there was a light switch on the end of a cable for the room lights. He got into bed early with the switch under his pillow, ensuring that Ray had to turn out the lights from the wall switch. Ray was really tired and threw himself into bed, whereupon the lights came back on. Naturally he thought that he had not done it properly, and so with much swearing (quietly), he went and switched them off again. Back to bed, Dick still snoring, and the lights come on again. Loud swearing now as he trogs over to put them off again. At this point the laughter outside alerted him to a set-up. We had all been briefed to await the joke.

In the same hotel, it was found that on a certain floor, the down button would send the elevator down without the doors opening. By moving the foliage you could hide alongside the elevator and as it arrived, press the button unseen, and send it down again. What a set piece that was. I guess you had to be there, but this humour was certainly a tension reliever and it defused any conflict through a process we all accepted.

Thorney Island was a well-known airfield to us and the site of two incidents. Roy on a return to UK was suffering from a bout of the shits. It is worth commenting that in my time we never lost a show through sickness, such is the power of adrenalin. We were over Thorney when Roy said that he had to land immediately. Ray dispatched another aircraft to go with him, and the rest continued to Kemble. The airfield was not really open and customs was not available. The two Gnats were met by an irate Wing Commander, who demanded an explanation. He did not get one as Ray sped past him heading for the nearest toilet. The rest of the conversation was carried on through the toilet door.

Incident number two was after a show at Brighton. There had been a major rain shower at the end of the display and Thorney runways were glistening in the sunlight as the rain ended. We broke into our usual landing routine with five landing from the right and four from the left. Dickie landed first and promptly went off the end into the barrier. Number two to land could not stop either and so went through where the barrier would have been, followed by number three to land. We usually had all the aircraft on the runway at the same time, each keeping to one side or the other for just such situations as this. The call of 'coming through' was further encouragement to keep well to one side. So Dickie was firmly in the net, two and three managed to keep going and bounce there way back onto the taxiway, several others had slid onto the grass in their efforts to stop and so Ray and I went around to prepare for a careful landing. We stopped, using the drag chute, but only just.

What transpired was that the surface had been treated to protect it from fuel contamination. It was the slippiest surface ever tested on RAF fields. Now to prepare for the next display due in less than three hours. The top wire had penetrated the fin area, but caused only skin damage. More serious was the loss of a gear door, which could not be replaced. They hand-shaped some new skin, resprayed and that took care of that. Ray then flew the aircraft without both doors, to see if it would perform its mission. It did.

One of the magic moments is when it all comes together as planned. We had a procedure for the loss of radio by the leader; rarely practiced if at all, but the cute bit was to recognise it quick enough so that there was no interruption. When it happened, Derek B picked up the R/T and was able to do all the calls that Ray would usually make.

Good R/T discipline is vital, for some of the calls initiate moves by several aircraft simultaneously into slots that are occupied. It is a dance routine that does not allow bodily contact.

We worked hard at the Big 9 as an arrival formation. Big 9 is a Vic (Vee) formation of all nine aircraft that arrives from behind the crowd, and pulls up changing into the well-known diamond. This change moves four aircraft from the edges of the Vic very fast into the rear of the diamond. That kind of movement calls for large control inputs to move and also to stop. Roy and I go for the centre of the diamond, but from opposite sides, and I must rely on him to get there just before me so that I can slide in behind him. The other two must expect that we will be in place with no overshoot, to enable them to fill the last gaps in the diamond. Quicker and quicker, it was the burst of adrenalin that an ice skater must feel when he does a triple jump at the start of his sequence, and it is perfect.

We left for another European trip with stops at the RAF bases in Germany. These were enthusiastic supporters of the team, my guess is because they are family units and all the activity is biased towards the flying wings.

Bruggen was a case in point, for we always got a super reception there and we tried harder because of it. All the families were out in brilliant sunshine as we did a display especially for them. The runway was the display line, but we discussed with Ray the plan of using the taxiway right in front of the tower as the line. The taxiway comes out of the trees from both directions, and if you could design a stage for a formation display, this would be it. The opposition stuff therefore burst onto the crowd with little warning, for the Gnat to a fault is very quiet. Travelling at 400 kts below the trees down a narrow NATO taxiway is quite a thrill, especially as you are usually taxiing at slow speed down the same piece of concrete. They were thrilled and complimentary, but were to feature in an unhappy episode in the following year.

We landed at a French Air Force base late one evening and were met by the RAF exchange officer. The Mess was empty and so it took a while for him to organise a meal for us. The tables were still set after the FAF had eaten and so the usual bread and wine were left out. We had been flying since early morning for an abnormally long day, and meal breaks were not on the itinerary. Faced with a wait for the cooks to rustle up something, we dived into the bread and wine. I had my share but it was like watching a movie in slow motion. The fatigue, elation, stress removal and just camaraderie added to empty stomachs and wine sent everybody into a happy 'high'. It happened

RAF Wildenrath, 1968.

Must be something he said.

Ready for the serious business.

so quickly that even if it was recognised that you were happily tipsy, it was too nice to do anything about it.

The FAF have always had wine with meals and they obviously can tolerate it; each to his own, I guess.

We were questioned at met briefing next morning by an overbearing FAF pilot. He wanted to know how slow we were able to loop the Gnat. Some wag gave a ridiculously low figure and he responded with the statement that he did the slowest 'loopings' in the FAF. The noise of a Mystere taking off took us outside to watch. He took off and began an aerobatic practice during which he came in for a very slow loop. It was painfully obvious that he was not going to make it, and he tent-pegged into the middle of the field. Hard to comment on a thing like that, but he was just pushing the envelope as we were.

The London-Sydney Marathon was coming along nicely in the planning stage and I was practicing in the Team Mini. Left-foot braking was new to me and I had been told that you will get slower before you get quicker. The front-wheel drive Mini was an ideal vehicle in which to practice, and on non-flying days I could be seen on the runway doing tight turns. The MT section were most perplexed at the tyre consumption on the team vehicle, but nobody enlightened them.

We had one visit to a German Air Force F104 unit at Cochem on the Moselle. They had a low-level role and were interested in our technique. We needed a practice and so as many as could be accommodated were taken for back-seat rides. The F104 is a fine but restricted aircraft. The US managed to pressure the rest of the operators of US equipment to have it, but they shied away from it themselves. It has little or no wing and is a testament to the fact that with enough power you can get a grand piano to fly.

To us, with a nimble small aircraft, it was an anathema. It needed 90 degrees of bank to even think of turning, which is kind of strange for a low-level fighter. We operated well below their authorised heights and so their reaction to our wanderings was disbelief. I flew up the winding road to their squadron buildings well below tree height, and they saw first-hand the security that comes from extremely low altitude in a war environment.

We began preparations for the Fiftieth Anniversary show at Abingdon. Such was the importance that a very senior officer was tasked with the responsibility of running it. He made several demands of us that were unacceptable, and when our umbrella supervisors got into the act, the restrictions were cancelled. Two remained, however: the fact that we could not overfly the Queen and the Royal Box and the need for very tight timing of each display item. Ray had said repeatedly that we would hold one minute and thirty seconds away. BUT, if we were delayed and had to start another holding orbit, it would be an added two minutes for that orbit. The very imperious senior officer demanded a check of the solo manoeuvres and Roy and I flew the sequence for him alone.

The vis was not good for the practice as we descended along Abingdon's main runway for the pass up the display line. We crossed at datum and the telepathic message was transmitted and received. Neither of us spoke, but there was a figure standing right at datum in an RAF greatcoat. The message passed, was, you go in one ear and I will go in the other. I cannot imagine what trying to keep two

Visit of
Her Majesty the Queen
to
The Royal Air Force
at
Royal Air Force Abingdon
on 14th June 1968
to Celebrate
the 50th Anniversary
of
the Formation of the Royal Air Force

A truly superb event.

aircraft in sight in poor visibility does to the senses, when they pass either side of you at shoulder height.

The show was quite climactic, and we held in orbit in Big 9. We needed to be in this formation as there was barely enough time to get set for the arrival. The dreaded delay was passed by Air Traffic, and we started another turn. It was immediately countermanded and Ray somehow corrected for the arrival. We were purposely off line to avoid overflying the Queen, and were lower than planned because of the adjusted flight path that was forced upon us. Ray got back on line in the pull up for the diamond change, and the show was a good one. Back at base, the review was favourable apart from a signal from 'Senior Air Force person'. Ray was to hold himself ready for a court martial, for violating his orders and arriving below authorised height. We were stunned, but calls to our directing staff set the ball in motion for a senior officer cockfight. When the delay was described to all and sundry, and Ray's sterling efforts to recover the situation explained, somebody had to back down. A Wing Commander arrived to collect all the copies of the signal, most irregular, but an effort to make it a non-incident. Naturally, we kept a copy and it resides in the team record.

Farnborough is the highlight of any flying career, and although I had already had my day there in the Belvedere, this was going to be a red letter day. We were the guests of British Aerospace, and under scrutiny from a very informed audience. The display line is complicated by buildings on the approach to the runway.

Roy did a double roll instead of a single on the U/C roll, and TV is a good witness to that. It was his last show, but told them that ultimate control over display pilots is never possible. Not a good point to make.

Pete E and I were sharing a room at the Test Pilots' Mess and preparing to leave for the last show. He was looking out of the window and he commented that the FAF Atlantic was going to crash. I looked up and agreed with him, as it spiralled into the famous black hangars at the end of the runway. The timing at Farnborough is very tight and if you do not make your landing slot time, you are diverted to another field. This is seen as a failure by most pilots and there is a lot of national pride at stake. The Atlantic had done a fly-by on one engine and was trying to start the other in preparation for landing. He was in tight and faced a strong cross-wind and a landing on one engine now. Turning in towards the dead engine is not a good technique, and he had the worst scenario of a strong wind from behind in the turn. The fire was quickly contained and we left not knowing whether we would fly the last display.

It was now very windy and bumpy at low level, with some cloud in the display area. We took off knowing that there was tension around, and Ray flew an immaculate display, compensating for this wind in a masterly fashion. The film record shows clearly the wind sheer as the smoke trails are cut into jagged pieces. Roy and I were forced into unheard of timing alterations to make it to datum together.

Experts like Bill Bedford recognised what was going on here, and praise from him was a fine end to the year. I left in the MGB to return to L Rissington to collect my wife for the dinner at BAE. It was a high-speed trip ending on wet roads made slippery by fallen leaves. I knew the road and was doing over a hundred when I set up for the first Roman bridge – over, on line and back up to speed as I saw the second bridge impossibly close. Braking with the wheels straight still caused the car to rotate and I was going backwards towards a tight old Roman bridge. Braking was all I could do, and try and keep the car straight. We stopped in the stone cut-out that has modified the original bridge, after a long noisy slide. I drove out and reversed direction back over the bridge. People were pouring out of the pub looking for the car that must have slid into the river after such a long skid. Did I learn from that, yes I did, but it was another one for the record.

Recall of the 'very exciting' bits would be different for us all, but if I am to identify some of mine, they would be as follows.

The Roulette at Bari in Italy was performed in poor vis and low cloud. The French and Italian teams had no sequence for such conditions, but we could try our 'Flat' routine. In less than 800 yds vis, with datum being somewhere in the middle of the grass area of the airfield, Roy and I carried off the lowest 'Roulette' I can recall, right in front of the Italian team's ground control vehicle. They were impressed.

Nurburgring is a magnificent site, and for a pairs solo act, a royal stage. We reportedly drove a cameraman out of a tree that sits

A great start to the year.

alongside the pit straight. There were 300,000 people watching and their intensity is communicated, even though you cannot hear it.

Similarly Brands Hatch in Kent is a display site that is forever with you. We had good memories from there previously, but to be down below the pit area at 400 kts is something even the Formula drivers could appreciate. What they did not know was that to make Manston we could not even join up after the show, such was our fuel state and I shut down on the taxiway, for fear of damaging the fuel pumps when they pumped air and not fuel.

Approaching on a GCA into Biggin Hill in a Diamond Nine is an electric memory. The weather was so bad that we had to try and arrive as one unit. Even then, the minuscule size of the Gnat caused the GCA controller to momentarily lose us all.

Brawdy was the Royal Navy base in South Wales, and their air show was a notable one. On the cliff tops under a sloping cloud base of, in parts, less than 200 ft, Ray was forced to use the extra height we gained when we popped over the sea cliff. Then he could turn the nine ships and reverse back to the airfield.

The sinking of the *Eilat* by a Styx missile had woken up the Israelis and most of NATO also. To simulate a Styx missile it was natural to look at the Gnat, so similar was its size and performance. The Navy requested a series of passes with us operating out of N Ireland They needed 650 kts at 20 ft, but were happy with 550-600 kts at less than 50 ft. The Gnat was on the edge of its controllability at 550 kts plus, and that low to the sea would have been a little rich for my blood. Derek and I did the runs, and I remembered these trials years later when I was involved in a project to supply 'Cruise Missile' simulation in the far north of Canada. Using the Dew Line radar, it was necessary to find out the gaps through which cruise missiles could penetrate the 'radar fence'.

The new season was approaching and all the new members were on board. Ray and Tim N had swapped jobs and so we were working up with a new leader. I now had the solo lead and a new Manager was in charge of our affairs. Pete M was an old associate but not my first choice for Manager. He turned out to be a first-class organiser and went on to run the Formula One team empire for several years. Just shows that with a narrow frame of reference, you can be quite wrong.

My number two was Ian D who had been No 5 in 1968. He was another New Zealander and generally very quiet. He was a superb pilot and never squawked at anything I did. We carried on the pattern used by Roy and I, and it was only necessary to get the flow and timing down pat. The new pilots were starting on the few aircraft that remained and progress was slow because of weather and lack of aircraft. We ventured far and wide looking for good weather and a place to train. Once Gnats started returning from the factory, we were able to get some of the problems ironed out.

What followed was a long descent into a nightmare for me, and inevitably for my family. I cannot fully identify the crucial turning points, for the process of getting a show together is always one of problem solving. Each problem that is seen demands everyone's attention to resolve it. Briefing and debriefing therefore are a way of life.

Tim was a social character and an excellent PR man for the job. The flying display did not progress very quickly, and debriefings were highlighting more and more problem areas. If everyone speaks as was our routine, we would spend the day talking not flying. As I sat under the leader and could see and assess what was going on, it was decided to restrict comments to the Manager, Pete E and myself. It solved the problem, but I should have realised that there was another side to this process. Although I was voicing the team's thoughts, from a distance it looked as if all the criticism was mine.

Tim was having serious problems controlling the axis of his display line. He was at full stretch just doing a clean manoeuvre and the exit paths could be almost anywhere. We solved that partially by relying on me to select a point for the solos to split off. We at one time had about four 'splits'. This is a brain-boiling situation, for there is no comfort in any of these scenarios, they are all struggles.

We could be dropped off with an extra 40 degrees to turn, or a 1,000 yds to cover. In some situations I took Nos 8 and 9 with me in an effort to help Tim. Personalities are almost irrelevant at such times, for it was the Red Arrows that was at stake here. Frustration was on everyone's face, and I foolishly flew the pattern to see what Tim was doing wrong. Again, it was find a solution, who cares whose idea it is. It is amazing what can be achieved, if it does not matter who gets the credit.

Because you are reacting rather than acting, we probably did not persevere in instances when we should have. We tried to give Tim more freedom to manoeuvre, by trying the five and four routine. This involves splitting the nine up into two sections initially, then joining them prior to the two solos separating.

It was on such a routine that we had our first fatal. I was flying down the back straight with 7, 8 and 9 to join up with Tim in an interlocking turning manoeuvre. In this situation, those following me keep their own separation and ground clearance. We were almost over the squadron buildings when No 9 flew into trees. He was ejected by the impact and landed on the fence alongside the parking area, in full view of all the groundcrew. As before, this was the danger period, and it is believed that he was doing a bit of low flying that did not have his full attention.

The Court of Inquiry was set to be straightforward, but it took a nasty turn when a farmworker was interviewed and claimed that we were all below the trees. There were many witnesses to the contrary, but it took some tricky geometry to disprove his line of sight. It was an upset for Tim, who appeared to be publicly unaffected by it, but I am sure, was limited by it. The first true outing for the season was a display at the factory for the workers and their families. The weather was on the edge of a full display limit, but I had no real fears about it. We got into the sequence and along the line pulled up for a nine-ship loop. Going into cloud at the top of a loop takes a steady hand and lots of confidence. We had entered cloud with Ray many times and it had been as though it was a clear day, uncanny but true. In this case Tim lost his cool and pulled very hard, close to 6 'g'. Being under Tim I can see the altimeter, airspeed and g meter, for they are in my line of sight.

The formation exploded as everyone hung on until the last second before giving up, and then made some sort of escape. We came out of cloud in the act of separating, with Ian and I still hanging on under the boss. The line astern slots are the only tenable ones in such circumstances. What we now faced was that on a good day, Tim could pull off a basic show. Gone was the flair and panache for which we were known, and on a bad day we would have problems.

Hucknall came and went, but the variations in heights and speeds were not lessening, As such, I can tell that this or that manoeuvre is going wrong, almost before Tim knows. With a loop, if you do a 4,500-footer on the way up, it is quite easy to do a 5,000-footer on the way down. I could see them coming, and the responsibility for doing or not doing something, weighed heavily upon me. I had dreams of being in a loop that must impact the ground, and being the only survivor. One's personality cannot stand this kind of pressure, for my loyalty was to the team and I did not want to be associated with a disaster. I am sure that I became impossible to live with and that my character started to change.

I could tell nobody but Ray and Lew the former manager, and it was not a burden that they relished being placed upon them. I said that we were facing a major accident, and that I could just as easily cause it as save the day. I had decided to go in with everybody else if I was faced with the awful choice.

Tim and I flew to Paris to discuss the show with the Prefect of Police who runs the show. It was a French farce, as some comprehension of aviation is required, rather than civil law.

We said that we could not comply with the height and angular restrictions that they proposed. He was unbending, for after all the French team complied, why not us. We explained that we could not just change the show, it was a sequence that was not altered for just such safety reasons. His mandate was safety, but the application would have the reverse effect. We left telling the Ambassador that we would need at least a week to prepare a new show, and then another week to change it back again.

National pride creeps in here and we were given the time to change the show, and told to go ahead and do it. One of the least understood aspects of display flying is that there is comfort in being close to the ground. All the references are there and it is easy to always be angled upwards, away from the ground. It is so slight as to be unnoticeable, but it prevents those silly barrel rolls angled downwards that year after year, kill people. The solo height at Paris was 300 ft which, for the Gnat, was a difficult altitude. You are above it all, and level or inclined-upwards assessments were far from easy. At 400 kts a slight downwards angle can have a high rate of descent build up very quickly.

We were not the problem, however, for Tim had also to adjust for the new heights, which were measured and reported if you broke them. We flew the biggest loop I had ever tried in formation, over 5,000 ft. It was awful and the descent was going to be a test. When you are working in such conditions, the combination of fear, frustration, helplessness and finally shame are acidic. Gone was the happy atmosphere, the jokes; it was a daily emotional tussle.

The trip to Bruggen was not one I looked forward to, and so it was to be. We did a very half-hearted show on arrival, in part due to the weather. We were dispatched to fill in with a solo display, which of course focuses more attention on why we were unable to fly some kind of a formation display. Cologne asked us to do a fly-by, but we managed to miss the place in poor visibility. I think that by now Tim was being weighed down with the sheer magnitude of his problem. I had called Ray to tell him that it was all going pear shaped and that I did not know what to do.

The Wildenrath Air Day is a monster NATO event with huge crowds. We flew from Bruggen and began our display. At the top of the loop, we were slow and low. The nightmare was before me for this was going to be the lowest break Tim had called. In slow motion I considered calling 8 and 9 to stay with me, or even giving some kind of warning to everyone, as Ian and I split off through the top of the formation. Tim called the bomburst and we pulled up into a flock of birds. I knew that I had swallowed a few and after a moment's hesitation I said that I was hit and going home. The bomburst had put the wing men in a terrible position, as they had to roll away from the rest of the formation and at the same time pull out of the dive. Euan was presented with an oak tree as he struggled to pull out. He went under it. With this kind of angst, the strength that keeps it together was gone. Pete, as number two, brought the right-hand side home and left Tim. Ian stayed for one solo manoeuvre and the left also. Tim now had the left-hand side only, and he finally gave up and returned. When Pete landed I said that I was quitting, it had to be an individual thing, but he said that he had had it also.

Euan was really beside himself, having stared death in the face and he was persuaded to go away and cool off. All were so ashamed that they took off the red flight suits in disgust. Pete and I were left to tell the boss that it was over. We stood on the grass, whilst the rest kept out of the way in the trees. That piece of grass became noteworthy and featured in the crewroom as a sign of the rebirth of the dream when we finally recovered from the nightmare.

The conversation was short but powerful. He had tried his best, but there was enough honour left in the situation for him to just resign. I called Ray and told him that we were coming back to UK the next day. I told the troops what was happening and it was all in the newspapers the following morning. So as not to have the appearance of a mutiny, it was agreed that we would meet the boss at his request. He wanted to continue with more training, but with one exception, it was unanimous, it was over. The exception was more of a career choice. I never minded that, for you always knew where you stood with somebody who feared for his career. The next day Tim wanted to lead us home, but that was not accepted and in fact those who wanted to return came as a group, leaving several behind.

It is almost impossible to convey the depth of emotion that is tied to something like this. You are involved in the problem and almost certainly will be seen as part of the problem, if not actually being the problem. It was the longest trip, most emotionally draining, most physically and intellectually testing period of my life. As I landed to face the music, the overpowering sense was failure. I could not reconcile the fact that we may have prevented a disaster. That is, and always will be, supposition to all those who did not have to live through it.

Pete went home, unable to speak and I was left closest to the inquisition that must follow. The Wing Commander in charge of flying at L Rissington called me in that afternoon and it started. My approach was that we had given it our best shot, and that nobody would fly with Tim any more. How they wanted to resolve that was up to them, but surely there was still enough honour in the situation for Tim to resign.

As is ever the evolution of military supervision, it came down to: 'Why did we not know? Why did you not tell us?' Nobody likes to be told that you would not understand, or that trying to inform any supervisor would have made it a personal problem. The team had always guarded its affairs and remained a very tight-knit community. We solved problems rather than generated them. The exception was keeping senior officers off our backs by deflecting them to the very capable people at MOD charged with our welfare. This routine was known as putting the boot in, and Ray was a master of the casual telephone call when somebody was interfering. He would call the AOC or even MOD and start a turf war that left us alone.

The next meeting was with the Station Commander, which was a trifle strange, for although we were based at L Rissington, we were run by the AOC 23 Group, by chance also based at L Rissington. I guess the protocol required it, but it put a man who had had little to do with the day-to-day running of the team, in the hot seat. I began to feel that the spotlight was too much on me, and it became evident that Tim saw Pete and I as the force for his demise. The basis of this harked back to our debriefing procedure, in that to save time we had restricted comments to Pete, the Manager and myself as the key observers. The initial tone of the meeting was not to my liking, for a question and answer routine was not going to get to the root of the troubles. I had little to lose at this point and so I took a deep breath and made a stand that the rules allowed. It needed respect, an understanding of the military system and an eloquence that I was not sure that I had.

First, I had to be able to speak freely, without fear of recrimination. It was a story that needed telling without interruption, and brutal frankness is sometimes hard to swallow. I covered the deep emotional bond that goes with such a close-knit group. That loyalties are not to the Queen, the Air Force or even to any of the supervising staff. They are to each other, to the whole idea of the team and through that to the Queen and country bit.

He let me ramble on, through the reasoning behind the debriefing system, the multiple changes to cover Tim's problems with display orientation, and the fact that I had real fears for the safety of the team which had been communicated to Ray and Lew. He could not grasp the fact that we had not told any of the directing staff. I hope I was not rude here, but told them: how realistically do you do that and still retain the loyalty to the group? What he saw was that he was not in control of anything and that this big superstructure actually prevented them from having the faintest idea what was going on. He reasoned that this was all my perception, and that they all thought that the show was acceptable. I seized on that to say that rarely, if ever, did any of the supervisors fly with us and what would they discover if they did. His background was in heavy transport aircraft, not an ideal position from which to critique display flying in fighter-type aircraft. At one stage I felt sorry for him, for the more powerful and articulate was my story, the more burdened he was with the responsibility.

I know that Ray and Lew were contacted for confirmation of the facts, my facts, but impressions that gained momentum with every other person that was interviewed. Tim unfortunately did not see that he could recover his self-esteem by honourably resigning. Whilst he fought to return to the leadership, there was a dilemma for the brass. The sensible thing was for Ray and Tim to switch jobs again, and the season would be recoverable quickly. The press announced that we were going back to school for more training, as MOD did not think that the show was up to standard. A nice face-saver, but Ray was back and in two days of training we had a show.

The new members were flabbergasted at just how easy it was. It was hard to comprehend just how far into the nightmare we had travelled. The directing staff now had to get involved and it was inevitable that we would have someone breathing down our necks for some weeks to come.

The Station Commander came to fly with us and was put in the back with me for his first ride. This was done on purpose, for the very high 'g' was going to force them to face their own inadequacies. We did a practice at Kemble and as I ran in for an opposition manoeuvre at and 50 ft and 400 kts, this voice from the back said, 'My altimeter is misreading, it is reading 250 ft below ground level.' I said that I would discuss it later and we entered 25 minutes of serious high 'g' work. The solos could, during the course of a season, use up 9-10 per cent of the fatigue life of the aeroplane. We had far and away the highest 'g' count in the Air Force. A full display would rack up 20-30 counts of 6 'g', double that of 4 'g' and maybe close to 200 counts of 3 'g'. We did not wear 'g' suits for they were prone to failure or disconnection under the wriggling around that was necessary as you looked for the other solo. A disconnection would have serious consequences at low altitude and on balance it was better to deal with effects of high 'g'. My 'g' limit was that of the aircraft, and so I had a built-in limiter that prevented me from overstressing, a condition the engineers were none too fond of. If you did overstress, the aircraft had to be taken out of service and checked and it was a lot of work.

When we sat for the debrief the Station Commander brought up the point about the altimeter. In his mind it was as though we were carrying unserviceabilities, a practice he would wish to stop. When Ray told him that the Gnat has a pressure error at that speed of up to 350 ft, he was stunned. How then can you be authorised to fly at 50 ft if you do not have an altimeter? We all looked at each other and knew that the next response was crucial. Trees, buildings, bicycles, telegraph poles even people, I said. He did not know what to say, for all that finely worded paper was so much rubbish. Whether that was the moment that set them off to rethink the whole idea of a display team that is operating at limits unheard of to anyone else in the Air Force is not known. The net result was that the AOC, a very smart man of infinite ability, determined to plot and authorise each aspect of the show and even training, so that they recognised realistic limits and we could at least feel covered. With Ray at the helm, they were in the best possible position to make this step.

What was done was to take what we did and commit it to print, rather than design an arbitrary set of rules and ask us to live by them. Inevitably there were areas that were sensitive, and the run-in for the solo opposition barrel roll was eventually negotiated to ground level. I believe that we were the only pair ever authorised in such a manner. The flat show required that we have the ability to rejoin all nine aircraft in a 500 ft cloud base. Obviously, those manoeuvring underneath could not be restricted to 200 ft. There was just not enough room for all those aircraft in the difference between the cloud base and 200 ft. Similarly, Ray had many times concluded a show in poor weather and manoeuvred the Diamond under a low ceiling. The Diamond can be likened to a large aircraft with a 100 ft wingspan. It is self-evident that the bottom aircraft is going to be below 200 ft at times, and that does not take into account variations in the base of the cloud and unevenness in the terrain. Air Commodore Ivor B coped with all this, and we believed that for a change, we were all facing the same direction. Without the power that Ray brought to the leadership, I think it would have gone the other way.

Successive leaders had their wings clipped and I think that the freedom that we had will never be repeated. It was the 'vintage years', a coming together of talent and leadership that blossomed when opportunity presented itself. The release from all the mental gymnastics required a short time earlier, allowed the two pieces of the team to operate in concert like never before.

Ray had several mannerisms that were hilarious and frustrating. He would start a descent and expect me to have the back four in position for anything that he might decide to do. Case in point, southern France, Nice airport. We were unable to let down there as they did not have an instrument approach that we could do. We had to let down, below cloud out to sea, and then turn back towards land when we were safely underneath. Time was pressing and so Ray suddenly started the descent. I raced in with my group, to position at 1,000 yds astern of the front five. Once in cloud I am at the mercy of any changes in speed or heading that he might make.

There was never very much chat on the RT and I might get a grunted, '350 kts' if that was an alteration. This is where the 'simpatico' means everything. You more or less sense that something is changing. He turns, says going left, and we pop out of cloud at 400 ft. Nice is ahead and we must be able to join the front five in time for some arrival or other. The pressure is the caustic comments that will follow if you are unable to join up quickly enough. We break into the circuit for a landing and a radio sequence follows that is a classic. A Swissair airliner calls long finals for landing. The tower answers, 'You are number ten to land.' 'Number ten?' he questions. 'You are now number six.' 'Number six?' he queries. 'You are now clear to land,' says the tower. He never did get it.

We sometimes needed to fill in with unplanned routines. The five versus four provided a great backdrop, especially enhanced by smoke trails. We actually were working two groups in a combat situation, manoeuvring hard to gain some advantage. This competitive testing matured into a solution for the problem we had when displaying at the airfield you took off from.

Normally, the aircraft would go away and reform for the arrival. What we needed was a way of getting the five and four together straight after take-off. We had tried putting more aircraft on the runway at the same time, but at rotation the wingmen got spat out under the effects of the powerful wing vortex generated by the Gnat. Therefore it was always a five and four separated by about five seconds. It was discussed that Ray could pull up and commence a slow 270-degree turn, to arrive back over the runway you have just left, at 90 degrees. In that time, I had to cut the corner, keep inside the five's jet wash, and then slide under and outside that jet wash, to join in the back to form the diamond, ready for the diamond loop.

Very spectacular if you can but an awful obvious mistake if you mess it up. We tried it and provided Ray called his speed, I could anticipate and get rid of the 50 kt overtake I needed. When one is asked for the high spots of a flying career, this for me is always the answer. I do not think it had been done before, and getting three other aircraft to stay with you as you need to judge the moment of join up, is a high I can never forget. The call of 'all aboard' allowed Ray the freedom to get into his routine, and he would question that I was really on board if we were particularly slick.

The originality of the 'Ray' display was that we were always in front of the crowd. It got to be so tight that by the end of the season the show would be reduced to 17 minutes from the original 22. Thus the rapid join-up fitted beautifully with that concept.

The AOC decided to come along on one of our overseas trips. We were heading for France and just leaving the London Control Zone when he called up that he had a hydraulic failure. Normally for one who flew so little, it would be expected that he would have an experienced pilot in the back seat. In this case he had one of the young airmen from our 'flying circus'.

Ray told him to return to base, and he was forced to pick up the pieces and leave the formation. He flew gently home and performed the drills related to a hyd failure. He elected to go to Fairford which had the longest runway, and flew around burning off the excess fuel to lighten the Gnat.

The drill calls for the elevators to be unlocked by pulling the 'unlock handle'. This would give him the extra control that he needed in manual. When it is unlocked, there is a light to confirm that the locks are actually disengaged, although you can feel the difference on the stick. He was flying around the circuit at roughly 180 kts, preparing for the landing and the speed was not varying

The AOC in his wheelchair, following the 'incident'.

very much. As he came in to land, the nose started to fall and he was unable to keep it from entering a descent that impacted outside the perimeter fence. The Gnat struck a large pile of manure, bounced over the fence and came to rest, on fire just short of the runway. He had broken both legs and was trapped. His backseater, using remarkable foresight, got him out although burned himself, and they were both able to get clear of the wreckage. For this noble deed he was awarded a medal, richly deserved, for he had little training to prepare himself for such an event. The AOC recovered to greet the Queen on her visit to L Rissington a short time later, albeit in a wheelchair.

We continued with our tour and ended up in Lyon with the usual bane of our existence, transport and hotels. We usually could expect two buses, one for the ten pilots, and the other for the groundcrew who would follow later when the Gnats had been put to bed. The

Royal visit, Little Rissington, 1969.

potential for a cock-up now gets bigger when you add in two lots of baggage. We could get to the right hotel with the wrong baggage, or various combinations thereof. The Manager would get all the flack associated with these dramas, but he was at the mercy of other people's organisation, or lack of. Nice was a favourite place for the transport not to turn up. All the tricks in the world cannot suborn a French bus driver. We found, however, that the authorities are open to blackmail. By stripping off and sunbathing in the most conspicuous places, they would appear from everywhere and magically the transport materialised. So if you have ever seen twenty or thirty semi-nude men sunbathing in a drain somewhere, it is really a transport problem.

Frank H was a large Welshman with all that goes with that. He loved his food to a fault, and naturally that provided many hours of humour as he was prodded about it. Gravy was a passion for him, and so we would all comment on the Welsh gravy mines any time we were in Wales. He was seated at a banquet one night in France, and the harassed waiters were struggling to deliver the food. The steaks had been brought, and we awaited the rest. Henry crawled along underneath the table, and all we saw was a hand vanishing with Frank's steak in it. This was too much, taking a man's food, but you are 'kinda limited' in your response.

Gravy, to this day, still features wherever we meet. With the end of 1968 approaching, a show at Biggin Hill led to another phase of my life. We had the MGBs there and parked alongside was the SIAI Marchetti SF 260. This little Ferrari of small aircraft was being marketed by one, James B. The London-Sydney Air Race had been announced, and after our success in the London-Sydney Marathon we thought that an Air Race would be a challenge. I flew with James that night after the show and we began a friendship that resulted in us using that SF 260 for the race.

The last show of the year was Blackpool, and I was very aware of 'last show' indiscretions. A lapse of concentration, just a feeling that it is all over, can have disastrous results.

We left from Valley as the weather was not good at Blackpool. The famous Blackpool Tower was standing tall in the fog, but we needed to get underneath, and quickly, for fuel was short. The Gnat had the ability to perform a show 47 miles from the departure airfield and return there. At this distance we would often return individually, as joining up took too much fuel.

The low state light came on at 250 lbs, and it would be on for the solo aircraft as we entered the final loop for the bomburst and landing. Each Gnat was calibrated individually, so that for example, 76 lb was 76 lb, meaning readings below 250 lb could be trusted. The front five all of a sudden closed up and in a wing over, dived below the fog. I looked at the altimeter, 1,500 ft, and knew that I could not emulate that. Leaving half the team at Valley and half at Blackpool was not on the cards, and so I let down out to sea and broke out under a very low ceiling. The back three stayed with me as we turned back in and heard the five landing. I had to hit the sea wall at a shallow angle, which we did well below the famous Blackpool illuminations. The end of the runway is just the other side of the road, but we had to be able to climb over the railings to get there. Over the airfield they streamed out behind me as I struggled to land off a very tight circuit. Thank goodness for the forgiving quality of the Gnat wing under such demand. So we were all down, even able to taxi in together.

The show was only slightly better weather, and as the runway pointed out to sea, there was a distinct lack of horizon. I thought through my display and was running at higher mental rpm than usual. I had Carl B in the back, a civil aerobatic champion. We completed most of the sequence and I made sure of my exit line of the barrel roll. This simple precaution was an extra, for with the lack of horizon I had not fully arrested my descent from the roll. We sank into the ground, so low that I could not pull too hard for fear of putting the tail in the ground. It was a case of pull, check forward to hold it level and a gentle climb away to get some ground clearance. The watching Manager said that I was lost behind all the grass that was blown up. My passenger was most complimentary, for he thought it was all part of the show.

Chapter VI

THE END OF THE SEASON brought about much soul searching on my part. Ray was definitely on his way, and the new leader scenario was not something I could go through again. There were two possibles: one who was not desired by anybody, and Denis, who was amply qualified for the job. I had my heart set on Harriers, and the powers-that-be usually arranged a job of your choice. When the dust finally settled, I was to stay on and help with the training, and until a leader was chosen. Ian was leaving and two new solos needed to be trained.

My posting was delayed, and despite all the promises, when it came it was to 92 Squadron in Germany on Lightnings. I was not happy about that initially, but I was massaged into accepting all sorts of things that went with it. Solo display in Germany, station QFI and a hand in the low-level role that was supposedly being given to the Lightning fleet.

The Air Race consumed much of the winter, and I returned to a short period of Gnat flying before I left for Coltishall. Along the way a request came in for a pilot with a civil licence needed for a TV advert for the Central Office of Information. I, being spare and having the right pieces of paper, was selected. The COI had a film crew available for a three-part advert on seat belt usage. They showed me in the Gnat strapping in, also in a coupé Triumph doing the same thing in a set piece where there was a conflict between the car and an aeroplane. The third bit was to show the use of seat belts in a Tiger Moth. We tried to find a Tiger Moth, but the only one quickly available was at the London Transport flying Club.

Here, insurance was a problem for me to do the aerial work with the helicopter. The Chief Instructor, a very large man, had to be on the aircraft. We solved the problem by taking out the front stick so that he could cover himself with a blanket and hide with his head under the instrument panel. Most uncomfortable, I would have thought, but the video went out on national television as a government campaign to promote the use of seat belts. I was paid a fee for the time, but not allowed to keep it, even though it was my licence that they were using, obtained with my own money.

I had retained the SF 260 for occasional display use at L Rissington and was deeply involved in the service requirement for a light trainer to replace the Chipmunk. The whole training scenario was being rewritten and there was no doubt that the Marchetti could do it all. In the end I took it to White Waltham for it to be viewed by MOD people. It became obvious that there was more to selling aircraft to the Ministry than just having the best product. My naivety had led me to believe that the Service was above such corruption. A conversation is recalled where I was pushing the virtues of a retractable undercarriage as being stronger than a fixed gear. This was resisted as the competitor was the Scottish Aviation Bulldog. Generally held views were not going to survive here, and I retreated realising that there was another agenda that I was not privy to.

I did however manage to get it to Boscombe Down by the back door, and let Handling Squadron have a look at it. Being at CFS I was able to organise a flight review by the Standards Unit and set the scene for another memorable day.

We took off early in the morning and immediately there was something wrong as the gear was selected up. With a loud creaking noise and then an alarming bang, the electric screw jack started to flail about between the seats. This jack is also the manual gear system and it has upon it the circuit breaker to cut off power to the jack. There is a weak link designed into the unit, but it had not failed at that point. As it flailed about, it took out much of the wiring between us, restricting communication with the tower. I felt that we had a major failure and that putting the aircraft on the ground, pronto, was the requirement. The gear was not up or down and a landing on the grass seemed sensible. I continued the turn and shut off the fuel on short finals, but selecting the mag switches off did not stop the propeller, which continued to run through a couple more revolutions. We hit quite lightly and slewed to a stop. A great intro for a superb aircraft.

The nose oleo retracts into a slot, and as such has a centring mechanism to ensure that the wheel does not go up sideways. This small piece of metal sits on the front of the oleo. It had cracked and broken off such that the front leg went up sideways. This strained the retraction mechanism enough to cause it to fail, but not at the weak link. We landed with the wheels partially up and caused only superficial damage to the airframe. After a prop change, I flew it at Hullavington for a display at the World Aerobatic Championships two days later.

The Fiats had come and gone, mostly used up in the planning of the Marathon and the Air Race. We settled for a brace of 850s, so that the drive to and from Coltishall would not be too expensive. I retained my married quarter at L Rissington, as is usually the case when you are detached on a course. This is a fairly commonplace circumstance, and I had no need to expect trouble from it.

The AOC had departed and the new incumbent was a different beast altogether. The Headquarters building housed the Station Commander and also the AOC. They took a strong dislike to each other and even built a wall down the centre to identify the 'separateness'.

I had spent almost three years in the casual uniform of the Red Arrows, and the two winters had been high profile events, closely tied to higher authority who were intimately involved in our participation in them. The new Station Commander took exception to my non-aligned state, and I often fell between a rock and a very hard place.

I invited Arthur G to the Summer Ball, something that I was perfectly at liberty to do. The AOC had asked if he was coming, for he had done so much for the Royal Air Force. He had intended to invite him himself, but was happy for me to do so, for Arthur and I were both fresh from the Air Race. The event had much Air Force content and so it was a natural follow-on.

I motored back to Coltishall one Sunday night to be told that the CO of L Rissington demanded my presence Monday morning. Technically I was not under his command, but my boss said that in the circumstances I had better go. Another four-hour drive and I presented myself to this bitter little man. He was indignant that I had invited Arthur to the Ball and presented such a confused stream of indignation that I knew that it had little to with me, and all to do with his conflict with the AOC. I could hardly relate the conversation that I had had with the AOC, and so I took it and left.

He wanted an apology in writing, and so the boss and I concocted a beauty that said everything and nothing. He was at the end of a career, crippled by alcoholism, but still a formidable barrier to the advancement of common sense.

Coltishall had all the makings of another Chivenor. I knew that I was a marked man and again tried to stay out of the spotlight.

First problem that surfaced was the Arrows training accident. Four pilots were killed doing the Roulette. The guys in the back were observing engine parameters and would not normally have been there. It was a classic training accident in that they were not yet able to operate within the narrow framework and only concern themselves with things that matter. They apparently lost contact somewhere around the Roulette pattern, broke it off and collided at datum. They were not sensitive enough to the danger of loss of contact and did not have an 'out'.

The TV contacted Coltishall for me to appear on a nightly news programme as a former solo pilot. MOD said go ahead and I was released to comment on the accident.

Next came the difficulty of converting to the single-pilot day/night fighter role. There was so much to absorb and I found it really taxing. I determined to do my best and let the chips fall where they may. The final straw came when I was asked to demonstrate the SIAI Marchetti at the Battle of Britain air display. I relayed the request to my boss and knew that whatever the outcome, it would be prone to misinterpretation. Some understood, even the Station Commander who was the brother of Pete J of Syerston fame. He had told his brother to give me a hard time, but I never voiced one word of that association. However, I was told to go ahead with the display, and I guess some of the supervisors must have been suspicious. I certainly kept pace with the course curriculum, but was not trying to make a point.

The final check ride was to be flown and I prepared for the trip. One issue with the staff there was the briefing system. CFS had for years pushed the idea that briefings refer to standard procedures, but itemise any differences. They, being somewhat removed from mainstream thinking on this matter, used to cover the blackboard with data that was impossible to remember. I quietly did not go along with this, and referred to the mission plan number, and then any variations. My ride was exercise number 39, which was a set-piece subsonic intercept.

I briefed, and covered the differences for the ride and the usual weather and fuel pointers. GCI vectored us into position and I struggled to fly an intercept using the Lightning radar. I picked up the target and began to manoeuvre for the attack. As I turned in, the target disappeared. I was not successful in locating it.

When we began the debrief I was asked if I knew what had happened. No, I thought that it was just poor ability on my part. The point they were making was that I had not briefed the target NOT to go supersonic. Despite the fact that that exercise had a different number, they were just making a point. I said OK, but we never brief on things we are not going to do, so was all this not just a waste of time. They were very grave and talked about failure, and I said that that was OK by me, if this was the way they wanted to play it, I am sure the hierarchy would understand.

A new flight was suggested and I said that I was not sure that I wanted to be set up again. There was a lot of disagreement amongst the staff, and I remained sidelined by the issue. A new bunch of instructors supervised the next ride and I purposely repeated the standard CFS briefing pattern as before.

After the ride I began clearing for my new job in Germany, and a tannoy broadcast was heard requesting my presence in the Station Commander's office, right now. Group Captain J and I had only met during his greeting to the course, and I was surprised by his request. He wanted my assessment of the teaching staff and the course in general. This is always a trap, but he calmed my reluctance by saying that his brother had said that if you wanted a straight answer, I would give it.

I really had little to say about personalities, but the issues of briefing standards and the arrant foolishness of my check ride were covered. He was furious that such a time-wasting approach had been used, and I have no doubt that he managed to put his point across after I left.

92 Squadron was a very operational outfit, guarding the northern

border of W Germany. NATO broke up the border into two sectors, with the US covering the prettier half to the south. As a new boy, I needed to become combat ready as soon as possible. This involved a series of exercises that generally took about six months to complete. I was expected to hurry through these as they needed a deputy flight commander, a squadron training instructor (QFI) and finally a QFI for the Lightning wing of two squadrons.

The boss was a stern no-nonsense operator and he made sure that I understood what was expected of me. I was given almost double the hours each month to speed my route to combat readiness.

He was tasked with a fly-past for the AOC's visit, and had decided to put up a four-ship to represent the squadron. His display was very difficult and there were few qualified to fly that kind of formation.

I was impressed into the show, and made no comment. The routine severely stressed the No 3 slot on the left as he was rolling into the turn almost viciously. In that slot when you have the leader rolling towards you, it is quite easy to finish up with severely crossed controls. Heavy use of rudder is about all you have left to balance the equation. What could I say, but in the end I think he was amazed that with so few hours on the Lightning, I stayed there. The display went off well and coincided with my elevation to 'combat readiness'.

He had a grave face when I was called to his office and pointed in the direction of the report from Coltishall. How can this be the same person? he asked. 'Don't complain, don't explain' has always been a maxim, but I was pressed to disclose my side of the issue. He did note the Station Commander's comments, but of course the training report could not be altered. He accepted my views, but in true political fashion deferred his assessment of my performance. The new CO was coming, and he could avoid any involvement.

The role was interesting and thoroughly enjoyable, but it was many years since I had been on such a young outfit. There were many first tourists, pilots straight out of training, and so the social life took some time to adjust to. Beer and loud music were not my scene, and I had no wish to appear remote. The settling in therefore, took some time.

The arrival of the new boss, Wing Commander John M was a high spot, for we had been on the same wing together at Acklington and

Middleton St George. I was appointed deputy flight commander to a young fast mover and received the standard speech of 'glad to have a someone of your experience on board'. I was cautious about being too close, and tried to alert him to the fact that I saw my position as a balancing act. I would support him, but trying to compromise loyalty and strong views was a difficult task. If he would respect my freedom to speak up, I felt that I could be of use to him.

The squadron training became an issue after a visit from the CFS trappers. Several of the first tourists were observed as being in need of further training. The boss asked me to set up a training environment and most importantly, I reported directly to him. On an operational unit, training and op requirement come quickly into conflict. You are always forced to face the fact that in a wartime scenario, many of the rules are discarded. However, in peacetime you must try to get as close to the real thing as risk will allow.

I took issue with subjecting young pilots to bad weather that they were not qualified to fly in, just because we were playing 'war games'. Surely they could taxi their aircraft and indicate to all that they would have taken-off, but avoid the risk that would be accepted in the real thing.

Higher authority approved my participation in the London-Victoria Air Race, and I was absent for ten days to compete. When I returned, we were preparing for another squadron visit.

The boss had much formation display experience, but to put nine squadron pilots up was asking a lot. All were perfectly capable of basic formation work, a fighter pilot's bread and butter. A large formation was not the same. We began working up over the airfield in a Diamond 9. The first manoeuvres were slack as the boss tried to make it easy for all. He asked for my comments, for in the No 6 slot again, I could see what was going on. He tightened the next wing over and I felt someone pushing me. I knew that an aircraft was interfering with the airflow over my aircraft. I tapped the throttle to make sure that I was clear of the boss ahead of me. The load increased and I was forced to use both hands to steady the Lightning. I could not transmit in this position and the blow, when it came, was severe. We were in a steep banked turn when I was hit, ejecting me through the top of the formation. I stopped upside down, having lost sight of the rest of the formation. I transmitted that I was hit and tried to roll the Lightning upright. A quick look in the rear-view mirrors showed the damage. I tightened the straps in preparation for ejection, and set about assessing the situation. The aircraft was in a continuous left turn with the stick fully forward and half aileron applied. We were over the airfield, but the city of Gutersloh was in my orbit. If I was going to eject, I had better plan it for open spaces. The immediate danger passed as the Lightning was obviously not going to fall out of the sky right away. John B, who had hit me, was damaged but OK, and so the boss appeared on my wing.

My right wing was folded over jamming the aileron, the fin was bent over at the top restricting rudder movement and worst of all, the tailplane was bent down about 20 degrees on the right with a large piece of it missing. The force to roll the aircraft upright had sawed a hole in the fuselage which was flapping in concert with a piece of metal high up on the upper fuselage. This vibration was getting all my attention as I tried to convince myself that what I could see was all the damage that I had to contend with.

A slow speed check was performed down to 180 kts, but each knot that I lost caused the nose to come up and with the stick fully forward, I doubted that I could continue to control it. The next problem was to work the aircraft around so that I might be able to land. I could not turn right and even straight ahead was only marginally possible.

By slackening the orbit or tightening it, I could walk the orbit towards the landing end of the field. Fuel was not a problem, for I needed to be as light as possible if I was to try and land. The boss had a good look over the aircraft and said what he could see. The high landing speed was a slight problem, but the loss of forward stick was my major concern, as was my ability to be able to keep it straight for the landing. I decided not to try and trim out the out-of-balance forces, for at least I knew what I had to contend with.

We discussed the landing as I circled the town and with the Lightning flying very sideways, started the approach. At 200 kts the vibration became worse, so much so that I kept the speed at 190 kts. I could see the fuselage skin flapping in the breeze, and with some rudder pressure and the stick hard in the top right-hand corner, I wobbled down the approach. The landing was uneventful.

When I surveyed the damage, many things came to mind. He had inserted his wing under mine, until it overlapped my tailplane. When control was finally lost, he rolled over the top of me, canopy to canopy, banging down hard on the tail, folding up the wing tip and also the top of the fin. We must have been very very close in the canopy moment, and I guess my hanging on until the last second saved us from making one aircraft out of two.

I felt OK, but a look at the 'g' meter showed it jammed at 14+ 'g'. The following day, my legs were stiff and my back ached. It was to reveal that the bottom three vertebrae were crushed, and it leaves a legacy that I have to this day. The blow to the top of the fin had levered the fuselage under me to pass a vertical shock that crushed my spine.

The Board of Inquiry was fast and straightforward. John received a minor reprimand, but it was put down to inexperience. My Green Endorsement is a treasured remembrance of that moment.

Battle flight is the monthly duty held by each squadron in turn. It requires that two armed aircraft be ready 24 hours a day, 365 days a year. They are kept in a special alert facility, and the crews spend 24 hours on shift. Preparing for this ordeal is not to be taken lightly. Each day/night there are two practice launches, and it was not uncommon for there to be several 'real' ones. From bed in the middle of the night, the requirement is to be airborne in 5 minutes. The usual response time was 2-3 minutes, so that we could be at the border 5 minutes from the order being received. The younger element were often airborne in less than 2 minutes, and so Battle Flight was a high point on a Lightning tour. Living under the alert bell actually changes your psyche, as for many years afterwards I would awaken instantly when the telephone rang and rush around until I recognised my surroundings.

I had a left foot that would go to sleep if I tried to sleep with my boots on. I therefore slept with only one boot on, which could be embarrassing if you did not get it on before flight. I was diverted to a German AFB from an alert scramble, and they must have thought that the RAF was running short of money if it could only issue its pilots with one boot each.

The technique for getting strapped in whilst starting the engines and staying on the narrow taxiway was personal, and it inevitably led to a few interesting moments. Tex J taxied close to the edge of the taxiway and the very high pressure narrow tyres (270 psi) cut through the concrete stranding him. Both aircraft would start, so that one was always able to go.

Vic L had an occasion to reflect on his technique when he scrambled and was alerted to a strange noise as he lifted off. He had not done up the shoulder harness and the straps were trapped by the canopy and were flapping around outside in the airflow. He could now not eject and the metal ends of the straps damaged the aircraft skin.

Battle Flight was run by four pilots on each squadron, and I for one felt the responsibility severely. The rules were well understood, but application of them could have far-reaching implications. For instance, a full scramble ignored the weather conditions and the potential loss of an aircraft was factored in. If the first aircraft crashed on take-off, then the next one would be dispatched instantly. We could expect to have a tanker up for flight refuelling if there was nowhere to land, but often there were no tankers available. The armed nature of the alert status needed to be continually brought to your attention, for otherwise you would end up forgetting that it was not just a routine sortie.

Border incursions were fairly commonplace and we were allowed into the ADIZ, but obviously not so close that an inadvertent crossing might take place. It was possible to see the East Bloc opposite number on radar, as they conducted identical flights.

I was Battle Flight Ops Officer (BAFOO) one night when there was much activity over the Harz mountains. We had two aircraft up to maintain a continuous patrol, and I had to call out the groundcrew to prepare another couple of aircraft. More pilots were needed and I scoured the Mess to find them. It looked like it was helicopter activity at low altitude and so a full air and ground alert was in being. We kept up a continuous stream of Lightnings and I was at the alert hangar for most of the night. The visual identification (VisIdent) was quite a tricky procedure to fly, especially on a low and slow target. It entailed a radar approach to the target, slightly offset, so that you could hopefully slide by and identify the target. Several passes might be needed to collect all the identity marks. With a helicopter, you could easily have an overtake of 100 kts, and on a pitch black night, it was tricky to say the least.

The role was really an amalgamation of two responsibilities, a NATO one and a Tripartite nation agreement. We should therefore have had four aircraft on state, but we never did. The armed state was likely to be tested by a scramble to the Valley missile range in Wales. This meant that your aircraft had to be fully serviceable, for to be dispatched to the range and have a misfire or some other unserviceability was a severe indictment on the squadron. The live exercise was rare, but there was little time to overcome mistakes, for Valley was at the limit of the Lightning range and the stress level was high if you were going to get it all right the first time.

I had a misfire and the second pass cut deeply into my fuel reserves. The tension does not go away until you find out that it was a missile problem and not finger trouble.

The long-expected role change to low level came later than expected, but it was of great interest to me. We had contingency plans for all manner of war scenarios and the basis of most was a series of race track patterns, flown by defensive aircraft in concert. This kept all aircraft at the north end of the patterns at the same time, so that they orbited in unison. Otherwise there would have been conflict on targets and big gaps for the attackers to sneak through. We would keep up a continual manning of the patterns as aircraft ran short of fuel and were replaced by new fighters.

The Lightning would orbit at 360 kts and 250 ft. Navigation was by map, and if you left to attack a target, you had to find your way back to the pattern, no mean feat in the normal central European weather. I was continually amazed by the rapid grasp of the essentials shown by first tourists, but full freedom in those conditions was not achieved by many.

We worked a little with the Hawk batteries who had good radar and could be utilised for certain intercepts. On one terrible day it was important to show some results and the controller was known to me from Odiham days. He requested that I do it, for it was going to be significantly under 250 ft. I found the battery, camouflaged though it was, and began the radar runs they needed. It took all my concentration to stay out of the foliage and, more to the point, navigate back to the start line.

I had devised a series of sorties for combat and low-level training. The boss liked it and it became the standard intro to theatre operations. There was some reluctance from the flight commanders to subject themselves to this, and inevitably minor conflicts arose. I had direct access to the boss over such matters and tried to put myself to one side when there was conflict. It started coming to a head with the pressure to achieve an operational status for the whole unit.

A NATO team travelled around checking the readiness of all units, and an annual full-scale test was the norm. We therefore would go on full alert once a month for practice. Typically the horn would blow at three in the morning, and the base would be sealed as the war plans were tested and exercised. The first pilots to reach the squadron would take the first aircraft made ready to the dispersal area. These 'revetments' were bomb-proof parking areas for two aircraft at a time. One squadron operated from each end of the runway, which is tailor-made for cock-ups.

Operations would then be carried out from the war facilities, testing all the elements of the station. On one of the first high-level defensive deployments, I noticed that the navigation data was poor, if not wrong. When it was checked, a basic mistake was uncovered. The alignment of the TACAN beacons was drawn to true north, not magnetic. A small error, but it could have compounding problems. It was, I found out too late, the brainchild of my flight commander. We had different views on many things and my protective attitude to the training element was not really understood. He was a very career-minded individual on his second flying tour and could not be expected to have the depth of knowledge that the position sometimes demanded. We clashed heavily over 'revetment' operations for the rules required that in full Nuclear/Biological/ Chemical (NBC) gear, we carried all the protective equipment. One of these items was a 'tin hat'. This weighty, sharp object, more suited to its original use as headgear for a soldier, was supposed to be carried in the cockpit. After completing the drill for entering the aircraft in the protective suit and plastic protectors, I would discard the 'tin hat', and leave it in the revetment for my return. He took exception to that and demanded that I keep it in the cockpit with me for the flights. Fight or flight was something I felt I knew how to handle, and it was clearly 'fight' at this point. I tried to soften the argument by observing that we would never consider flying with a heavy, sharp, loose article in the cockpit in normal circumstances, could we not accept that in wartime we would, but for now the risk outweighed the gain. It was not solved and I am afraid that our relationship weakened from then on.

The combat phase was with us and this was quite a personal aspect of the squadron. It was still a hang-back to 66 Squadron days that never again would anybody get on my tail. I moved up the ladder and was never beaten, which although it was significant to me, I never pressed for recognition. In fact it was almost taken for granted, and some of the younger guys would plead for more training and information, which I gladly gave.

Pete N, son of my Wing Commander Flying at Church Fenton, was a case in point. He would press for more demanding flying and ask to be on my sorties. The low-level role had its interesting moments in that if we were not to be cleared below 250 ft, the same height as the targets, we could not theoretically bring our guns to bear. The sight line and installation of the guns was inclined upwards 7 degrees. This meant that you were significantly below the target at firing range of 300-350 yds. I devised an attack profile from the side that kept the fighter from an underneath attack. On one exercise there were many targets and I inverted the Lightning and obtained my film from above. The boss did not think much of that idea, and the other profile was safer.

Life on the unit had become full. I had the SIAI Marchetti to display and would drive to Gosselies in Belgium to pick it up. The station had an excellent magazine and I volunteered my services as a motoring journalist. Using my rallying credibility, I obtained a whole series of vehicles for test, for NATO was where everyone took advantage of cheaper car prices and thus there was unflagging interest in such things. I also started a motorsport club which evolved into a full-blown autocross circuit. From small beginnings, it blossomed to involve friends and families alike. We used the ground outside the perimeter of the airfield, and so I could run the events whilst still operating as BAFOO, using the Ops vehicle.

The new low-level role demands were to focus on the lack of gun-firing experience that the Lightning force possessed. As such an air firing detachment was organised to Decimomanu in Sardinia – 19 Squadron went first, and their results were, to say the least, abysmal. Air-to-air is practiced as a pattern against a towed target, in this case by a Canberra. The target is a fabric banner, some thirty feet long and twelve deep. It is kept vertical by a spreader bar that attaches to the tow wire. The pattern is designed to keep the towing aircraft out of the firing zone, but the angular separation is not very great.

We flew down as a squadron, and flight refuelled at the Austrian border. This detachment was important in that I had never really had sufficient practice to identify a technique that worked. The competition was going to be fierce from the young lions, and I knew that the boss and flight commanders were feeling the pressure also. The fact that 19 Squadron had failed to make any impact was impetus enough.

The first sorties are merely camera ones to adjust the firing position so that the towing aircraft is not put in jeopardy. I settled on a technique, but did not take any film as I explored the potential. The flight commander was adamant that he needed film before you could be released to live firing, quite rightly. The film I brought back was right on the money at 12-15 degrees angle off and 350-325 yds range.

19 Squadron had averaged less than 2 per cent hits, so much so that all our gun harmonisation was checked very thoroughly. The boss had some excellent film but no hits, which was seen as a bad omen, for if he could not hit it with such good film, what chance the rest of us. My first run was 30 out of 95 bullets fired. Several others had double figures, and so we knew that it was possible as the scores began to mount. I kept up my average over the next sorties and finished with a 24 per cent score. The best single score was made by my flight commander, but mine and several others made Air Combat Europe (ACE) standard. It was a personal achievement that I had long needed to complete, something left undone for so many years.

The boss had flown his own aircraft all along, and with such good film, something had to be amiss. The gyro input was faulty and we therefore lost his scores to elevate even further the squadron average.

Deci was a joint-run range between the Italians, Germans, Brits, Canadians and the US of A. The cost equation was 50 per cent Italian and the other 50 per cent split between the rest equally. Simple you might say, but it translated into 12.5 per cent of the seats on the bus, in fact 12.5 per cent of everything. This kind of put a tone on the detachment that left the Italians open for all kinds of abuse.

They were serious about security and had a guard detail that responded only to their officer. This Pavlovian situation was ripe for humour. Between the officers' quarters there was a bell tower, set about 20 ft above ground. The Germans, during a non-flying period, wired a thin cable to the bell and started ringing it for all it was worth. The guard was called out and they arrived, armed to the teeth, to slay these malcreants. They scoured the bushes and, when nothing was found, climbed aboard their vehicle to return to their cages. As they departed the bell began to ring again. Same situation, but much laughter from the watchers on the balconies. In true Pavlovian fashion they could be kept coming and going endlessly. This and tennis ball mortars were the weekend's entertainment. It is amazing what can be achieved with a little ingenuity and acetylene.

A conversation took place between the Italians and the Germans, discussing the courage and skill of their respective Air Forces in the Second World War. The Germans were berating the Italians for always running away, and the Italians were protesting their courage. After a heated exchange, the Germans said, 'Anyway, we came second and you did not even qualify.'

The final party was enjoined at the best restaurant in town. The young lions were intent on having a 'party'. We ordered 'O Sole di Marinara', a local fish soup delicacy. It was promptly revised to Arsehole di Mariner, and came in a huge tureen. The seafood was cooked in seawater and spices, mainly garlic. When the offering was consumed it left the sauce, seawater, sand, bits of shell and garlic. Vic, not to be outdone, promptly upended the tureen and drank the liquid in front of a horrified waiter. The fumes preceded our arrival at Gutersloh on our return.

The demands of Battle Flight were ever with us, and to survive the boredom of a long patrol, I had devised a method of extending the sortie. When I arrived at Gutersloh, the usual patrol was just over two hours in duration, provided you obeyed the rules and landed back with the minimum required fuel. I found that by planning for the least number of turns and being ultra precise with the throttle and climb schedules, it was possible to add considerably to the length of the sortie.

I planned a climb almost to the Swedish border, shut down one engine and very slowly descended into the twenties, whereupon I relit the engine and climbed back up to altitude. A large gentle turn would take you south to the Austrian border, all the time repeating the climb and descend process. Using this technique I extended the sortie to about 2hrs 20 mins, and after I left I know that others milked even more time out of the aircraft.

I now had so many things going on that life was full and enjoyable. The SIAI Marchetti was used for several demos, with one at the Gutersloh open day. I had a ball practicing before met briefing each day, for nobody knew what limits were applicable – a NATO/RAF airfield, Belgian registered Italian aircraft, flown by a UK licensed pilot with Belgian and Italian privileges. For the day, I had practiced a low-level sequence that included an approach up the taxiway and a sharp turn through the light towers illuminating the main parking area. It was to be followed by a loop along the runway and a roll, off which I landed. The SF 260, unlike the Gnat, could not gain height in a loop, only lose it if you were careless. I started the loop at 200 ft and exited climbing to 250 ft slowing for the roll and the landing. The gear for some reason went down very slowly, and I had visions of a wheels-up in front of my peers. I checked the engine slightly to see that after all this time at idle power, it would accelerate. Of course, it did not want to accelerate at all and so a go-around was discounted. Using up runway fast, I held off till the last second before putting it on the ground. Some very heavy breaking saved the day, but the incident stands out in my mind as yet another example of how quickly things can go pear shaped, and as Murphy says, at the most inconvenient moment.

My first retirement point was fast approaching and a career path was rarely relayed to you by MOD. They needed to know six months in advance of your release date whether you intended to stay on in the service. It had been my life for almost twenty years, and shaped my attitudes to many things. I believe that after such exposure to the military mind, the free thinkers find themselves in a rebellious state. I had a hard time doing on Friday what we could not do on Monday. There are so many times that 'just do it' is applicable. This spirit is misused and often misapplied. We have never had problems with the legal order situation that plagued the US in Vietnam, and more to the point the Nazis.

The war games scenario obviously highlights these potentially troubling moments. The 'tin hat' one and Chris's accident left a nasty taste in my mouth. Chris had been night-flying and left the mess after a few beers and a night-flying supper at 1 a.m., all very normal. The alert hooter went off at 3 a.m. for a Tactical Evaluation (TACEVAL). Chris was in the cockpit from then until 9 a.m. having flown three times. On his last sortie he hit a tree on the low-level patterns. My view was that if you are going to expose your operators to this kind of fatigue, a certain level of operational accidents are a given. You can argue until you are blue in the face, but accidents are a fact of life, they will never be zero, and the more you venture into the grey areas, the more will be the likelihood of an increased rate.

Chris asked me to be 'an officer's friend', a cheap legal assistant that is allowed by the rules. I read up on micro-sleeps, sleep deprivation, fatigue affecting vision and co-ordination and referred to my notes from the telemetry backed drives that were undertaken for BLMH when we were preparing for the non-stop rallies. Some of the Red Arrows exposure was enormously fatiguing, but as I have stated, we all seemed to have the ability to concentrate for a short time, no matter what the base state. In Chris's case, the motivation was probably not there, it was after all a synthetic exercise. When all the Boards had reported, we were summoned to the office of the C-in-C.

Our brief was that we would be given a chance to explain and that it should be as short as possible. The Commander-in-Chief was an ex-Dam Busters pilot, suffering from back trouble and a short temper. And so it was to be, he was slumped in his chair and dismissed any attempts at explanation with a wave of his hand. You hit a tree and damaged an aircraft, you will pay with a fine and loss of seniority, get out. As a rider to this incident, a dictate had come down from on high, that there were to be no more witch-hunts after accidents, and that whilst a certain risk was accepted, pilot error (stupidity) would not be condoned. Which was this? I wondered.

A careers interview was organised and a Wing Commander came over from MOD. He was pleasant but not very informative. If I would commit to signing, they would let me know what was in store for me. I could not believe that this was how twenty-year careers are handled. The Army could at any time discuss their future with a career counsellor, and know where they would be at any given moment. They had a pile of personal and professional data on me a mile high, and it seemed fair to trade that for a career statement. My boss tried to influence the process, but was unsuccessful.

About this time I had received a letter from Canada with the offer of a job from an associate on the Air Race. I had researched the job market all over the world in preparation for a possible move, but Canada was never on the list. I had contacts from my earlier 'quiet employment', and with Air America, now known as a CIA front. The job was very well paid and certainly within my capabilities. Australia, after two visits, beckoned strongly, but private flying was not very developed there. After many agonising nights of argument and self-examination, I realised that I was at the end of a mutually satisfying employment.

To balance your value as a pilot against the career view was always going to be a struggle. On 92 Squadron, I had established a niche that left me alone to do my thing, with direct access to the boss. He condoned this as long as I did not let him down and I worked at elevating the standard of flying on the squadron. I brought some unusual experience to the wing, and was gratified that for long after I was gone, some of the landmarks and viewpoints remained.

I had been one of the first pilots to accept special aircrew as a means to keep flying and open the way for those bent on promotion, to accelerate past you. This plan paid flight lieutenants an increased rate, so that those being groomed for stardom did not have financial advantage until much later on the promotion ladder. I could realistically expect to be promoted to Squadron Leader on my next tour, but it was not a given, for openings had to be available.

I discussed the Canada offer with Pete E who was at his first retirement point, and he accepted it after turning down a job with Volkswagen. I did not want to leave, but the fear of being grounded was real, locked in until age fifty-five, against a new life in civilian aviation, biased my choice to Canada.

Emigration is a stressful decision, and to see how many people do it twice, shows that it is almost impossible to adjust in one step. We met innumerable families who emigrated, got homesick, returned home and then found out that they were better off as emigrants, and so turned around again to finally change countries for good. With my choice now public, I discussed with the boss giving up all my responsibilities and by so doing, providing the younger element with the chance to take over. This was done, but even though the boss made the announcement, it always felt as though I had been demoted.

I backed out of everything and concentrated on my civilian licences and the emigration process. When I recall what took place, I realise that to move on such slim data and knowledge was almost foolhardy, but sometimes you have to go on instinct and this was one of them. The job offer was to fly a Citation for Alcan, operating out of Oshawa, a suburb of Toronto. Grant D kept up the correspondence, and so I was comfortable with the move and of course Pete was going to be there six months before me. I took the time to test some superb motor cars and also fly as many NATO aircraft as I could, F5, F104, Mirage, even G91.

I had driven for BMW in a European event and so when an open day at the Zolder track was offered, I took it enthusiastically. I spent the whole day in the 2000Tii, a turbo rocket ship, that on the wet track gave me some interesting moments. The other vehicles were tested, but for sheer entertainment, there was nothing to touch the Tii.

I had prepared for my Canadian licences, but needed to go to Canada House in London to take the exams. The T4 Lightning was an ideal vehicle for a quick whizz over to Lyneham, hire a car, drive to London, study the exam guide, take the exam and return to Gutersloh before you were seriously missed. The boss was most understanding in allowing this 'training', which ceased when the AOC happened to land at Lyneham and see a 92 Squadron aircraft parked there. We fended off his enquiries, but my exams were over satisfactorily.

On the last trip I was asked if I could make 29,000 ft thirty miles from Lyneham by Air Traffic. I made it and went into a ballistic supersonic run home to Gutersloh. The T4 needed to be pointing at the intended landing point whenever it went supersonic, as fuel started to disappear at an alarming rate. The two hundred and odd miles were completed in just over fifteen minutes, including an arrival at base in a dive at well over 550 kts. Very satisfying.

The RAF had a transport aircraft travelling to Canada frequently, taking soldiery to the Canadian training area at Suffield in Alberta. A trip was organised for me to visit Ottawa and Grant, to view the job and the city. I landed in Ottawa, took airlines to Toronto and drove to Oshawa. We had a good meeting and cemented the job offer. Back out to Toronto, airlines to Calgary to link up with the VC10 transport. The VC10 was not to be found, nor did anyone know anything about it. Finally, I found that it was twelve hours late, which meant hanging around for the ten hours.

The idea of being trapped in Calgary with no alternate plan was most unappealing, but there it was, I was at the mercy of Transport Command. Having not slept for three days, I do not remember much about the flight back to base. I was tour-ex almost three months before my release date, which was my birth date. It would have been sensible to stay on until that time, but they needed the post for my replacement. I was posted to Uxbridge, with the ability to study the UK licence requirements at the London Polytechnic. This demob perk was available in certain circumstances. When I arrived at Uxbridge, my new boss was unaware of the arrangement, but saw little point in me hanging around for such a short time.

The bureaucratic nightmare then started in earnest. I had passed my Canadian licence, which legally I could convert to a British licence of lesser standing. When I tried to do this, they needed to have sight of my Canadian licence. Canada agreed to telex the details properly validated. This was unacceptable to the mandarins at Shell Mex house, and the Catch 22 was that Canada would not release my licence until I reached Canada. It would be alright if this kind of bureaucracy served some purpose, but it was a true representation of the Britain of that period.

Fuel shortages were crippling industry at the end of 1973, so much so that I could not accept a job as a test pilot at Shorts in Belfast, even in the short term. I had tried for this job, just in case one of the many pieces of Canada and emigration was unobtainable.

I retired on 22 November 1973 having served since 1954, which with the altered rules, gave me more than the sixteen years over the age of twenty-one, that I needed. The flight to Canada was on New Year's Eve on one of Freddie Laker's specials.

Chapter VII

THE YEARS 1968 to 1972 were a period of such high activity, that looking back upon it even I sometimes wonder how we did it all. The London-Sydney Marathon was announced in early 1968, sponsored by the *Daily Express*. I caught the announcement by chance and wrote for details. The cost was beyond our modest means, and so sponsorship was the only chance we had. As soon as I had enough detail, I asked Derek B to join me on the venture. We would try to parlay our RA publicity image into a fully financed entry. The need for a third driver was indicated and so Pete E was asked to join. He was a motorcycle racer of repute with a long history of enjoying fast cars. He also had the mechanical knowledge that we thought we needed.

Raymond Baxter, a TV personality, was a friend of the team and also a director of the British Motor Corporation (BMC). He was contacted and advised us that he would do what he could. The *Daily Express* was also closely connected to the team, but their basic sponsorship of the event precluded them from helping us. The RAF had long had a special fund called the Trenchard Memorial Award scheme which sponsored all kinds of endeavour, be it mountain climbing or underwater exploration. Whether this fell into that category was unknown. I wrote a paper for the directors of the fund including all the spin-offs such as testing flying clothing, assault rations, telemetry of neural activity under stress and fatigue etc. We went to Arthur G, being a Fleet Street advertising agent, for commercial avenues. He quickly came up with a shipping and packaging company called Evan Cook Ltd. They were prepared to fund 1,500 pounds which left us well short of the required entry fee, and we did not even have a car at this stage.

Deadlines approached and it started to look feasible, especially as BMC had come up with an Austin 1800, prepared by the

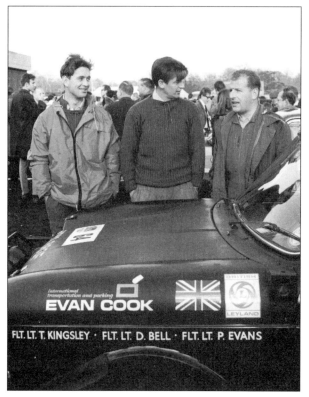

EVAN COOK

FLT. LT. T. KINGSLEY · FLT. LT. D. BELL · FLT. LT. P. EVANS

It starts – 1968.

competition department, but no financial assistance. We were forced to send in our entry without full funding, in expectation of the rest of the cash. Not a desirable situation for three air force officers, who collectively could not find the final payment. The Memorial Fund, steered by Sir Andrew H, came through with the money on condition that we supply all kinds of reports and data. With the usual intense period of activity at the end of the season, we could do little other than plan. Extra leave was requested and approved in view of the lack of opportunity for regular leave that went with being a team member.

As soon as the aircraft were headed for winter maintenance, we divided up the daily routine into three parts, usually meeting each morning before driving off to London for a round of PR/Admin meetings. Peter B, the competition manager at Abingdon, was

Publicity blurb prepared by Arthur G.

quickly very helpful, and we began to collect information on the cars, the teams and the task. Six cars were being hand built, one mechanic being responsible for each car. We made contact with our builder and he saw that we were approaching this event seriously. Pete was responsible for knowing all about the 1800, and we all tried our hand at changing the various components. Being serving officers, there were more hoops to jump through than normal; it was, after all, 1968 and Hungary and Bulgaria were not on the tourist route. We were required to speak to all the attachés, and assembled masses of data which, whilst it alerted us to the potential problems, mostly went unused. The Marathon went by at such speed and the borders were never an issue on the day.

The BMC package really was very basic, but slowly evolved into much more. We became part of the 'B' team and as such were to be given roadside service, the same as the professional effort and also the very important route notes. There was much joking about the fact that the mechanics had a bet on that we would not get past

Dover, although we did give them plenty of ammunition by severely bending two vehicles during the development phase. The major testing consists of putting destructive mileage on the test car, redesigning it, and then working towards a total test mileage of 10,000. This gives a ratio of 10 to 1 in rally terms. The test site has to be understood to see why this ratio is seen as significant.

The Fighting Vehicles Research Establishment (FVRE) is a torture track akin to the rock and rubble that are laid before a normal road is constructed. Rally tyres last 40 miles on this surface, and no production motor car had ever lasted more than 47 miles before it returned to its component parts. It has hills, washaways, flooded concrete structures designed to test any suspension. Army vehicles were our constant companions. The mechanics take a representative 1800 and put in as many miles as possible. When it breaks, as it surely will, it is back to the drawing board and a new round of test miles. BMC had an attitude of strengthening their cars, whilst Ford used to lighten theirs. Both techniques work, but it shows the philosophical difference in approach. We finished up with a very heavy motor car, and the 'Landcrab' was known for its robustness. We were able to put in plenty of hours at the track, and started to get close to the times of the mechanics. I was having an exhilarating time pounding this noisy vehicle around this magnificent site. Each lap was quicker than the last as I came to believe in the strength of the 1800. The front-drive shafts were a source of trouble and so it was normal to stress them as much as possible. At each hairpin bend, a wheel was dropped off the edge to help pull the car round the corner. As I exited, the 1800 slid across the track and we mounted a very large boulder to complete a perfect barrel roll onto the roof. The 500 lb of sandbags hit me in the ear and I dismounted rapido. They knew something was amiss when at the due time I did not appear.

Shame and ignominy, but the damage was repaired quickly and testing continued. The second black mark was during a night drive to work up some sort of a system for navigating, changing tyres, etc. Derek was executing a pass on a wet night up a narrow country road when a Ford appeared coming towards at high speed There was nowhere to go and the brakes option was not really an option. We met head-on, with mental and metal damage, but no physical. I guess damaged motor cars are a fact of life in the rally world, for without the ribbing we would not have known that anything had happened.

Dividing up the responsibilities into nav, technical and admin certainly allowed us to prepare in an organised fashion. We were ready by mid-November. The car, however, was not. The extra cash had been obtained through Graham Hill and Brands Hatch Motor Racing Circuit, both good friends of the RA.

We took part in a press day at Thruxton race track and met the famous names of the BMC entry. I managed to sit in with Rauno Aaltonen as he made his acquaintance with the 1800. This magic drive was to open my eyes to the elevated skills and knowledge possessed by top-line rally drivers. He was so smooth in his treatment of the car, with the brilliant anticipation that goes with it. I learned a great deal from Rauno. Tony Fall was putting the 1800 through its paces driving over cliffs and in general treating the car in a manner we found incredible. Having seen what the rally world can do, we were more than chastened, for you do not learn that stuff overnight.

To bolster our spirits we had to consider our strengths and weaknesses. We could work under stress as a team and I knew that we had more than the average amount of stamina. Drive within your capabilities, no mistakes and the car was certainly better than we were. The hard part was deciding which spares to take. When it was laid out on the floor at Abingdon, it was a mass of items, much of which was beyond our capabilities to deal with.

We considered weight and tyres carefully, settling on four wheels and tyres so that we could carry them in the car and reduce fuel consumption. The battery was a major point of contention from the drivers, for it and the alternator had given trouble on previous long-distance events. Strangely, the six engines varied between 95 and 108 BHP when they were tested; ours needed little or no adjustment to obtain peak power. There were two items that were unusual, a jack that was used to recover the car from a ditch, and a winch. By jacking the car up and then removing a pin, the car could be walked up surprisingly steep slopes as it fell sideways off the jack.

Black Friday, 22 November 1968 was a never-to-be-forgotten day. I was to collect the others en route to London for the final briefings. On checking the oil, I noticed that the dipstick was foreshortened by about three inches. It had been notched to better indicate the increased oil capacity and broken at the notch. The Administrator was forced to get his hands dirty as I tried to recover the broken piece. It was inevitable that the car had to be returned to Abingdon, and so Pete and I commandeered an Air Force truck to deliver it to BMC. They worked into the night to retrieve the piece of spring steel from the sump and put out an alert to change all the other dipsticks.

We arrived at Biggin Hill in the early hours of the morning. Crystal Palace was packed for the start and we were on our way to Dover. Down the Dover road traffic was heavy and a black Citroen was observed carving his way through the traffic behind us. It was Arthur hanging out of the car taking pictures for the record.

The French section was fog bound and we were driving fast as the professionals whizzed by as though we were stationary. A certain 'press-on' attitude adjustment was necessary and we settled to a group of vehicles travelling at our speed. Belgrade allowed us some sleep, the border crossings were uneventful until a large rock was lofted out of a ditch just after the Bulgarian border, breaking the windscreen. Turkey was entered and we made our way to Sivas for the first special stage, a distance of 186 miles to be covered in 2 hrs and 40 minutes. The special was not going to be covered by us in that time, and so it was more a matter of working out what was a reasonable amount of time to lose. Pete drove the section, over a mountain with many miles of Alpine hairpins and narrow bridges. The BMC notes were detailed, but a routine was needed to deal with them and the HALDA, the very accurate odometer.

The intercomm was useful in reducing noise fatigue, and the superb lights made night driving into day. They were rigged in rally style, two ahead, two crossed to look around corners, one up one down to take care of brows. Even with this lot, a fast right-angled bend put us into a Turkish garden, one of eighteen cars to effect this detour. We caught the tail lights of a car just as we left the road and jumped into soft soil alongside another rally car digging himself out. We continued around the stalled car back onto the road, a loose term.

The trip to Tehran was uneventful, but we never saw another rally car for 600 miles. Tehran was well organised and the Air Attaché was kind enough to offer a shower and a meal in comfort. The route to

Kabul was going to be significant and most of the teams had spent considerable resources preparing for the arrival of the Marathon. There were really three ways that you could drive to Kabul, actually to the Afghanistan border, all with their distinct advantages and disadvantages; the total distance was 1,500 miles, to be covered in 23.5 hrs: Route 'A', over the mountains on a fairly good road, but with weather problems; Route 'B', the southern desert road; and 'C' a combination of both. BMC had covered the routes with a service vehicle prior to our arrival and the choice was Route 'C', some 40 miles shorter than the other two. This choice was followed by BMC, Rootes and Citroen, nine cars in all. Only 32 cars escaped penalty to Kabul and this was a major factor in our position at Bombay.

The mountain hairpins and desert washboard claimed two BMC cars, and but for the ingenuity of Rauno Aaltonen, he would have been excluded. He misread a hairpin bend in the dark and flew over the precipice to arrive at the other side sans front suspension. It was all folded back under the car, but using the winch around the cross-mounted engine, and the 'kangaroo bar', he was able to drive 3,000 miles to Bombay. From behind, he could be seen to jerk to one side as power was applied, and vice versa as it was taken off. Tuning was achieved by striking the winch cable and listening to the note.

We had never experienced any surface like the desert washboard. Vibration would build up to the point that the instruments were unreadable and something had to break. By bouncing off the edges of the track you could break up the frequency and then try and find a speed at which the vibration harmonic ceased. Our problems were twofold: in that in soft sand we could not achieve a speed high enough to end the vibration, or if we could it was too fast for the hazards.

We started having electrical problems from a broken battery and a loose dashboard. The Afghan border was reached and a large muddy river crossing was undertaken. We watched the experts and then lined up for a high-speed charge ourselves. As long as you can hold the front wheels straight, you generally can skip across. The good US/Russian-built highway was 700 miles to be done at 62 mph, if we were to escape penalty. Apart from the concrete drainage channels across the road, it was do-able. We slid into BMC service with five minutes to spare and a broken battery. The regulations forced a halt of 7.5 hrs in Kabul, so that the Lataban pass would be tackled in daylight. So, we had driven 3,000 miles from Istanbul to Kabul without sleep.

The cars were locked in Parc-Ferme and could not be touched until your start time in the morning. This meant a push start in minus temperatures at 9,000 feet in the early morning hours. The Lataban had been hyped up so much by the press that the authorities had graded the goat track and posted soldiers on the edge of nearly every drop-off.

With a cold engine and no warm-up possible we took it easy and wondered what all the fuss was about, but then we were going relatively slowly. Running down the Khyber Pass in the early morning hours was a visual treat. Two battery changes were accomplished at the borders, finally settling the electrical troubles.

The run into Delhi had its own treat: crowds, not the football density kind, but millions packed into the roadway. They were happy, but the kind of happiness that verges on hysteria. Everything that could be removed from the outside of the car was taken, and eventually they were swarming all over the vehicle. You lose sight of the road, and stopping is fatal. The temperature rises rapidly in the car, and the lack of oxygen is noticeable.

After negotiating one huge crowd, we joined the Aussies in preparing for the engagement with the next one. They opened the doors to make the car as wide as possible, and then ran at the crowd, which divided to allow this wide vehicle through. At the last minute, they shut the doors and used the momentum to carry them through. Legs and feet were certainly run over, as those at the back pushed those at the front into the traffic. It would not have taken much to change the mood of such a crowd, and no help is possible in such circumstances. You are an ant in these situations, and reading the attitude of the mass is not a Western skill.

We joined a convoy on entering the outskirts of Delhi, with police lining the road. A diminutive Mini-Minor sneaked into the parade and was savaged by a policeman for his pains. This very large officer was carrying a pace-stick of the cane and brass variety. He swung at the dodging Mini and caught it down the centre of the roof, bifurcating it into a Mi-Ni.

The run to Bombay was fatiguing in the extreme, but the clean-up of the car was magic on the roadside. Where there were no people or dwellings to be seen, turfing the spare food items in their foil wrappers overboard instantly attracted scores or people, seemingly out of nowhere. We tried to make as much time as possible to Bombay in order to work on the car. We needed to change the windscreen and the battery and complete a service.

Fatigue was so great that we could scarcely carry out the clean and wash demanded by the Australian authorities. Pete was running a fever and almost unconscious in the back, whilst Derek and I tried to change the battery. We were too tired to lift it, and Alec P, another BMC competitor changed it for us, along with the windscreen. They would not allow Pete to go to the hotel unless we all went, and we could not go until the car was cleaned. Catch 22.

Two nights in a hotel raised our spirits, as did our position at thirty-two, with a ninety-four minute penalty. The boat trip was my first and last cruise ship experience, but nine days with almost 200 rally people was certain to have its moments. It did.

The poker game was too rich for mine and many others and so I introduced the 'Lurgi' from Benson days. A simple game, such that you are not trapped into contributing large sums of money. You can stay or fold, risking initially only the 'ante'. At ten that night, it suddenly got expensive when I risked over one hundred pounds on an almost sure thing, and lost. I rushed back to the cabin to ask Derek for the TCs, and left before he could focus on what I was doing. By six in the morning I was fully recovered and operating at a small profit. The wealthy came to join the cheap game in the early hours in view of all the noise and interest we were attracting.

The Victorian atmosphere of the P & O ship was not conducive to rest and relaxation, rally world style. The poolside parties were noisy affairs and an attempt to close the bar was met with derision. We all trotted off to our cabins to order room service and then take it back to the pool. The next move was to close the pool by placing a net over it. In the process, one of the officers was nudged in. We then all entered the pool beneath the net, defeating the purpose entirely. Finally, they tried to empty the pool, but I noticed where it was done and promptly reversed the flow. Peace broke out when they realised that this was not going to be a normal cruise and some attempt was made to soften the rigidity under which they operated.

The crew normally ran a 'fixed' Casino night, with a betting system. The various rally teams were competing in the horse race, when we decided to beat them at their own game. The crew set the odds after the heat races, and we all agreed that BMC would win in the final. With much serious winding, our horse won and paid handsomely, thank you very much, mind your fingers. The crew changed to a new Goanese one, and they appeared to bring aboard a new round of infections. I used up my comprehensive medical kit as people asked for me rather than the ship's doctor at five pounds a time. If I had charged anything at all, I could have repaid the Trenchard fund in full.

Australia was a warm welcome in both senses. They were very aware of the RA entry and had a close relationship with the Royal Air Force. The climate was superb and we departed from the trotting track and huge crowds. BMC service was outside Perth and it was a relief to see the rapid check of the 1800 accomplish so much. We had not counted on their assistance, but could now lighten the car and use their fuel arrangements.

The 1800 had an identification light on the roof and a siren to alert the superb BMC car club support which opened the many gates, moved trees aside, and pointed the way when there were multiple tracks to choose from. Some of the volunteers had driven from Sydney, 3,000 miles, to attend the briefing and then return to organise their response.

With a fresh-sounding vehicle, we drove 300 miles north to Youanmi, a crossroads in the desert. As we approached the area, lights and activity could seen, for there was now a tent city and hundreds of people to witness the stop. The run south was 'bush', and made increasingly difficult by the talcum powder-like dust which penetrates everything. The changed rules for Australia meant that collecting too much lateness per section could mean exclusion. Whilst we could accept a certain amount, we were very conscious of getting too far behind schedule.

The Lake King was a car breaker, being an old ox cart track, unused for forty years. It had every conceivable hazard: dust, rocky outcrops, hidden gullies, fallen trees and navigationally troublesome crossroads. With the requirement for a 66 mph average, many were not going to make it. Overtaking was impossible, sometimes for many miles. Our windscreen bore witness to that, for it was again broken along with almost all the lights.

The Nullarbor was a straight run of 900 miles, during which we made up enough time to enjoy a shower at Quorn. One of those 'nearlys' slowly unfolded on a dusty stretch of the Nullarbor, as a road train came into view. These incredible haulage systems are easy to identify, but the road was narrowing to a collection of ironmongery that passed for a bridge. It was going to be close, so close that I decided to give in to the gross-weight-wins argument. Attempting to slow, I made contact with the ridge of dust in the edge of the road left by the graders. We popped over it and were channelled straight into the bridgeworks at slow speed. We crossed exactly at the bridge and he stopped a mile down the road, unhooked and came back to pull us from the dust pile.

It was to be our last rest, as the stages from then on through the mountains of Australia were acknowledged to be the deciders. We crossed the Flinders Range three times with its dry mountainous bush country, criss-crossing creek beds three or four times per mile. It was here that the temperature became noticeable, but either our insulation was superb or we were too occupied for it to be a problem in this sandy sheep country. From there on we followed the high route on unsurfaced roads with severe drop-offs, ready to catch the slightest mistake.

Sightseeing traffic unbeknown to us took out Bianchi when he was leading. It is most disconcerting to meet traffic on a closed road, for you are almost inevitably using all of it and the corrective action can be fatal to both parties. We were on the inside of a turn hugging the rock face, when a sightseer appeared and to avoid a head-on I was forced to the outside putting one wheel over the edge. Front wheel drive pulled us back on, but it was so close that we had a short discussion about how to handle the next idiot. We all agreed that a head-on was preferable to going over the edge, and we had a strong car to support that decision.

We incurred our worst penalty in the fog near the ski slopes of Falls Creek. Cars could he seen going in all directions and 'a' road was as good as any other road. There was no letting up as we were given a message from Peter Browning that we were in the first twenty and to finish at all costs as the two BMC teams were lying first and second. One of the Ford Falcons was upside down in a field penalising their team, but they subsequently restarted and claimed the first team slot.

An excursion into the branches of a fallen tree caused some consternation to a photographer, but slowed the car only slightly. And then we were through to the end in a creditable way, first non-professional crew, and the best effort from the services. There was the euphoria that is so much a part of finishing these types of events, a bit like the end of season for the Red Arrows; what next is the recurring question.

Well, the immediate problem was the return of the car to the UK. RAF Transport Command was to carry some of the service-entered vehicles, but we needed our car back for BMC publicity as part of our arrangement, and we had not funded returning it any other way.

We did manage to visit Gelignite Jack's Shack on the Hawkesbury river. This unforgettable character had lost a wheel in the desert and received one thrown out of an aircraft to get them going again. His 'Shack' was set in an orange grove on the banks of the river and was a meeting point for all the locals. He was firmly in the belief that we 'poms' needed feeding up as we were too pale and weedy.

Male sport for his crowd was only a success if at least half were bleeding or nursing some major wound. I was cajoled into water skiing behind his 700 hp boat and unaware of the implications. The river has willow trees all along the banks, plus a fair amount of fallen logs on the edges. The first turn in the waterway whiplashed me into the assault course along the banks, where it was safer to suffer the lacerations from the branches than risk falling in. They were all laughing their heads off in the boat as I took their punishment. I tried to disengage as we came past his shack, jeered on by the beer drinkers on the dock. Perfectly timed, he hit full power and yanked me straight out of the skis. The photo shows me imitating 'Sylvester' the cat, horizontal, two feet off the water, desperately trying to let go of the rope. It does not show that we were accelerating to some humongous speed that solidified the water when I hit it. Such is the entrance exam to the 'club'.

One of the visitors was a 'parasail' expert. He had built a 'delta' sail contraption on two large floats. It was well built apart from the 'Jesus nut' that held the sail to the 'A' frame. He had severely broken his arm and could not fly for the moment. Yes, of course we would fly it, etc. etc. Having no tail surfaces at all, it possessed little in the way of directional stability. The boat was very capable of pulling it, and so when I popped out of the river valley, we slid over the land and only a steep slipping turn could put me back over water. As Jack made a reversal in the waterway, it was necessary to dive off all the height and try and co-ordinate both our changes of direction. It was so buoyant that any impact with the water caused it to fire back out as if it were rocket propelled. Derek B had a go and the rope broke just after he left the water. He nosed in, to the chagrin of the watchers who were expecting blood.

We were taken around by Grace Bros, the Australian end of our UK sponsors and the car was on display in their huge shopping centre. A visit to the flying club gave us a chance to fly the Victa, an indigenous training aircraft that was popular in Australasia.

The trip home for Christmas was long and boring; a C-130 is not the most comfortable mode of travel. It has a frontal system all its own, a dividing line that separates the warm air from the cold. To cool off you just move a couple of seats towards the rear and vice versa if you are cold. It turned out to be more comfortable sitting in our car than enduring the sideways facing paratroop ones. Nevertheless, we would be home for Christmas, reflective, and forever changed by the events of the past few months.

Chapter VIII

THE LONDON-SYDNEY Air Race was a repeat of the 1919 event, but run under the Royal Aero Club handicap system. This tried and proven system has plotted the performance of competitive aircraft since air racing began. It purports to be the ideal formula by equating installed horsepower to wing area. As we shall see, its basic hypothesis was tested by our entry. After flying the SF-260 at Biggin Hill in May, and cementing a friendship with James B, we looked no further for a race aircraft. It was the Ferrari of small aircraft, a piston-engined version of the Gnat. Tiny, fast, acrobatic with an excellent wing, it had enough range to place it on a par with other potential entrants. SIAI Marchetti were sold on the idea of a Red Arrows entry using a new SF-260, and we were to co-ordinate our planning through James and the sales base of Gossellies in Belgium.

As for the Marathon, we could do little to prepare until the RA season was over, but the Race regulations demanded much administrative response. Arthur and Pete were to accompany me as crew and we used every available spare minute to comply with the regs.

The first major barrier was that the two classes were divided into those who were instrument rated, and those who would be restricted to visual conditions. The venerable Civil Aviation Authority (CAA) did not recognise military instrument ratings, nor did it accept the long hours of instrument training that are so much a part of a service pilot's lot. One of us needed to possess a civil instrument rating, and there was no time to obtain one. All our attempts to coerce the CAA to give us a waiver were failures and so I went to the AOC, of Gnat crashing fame, and asked for his help.

We were far enough along with publicity that for an RAF entry to be refused on such grounds was not going to be good politics. I was directed to return to Shell Mex House, the CAA HQ, and restate my case for a waiver. With much sharp pencilling, I was given a one-time instrument rating for three months, a success story that I believe has never been repeated or equalled in the annals of a bureaucracy like the CAA. It is a treasured possession.

As soon as the RA season was over we set about sifting through the mass of information for the route. We worked closely with Aeronautical Information Services (AIS), the Board of Trade, the Royal Aero Club, and the Royal Air Force departments overseas. It is perhaps worth noting the original route we selected, seen against the compulsory stopping points of the event. Race stops:

    Athens
    Karachi
    Calcutta
    Singapore
    Darwin
    Adelaide

Having flown over much of the route in my service career, I was well aware of the geographical and meteorological hazards that prevailed. Our initial choice of route therefore was as follows:

    London-Northern Italy-Athens
    Athens-Diyabakir
    Diyabakir-Zanzan
    Zanzan-Karachi
    Karachi-Nagpur
    Nagpur-Calcutta
    Calcutta-Port Blair
    Port Blair-Butterworth
    Butterworth-Singapore
    Singapore-Semerang
    Semerang-Kupang
    Kupang-Darwin
    Darwin-Alice Springs
    Alice Springs-Adelaide

As many of the stops possible were organised through the air attachés to be at military airfields, some very slick organisation was anticipated. In late October, however, three problems arose which were to cause a tremendous amount of extra work before the route was finalised. These problems will be discussed under phase two.

A further visit to Belgium showed that no aircraft was likely to be available before mid-November and to compensate I was given funds to hire another Marchetti based in the UK. This aircraft was G-AXKA and as the world found out, it was the aircraft eventually used in the Race. Virtually new, it had only completed 100 hrs when we collected it at the end of October. From this point on the planning and organisation turned into something of a nightmare.

We flew from Little Rissington in the Marchetti owned by the Honourable James Baring, on to Abbotsinch to collect the aircraft G-AXKA and I offered a seat to my wife as a demonstration of the capabilities of the SF-260. We ran into heavy snow en route and the turbulence over the mountains south of Glasgow was quite something. As this was my first solo in the 260, we decided to fly back in formation. The snowball of minor problems caused us to leave Abbotsinch very late and it was nightfall before we reached Nottinghamshire. Suffice it to say that after a series of radio problems we reached Little Rissington and were very lucky to find it open.

In an auspicious start we carried out one long-range nav trip, as the maximum range fully loaded was not really known. Pressure of work prevented us from carrying out the rest of our planned series of test flights. However, much useful information was gained from just operating the aircraft locally. Radio troubles and an undercarriage snag, all were to provide valuable learning experience.

The most significant incident concerned the starting and on a visit to Manston the prompt reaction of the RAF ground crew prevented serious damage when a starter fire occurred. The same fire occurred at Little Rissington and with these facts in mind the cowling was modified.

Forewarned as we were, we could only stand and watch as our race aircraft was ignited at Gosselies some weeks later from the same fault. I had been unable to start the engine in the cold, and the mechanic leaped in and did exactly what I had been trying to avoid.

Route planning progressed on a day-to-day basis, but the serious strikes in Northern Italy were obviously going to cause delay in the production of our special race aircraft. Its new arrival date was pushed back to 20 November 1969. It was at this stage that the idea of using G-AXKA first materialised and so we could continue with our planning assured that we would at least have an aircraft no matter what.

In late November a pilot was dispatched to the factory in Italy to pick the race aircraft, OO-HEV and we were dumbfounded to hear that it had been involved in a taxiing accident. Another aircraft was promised and we could smile yet again. Our concern over OO-HEV was entirely due to the fact that on arrival in England it would need a minimum of eight days to install the radios and nav equipment. Time was now short and the deadline for OO-HEV was set for 1 December 1969 as we now learned that 40 hours flying time would be needed to run in the Lycoming engine. It was not so much a matter of running in the engine but of changing the type of oil along the race route.

The weather over the next few days was atrocious and despite our attempts at getting to Belgium the delivery flight never took place. In desperation we flew to Gossellies and were fog bound there for three days. OO-HEV finally arrived from Italy and was promptly set on fire again by the same mechanic, ensuring that G-AXKA was to be our race aircraft.

The extra burden of obtaining the civilian instrument rating caused me to motor some 4,000 miles in six weeks and extended our working day well into the wee hours.

In routing a small aeroplane in standard form to Australia, we had no time to consider the problems of others. This isolation was to prove costly in the end, as we should have known how much the handicap favoured the long-range aircraft, particularly those carrying extra fuel tanks.

There were three problem areas on our route: Turkey, India and the Malaysian Peninsula. In flying from Athens to Karachi there are three basic routes available: via Beirut and through the Middle East, a very troubled area at the time of the race; Athens-Cairo-Saudi Arabia, a much longer route with potentially many diplomatic problems; and the northern route over the mountains of Turkey, well known to many RAF crews.

We dismissed the Cairo route from the time factor alone and we did not wish to be involved in the diplomacy of the Arab countries. An outside alternative was an overflight landing in Damascus, but a summons to Whitehall ruled out any possibility of a Royal Air Force crew entering Syria. To enable us to fly the Turkey route I sought diplomatic help and was granted permission to land at Diyabakir. This meant I could follow the Mediterranean route to Cyprus and use the lowland route to Diyabakir.

It must be stated here that the terrain clearance on the Turkish routes required altitude of 13,500 ft minimum and at one stage 15,500 ft. Our aircraft was stated to be capable of 21,000 ft, but we had serious doubts whether it would achieve this fully loaded. The next body blow occurred when the Turkish authorities withdrew permission for Diyabakir, forcing us into the highlands of Turkey, a frightening prospect.

With these facts in mind I approached the Royal Aero Club for a dispensation of take-off time to enable us to cross 450 miles of mountains in daylight. This was refused, and the prospect of a night flight from Ankara into Iran caused many a sleepless night. A night trip would sensibly require oxygen and so we set to work to chase up some portable equipment, capable of taking us through Turkey. No ideal equipment was available, but the British Aircraft Corporation (BAC) through Arthur G was able to offer the loan of some equipment giving us six hours oxygen for one man.

The next issue concerned the stopping points in India. The race compulsories were Karachi and Calcutta. This distance dictated a stop somewhere in the middle of India. Investigation showed that Nagpur was ideal for our requirements. However India has port-of-entry rules necessitating a landing prior to Nagpur and in our case at Ahmadabad. Through our military contact we were able to obtain a waiver of this first point of landing, as Ahmadabad would have forced us to make two stops between Karachi and Calcutta. With such a short-range aeroplane this move was vital. The mass of communications needed to organise this were eventually to be wasted as in due course the Indian government allowed race traffic an unimpeded flow, so away went our first advantage.

The second and most long-fought idea concerned our route from Calcutta to Singapore. Regulations allowed two intermediate stops on this leg. For us, this meant an almost straight line route had to be followed. However, the weather in this area in December could cause many fuel-consuming delays, besides which the requirements of the civil air authorities of Burma, Thailand and Malaysia were not conducive to a direct flight. We therefore investigated the idea of using Port Blair in the Andaman and Nicobar Islands. This involved a flight of close to 700 miles south from Calcutta to this small chain of islands. If the prevailing wind is sufficiently strong we could make Car Nicobar some 160 miles further on. A great deal of effort was put into this project by the Ministry of Defence, the Air Attaché and ourselves. With the detail known in the initial planning stages it could have provided us with several hours advantage. We had planned to fly in fuel and a fuel pump as no acceptable petrol was available on the island. As a safeguard, I had also very quietly, through the great help of Mr Ken H of Castrol Ltd, had 50 gallons shipped in and this arrived of 28 November 1969.

We were in a very powerful position as no other aircraft could possibly use Port Blair and we had the only 100-octane fuel on the island. These islands are a very sensitive issue with the Indian government and in the end permission could not be obtained for a landing and we were forced to revert to a mainland route.

Compliance with all the rules and regulations necessary for flying an aircraft from country to country is a long-winded business. No short cuts could be taken for fear of delays on the ground. We therefore wrote and established contact with the authorities in every country concerned, and this of course involved countries other than those on our planned route, for we had to cater for diversions. We telegraphed all the Civil Aviation Authorities and all the fuel companies, although ShellMex and BP London were able to supply the bulk of our requirements. In view of the communication delays we followed the same process through the air attachés, a double insurance against foreseen problems.

Preparation and training on the aircraft still continued, although we were never able to fly the first leg to Pisa, as was our intention, nor were we able to complete the extreme range trip we had planned in UK. To show how daily incidents seemed to beset us, I was called by the Hon. James B. to fly to Redhill to meet him. Weather permitting, we would fly to Belgium in the hope of collecting our race aircraft. I left Brize Norton where my aircraft had been parked for the weekend, and in very poor weather flew to Redhill. I skirted Farnborough from the south and set off along the corridor for

Redhill. In heavy rain, low cloud and extreme turbulence from a strong wind, I spent an hour and a half trying to get through. Near Guildford the cloud lay on the trees. Shortage of fuel forced me back to Blackbushe where I refuelled and set off for another try. No communication with Redhill was possible and an hour later I was able to sneak in on the A25. In so doing I was just able to prevent James from alerting the SAR services. A simple but urgent thirty-minute flight had taken nearly four hours.

We sat and stared out to the south, intensely frustrated at the weather and the lack of contact with Belgium and our race aircraft. When we finally did reach Belgium a few weeks later the fog and snow arrived behind us forcing yet another three-day wait. We made strong overtures to the airport authorities at Gossellies but they were unmoved. We could not take off until visibility was 500 yds, even though the fog layer was 50 ft thick with blue skies above. The moves and counter moves, start up, taxi here, taxi there, proved conclusively to me that I would never suffer a nervous breakdown.

Such is the procedure at Gossellies that with poor visibility the airport commandant must, after consultation with the meteorological office, order a physical inspection of the conditions. Transport is therefore ordered and an officer of the air traffic services motors down the runway to check the visibility. This frustrating process successfully overtook the only break in the weather and therefore approval never came close to being given. The return trip had its moments as we were diverted into Lydd before finally reaching Gatwick. Even there the go/come back saga did not stop.

Pete drove from Gatwick to Brize Norton to collect me on my arrival from Fair Oaks and James and I were to fly to Fair Oaks from Gatwick, where he had his car. By the time the formalities were over it was too late for us to fly to Fair Oaks. I lent him nearly all the money I possessed, so that he could catch the train to his home in London. He left for the train and I taxied out to fly to Brize Norton. At the holding point for the runway at this international airport, I found that I could not release the brakes. Two hours later with help from Dan-Air we managed to push the aircraft into the park. I now had sufficient money for two phone calls and possibly the train fare to London. My second telephone call was the right one and I arrived at Little Rissington by train some four hours later having been conveyed across London by James who met me and returned the loan.

Race regulations allowed for record-breaking flights during the race and it was necessary therefore to have the aircraft weighed and certificated. Having completed its overhaul with Mann Aviation at Fair Oaks, I flew it to Wisley, the home of BAC and there it was weighed. The final figure came as something of a shock and it meant yet another weight reduction had to be carried out in order to keep the aircraft within its ferry limits. From Wisley the aircraft was flown to Little Rissington in early December with the intention of carrying out some night-flying that evening. However all the miles of driving and the frustrating hours in and around the aircraft dictated an early bed.

The following morning the weather at Little Rissington proved true to form – poor visibility and the airfield a sheet of ice. We were unable to leave for Biggin Hill as planned and the following day it was necessary to slide the aircraft out of the hangar and take off straight across the airfield, as taxiing was impossible. We overflew Brize Norton and headed for Biggin Hill. Low cloud and icing conditions forced us to return to Brize Norton and we were unable to reach Biggin Hill until the day of the race.

It was necessary to check in to Biggin Hill prior to being called forward to the start at Gatwick. A very worrying factor at this time was the lack of funds which had somehow been delayed in transit and I finally received the money in dollars on 16 December 1969, after many telephone calls and several bewildered bank managers. By now several factors along the route caused a series of changes to our stopping points, the route now being Gatwick-Pisa. This last-minute change from Grossetto, an Italian Air Force base, was necessitated by work in progress on the airfield.

From Athens onwards the only available Turkish airfield was closed on Friday and it was decided to assess the alternatives on our arrival at Ankara. The route from Calcutta southwards was to be a series of alternatives dependent upon the time of day and the weather. Following the final briefing we approached the race committee with a view to bringing the start time forward by six hours. This would have allowed an overflight of the Turkish mountains in daylight. This was not allowed, but by claiming an extra three stops we managed a 1.5 hrs earlier take-off.

When Arthur G arrived at Gatwick with his camera gear, it was obvious that sheer volume as well as weight was against us. The bulk of the O2 bottle increased the problem tremendously and it was not until Catania that we finally compromised on the storage of equipment in the back. To save weight we were now down to one flying suit each with a change of underclothes and comprehensive safety equipment. Even so we were 400 lb overweight.

Following the initial delay with the early starters we had kept a wary eye on the weather over France, but it seemed all right, the worst weather being well to the east of our route. We spent the last hour filling in innumerable copies of the paperwork of travel, and I could produce twenty copies of everything at the drop of a hat.

We left at half past midnight and settled at 9,000 ft at a temperature of minus 25 degrees C. The aircraft was well up to expectations on the first leg, very cold until we placed some plastic tubing around the canopy seal, although still below its race handicap speed. The SF-260 acquired much of its lift from the canopy curvature, and therefore that formula could never truly apply to this aircraft. If the canopy area had been included in the wing area factor, the performance index would have been perfect. Our handicap speed was 178 kts, 3 kts less than the maximum speed according to the manual.

We approached the Italian coast from Nice and were startled to see flashes of electrical storms over Genoa and through the lights of the coast, rain and low cloud. We landed at Pisa in pouring rain and the turnaround was accomplished in 20 min. The weather information indicated poor weather ahead, but after t/o we climbed into low cloud, heavy rain, extreme turbulence and severe electrical activity. The aircraft began to ice almost immediately and due to the electrical activity no radio beacons could be used up ahead. With the onset of carb icing and the heavy aeroplane we were unable to climb beyond 6,000 ft. To continue would have been irresponsible as the terrain clearance a short way ahead was 10,000 ft. With disbelief we turned back for Pisa. In the heavy mental stress of turning back to Pisa an engine stoppage caused by icing altered our breathing but little as we flew the ILS. The engine started as soon as we hit the runway.

We were very despondent, sitting in the aircraft for nearly an hour to avoid getting drenched on the run to the airport buildings. We had lost the race with the weather system and a very difficult run to Athens was obviously inevitable. We could now only wait for daylight and attempt a low-level flight down the coast of Italy en route to Athens. Such a flight would entail an extra stop as we did not have the range to make Athens at low level.

Refreshed by Italian rolls and coffee, we left at dawn and caught up with the bad weather some 40 miles south as expected. By staying low and flying for the light patches we managed to keep heading south but even so, we were forced many miles out to sea.

Towards Naples fuel dictated a search for a landing field, although no contact could be established with the Italian facilities. Our flight plan destination was Crotone and although Naples airport was shut we could not make contact with any other airfield in the area.

Finally in very heavy weather we heard an American aircraft departing Grazzanise and he was able to relay our requirements. We were identified on radar and with conditions deteriorating rapidly at Grazzanise, landed as a peculiar layer of mist settled over the countryside. As we popped out of the gloom they were most surprised to see that we were a civilian aircraft, as Grazzanise is a military airfield.

We were allowed to leave the runway, and after much radio conversation, a vehicle appeared and we were instructed to fly to Capua, a local airfield. A very low-level flight following erroneous directions brought us to a lake through which the grass was visible, Capua. A landing was obviously out of the question as the whole area was waterlogged, and we returned miraculously to Grazzanise. When we were able to explain the situation, particularly as the Italian Air Force had been involved in our race planning, all the problems disappeared. Yet again this classical weather system had passed us by and lay between us and Athens.

We discussed the alternatives and decided to attempt to fly well to the south around the bottom of the system. We therefore set off for Sicily and the airfield of Catania. A relatively uneventful trip to Sicily was made up for by the problems at Catania. Being well off the air race route they had no news or information on competitors and a comic opera situation was played out for the next few hours with language problems, inability to change money and a Napoleonic telephone.

We assessed the weather ourselves as the met man spoke no English, and from the look of horror on his face as we indicated Athens as our destination, we concluded that we had lost to the weather system yet again. Had there been enough daylight left we may have attempted Athens. As it was we went downtown for a clean up and a meal.

We returned at midnight determined to wait by the weather teleprinter for its hourly discharge. We were swept up or moved from a variety of quiet corners and finally there remained only the seats between two sets of double doors, through which there was a constant stream of traffic. A comical brawl occurred in the restaurant and provided entertainment for a brief period. There was much pushing and shoving but the 'macho' shoulder-flexing combined with Italian body language, ensured that no blood was drawn.

We left at dawn dodging the storms and arriving in Athens just prior to a massive cloudburst. Two exceptionally good met officers showed quite clearly that the weather system was passing through on its way to our next stop at Ankara. We had lost again.

In company with Major Somerton-Rainer and the Naval Attaché Captain D, we left for a hotel and the funny side of the saga soon appeared after a few drinks. Had we been able to overfly Syria, we would have left immediately. Several other competitors had been grounded at Athens that night and a memorable face was that of an Australian whom I shall call 'Geelong Jack'. He was a great character and used up co-pilots at a great rate. Now on his third he was faced with a solo trip home. He had force-landed in Turkey on the way out to UK, and damaged his Cessna. Overcoming much local 'aggro', he tried to take off on the road and hit a pole. He cut a large chunk off the prop to balance the damage and ignored the hole in the wing. I do not think that the CAA were impressed.

With the very high ground between Athens and Ankara there was a chance that by routing via Nicosia we might beat the weather to Ankara. If not, there was always the questionable alternative of Diyabakir. We had to weigh the furore our arrival would undoubtedly cause. We arrived at the coast of Cyprus in lowering thick layer cloud and despite our distrust of the radio compass we allowed ourselves to be swayed, the only time along the route, and headed off too far to the south. We were letting down through the holes in the cloud but eventually underneath it got very black. Well south we found ourselves on the edge of the Troodos mountains, an area I vaguely recognized. We flew up several valleys and on the final ridge experienced the worst turbulence that any of us had ever felt in our flying careers. The aircraft was heaved around by a mighty hand and pitched end over end towards a rock face, and were it not for the sound construction of this aerobatic aircraft we would have been but a pile of splinters. Arthur hit the roof with his heavy camera but managed to contain everything, although I was far too busy trying to stay out of the scenery to be of any assistance.

We landed at Nicosia expecting the worst but it appeared that we might beat the weather into Ankara by a scant hour. Of all the many stopping places en route Athens and Ankara provided me with the most worry. We set off therefore extremely alert to the hazards ahead, but could only laugh at the ridiculousness of flying north for three hours on our way to Australia. Some 50 miles from Ankara the bad weather was visible and we descended towards Esenboga in a very flexible state of mind. Icing in the low cloud and rain beneath caused a very non-standard arrival and we appeared in true Red Arrows fashion at about 50 ft.

The airport was promptly closed for one hour because of the arrival of the President of Turkey. Arthur filmed the ceremonial arrival and we had to stop and stare as all the ambassadorial cars, their country's finest, seemingly competed in a Le Mans start for the presidential aircraft.

We refuelled and planned the next leg, the one we feared the most. Time was of the essence and it looked like that vital hour of closure would force us to stay the night, in fact two or three nights if we ever allowed ourselves to be overtaken by that weather system again.

The bad weather rolled in and I stood on the wing for twenty minutes torn by indecision, but looking at the light patches as they came and went. In order to make the height necessary for a flight over Turkey, particularly with the risk of icing, some of the weight had to go and the luxury of oxygen carried so uncomfortably from England was the choice. We gave it to the Air Attaché.

Our destination was to be Tabriz or Baghdad. Both had their own peculiar problems, but the met man interpreted his charts completely differently to us. Where it said rain, he said 'OK', where it said fog, he said 'OK' also.

We had just the minimum two hours for the flight over the mountains in daylight but a night let-down into Tabriz would have followed. The alternative was an extreme-range trip to Baghdad with a chance at better weather at the other end. We left Ankara in a spiral climb collecting ice with every brush with the cloud. A photograph from the met satellite had indicated cloud for at least 400 miles. We climbed to 13,500 ft, but the steadily increasing ice affected our artificial horizon and we faced the rest of the trip on limited panel instruments. The engine performed well, although at one stage we lost an awful lot of speed due to the very visible mass of ice on the wings and tip tanks.

The cloud thinned out and we could occasionally see the snow-capped mountains only 2,000 ft below us in places. It was a nerve-racking experience and very, very careful calculations indicated that we would have 4 gal. left at Baghdad. As we turned into Iraq the skies cleared and we flew down the Euphrates with tremendous electrical activity away to our left in Iran and over Tabriz. In order to use all the fuel in each tank they had to be drained in turn, each time causing a momentary stoppage of the engine. Mental fatigue did not increase my liking for this operation. With straining eyes we eventually saw the lights of Baghdad although the airfield was not visible amongst them.

The weather was now excellent as we had been informed by a Qantas 707 with which we had made contact while over the mountains of Turkey. Flight 174 was a great help to us with its superior radio equipment, as were two other Qantas flights we made contact with during the race. Not until they turned on the airfield lights were we able to locate the airfield and spiral down for a landing. Their main concern was that we would pay for the cost of turning them on.

We were met by the Air Attaché, his wife and family with food and hot coffee, for they believed that we were still in a great hurry. Having explained our delayed arrival, we accepted his offer of a shower and went to his house to eat our sandwiches in peace.

On our return we found that we had approximately 2 gal. on landing and that an extra charge had been levied for turning on the airfield lights. Thus it could be safely stated that the aircraft range was 750 miles, heavily laden with some considerable time spent in icing conditions.

We had provisionally planned to fly to Sharjah non-stop, but decided to route through Bahrain as the risk of another extreme-range flight was outweighed by the now lack of urgency. A lot of fog was visible down the Gulf as we arrived at dawn and the airfield was promptly closed by the bank of fog. This gave us time for breakfast although a pound a head for egg and bacon removed the early morning dew from our eyes.

We pressed on to Sharjah hoping to rectify what appeared to be dirty plugs, on landing there. Support here was superb although the plug change did not clear the mag drop. Whilst in Baghdad we had timed the route so that we would be in Calcutta just before dawn hoping to ease our passage down the Malaysian peninsular to Singapore with a daylight flight.

The flight to Karachi was uneventful, so much so that we decided to have a go at the record from Karachi to Calcutta. We left in high spirits and were airborne again from Nagpur after only 20 minutes on the ground. Dirty fuel caused some heart-stopping moments shortly after take-off, right over the middle of the town, when the engine stopped again for a brief period.

Between Nagpur and Calcutta problems with radio and navigation aids, and a wall of fog in the moonlight, caused much consternation as it appeared to be the eastern coast of India. A hurried search for topographical maps turned the cockpit into a waste paper bin and we continued with much distrust of our position. A kamikaze approach into Calcutta airport necessitated by a radar positioning of doubtful value put us on finals at 3,000 ft. We discovered later that we had set a new record for the Karachi-Calcutta run, in class C1c, and with the present state of affairs between Pakistan and India, it is unlikely ever to be broken.

The nightmare squalor of Calcutta afforded us a reasonable met forecast although a visit to the tower where the SATCO was asleep in a blanket on the console did nothing to change my opinion of the place.

We left for Rangoon with a little information from the dustbin called the met office. Having followed the schedule from Baghdad we completed the sea leg to the coast of Burma in darkness arriving at the coast just right to make full photographic use of a magnificent dawn.

For the first time Arthur was able to earn his keep, in fact use his camera at all, as until that point we had either been in bad weather or at night. The beautiful greens of the jungle, the many waterways and the never-to-be-forgotten gold of the rising sun occupied our minds as we flew for the capital of Burma.

We arrived in the circuit of Mingaladon shortly before another race aircraft and realised that the T33 jet trainers flying near the airfield were flown by Burmese student pilots. Despite clearance to land, we overshot and won a turning race with a T33 close behind us.

The weather was still excellent and we pressed on to Phuket in Thailand, a flight down the superb coastline of the peninsular with its fascinating and numerous offshore islands. It was on this leg that a comedy of coincidences set our hearts pounding again.

I was sitting in the back operating the HF radio. This, in the confined space of the rear seat, was quite a complicated business as it required the operator to wind out the HF aerial from a drum situated at his feet. The cable was withdrawn by the pull of a small drogue situated at the centre of the aircraft. Once the required length had been played out, indicated by a light in the cockpit, the handle was locked in position by a small friction nut. Whilst playing out the aerial I was conscious of the fact that the cable was banging on the rear fuselage. It must have knocked against the radio compass antenna, also strung beneath the fuselage. Pete noticed its effect on the instruments and turned round to speak to me. Whilst attempting to converse I knocked off the friction nut causing the cable to release and wind out noisily and at great speed. I attempted to stop it with my foot and broke off the handle on the drum. The noise awakened Arthur and he turned round with a start. At this point the intercom packed up and we apparently had no radio compass.

I switched off the HF and laboriously wound it in by hand as we set about finding the cause of the radio problems. Unpack the luggage compartment, find the technical manual, repack the compartment and read up on the electrical system. I tried to communicate what I wanted from the front, but in the end had to reach through and check all the fuses myself. I checked the booster pump and that was apparently not working. We were many miles out to sea, although in reach of at least a dozen islands. By the look on my face they realized that I had discovered the reason for our troubles. Arthur in turning round had knocked off a bunch of switches and by returning these to their rightful position we could actually hear each other laughing.

The coastline was now fantastically beautiful and it could only be said that Phuket is an airfield in the most beautiful setting I had ever seen. The only runway ran straight inland from the beach into low jungle hills and was rounded off by a very modern but tiny airport building. It was very hot and these gentle people were overwhelming in their desire to be of assistance. We were offered food from a large sweet jar, sandy ping pong balls I thought. They were in fact a rare delicacy, turtle eggs.

Arthur wished to stay for some photography, but with several small defects to rectify, it would be better to press on to Singapore straight away. We left with a picture of Phuket stored away in my mind as a haven to which I might one day return.

The first part of the run to Singapore was uneventful until Arthur noticed oil beginning to streak up the windshield. At this juncture the oil pressure was fluctuating badly and the oil temperature was higher than usual. Logic produced a number of reasons for these facts, the major suggestion being that the oil cap had not been replaced properly. We reduced power and attempted to run the engine as cool as possible. This was successful but the oil leak still continued. As it was mid-afternoon, the cumulo-nimbus activity was at its height. We altered course continually avoiding these towering structures. Conversation with the Malaysian radar forced us to declare an emergency and I, for one, was none to happy about the situation.

We arrived at Singapore at dusk, and completed a glide approach as the oil problems had affected the propeller and I was unable to adjust the rpm. We were met by Pete M, the Red Arrows team manager who had been sent to Singapore to organise our passage in the Far East.

I handed over a long list of defects to the aero club servicing department, and we retired to the bar for a succession of steak sandwiches. Sleep was organized for us in a nearby building as the ideal departure time for Djakarta was 4 a.m. I had apparently carried with me from England a latent flu bug and at this point had almost lost my voice. A visit to the airport doctor produced penicillin, although he tried to give me tetracycline to which I am allergic.

Fear of oversleeping, concern for the aircraft and the fact that no matter how I tried I was unable to work out the time from my watch, caused me to wander around in the early hours. I drank copious amounts of fresh lime juice and carried out the first of the engine runs at 2 a.m. The mag drop had deteriorated into a dead cut and I left them shaking their heads as to the cause. They eventually located a plug lead that was shorting out, and with a new HF radio set-up, reset brakes and a very smart engine we were ready for Indonesia.

The weather ahead of us, commonly known as the monsoon, is amongst the most revered in the world. Properly named the Inter Tropical Convergence Zone, nature's power must be seen to be understood. Towering cu/nims boil up from very low altitudes shooting sometimes to over 55,000 ft in minutes. This rapid upsurge produces extreme turbulence, very heavy icing and from its base the tropical rains, for which it is most widely known. A look at the size of the monsoon drains in Singapore and Indonesia will give one an idea of the volume of water that can be discharged in seconds from an active cloud. In daylight these colossal towers stand out, so that one can sometimes choose a course between them. Near dawn their activity is at a minimum and it is thus the time at which the convergence zone should be penetrated. Rarely more than 120 miles wide this band of weather lay between us and Djakarta.

The very essence of the Air Race for us was to begin in Singapore and prior to our departure in Indonesia we were shown a telegram from the only solo female pilot in the race, Miss Sheila Scott. She had attempted the long flight from Singapore to Darwin. This non-stop route over Borneo took her well north of the route followed by the shorter range aircraft. After a very harrowing flight she eventually landed at Makasser, the capital of the Celebes, some 11 hrs after leaving Singapore. She was now stuck on the ground there, having had severe radio trouble, and from her telegram, was in desperate need of assistance. Behind us were only a few more race aircraft, and for us the race had deteriorated into a flight of maximum safety with only sufficient urgency to get us to Adelaide by 29 December 1969, where the second half of the Race began. It was now 23/24 December.

We were asked therefore if we would consider going to Makasser and if necessary escorting her to Darwin. This would involve flying 1,000 miles from our planned route, and to land at Makasser we would need the permission of the Indonesian authorities. In view of the communications time lag, we tried to confirm whether she was still in Makasser. This proved impossible in Singapore, but was a possibility from Djakarta. We decided therefore to bypass our scheduled stop of Semerang and fly to Djakarta. There we hoped to get permission for Makasser and confirm Sheila Scott's location at the airfield. When dawn broke, a look behind us showed us that we had passed through the ITCZ and we made Djakarta untroubled. The decision we had hoped to make at Djakarta was impossible, as communication with Makasser would take two hours. However, we did get permission to fly to Makasser should we require it and the Indonesian authorities were incredibly helpful in organizing the information to be passed to Surabaya, an airfield some three hours away.

We planned to overfly Surabaya en route to Bali and when in the vicinity of Surabaya we could radio for the information. If she was still at Makasser, we would land and refuel before flying to her help. Surabaya came up loud and clear with a message for us and we landed prior to a trip that we would never forget.

Arthur disposed of the last of our fresh lime juice from Singapore, having accepted the offer of some local jungle juice. To Pete and I this was akin to sabotage.

The flight to Makasser required some very accurate navigation as it was a sea leg with no diversions whatsoever for our short-range aircraft. With luck the second crossing of the ITCZ would be made midway in the flight and we could therefore fly through the rain at low altitude without the fear of finding a hard-centred cloud. Just beyond the point of no return, the expected deterioration occurred and we were flying at 200 ft in heavy rain. A despairing check of our fuel reaffirmed that we must go on as to return was impossible.

Our radio compass picked up Makasser, although we knew from

previous experience that it must be treated with suspicion in view of all the electrical activity. We were in an area of many coral atolls, the kind you see in cartoons, none of which were of any use for navigation. The ITCZ proved to be 120 miles wide and Makasser came into view as the visibility started to improve.

The rain abated and in a 200 ft cloud base we skirted the town for the airfield of Hassanuddin, some 15 miles to the north. The airfield appeared in the midst of the flooded landscape of rice field agriculture, and as we turned in for landing we could see the Comanche of Miss Sheila Scott. When we were able to view the terrain around the airfield as the low cloud lifted, it took on quite a forbidding appearance.

The facilities at the airfield were not great, but the local air force commander and his staff were very friendly and intent on doing all they could to help us. Sheila had been aided by a local American missionary by the name of Maury B. He had stayed with her in those desperate hours, while she had tried to continue with the race. I do not think that his training had prepared him for a personality such as Sheila's, and I am sure that we provided a friendly opportunity for him to disengage.

The change from the speed and bustle of the air race to the pleasant Indonesian lethargy took much adjustment, but we were able to busy ourselves with flying problems, photography and cross-checking local knowledge on the ITCZ.

A Garuda Airlines Electra disgorged its load of Auri officers and several of them came over to speak to us. We were able to confirm the position of the ITCZ, and were advised to penetrate it as early as possible. The air force mechanics were still working on Sheila's aircraft and they borrowed our supply of fuses and radio parts. She was still unsure of the serviceability of some of her radio equipment, and we could not find out what work the mechanics had done. It was apparent that she had landed with her HF antenna still trailed, and hopefully this was the cause of her problems. We assumed therefore, that for the flight to Kupang, we would have little radio contact and planned on a formation flight for the next two legs.

The nearest hotel lay in the capital town of Makasser some 20 miles away, but before leaving we were able to pay for a night guard on the aircraft as hundreds of children and onlookers were our constant companions whilst we were there. We left for a very bouncy ride into Makasser arriving at supposedly the best hotel in town. We were very tired and not ready to be tempted by some of the local dishes. Surprisingly the bar was full of English and American engineers. We booked an early call for 4 a.m. intending to be airborne 30 minutes before sunrise. The barefooted staff, however, only left our breakfast outside the rooms and I awoke at 4.15 a.m. I woke the others but regretfully we were late, very late leaving the hotel and unable to take off until about an hour after sunrise. Sheila had a mind of her own and did not readily accept the urgency we felt, nor would she countenance one of us flying with her to help with the formation work. I had briefed Sheila on the requirements of formation flight and we set up both the VHF and HF radios so that we could communicate if the systems worked. Her aircraft had been refuelled 'in error' and probably had in excess of 10 hrs fuel at take-off.

The Marchetti was considerably faster than the Commanche, and she therefore took off first in order to save time. The weather was reasonable and we climbed to 9,000 ft. We approached the island of Flores and Arthur was able to photograph her aircraft against the background of some active volcanoes. Maumere, our only alternate airfield, was clearly in view as we crossed Flores and set our watches for accurate timing from the coast for the hour-long flight over the sea to Kupang. The clouds were beginning to build up ahead and several alterations to course were made to keep clear of them. Some 90 miles from Kupang we were forced to descend, eventually reaching 200 ft over the sea, in rain. The visibility was now deteriorating and I descended to sea level to accurately set the altimeters.

Kupang lies at the western end of the island of Timor on some fairly low-lying ground. Beyond it lies the Timor Sea and the western coast of Australia. If we did not sight land after our 1hr 10min flight, then we would have to turn back for the island chain and Flores. It is very difficult to estimate visibility in these conditions as the sea disturbed by heavy rain offers no horizon. Forward visibility in rain in the Marchetti is very poor and so we could only guess at 1,000 yds.

No sign of land appeared although we should have been able to see the high ground of Timor to our left. This fact was most disturbing and we had to assume that we had been blown off course. After one hour and eleven minutes I called to Sheila and we reversed our direction and flew northwards for the island chain and Maumere. There was no let-up, and the weather deteriorated even further. We assumed that we had been well to the right of our intended track on the way to Kupang, and therefore corrected carefully in estimating a course for Maumere. In terrible visibility Sheila lost contact with us twice, but three pairs of eyes are better than one and we were able to locate her again. She was having trouble with formation anyway and in effect we were formating backwards on her although she did not know it.

When we estimated that there were a few minutes to run to the coast, we were down to 50 ft in torrential rain. Pete was urgently speaking of contacting the land anytime now, and his strangled shout of coast ahead, breakers, was right on. I saw the breakers and simultaneously turned left, calling Sheila to climb immediately. The sheer rock face rising from the sea had shown the visibility to be about 200 yds. What followed in the next minutes will remain forever fixed in our minds.

Arthur in the back seat had a clearer view ahead through the bubble of the canopy then either Peter or I, and the rapid alterations to course as the fingers of the rock appeared ahead, say a lot for his courage and nerve. The workload in the front was now extreme, but we were able to contact Sheila Scott and were overjoyed to hear that she was at 7,500 feet. I advised her to return to Makasser and informed her of our intention to try and make Maumere.

We were still unsure that the land was the main island of Flores, as the visibility precluded any map-reading at all. We were forced lower and lower and had to make two desperate circles out to sea and away from looming obstacles. This would have been beyond the capabilities of a solo pilot for it needed rapid information on aircraft heading, speed and height. These turns so unnerved us that a ditching was imminent.

We had one hour and fifteen minutes fuel remaining at this stage, insufficient to fly all the way round Flores assuming that this land was Flores. Sheila Scott had many hours fuel left, and therefore was right to climb. Fatefully the rain abated a little, and we flew into a clearer area alongside a small bay. Hoping that this was the beginning of a general clearance we flew on straight into the bad weather again. It would have been suicide to continue, we therefore reversed to the beach that I had seen. We had been able to make out a house close to the beach and so the area was obviously inhabited.

There was very little time to plan the landing as the black clouds we had just left were racing towards our beach, blotting out the landscape as they did so. We made one run down the beach a few feet above the sand, picking a touchdown point and checking for any obstacles that might damage the aircraft. A curving approach would allow us little room for error and there appeared to be about 250 yards of reasonable flat surface. One small bush in the vegetation alongside the sand strip gave us an aiming point, ideally some 20 yards beyond it. We turned downwind with Arthur completing the frantic activity that had been necessary for him since we had turned back for a landing. In those few minutes he had packed the many rolls of valuable film in polythene bags, blown up the bags and stowed them in the leg pockets of his flying suit. He had dug out the shoulder harness for the two front seats, a far more difficult task than it appears, and had then stowed all the heavy equipment around himself, as his only security was a lap strap.

We turned in for a landing just inside the high cliffs limiting the bay, and I remember feeling relatively unconcerned, just mentally going over the requirements for a landing such as this. I had time to notice that the run was relatively smooth, if narrow and that a small grass hut was off to one side of the 'runway'. We touched down on target and I had a mental argument with myself as I considered the effects of a steerable nosewheel in soft sand. Nothing untoward was noticed initially and we seemed to run on for an age; fortunately the sand was reasonably firm. Suddenly a large driftwood tree was seen some yards ahead, which I cannot remember seeing as we flew down the beach. There was no room to pass it on either side, we could only hope to stop. I tried full brake and the aircraft slewed to the left. I now felt the effects of the soft sand on the nosewheel and was critically aware that we were about to lose it unless I could keep the aircraft straight. The pressure on the rudders forced me against the shoulder harness, which as luck would have it I had adjusted exceptionally tightly. The aircraft came to an abrupt halt some 15 to

20 feet from the log, about 20 degrees off line. Everything was switched off and apart from a few grunts I remember little being said.

A feeling of intense disgust at being responsible for placing us seemingly forever on an unknown beach clouded my mind. Peter and I made as to get out, as a few natives were appearing on the scene. Arthur, forever the professional, called us back and said, 'Hang on a minute, mate, I'm not going to miss this.' He was actually taking pictures before our feet touched the ground. The first group of natives arrived at the aircraft as we were putting on our anoraks, as the rain was now upon us.

The landscape disappeared and we wandered or were led into a grass hut on the edge of the jungle. We were saturated before we reached the hut, but at least the population appeared extremely friendly. They prepared a place for us to sit down and amidst a few laughs as the funny side struck us, we sat down to discuss the problems.

No one spoke English, and we were obviously many miles from civilisation, although there was that house some miles back along the coast. As bright ideas came to us we said 'telephone, house', made faces, but only succeeded in making ourselves laugh at their uncomprehending looks. Arthur set about drawing a telephone, and then a house, on the RAF sick bag, our only dry paper, but this too achieved nothing. We then decided to try to communicate the need for an official, and settled for the doctor. This they understood and changed it into pastor, indicating his location by pointing along the coast. We discussed where we might be and mentioned Maumere in the course of the discussion. Surprise, surprise, a bright boy from the front row repeated Maumere, and pointed to the north-east. By pointing in the opposite direction we were able to tie down the location of Maumere and that it was in kilometres four hands and four fingers away. He repeated the word Leilo which we later found to be a town along the coast.

We tried to communicate our need to get to Maumere but eventually settled for the pastor who was apparently much closer. I was sure by this time that the aircraft could be flown out, but intended to check the undercarriage before making a decision.

Arthur was in a photographer's Utopia and so Peter volunteered to go to the pastor. He eventually left with a guide for a round trip of some six miles through very difficult terrain. We returned to the aircraft and collected our immediate needs. The aircraft had sunk fairly well into the sand, and due to its final swing, the tyres and oleo legs were under some strain. I therefore set about digging them out with a long piece of wood and encouraged the locals to follow my example. As the crowd was increasing at a fair rate, I was able to get enough manpower to push the SF 260 out of the holes so that I could check the undercarriage. It appeared serviceable, the undercarriage being unmarked. The propeller tip had been sand blasted, and I saw sand in the air intake, mentally noting that it must be cleared before flight, that is if it were ever to fly again.

As the natives stood around and watched us, I noticed that they were using large green leaves as umbrellas, which later turned out to be banana leaves. I borrowed one, laid it in the sand and jumped on it. I could not get my foot or heel through the fibres. When Arthur realised what I had in mind he was aghast, but he was still able to remind me that Ross and Keith Smith in very similar circumstances had laid a runway some fifty years previously on their epic flight.

I searched for a better material for a runway surface, but it would obviously need to be reasonably soft or the aircraft stood a chance of being damaged. Looking at the problem showed me that it would take many hours to lay a runway of sufficient length with banana leaves. We planned on a morning take-off and considered our food and water supplies, as for us the local produce was obviously suspect.

I continued to organise the labour force, and about 50 yards of banana leaves was laid by this time. The local headman, who was also the policeman, had appeared to take control. He had a sort of uniform and with the aid of a large stick he was able to induce them to work for us. Shortly afterwards a youth appeared on a very mangy horse, and with the aid of his very small amount of English we were told that he was the headman's son. He had with him a note, in fact, the note that we had originally written in the hope that it could be taken to somebody who spoke English. He had met up with Peter along the trail, been given the note and brought it to us. We prevailed upon him to continue to the town and he confirmed that Leilo was nearer than Maumere.

Many more people appeared, in fact, they could be seen appearing over the rocks at either end of the bay in a steady steam. Several wore European clothes and were capable of the odd word of English. Our original request for a doctor had brought a nun, believing we were injured. She spoke no English and was soon on her way when she realised we were not injured. She was followed by the headman's wife who appeared with an ancient kettle containing tea or coffee or both, and a plastic bag full of sandwiches.

Arthur's fears for his constitution caused a charade in which he filled his cup with drugs under the guise that it was sugar. Their kindness was extreme, but the local bread and its contents were bitten in public and discarded in secrecy.

Luckily we could both busy ourselves with the tasks in hand. I brought out our search and rescue beacon, knowing full well that no search aircraft would reach us for many hours although there was a chance that a routine flight might pick up our signals. We discussed using the HF radio and withdrew the aerial, raising it high on a long bamboo pole. In order to get sufficient power for the radio, I restarted the engine, but the sight of a single native clasping firmly the bamboo pole surrounded by his admiring friends is a picture I will treasure.

No contact was possible on the radio so we returned to the task of building the runway. Peter, by this time had reappeared with the pastor who by chance was in the area. It must be remembered that the island is almost totally Roman Catholic and that it was Christmas Day. When I saw the rate of progress with the banana leaves I realised what a long job it was going to be. We still had to turn the aircraft around, as the take-off would have to be carried out in the opposite direction to that of the landing. Whilst clearing the sand off one of the many piles of coconut husks I saw what I believed to be a bush with some very large fern-like branches. I requested some of these from the headman, and with much shouting I was eventually presented with a few branches.

They were coconut palms, each branch being 5 to 10 feet tall, the fronds being far tougher than the banana leaves. Only the top 5 or 6 feet would be useable for the runway, as the stem was as thick as a man's arm at the base. This was obviously what was required, and I urged them all to collect these branches for me. There was initial reluctance, the reasons for which I did not discover until later. The bush I had seen was in actual fact the top of a palm tree some 80 feet high. However the main part of the palm was invisible, being in a hollow at the back of the beach. Evidently climbing these trees when they are wet can be quite dangerous, besides which, it was very tiring work.

The branches continued to appear and when we had reached what I estimated to be 230 yards, there was a lull in the proceedings. There were many piles of driftwood to be removed and I had to interlock the branches and realign the runway many times. The crowd was now some 500 strong although only about 5 per cent were actually working. My conviction that a take-off was possible got stronger as did my concern for the aircraft, which was now hemmed in by this dense mass of people. I tried desperately to keep them away from the delicate parts of the aircraft, and enlisted the aid of some of the more militant locals.

The local madman appeared on the scene and amused the crowd for a while. Not a time for philosophising, but Peter and I discussed how happy the people appeared, and how this one unfortunate was accepted and tolerated without interference. Such an existence would be impossible in our society, yet from his appearance he was quite happy.

Arthur had been unable to find his waterproof and was now feeling the cold through being soaked for so long. I unpacked our space blanket, a large sheet of tin foil which has the feel of polythene. It was designed for such an occasion as this, and wrapped in his metal blanket he warmed up rapidly, followed wherever he went by an awed crowd.

Pete and I looked at the filter and decided it would have to be removed and examined. We had no Phillips screwdriver with us, but it had to be removed. With great care we extracted the screws knowing that one slip could put us in a very difficult position. My Swiss Army knife did the trick, and is a prized possession even to this day. The filter was dirty and a little sand had penetrated it. It would need a clean. We searched round for some way in which to carry this out. A hole was made in the sand underneath a tip tank and borrowing the space blanket from Arthur, we laid the blanket in the hole. Fuel was drained from the tip tank providing an ideal bath for the filter, which was refitted very carefully.

A few coconut fibre sacks had been found and my request for more, in fact enough for the runway, brought peals of laughter from Arthur. 'It has only taken them twenty years to make those,' he said. However there were sufficient to manoeuvre the aircraft and with many willing helpers I set about turning it around. There was only room for four or five on each tip tank and I had to be extremely careful to prevent them from pushing and pulling in the wrong places and irrevocably damaging the aircraft.

We managed to turn it round without using up more valuable runway space, but I could not quite align the aircraft with the line of vegetation we had laid. Pete and I paced the strip several times and discussed the length of a pace. Having experience of this task some years previously, we were able to conclude that we were still in need of at least another 100 yards. Book figures for the aircraft show a minimum requirement of 300 yards, which we just about had, and then the undulations of the beach became excessive. A fully loaded take-off was out of the question, and so Pete and Arthur and all the equipment would have to be removed for the flight.

The weather this time had improved although there were still clouds over the high ground behind us. The island of Flores has an area in the centre of it which is considerably higher than the peaks which we could see behind us, and although we had identified our position there was still some debate as to the weather over Maumere.

The final burst of energy from the tree climbers had given us our 325 yards of runway. Apart from a few sweets, we had not eaten a proper meal since Singapore. We were suddenly hungry and very thirsty. Coconut palms, a ready drink we thought. It raised a laugh as Peter recalled the words of the Survival Manual. In such a situation, send a native up a tree for a coconut. No sooner said than done, and we were presented with a large green melon-sized object. A machete was used with medical precision and we had about a gallon of superb liquid. When we had drunk our fill the nut was opened and a piece of the outer skin used like a flint knife to scrape the white meat for us to eat. It was delicious.

When we mentioned our coconut meal to the Airport Manager at Maumere, he was most concerned. Evidently malaria is prevalent on the island, caught mostly from coconuts and mangoes, virtually the basis of their diet. We were grateful for Paludrin.

Although I was convinced that a take-off was possible, this conviction was diluted somewhat as the possibility drew near. We had been working for nearly eight hours and there seemed no reason to hold until morning. The adrenalin challenge was keeping us all going. Several more officials had appeared, including a policeman from the town of Leilo and a local official of unknown background.

The equipment was unpacked and the aircraft made ready for departure. I was concerned for the security of our possessions, for immediately they were placed on the ground away from the aircraft, they disappeared under a mass of bodies and legs. It is refreshing to note that throughout not one item vanished or was even remotely borrowed, such was their character.

Peter was to remain at the take-off point and marshal the resources there, whilst Arthur repaired to the end of the strip clutching his camera. As a final gesture, I unpacked the Wilkinson survival machete and told him to keep it handy in case the take-off was a failure. The strip was barely 12 feet wide and should one wheel enter the soft sand it was doubtful that I would get airborne. Should the take-off look like failing I determined to go into the sea rather than the trees.

I checked the aircraft over and started up, having sign languaged six islanders to be ready at each tip tank to release me at the drop of my hand. Pete supervised, and I needed a warm engine, although I could not afford to do a full run-up in view of the sand and the risk of lifting up the leaves into the propeller.

As I opened up the power, the nose wheel sank through the leaves and the prop tip turned green as it chopped up the vegetation. I throttled right back and conferred with Peter. For me to get the nose wheel out he would need to hang on to the tail, reducing the load on the nose wheel as much as possible. I applied the power slowly and must have finally finished up at full power. Nothing was happening, we were still in the hole. Then it happened, the aircraft shot forward and I was on my way, unprepared, as I did not intend to commence my run like this. The 260 was almost ready to go but I had no flap down – flap, the very thing that could reduce my take-off run. I dared not brake for fear of leaving the strip, besides which we would probably have to rebuild the strip all over again. Using large lumps of coarse rudder, no brake please, to keep on the strip, the 260 was accelerating far better than I had expected and so I continued, with my hand on the flap switch, hoping that the electrics would give me some flap before I reached the end. The run was remarkably smooth, although the 260 decelerated noticeably in the bigger undulations of the beach. I dared not try and lift off too early, but I had to reduce the load on the nose wheel. The end of the strip came up and we were still not airborne and I probably bounced just once on a slight rise in the beginning of the dunes. I tried to re-assess my thoughts during the run, I have no idea why such a thought process should appear at such a time, but they were discarded in my concern for what lay over the mountains.

I circled over the beach whilst Peter and Arthur tried to keep the large crowd away from the strip in case I had to return. I left the gear down for fear that it may have been damaged, with the hope that we might raise it just once on the trip to Darwin next day. The high centre of the island was soon cleared and I picked up Maumere almost immediately. There is no radio communication with the ground in this part of the world, and so I flew up the runway to warn of my arrival. I approached the strip, a grass one cut into the hillside, and landed to be greeted by the airport manager, who followed me up the strip in his jeep. He spoke excellent English, but was speechless when I explained the situation.

I questioned the availability of communication facilities, for there was an urgent need to get the word out that we were safe. I asked for the 260 to be refuelled and this was done from a pile of drums alongside the runway. A very young Indonesian air force officer appeared on his motorcycle and through Mr Tomaru, the airport manager, I was able to learn that there was a total communication failure on the island. I could tell no one of our position, and they did not expect to repair it until the next morning.

I inquired about my friends who were faced with a long climb off the beach, and asked for a vehicle to go and fetch them. Whilst waiting for the transport, I thoroughly checked the undercarriage and cleaned off all the sand. There was no sign to indicate that it had endured anything other than normal usage.

I expected to have to stay overnight with the 260, but Mr Tomaru insisted that we enjoy the hospitality of his house nearby. He organised a guard for the aircraft and I paid him there and then.

When his sons returned, we went back to the house for a drink. I showed my concern for the whereabouts of Peter and Arthur, but we evidently had to call in at the police station before anything could happen.

This was a long-winded business and I finally got away in a jeep to search for them at about 2130. We had landed in the bay at 0820 and I had arrived at Maumere at 1640.

The road, a very loose description, climbed into the jungle-clad slopes and the next vehicle we saw was a jeep carrying Peter and Arthur and all our gear. The natives had accompanied them and even the tiniest bit of useless equipment had been lovingly cared for. We gave away all but the absolutely vital pieces, and I realised that the survival knife that I had signed for was also a 'lost' item. I did not think that 'given to native on beach' would be an acceptable explanation for its loss.

We returned to Mr Tomaru's house for a slice of Christmas cake and some troubled sleep in the bedroom from which he had removed his sons. We planned an early start for Darwin, as this was the leg that had always concerned me most, and it was becoming very much the last hurdle for us.

We awoke early and donned some very wet clothing. Before going to bed we had attempted to wash the few items of clothing that we possessed, but I am afraid that the humidity of Flores had not allowed them to dry. We were driven across to the 260, and with a growing audience, repacked the aircraft. It was checked over very carefully, and we were meticulous about the fuel drains as the bulk fuel supplies appeared to have been in situ for a long time.

We made our goodbyes and with the weather already starting to build, we climbed away circumventing a 5,000 ft hill already enveloped in cloud. Our concern for the take-off and the possible conditions ahead slowed our reactions and it was Arthur that noticed that the gear was not retracting properly. This alone would have been enough for we were not gaining speed readily, even allowing for the half-retracted gear. We must obviously return to Maumere and with very heavy hearts we turned for the airfield. At this juncture all the pressure instruments went haywire and we lost both altimeters and, more important, our airspeed indicator. Silence showed the mental turmoil as we considered the reasons for the

253

failures and we were now faced with an overweight landing without instruments onto a small grass strip.

The landing was uneventful and we left the 260 to look at the manuals. I took a deep breath and set about searching for the cause of our troubles. We scanned the technical manuals and removed the inspection hatches with the thought that we were faced with major technical problems. We had very few tools, but the tool kit from a Japanese motorcycle looked like being our only other source of supply.

On considering the instrument problem I remembered a similar incident before leaving England. I said that I believed that there was an airspeed switch in the undercarriage system, and this was seized upon as the reason for the failure. We checked all the micro-switches and Peter having removed the front seat, disconnected the altimeter to blow out the static system. We were very happy to see water spurting out from the vent holes and after many minutes blowing, water was still being expelled.

With new-found energy the 260 was made ready for take-off and we were not to learn until later that there was no airspeed switch in the system, although it appears that some obscure electrical defect, through the saturation that the 260 received on the beach, was the cause of our troubles. We now needed fuel, but on looking at the weather building to the east decided to risk it and fly to Kupang. Remember we did not have the comfort of any weather information. The fuel operator could not arrive at the airfield for at least thirty minutes and this wait would have been intolerable.

We left for Kupang and I for one felt that any more problems would finish me. I did not enjoy the flight to Kupang, for the intense mental activity of the past two days had taken its toll. I was so drained that my immense fear of sharks never even surfaced, and this was the leg that I dreaded. But our fears were groundless as Kupang came up on the nose. The refuel was quick and with the worst weather apparently behind us, we left for Darwin.

On leaving Maumere finally, Peter had contacted Darwin on our HF radio. On hearing all the chatter he realised that they were discussing us. Darwin was very pleased to hear from us and the search was called off although we continued to make contact on the HF until we were approaching the city. We realised as we coasted in to Australia that our one topic of conversation in the UK about this area had been sharks, and yet from Maumere I do not remember giving it a second thought.

On landing we were met by the press and the RAAF Station Commander who gave us the details of our epic as released to the outside world. The local Aero Club were very kind, and we made up for the lack of food and water over the last two days. How about a plate of Christmas pudding and custard in a temperature of 90°F?

We decided to take it easy across Australia, and planned on a night stop in Alice Springs. There was little energy for talking, even though strong winds forced a fuel stop in Tennant Creek. I was relegated to the back seat, but paranoia kept me surfacing from bad dreams of being lost, in an instant alert mode. I had asked that we follow the road south out of Darwin, even though the VOR radial departed from this. My instant awake mode started me panicking when I saw that the road had disappeared. 'Shut the hell up', was to calm my overworked reflexes.

Alice Springs was reached after dark and our stop was made memorable by the hospitality we received from the Aero Club and from the people of Alice. The three of us reckoned that the steaks were the largest we had ever seen, after which we went to sleep in a proper bed for the first time since Athens. This was indeed joy everlasting.

To reach Adelaide we had to refuel in Leigh Creek, and with an 0800 start we hoped to be in Adelaide after lunch. It was an enjoyable run, the changes of the countryside being unforgettable. The great salt lakes, mushrooming mining sites and the single railway kept us occupied. We stayed for an extra trip at Leigh Creek to complete Arthur's photographic requirements, but were far happier in the cool of 7,000 ft than the temperature on the ground.

Adelaide Parrafield is a very busy civil airfield, but as we turned in for landing we realised that the crowd on the ground was waiting for us. They parked us very close to the public enclosure and we were immediately engulfed by well-wishers and cameramen.

We were very happy to have made it to the end of the first part of the race, although the mental battering seemed a high price to pay. All we wanted now was an air-conditioned room and the chance for a relaxing swim. The organisers bundled us off downtown to an excellent motel. We had intended to buy clothing in Australia, and on our original schedule this would have been before Christmas. However, it was now a holiday period and all the shops were shut. With apologies, we were therefore restricted to the clothing we stood up in. We borrowed swimsuits and wallowed for a few hours in the restful rays of the sun. Arthur already had a constant stream of telephone calls over his film and it was therefore decided that he should return to UK immediately. He managed to get on a flight the next morning, and by 7 a.m. was en route to Sydney.

There was a great deal to be done to the aircraft and interspersed with changing to less pricey accommodation, we spent most of our time at the airfield. The 260 was washed and cleaned, and emptied of much of the unwanted gear and two items of radio equipment that did not function in Australia.

We made many friends, but after the intensity of the last days, inactivity was hard to accept. After the first glorious days the weather became very English, and without the transport loaned to us by British Leyland Australia, we would have gone mad.

Memories of the Marathon were still clear in the minds of many Aussies, and in many ways it was almost as if we had never left. The Race restart was delayed by bad weather and the guesstimate was that it would be delayed for at least another day.

With only a reasonable forecast for Griffith, the race was restarted a day later. We were none too happy about our handicap, because instead of improving our position in relation to other aircraft, we were now worse off, in fact we were sixth from last to start. This was laughable in view of all the expensive machinery around us. We had a good store of maps, a rarity it seemed and planned a map-reading exercise to Griffith. We took off, stayed low and then commenced a high-speed climb to our best altitude. There were two other aircraft taking off within seconds of us and we were amazed to see them disappearing, one to the left and the other to the right. So much for handicaps.

We held our course intent on not losing a second by being off track. Some time later the aircraft to the right crossed over us and flew out of sight. So much for navigation, but then again they were probably following radio aids towards Griffith.

It was very hollow laughter that filled the cockpit as bad weather again forced us to descend until we were back in the groove at 200 ft, in poor visibility and rain. Although an instrument trip would have been quite acceptable to Griffith, all competitors were warned that this would consume a lot of time at Griffith itself.

For about an hour there were very few features by which to navigate, the terrain being salt flats and scrubland, criss-crossed by many tracks. When one remembers how many race craft were using the radio, it can be imagined how impossible communications became. The weather remained as bad as ever and we picked up a pinpoint some 60 miles from Griffith. We managed to call at 60 miles, although by now all thoughts of controlled radio com-munication had been discarded. There were aircraft circling to the north and south of the field waiting to get descent clearance, and at two miles from the field an attempt was made by the authorities to close it in view of the weather deterioration. From the sheer collision risk alone we got down as low as we could and flashed across the field for a fighter-type approach and landing. The weather had meant that we were the only aircraft over the field and we taxied through the mud to the hundreds of parked cars at the control point. To continue was out of the question and the race was held at Griffith for 24 hours, which subsequently turned into 48 hours as the weather worsened.

We learned that several aircraft had been diverted, including Sheila Scott. The leading Bonanza had run out of fuel and was very sick in a field some miles away, although the crew were uninjured in this performance. Years of training had taught us to sit back and wait whilst others panicked for hotel accommodation; we resigned ourselves to a night in the 260. Local families eventually accepted the overflow, and we were fostered to a family who were very proud of their country.

They were very kind and offered an interesting insight into the social fabric of Australia. They asked what we wanted to drink and seeing a lemon tree in the garden we requested fresh lemons. They were non-plussed by this as they never thought of using the fruit this way, preferring the ever-present Coke or other canned drinks.

Griffith is the garden of Australia being in the Murray-Murrumbigee irrigation area. They grow virtually everything, even to rice and grapes. Living off the land was not our hosts' routine, for they favoured tinned or prepared foods, most strange.

In some ways it helped to understand the itinerant nature of the Australian work ethic. The man of the house would work at several jobs, even though he could have committed himself and stayed in one place. They were all happy to go north for work in the sugar cane industry, earn enough to move on and then travel to another short-term job. All of these had had sporting activities associated with them, and the house was filled with sporting equipment.

We met up with a co-competitor from the London-Sydney Marathon, Bruce Hodgson, who took us around in his high-performance truck. We repaid him with a flight in the 260 which he remembered well when our paths crossed 25 years later during the re-run of the Sydney and Mexico events. The restart for the short leg over the Australian Alps was noticeable only for the ruggedness of the terrain and the ridiculous handicap, even worse than the last one. Within one minute from take-off we were overtaken by another competitor with a speed at least 30 kts in excess of ours.

We ran to Sydney in the company of at least six other aircraft and on crossing the finishing line were ordered to circle the airfield. It was like Hyde Park Corner in three dimensions. There were massive crowds on the ground, and after a little formation with a colleague in an Islander we were called in to land. There were many friends to meet us, too many, as it was impossible to speak to them all.

However, we had done it, the aircraft had been delivered in excellent condition and unmarked. It had not been ill-used and never once flown outside its limitations. It stood the test well and I for one would buy one.

Our stay in Sydney was accomplished at high speed as there was much to be done. With the help of Evan Green the publicity head of British Leyland Australia, who provided an Aussie version of the Austin 1100, we were able to go for a day to the shack of Gelignite Jack Murray, on the Hawkesbury river at Sackville. He was an unforgettable character, as was our stay with him.

I attempted to again fly the para-sail contraption towed behind his very powerful motorboat. I had flown it previously (1968), but it had been in several scrapes since then and was in need of careful scrutiny. The mast and 'Jesus nut' were bent and after a fashion were straightened for my flight. In the narrow confines of the river, I spent a very harrowing ten minutes trying not to kill myself. Having briefed Jack to please have some response to my hand signals, I tried to gently ease it into the air. It snapped off the water into a steep climb, and even with my arms jammed between the 'A' frame supports, I could not control its oscillations. Each movement of the pitch control caused a massive change, and I knew that if the rope broke, it would be disastrous. I avoided hitting the water at the end of the dive phase, but the phugoid just got bigger. The watchers in the boat were enjoying my discomfort, not knowing that it was building up to a serious accident. I could not wave as agreed as the loads were too great for me to relinquish my grip for a second. I needed to strike the water at a survivable angle and hope to either break the rope, or cause them to cut the power. The immense buoyancy of the floats made the impact less, and they must have recognised the white face enough to cut the power. With so little to see in the craft, it is hard to understand why its flying characteristics had changed so much.

The trip home was something of an anticlimax and it was only when we reached the UK that we realised the massive publicity that had followed us to the beach. Christmas news is often scarce, and as the Chief of the Air Staff wrote in his letter, 'Now that the hyperbole is over, I wish to thank you for your efforts and the contribution to the professionalism and good name of the Royal Air Force.'

Chapter IX

THE 1970 LONDON-MEXICO was a natural follow-on for us, but it developed with less fuss as BMC offered us a 'works' drive as a consequence of the results of our last two events.

It was to be the launch date for the Range Rover and that was the planned vehicle for our entry. The Rally, organised through the *Daily Mirror* newspaper, coincided with the World Cup Soccer Finals, and properly titled was The London-Mexico World Cup Rally. It was to be longer and harder than the London-Sydney.

Our initial meetings with the competition department in Abingdon looked at what we could contribute in the way of assistance. Peter Browning was still the boss at that time, thus he was well aware of much of the input that we could bring to the event for BMC. Outside partial sponsorship was determined to be a necessity, and in the end we associated with *Autocar* for our entry.

The high-altitude chamber at Farnborough was made available for all the BMC crews, for the Andes were going to take the Rally to over 16,000 ft. Whilst hypoxia was an unknown for most, the general response was indifference. Apart from the headaches, most crews got through the Andes without feeling that altitude training was necessary.

We were given two tasks to perform in view of our aviation expertise. First, organise air support with the idea that parts would be stockpiled in South America. The same aircraft would then roll up the pre-positioned mechanics as the Rally went through, as it were, collecting parts and people and taking them to the finish in Mexico City. British Caledonian was receptive to the idea, especially as the Red Arrows had collaborated in previous advertising ventures.

They provided a Britannia at an excellent price, which took all the spares to South America, and returned crews and equipment to UK after the event. I signed a cheque for many thousands of pounds on behalf of BMC, an enormous sum of money for a lowly Flight Lieutenant, and we carried the BCal logo on our car.

The Royal Air Force supported our entry, although there was some sour grapes from the official RAF motorsports entry. We were given extra leave and dovetailed all the work into the relaxed time at the end of the display season.

As the Rally format was still the continuous one, a reliable food supply was a must. The Royal Navy were very helpful in giving us assault rations. They were light in weight and more used by us than the other BMC, now BLMH, crews. The change to British Leyland Motor Holdings (BLMH) started the decline of the once proud Abingdon Competition Department. Lord Stokes sought amalgamation of the various marques and having finally created a monolith, bigness eventually became unfashionable.

Our involvement this time was more fundamental and we carried out many tasks for the department. I completed hours of tyre testing, generally driving around L Rissington through the weekend: 500 miles around the perimeter track through the night, change tyres and 500 miles the other way.

Fatigue for aircrews was not something that was well researched and as the Rally was going to be a severe physical test, a fully instrumented drive around Kemble airfield was considered, to produce data on human fatigue. Kemble was chosen as it was the Red Arrows home base, unused at weekends, and it possessed large run-off areas from the perimeter track. Planning was well advanced when the negatives from the medical fraternity surfaced, enough to cause the powers-that-be to have second thoughts.

By now it was known that the Range Rover would not be ready for the event and so we had switched to the Maxi, very much an unknown quantity. Testing at the Fighting Vehicles Research Establishment (FVRE) in Bagshot, showed up many deficiencies in the Maxi, which the first-class mechanics soon set about fixing. The five-door Maxi was not stiff enough at the rear and several fixes were tried. Finally, the rear door was cut and welded so that only the top half opened. Double shocks were added to complement the hydrolastic suspension and the system pressure upped to 240 psi. The 1500 cc engine pumped out close to 100 bhp, a slightly better power weight ratio than the BMC 1800.

An ingenious compensator was built in to the system to enable the drivers to know and adjust the fuel mixture at altitude. We had an altimeter and two levers, marked, so that ignition and fuel adjustments were made to preset marks as the altitude increased, and of course decreased.

On one of my night-testing sessions on a spirited hairpin bend, the front outside tyre blew, causing me to slide into the ditch. As luck would have it, there was a concrete culvert in the way. Here we go again, I thought. They will never believe a tyre burst. But when the car was returned, they quickly found a series of splits in the tread and my honour was restored.

The Rally route spent a considerable time in Europe going as far as Sofia in Bulgaria. These Communist country excursions necessitated extensive briefings with the security people, for it was at the height of the Cold War.

We were asked to do part of the route survey and prepare route notes for that section. On excellent expenses we flew to Nice to pick up a Triumph 2.5PI from Brian Culcheth and Evan Green, both of whom would be driving Triumphs.

Our task was to go east to the Yugoslav border, return and cover the ground to the Portuguese border. Pete and I felt the responsibility of this task and knew that any mistakes would not be well received by the other BLMH crews.

Sitting in a large traffic jam at a major intersection in Milan, we heard the sound of a high-performance engine at very high rpm. Seeing that the intersection was locked up solid, we were curious as to where this vehicle was going. A Ferrari arrived at speed, by-passed the intersection by crossing over and drove through the gas station on the corner. The gas station was busy and he was doing an admirable speed. Nobody even looked up from the job in hand of filling up their vehicles, and he zipped off down the side street as though that was acceptable behaviour for a Ferrari.

The *Autocar* third member was not known to us and did not put in an appearance till the final days of preparation. Michael S was a car tester, but without rally experience. His driving skills should have been acceptable, but he was not up to the task. I say that, although he did change an alternator in the dark at 16,000 ft, when the loss of one nut in the dirt under the car would have finished us. On that score he was invaluable.

A rear seat had been custom designed with the idea that one person could sleep on the humungously long stages. I think all would agree that a third crew member is a waste of time. The two-crew cars did just as well if not better, and without the added weight.

The start at Wembley Stadium was all hype to most of us just wanting to get going. Down to Dover where the infamous Kent police were at their finest. We were picked out of a stream of traffic and visually identified as exceeding the speed limit. At the subsequent court case, the constable identified our car as an Austin Maxi, but could recall nothing unusual about it. This was despite the fact that it had two tyres on the roof and was festooned with numbers and advertising material. He placed the car in the stream and judged it to be speeding. Michael S managed to confuse the judge fully with his recollection, enough to apply the revolving door technique for which the Kent police are justly known.

The car settled fine and Europe was covered in style. It was more nimble than our old 1800, but certainly far less of a performer than the Escorts. Works service certainly takes much of the stress out of long-distance rallying, but we needed little during the trek eastwards.

The ominous clattering in Hungary turned out to be a surveillance aircraft, an AN-2 biplane sitting right over the top of us. Were we just unlucky for the attention, or did all the military crews get special treatment?

The Yugoslav sections really opened our eyes, for during a night climb the road deteriorated to such a degree that we stopped in disbelief that this could possibly be the intended route. Lights could be seen ahead up high, but it was more like a dried river bed than a road.

The famous bridge incident happened around the time we arrived to cross it. I do not know whether Timo M jumped it before or after we faced it. The plank surface had so much missing that the group of entrants we happened to be with jointly decided that a 20-mile detour was needed. Evidently the Ford contingent restructured the bridgeworks enough to ease across, but Timo backed up and jumped over the not inconsiderable gap.

We managed to travel in convoy with several of the BLMH team and arrived on a muddy hillside, deeply rutted, to find two trucks jammed together, such that neither could move. Passing on either side was impossible in view of a steep bank on one side, or a large drop-off on the other. A Citroen was taking runs at the hillside using its adjustable suspension at the top of its travel, and I ran back to see if we could circumnavigate the obstruction by going around through the wooded area. Newer arrivals got together to push the trucks and the drivers of the trucks quickly got the message that they had better co-operate or else.

Whilst there was some latitude in start times on a prime, for the professionals this was a strategic choice, we just motored steadily on not really caring about day or night. By now we were on to the route notes we had prepared and there was just enough return from that to be comfortable. The fast guys were enjoying plenty of rest, whilst we seemed to be on the edge of a usable 'get some sleep' schedule.

Italy was crossed on the autostrada system and the Monza stopover was lost in a flurry of activity at the BLMH service point. The obvious retirements were seen, stuck in trees, or victims of road accidents. Our feelings were that attrition was running at a slightly higher rate than on the London-Sydney.

France and the memorable Monte Carlo stages were covered and we slipped into Spain heading for the Portuguese prime of note, the 'Arganil'. We had lots of advice from other team members, for it was a severe test of man and machine. Spectators jammed in tight on the hairy bits, so much so that they were indicators of spectacular hazards.

Autocar did a fine piece on us as we sat on the dockside awaiting loading instructions for the *Derwent*, that was to take all the remaining cars to Rio. I had a long, animated discussion with Roger Clark on the techniques of steering a car from both ends, a skill for which he was well known.

We had worked our way up the field and eased into Portugal positioned in the low thirties. No real surprises, but proud to be part of a very professional team.

Whilst the ship was carrying its valuable cargo to Rio, we enjoyed a stay in Estoril, and my wife and family flew in to sample the hard life of an international rally driver.

My two boys were completely entranced by 'Gelignite' Jack

Murray, who took them on an eating tour. He was an Australian Pied Piper, whose mannerisms and gift for the unorthodox were guaranteed to beguile all who came into contact. The sight of my two boys on the beach in the early hours, as the local fishermen prepared their catch, was an award-winning photograph. National barriers are meaningless in such circumstances. Without a common language, real communication was taking place right there.

Pete and I, plus wives, took a memorable horse ride along the coast. The pine forest was thick with a heavy perfume that I can recall to this day. So if anyone says that memories are only visual, I have evidence to the contrary.

Rio was just another city, but a backdrop that is known the world over. A few lazy days were well received, but then there was a general wish to get going again.

Pete was on the beach, sunning, face down on his towel with his clothes and valuables by his head. He was aware of running feet on the sand, but only looked up because they appeared closer than before. His clothes and possessions were en route to the major road system that flanks the beach. Giving chase, he may have thought that the young Brazilian was going to be cornered by the busy road. It was not to be, for the thief whistled through eight lanes of traffic, none of which made any attempt to avoid him. In fact, knowing that the 'Barrio' is just across the road, Pete is sure that the traffic tried to get the runners.

We were glad to be on the way, but somewhat alarmed by South American attitudes. The good city roads finish very abruptly, so that without any warning you drop off a four-lane highway onto the dirt. Road signs are rare, and so the route notes are vital. Road accidents were frequent, and the all-girl crews were somewhat unsettled by the sight of dead bodies still lying in the road, long after apparently being clobbered.

Some rhythm was necessary, if the tasks of driving, navigating and sleeping were going to be shared effectively. We never seemed to get it quite right, and inevitably arrived at a point where we were all incapable of continuing without a minor break.

It was heart-breaking to sit by the roadside to try and sleep for fifteen minutes, especially after running hard to maintain some schedule. The distances were so large and the speeds so high, that it was sensible to just try and maintain a pace that would not likely kill you and hope that it was good enough.

Michael really brought it to a head after he took over for a stint behind the wheel. It was very muddy and windy, but interesting rather than dangerous. He lost it on a minor bend and slammed into the bank, muttering about technique. He was obviously tired and seemed to be only able to drive for about thirty minutes before dozing off. His technique of closing on trucks at a high rate of knots, before realising that a powerful test of the brakes was going to be needed, denied all of us any sleep. It was prudent thereafter to limit his time behind the wheel.

We had few bad experiences, apart from a fast downhill section through the trees. The surface was very loose, but it looked as though the hill ended on a levee across a muddy plain. The levee was straight and raised off the plain by about 15 feet. As the surface was so loose I let the car accelerate, avoiding any real braking. Once the trees allowed us a clear view of the levee road, we saw a large truck approaching. At the same moment, a huge stockpile of gravel was seen, positioned on our side of the road. As ever the truck and the Maxi were going to cross at exactly the pile, by my frantic guesswork. With what limited room I had, the car was sideways as I tried to reduce speed. Aim at the pile of gravel and a 'Roulette' was performed as I whistled through the gap that was not there until a nanosecond before.

It was possible to travel for miles without seeing another rally vehicle, and quite unnerving at times. The prime that cost the leading Citroens dearly was very fast and open – pampas-like conditions, along fence lines, with many possible routes and tracks to follow. Rocky outcrops would catch the unwary, and the drainage was river beds deeply cut into the land. The roads crossed the rivers by rudimentary bridges, but descended into the cuts at an angle. You would come upon the descents very suddenly and be forced into changing direction, slowing and making sure you were lined up for the narrow bridge. The fast-moving Citroens managed to get across the bridges, but slid off the dirt on the far side, rolling the car end over end. A banana is not considered a reasonable shape for a rally car.

We did extremely well on that section, emerging around twelfth.

Service was available as we left the prime, and the route immediately entered a small village. On dusty tarmac, I overcooked it a little, buoyed by the last section. We slid along the edge of the corner knocking over a few parked bicycles and a motorbike. We were full of fuel, some thirty gallons of it, and I was quickly aware of the extra weight. Up a long tree-lined road, vaguely Napoleonic, with stacked piles of lumber being noticeable. A small, ancient Ford Popular was seen ahead, and with lights flashing, air horns blowing and finally a quick squirt on the siren we carried, we tried to alert them to our approach. The car commenced a turn through the trees and stopped squarely in the middle of the road. There was insufficient room either side, and a tree strike was not an option. Peter was not buckled in, as he was fixing the equipment after the prime, and he knew that we were far too heavy to successfully stop. I tried to squeeze by in the gap, but struck the Popular square on the front wheel with the right front of the Maxi. The Ford rolled off up the road to finish inverted. We all jumped out to survey the damage, and eventually to see what all the screeching was in the Ford. More cars arrived and the Uruguayan's were very sympathetic to our state as they could easily see what had happened. The small dog was making an awful din, but the occupants were unhurt. The old lady driver said that we had confused her with all that noise, such that she made the brilliant choice of stopping in the middle of the road.

Truck mechanics, and finally BLMH mechanics appeared, after Michael went back to town to fetch them. Our hydraulic jack would not work on its side, and so local know-how began beating out the wheel well area so that we could get the smashed wheel out and look at the other damage.

The steering rack was broken, the battery leaking and punctured by the impact. The stub axle was seriously deranged, but after beating back the wheel area about eight inches, the replacement wheel would turn, but at a ridiculous angle. It was possible to see the wheel from the driver's seat, such was the distortion. The police arrived and with much translation we were finally allowed to proceed.

It was 650 km to the boat and Montevideo, but at a reduced speed now just possible. It needed two hands to hang on to one side of the steering wheel just to keep straight, and our turning radius to the right was hopeless. With extra wheels given by other Maxi drivers, we set off at about 54 kph. This was never going to be good enough and so it slowly increased under the logic that it was pointless driving so slow that we missed the boat. Risking a suspension collapse was the only real choice. The new tyres chewed up the road surface terribly, wearing out about every 200 km. At one controlled crossroads, the policeman in his 'pulpit' was amazed as we were forced to drive completely around him just to make the turn.

With the tyre noise making us deaf, we arrived at the boat with some time to spare. Getting up the ramp was quite a test, but we were at least on, only to learn that the next BLMH service point was 200 km the other side of Buenos Aires across the River Plate, at Saladillo. The enormous crowds in Buenos Aires necessitated a police escort, but such was the speed of the cavalcade that we fell off the back of the procession into the enthusiastic locals. With the minutes ticking by, we arrived at service to find that we were well down the queue. In the end they had one hour to change the rack and front suspension. With minutes to spare we left the service area, now at the full extent of our lateness. The thick crowds obscured the rally control point, and so we left without the necessary stamp.

The car felt like new again after all the work, incredible work considering the damage, but it handled strangely, being lightning quick in right handers, but ponderous in left. With no margin now for any eventuality, we needed to create some buffer for the unforeseen. Spectator traffic was evident but slowly we caught up with back markers and those suffering terminal ailments. The red dust road was fast and full of brows and then it began to rain. The dust turned to chocolate and we slid all over the place in the stickiest mud I have ever encountered. A rutted section punted us off the road into a muddy low-lying area. The car started to slow and sink into the mud and the engine laboured as I sought to keep it running. Pete jumped out into knee-high mud and yelled to keep going as he pushed to assist the Maxi back onto the road. With much chugging in the too high a gear, I made it. He caught the still-moving car and jumped in, bringing in mud/dust that was with us for the rest of the event.

The route continued south to Viedma before turning west for the last road across South America. We had regained some of our spirits now, and believed that we had a chance of getting back into the fray. This road was a wide open track with numerous routes always possible. There was little or no traffic, or for that matter anything. In one of the hollows, Pete felt for the brakes, to find that the pedal went to the floor. Gear down and handbrake to a stop. Check fluid, no sign of a leak and so empty spare can into reservoir. Brilliant, for although we had brakes for a few applications, the problem was there again. Slow down, stop again and really look for the problem. The rear brake lines had an extra plastic tube protecting them. This arrangement caused the fine gravel thrown off the back wheels to impact on the bleed nut, wearing it away and finally it fell off. A service point was noted up ahead about 100 km and so we felt that we could continue without brakes. Pete noted that it was the first time he had knowingly driven at 160 kph without brakes. They were packing up to leave as we appeared, which gave added impetus for us to increase the pace, for to be without service would have been unthinkable.

The alpine area of Bariloche was reached and crossed before we joined the Pan American highway and headed north. A paved road at last, but a catch for the unwary as bullock carts without lights were not infrequent. One Peugeot, South American entered, hit a bullock square on, punching the engine back into the cabin. The animal was still whole, but minus head as an indication of its crash-worthiness.

We reached Santiago with the suspension being flat, but found service and a brief few hours in the Sheraton. The shocks were changed and the hydrolastic pumped up and it was as good as new. In view of the brevity of our stopover, we agreed to meet for a quick breakfast and a tightly scheduled departure.

Breakfast at 0600, checkout 0615, load/check car and on the road 0630. Michael arrived at 0615 and in true English style set about confusing the waiter with a complicated order. As we all had to be in the car to start, he was left in no doubt that punctuality was a virtue.

Fairly large changes to the route were necessary in view of mud slides et al. The recrossing of the Andes was by a rail tunnel that operated one way on alternate days. It was supposedly closed for the Rally, but we all felt very confined and expected to see the 'light at the end of the tunnel' and hope that it was not of an oncoming train. Down onto the dusty plains of Argentina and numerous walled townships named 'Mercedes', as a reminder of where many Germans fled at the end of the Second World War.

The Gran Premio prime was so long that mentally you had to keep reminding yourself that it was not another road section and that max performance was the goal. The topography was like a giant dried river bed, almost devoid of vegetation, with the 'road' winding along the edge of what had to be a winter flood area. It was incredibly dusty and cars way ahead could be tracked by the dust clouds separating them. Any attempt to overtake was fraught, for an error would put you into the river bed, a 15-20 ft drop. The drop-off was not the problem, just the large house-sized boulders that were strewn around in the old watercourse.

After a time of being in heavy dust, we backed off and suffered the restricted pace and the fine talcum powder that combined with sweat to make a misery out of it all. And then there was obviously an accident, two or three cars had stopped and we saw that a Triumph 2.5 was upside down in the river bed amongst some large rocks. Andrew Cowan appeared, blood-soaked and shocked. I ran for my medical kit, knowing that I might be called upon to use the morphine that I carried for just such an occasion. One of the Argentineans was a doctor, and Ken Tubman left in haste for the nearest town and help. Andrew's crewman was seriously injured when the car went backwards off the road and landed on one of those house-sized rocks upside down. This put a damper on our efforts for a while, but then we apparently were not travelling at those speeds.

Northwards to Bolivia and the rockpile it displayed itself as. In the foothills, the road often wound around cliff faces with enormous drops and angled tracks to trap the unwary. Where slides had removed some of the road it was necessary to check that there was road and an exit still there.

We were faced with one emergency stop to avoid a ski-jump departure, but generally retained an 'out', or thought that we did. One of the Hunters was passed, appearing to have lost an awful lot of the transmission and rear axle. The prop shaft had failed aft of the gearbox and dropped onto the road, digging in and punching off the back axle and some of the suspension. It looked hopeless with all those bits laid out behind the car, but I understand that they cobbled together something to enable them to continue.

Bolivia had an additional wrinkle in that the locals, seemingly stunned under the effects of too much 'coca', placed boulders in the road and then sat high up on the rocks to watch the result. To come around a fast corner to see enough rocks strewn around to rip your car to pieces, was not something that endeared them to me.

We had been enduring incipient electrical problems, no doubt as a result of our shunt, but an alternator change seemed to be indicated. High up, 15,600 ft by our altimeter, on a flinty road with not a light in sight, we set about changing the offending component. The emergency triangle was placed well back, and Michael began the change. We only had one alt lock nut, and little else would supply enough tension to the alt belt. With great care it was removed and by agreement the old unit tossed behind the car. All worked as advertised, a great job by Michael, but when we thought better of discarding the old unit and also collecting the emergency triangle, both were missing, Even using the car lights to cover the area, it was obvious that they had been taken. Scary stuff.

Early morning down a long straight, and something was seen coming towards us. Impossible to make out what it was and then I realised it was a low-flying aircraft, identified at the last minute as a P-51. Pretty good, did not know that they had such men.

La Paz to Lima was a nightmare. Not only was it mind-bendingly long, it wound around the mountains in a very haphazard fashion. The Maxi had little performance at those altitudes, made worse by some terrible fuel, no power, constant climbs and a barrenness that was stunning. I believe that the tracks were worn by inebriated locals, such that you could look down and see a village way below and feel that you might actually be going there. The road wandered and reversed itself time after time, making you consider driving straight down the hillside in the hope of intercepting the track lower down. I remember taking four hours to reach a village we had seen intermittently all that time. Soul destroying was all I could recall.

Several of the entrants who had been time excluded, but having managed to get going again were now sweeping up and lending a hand to all and sundry. They were able to jump ahead occasionally, and it was most disconcerting to find them in front.

By the time we reached Cali, there were only 26 cars still in the rally. We were still at the end but at least running with some of the fast rally traffic and creating a small buffer for ourselves. They were usually packing up the service areas as we arrived, and so we did get valued assistance which would have worn us out had we been forced to perform it ourselves.

It was a pleasure to descend off the high ground and into the jungle of Columbia. The run to the boat at Buenaventura was not without its incidents, several entrants falling foul of the truck traffic. Heavy jungle came right to the roadside, and it was wet and muddy with slides and rocky outcrops. The population wandered about on the quite busy route, so that dodging them and the trucks was a scary business. I could not make out if the truck drivers did not care or were just unaware and feeling secure in their large vehicles.

The port was vaguely Hemingway-ish steaming in 100-degree heat, such that nothing moved quickly and everything was overhung with creepers and mould.

The wreckage that presented itself for loading was unbelievable. The *Verdi* was capable of carrying 35 cars, but not set up for Rally cars only. In the end 26 Rally cars and 12 assorted were squeezed on board. There were so many tales to tell that it was certain that you never heard them all on the two-day trip.

Cristobal in Panama was the point of unloading and at the height of the rainy season. No work had been allowed on the cars on board and a 'Parc Ferme' was set up in Cristobal. The police controlled the paperwork at the dockside and so the drivers could take some time off.

We were taken by taxi to a hotel for a meal and a clean-up. Stepping from the taxi I found out why the storm drains were so large, as I tested a puddle and found it thigh deep.

We were now 51 hrs 30 mins from the finish at Fortin, some 200 kms from Mexico City. One of the Citroens driven by Paul Coltelloni was taken out by a local, and the co-driver killed. We came across the burning Citroen, but in the confusion did not learn what had happened until later. It was a silly accident, almost no reflection on the rally car and its crew.

So many frontiers, little or no delay and then we were in Oaxaca.

The Maxi was still suffering overheating and electrical problems, solved in part by driving with the heat full on and keeping the revs above 4,000. The final prime had a 113 kph average set on a road that was in the process of a rebuild. The bulldozers were not cleared from the track until one hour before the first rally car came through.

The Fortin hotel was a zoo with enthusiastic spectators and ecstatic crews. The pool was treated to a quota of dressed and undressed visitors. The last two cars arrived in the early hours to join the parade to Mexico City.

Led by the police, the drive to the Aztec Stadium was at a highly illegal speed with many locals joining in. We had made it and to hear from some of the competitors, had a relatively easy run – 23rd out of 24 to finish may not sound like a sterling effort, but then you had to be there.

After all the jeopardy I had been in, I fell foul of 'Montezuma's revenge' in Mexico City. The flight home was endured in a semi stupor, even though I was aware that the aircraft had managed to hit a large bird which demolished the windscreen and delayed the return flight. The carry-on baggage was a sight to be seen, for I am sure that a mechanic's tool kit weighing at least 60-70 lb was the norm and that the aircraft was accidentally overloaded.

Our Maxi was used in many more events in UK, but we slid out of the rally scene, being in Canada when the first reruns of the London-Sydney were organised in the late 1970s.

Chapter X

THE LONDON-VICTORIA Air Race came at a very inconvenient time for me, as I was heavily committed to the work of 92 Sqn. Being in Germany left me unable to contribute much to the planning, but Arthur and Pete shouldered the load and it was accepted that we would again go as a crew of three.

Arthur was involved in PR work for Britten-Norman Aircraft, and as the Islander had won the London-Sydney, we thought it a good choice. They provided a delivery aircraft that we would return to Ottawa after the race. Pete was able to perform most of the liaison with the factory on the Isle of Wight, and we conferred with regard to the specs for the race aircraft. It was a requirement that all entries have HF radio, not a usual fit for the Islander. Also, there were several mods available for Islanders that were purchased as required by the buyer. We wanted long-range tanks, which are fitted in wing-tip extensions, and also the 'speed kit'. This item was to dog us all through the planning stage and in the end it was a vital component of the performance or lack of on our aircraft. If more time had been available we would have discovered that all the kit contained was a paperwork and minor electrical change that permitted the lowering of about five degrees of flap in the cruise mode to reduce drag.

The Ottawa dealer would not accept the modification cost, but we could have achieved the same effect by lowering flap and pulling a circuit breaker to restrict flap travel. In all, our extras, tip extension, windscreen de-icer plate and wing de-icer boots cost us about 10-12 kts in cruise speed. We were not too concerned for it was part of the formula to amend the handicap speed for such components. Because it was the Canadian Aero Club's event, the Royal Aero Club formula was not followed. Here we go again, another handicap speed that is impossible to attain.

As before we needed to run-in the engines to avoid an oil change en route, and I nipped back to UK to help Pete with the fifty hours needed. I had not flown the Islander before and it became sensible for me to look after the nav rather than become too involved with aircraft details. Arthur was of course after a photographic record, and his excellent film work became a large part of the book of the event.

The rules stated that the race was open to both IFR and VFR aircraft. Fuel stops were mandated such that we hoped for a rapid turnaround at Lossiemouth in Scotland. We knew that we could be in and out far quicker at a military airfield, not open to many other competitors.

The briefing at Abingdon was to make us very concerned over the organisation and the quality of some of the competitors. Many questions were asked that showed a lack of awareness on the part of some of the entries, and of course our request for a proper handicap was refused.

We met a Canadian entry in a Turbo-Beaver who was calmly unmoved by the quality of the organisation. He was to feature in our lives in the not-too-distant future.

We left for Lossie and a planned rapid fuel stop. The Navy were ready on the runway to refuel us right there. The Islander had four 50-gal drums mounted in the cabin, with the fuel system fastened on top. There was not much room to manoeuvre, and getting at the middle two tanks was a contortion. The Wren refueller was slightly built, and the refuelling nozzle heavy and awkward. She dropped the hose into the tray under the tanks, and several gallons were discharged before we could shut off the flow and recover the nozzle. The hyperactivity slowed as we considered the implications. We could depart with all electrical equipment turned off, vent the cabin by opening the windows, and hope that we would not freeze to death before the fuel evaporated. Not the most admirable decision, but a risk we could quantify, we thought. It took forever to evaporate the gasoline, and there were three very cold and smelly crew members when we finally turned on the electrics. Iceland came up in poor weather, and several competitors were sitting on the ground considering their options. We fuelled and left in haste for Goose Bay, a planned 11.5-hour trip. The Atlantic weather lived up to its reputation, and we settled for a low-level crossing just below the cloud deck. The HF radio was resting in the radio bay, for we had been required to show it at pre-race inspection, but it was not connected nor was the antenna in place. All our radio calls were relayed through airline traffic without any difficulty.

A strange phenomena occurred shortly after departing Reykjavik. I could see through the rain a land mass off to our right. We were some 100 miles out of Iceland and there is no land in that position. Unless we were way off course and tracking up the coast of Iceland, it had to be a mirage. In those latitudes, the air masses can have vastly different temperatures causing a tubing effect that enables you to see much further than is normally possible. We were looking at the coast of Greenland some 300-400 miles away.

The tip of Greenland was expected at 5.5 hrs, the foreboding cliffs loomed out of the murk on time, but we were a little north of track, necessitating a crawl around the tip and over the sea ice. Narssassuak was a considered fuel stop, but in those days a visual airport only. It required a 90-mile flight up the fjord with a careful turn to avoid finishing up in a blind alley. There were three 'Mayday' calls on the air as we passed the entrance, from entrants in serious trouble trying to find Bluie West One, its old wartime name. One Viking was forced out to sea beyond the pack ice, in order to ditch his aircraft, which he did successfully. So much so that he was rescued by helicopter and his aircraft pulled to safety before it sank.

Others were led down through the murk by pilots familiar with Narssassuak. One fixed-gear aircraft crossed the ice cap in cloud at a low altitude. The wheels hit something solid and he realised that he had made contact with the ice field, fortunately propelling him back into the air. At that point it looked like the Race was going to turn into a disaster for the organisers.

Prinz Christian was behind us and a 5.5-hour was anticipated to Goose. Two NDB beacons are situated on the coast, almost equidistant north and south of our track. If the bearings were roughly the same it would indicate that we were on track. At roughly 150 miles by our timing, both beacons were identified and they were exactly where expected. They then both vanished leaving us somewhat anxious.

We eventually could hear race traffic on the radio, but we should have been receiving Goose VOR by now. The same wacky temperatures were causing havoc with radio communications, and we coasted in some 90 minutes late, having suffered unforecasted winds on the leg from Prinz Christian. Our fuel reserves were gone and the melee at Goose Bay did not calm us.

We queued for a GCA approach, for there were several entrants with less fuel than us. All the Air/Sea rescue aircraft were either in the air or being scrambled for race aircraft in trouble. It was right at minimums for landing, but not a deterrent for a rapid departure.

All aircraft were now restricted to normal fuel only and so another fuel stop in Seven Islands put us on time at Quebec City for the night stop, with an arrival through the very impressive bridgeworks over the St Lawrence.

We were very well entertained, this being a significant sporting event for the city. All competitors were taken aboard a new vessel for a waterfront tour. If I remember correctly it was a round ship, most unusual, and the captain was having trouble steering it, for we smacked the dock hard enough to knock people off their feet.

The next stop was Ottawa and a preview of the capital that I was to know well in future years. The route from thereon was Thunder Bay, Calgary and Victoria. All intermediate stops were at the entrant's discretion. We believed that the most direct route at the lowest altitude, in view of the prevailing westerly winds, would suit. The winds were generally 20 kts plus from the west at 2,000 ft, and therefore in the turbulent air above the trees, there was a chance to reduce this headwind component. Other competitors could be seen heading off for radio beacons, whilst we stuck rigidly to a carefully drawn line on our map.

I navigated, asking heading accuracy from Pete that was not really reasonable. We landed at Sudbury, having organised a quick turnaround. The fuel truck was right there, parking across the front of the Islander at an angle. In his haste, the young lad must have had full pressure before he was able to start fuelling. In any case, the hose blew off the truck with a bang, and 50 psi fuel soaked the ground around the aircraft.

Moving the truck was now not safe, and we were hemmed in by his parking. Pete started the left engine, in the vain hope that he could make the turn away from the truck on the one engine. Using a lot of power and brake, it was a jerky attempt to clear the truck, and it was going to be very close anyway. On the last jerk, he hit the truck a glancing blow, smashing the nav light and crumpling the wing tip. The truck driver was not impressed, but Pete supervised the refuel whilst I tried to reshape the wing tip and stuff the wiring back inside.

It went back to its original shape very conveniently, and the C/B was pulled for safety.

Heading for Thunder Bay took us to the shores of Lake Superior, where clouds were right down on the trees. With disgust, we climbed up, for a low-level trip all the way across Canada was a personal goal. The lake was in view from 3,000 ft, and so we began a descent back down to 300 ft. Several race aircraft were in sight, including another Canadian Islander. He was not encumbered by our de-icer gear, and the difference in speed slowly made itself noticeable – he was at least 8-10 kts faster than us. We reckoned that the headwind was 15-20 kts at around 500 ft, and so slid down to the wave tops. Here the temperature change gave us an IAS increment of about 8 kts, such that we started to gain on higher traffic. The Turbo-Beaver was right with us to landing.

Arthur was swapping places with us up front, and this was done by crawling in the narrow space on top of the fuel barrels. Although the system was tagged and marked 'OFF', there were occasions where some lack of performance was noticed. By rerouting the fuel flow, it was possible to try and fly on any residual fuel in the barrels. With much grunting and cursing, I managed to reroute the fuel. Expecting to see a drop in fuel pressure fairly quickly, they were ready to revert to normal fuel feed at the first sign of an engine stoppage. We waited and waited, finally realising that fuel had been feeding back into these tanks for some time, and that we must have been carrying an extra 60 gals as dead weight.

Calgary came up after a long blast down a country road, race traffic being scheduled to night stop before the final run to Victoria. I was amazed at the back country nature of Calgary and its many rail yards. The Race directors told us to assemble for a briefing tomorrow, for the weather up ahead was not good.

We examined our options and knew that whilst it would be an IFR flight, the big loss would be not being able to see the Rockies at close quarters. Quoting safety concerns, the Race authorities decided to halt the race until the weather improved. This was completely against the rules, and unnecessary. We, along with many others, had carried IFR equipment all through the race, and more to the point, been adversely handicapped for it. Now, when our gamble was about to pay off they wanted to change the rules. There was much heated discussion, and finally a large group of us had to tell the organisers that we were departing, as race traffic or not, but that when we arrived in Victoria they would have a hard time eliminating half the field. They asked for time to rule on the issue and we gave them until 1000 hrs to make a decision.

IFR race traffic departed without the formality of a decision, but the organisers recovered enough face to say nothing and let the race continue.

The sea was sighted on the windward side of the Rockies, and a slow let-down started for the brief crossing to Victoria. The beautiful islands in the Juan de Fuca strait, home to Ernest Gann who was flying in this race, were crossed and memorised for a later visit. And then it was over, not quite as much adversity as the London-Sydney Air Race, but a test nonetheless. We flew some publicity photo trips, with three Islanders and the Trilander. I flew the ladies' US-entered Islander, for although they were enormously experienced, they graciously bowed to my formation qualifications. It stands a rare and cherished memory of those times.

The return to Ottawa was accomplished at a lesser pace, but the Rockies forced us to divert well to the south, stopping in Medicine Hat for lunch. Here the refueller casually gave us his car to take to the diner some miles away. He could not know that giving someone your car is not a decision taken lightly by Europeans.

We delivered the Islander, somewhat damaged by leaving the keys in the door lock for the last leg. The flight home was supposed to be on Lloyd Air out of Montreal or Bangor. They had folded during our Race and Pete and I were now faced with some difficult choices on how to get home.

Arthur fled back to business by scheduled airline, and we settled for our alternate plan on RAF Transport Command. Ottawa was not on their immediate schedule and so we had to try a link-up in Bagotville. Hiring a car was easy, but the route only a guess.

The North American Ford was a monstrosity to us, loosely held together with poor tyres and terrible brakes. Its road holding was not on any graph known to us. However, the roads generally demanded very little of it, for they were straight and good until we left Quebec City. With only a rough idea of the C-130's departure time, we pushed on non-stop to the military airfield of 'Bagtown'. There were far to many people awaiting the Hercules, nearly all going to Goose Bay fishing. The smallest contingent by far was the RAF group.

When it arrived there was a rush to the aircraft, backing the air quartermaster against the door. It took a few anxious moments to make the point that we were returning aircrew, and as such we had priority. The Hercules eventually took everyone, but nightstopped in Goose for crew rest. I now had to make it back to RAF Germany. As before, the Herc was an uncomfortable way to travel, made more so by the fact that it was to make a stop at Waddington before our destination of Lyneham.

Constantly watching the clock did not help the acidity in my stomach. Nor did the attempts to restart one engine. It was apparent that a starter had failed, and we were amazed to see them back up another C-130, to attempt a start under the jet blast of the aircraft in front. I know it was supposed to be possible, but the size of the C-130 props gave little hope for success. A hurried change of aircraft put us on our way to Lyneham for an arrival in the early hours of the morning. Pete drove me to a friend's garage where my car had been stashed, but we needed to wake him up in order to retrieve it. A quick goodbye and I was off to Dover and the car ferry at a high rate of knots.

Of course they were very busy and I could not get on the desired boat to Dunkirk, having to accept Boulogne and the extra miles it added to my journey. The Fiat Coupe was driven flat out for most of the way, but still I was more than a day late returning for duty.

Arthur produced most of the photos for the book of the event, and all thoughts of further events were removed by circumstance. It had been a great six years, adrenalin highs that force introspection, but in some way encourage a separateness that can be burdensome. We are what we are, changed only by time and trouble.

Oshawa, Ontario in the winter of 1974 was extremely cold. To a neophyte from UK the learning curve on just how cold it can get was steep. I stayed with Pete for a few days, then organised a room at the old Genosha Hotel.

I went to work immediately, mostly flying with Pete on the freight runs that were the bread and butter of JV Aviation. Grant had an assortment of ancient machinery and the step-up to a Citation jet was going to be large. Whilst I learnt the ropes, there was little pressure to inquire where the Alcan aircraft was. We all knew that it was expected, but the arrival date kept slipping. Grant paid expenses only, and so after a short while finances became the limiting factor. Either there was a job, or I had to look elsewhere. It became sensible to return to UK, for I felt better able to find a job there than in the enormous reaches of Canada.

An opportunity had long existed with one Lofter, an Icelander, who ran a rather secret airline-type operation, mostly supporting US intelligence services. We had known about each other since my 'courier' days, and he was quite happy to utilise me on his DC-7, but it crashed in Switzerland before any real progress could be made.

I returned to UK and followed up on the test pilot position at Shorts in Eire. One delivery flight was made to Belfast before a letter arrived from Grant saying that the Alcan letter was on its way, please come back to Canada pronto.

I set about obtaining the necessary instrument rating as soon as I landed, but the examiner was more than upset to be asked to fly one more trip in an unheated Aztec. Grant had stuck him once too often and I was caught in the middle.

Piston flying was an interesting challenge for a while, diminished only by the quality of the aircraft that Grant operated. Nothing ever worked as advertised and he had some very strange attitudes to saving money on maintenance. All pistons need a magneto check before flight, and spark plugs will cause a mag drop outside limits if they are old or breaking down. Time and time again we would return to the flight line with a drop caused by plugs, and Grant would hammer the engines at full power to clear the drop; he must have known that it would occur again.

Both Pete and I instructed during the day on the school aircraft that Grant owned. General Motors always called at 1700 with their freight requests and so it was then usually an all-nighter delivering GM parts. The days were extending into 18-20 hrs of work and so

Pete and I went on a four-days-on/two-days-off cycle. Against the RAF monthly flight schedule of 25-40 hrs, this was something else. The Canadian rules limited one to 1,200 hrs annually and I could see that figure being easily obtained. It became obvious that the Alcan deal was dead and I kind of slipped into alternative employment as a necessary prerequisite for paying your dues in Canadian aviation. How easy it is to become trapped when there is little time to even research options.

The Chief Pilot was an Indian gentleman, remarkably officious and secretive. We just did the flying that was scheduled and in general did not come into contact with him. He was supposedly highly qualified, but there were too many inconsistencies. He always locked up his log book which he meticulously kept up to date. It had to happen and the day it was left out, Pete and I found out the depth of his experience. I had visited many of the places in India he talked about and the stories dried up quickly when he discovered how much I knew about India and the Indian Air Force.

Grant was larger than life in many ways, with a highly varied career in aviation. He was a stern taskmaster, but very dismissive of things that were still on my 'important' list.

One night Pete and I were scheduled to take the old Aero Commander on a freight run and after t/o the engines indicated that they were not happy with the plugs yet again. We returned and asked for a plug change. The Chief Pilot said it was OK when he last flew it and that he would do the trip. He took off and with much banging and back-firing struggled back for a landing. Grant now decides that we are all idiots and that he will take it as a show of ability (read stupidity). He ran up the engines in an effort to clear the mag drop and then took off to repeat Dave A's display. The plugs were changed and we left on the run several hours late.

The Commander 520 that was in use was previously used as a training aircraft. As such it could have spent much of its life on one engine practicing asymmetric flight. There was only one hydraulic pump, on the right engine, and therefore it does not take a genius to work out that the right engine will have been favoured much more than the left. It was a terrible night, really well beyond the miserable steam-driven equipment fitted to the Commander. A rush job, even though we knew that a return to Oshawa was impossible and therefore it would have to be back to Toronto, and still Grant insisted that it was OK.

February the 17th lies forever in my subconscious as the landmark it should be. We lifted off into the freezing air bound for Rochester across Lake Ontario. Not a long flight, but the lake in winter is most uninviting. We sneaked into Rochester and landed to pick up the GM cargo, usually odd bits that were holding up the production line. The weather was unchanged and therefore Toronto was our destination. We climbed to 3,000 feet and throttled back the geared engines as we levelled off. There was a change in the engine note, a sort of cough that caused us to look at each other. The bang when it came was loud and unmistakable. The right engine had failed and Pete feathered it. The side window was covered in oil as was the engine. We turned back for Rochester and radioed our predicament. Speed was falling too quickly and another check around showed that the undercarriage was down. Also, I did not like the look of the engine, for it was sagging on the wing, eventually hanging significantly nose down.

I started to pump with the hand pump, mentally working out whether there was more drag with the gear down or half down. It became irrelevant, for as soon as I rested the gear flopped straight back down again. We were in freezing rain right on the edge of the worst temperature conditions, but as Pete struggled to maintain control we were going down. I played with the carb heat for we needed all the power we could muster out of the left engine and the temps were starting to rise ominously.

I put out a 'Mayday' call but did not expect to be heard by Rochester. A British Airways flight heard our call and relayed for us. We sank through 1,500 feet with a rate of descent that would put us in the water before we reached the coast. No navigation was possible as we were too low to receive anything. Feverish activity on my part focused on the good highways that ran along the edge of the lake. I said to Pete that as a last resort I thought I could find the road or at least the water's edge. We settled at 800 feet and seemed to stabilise there. Pete had kept the speed just above the minimum safe with a few knots for manoeuvring. I played with the throttle and rpm trying to find the best settings, but we were still descending ever so slowly. At this point we had a discussion that was certainly character building. I had no wish to freeze to death in the icy waters of Lake Ontario, for there was no chance of a rescue if we did manage to ditch successfully. It was a simple choice, if he could not hold it, we would invert and pull into the lake. No heroics, just common sense in a very tight situation. We crossed the coast with a few lights being visible through the patchy low cloud.

With a limited ability to avoid anything, trying to map-read was pointless. The lights of the city loomed and we aimed for where we knew the airport to be. Now down to 200 ft it was going to be close. They cleared us to land on any runway and we needed only a slight turn to make the main one. The landing was uneventful is the usual phrase, until Pete tried to use the nosewheel steering. Pressure finally bled away and we shot off the runway down a taxiway that was conveniently placed where the aircraft was going.

We retired to a bar and I had more than was usual for me. The adrenalin pump was at least still working, for at the moment the engine failed, I received such a thump in my back as the 'fight or flight' circuit kicked in. The engine, on inspection, had split and was hanging in the cowling ready to fall out.

Grant arrived the next day to pick us up, seemingly vexed at the inconvenience of it all. He made one more pressure tactic decision that we readily went along with, and again there was much to be learned from the circumstance.

We were called out for a quick trip to Detroit, not unusual, but the weather was suspect. Grant had done all the flight planning and checked the weather, 'he said'. Rush, rush was the mood and we left for the trip down to the western end of Lake Erie. As we passed Toronto, the cloud base lowered and in this Commander we were not equipped for IFR flight. Radio checks confirmed that the weather was far from acceptable, but there was a chance that we could get through underneath.

In the limited visibility, map-reading is almost impossible, and to avoid the many aerials and antenna on the route, we flew right down the main Toronto-Windsor highway. The concept here is that they rarely, if ever, build aerials down the centre of a main highway. In the failing light, we could see the vehicle lights and the windscreen wipers, cold comfort, but it identified the direction clearly. At extremely low altitude we called a US military base just north of Detroit and their radar kept us clear of conflict. Across Lake St Clair, turn down the rail line that goes straight to Detroit City airport and a quick call to let them know that we are inside five miles.

With the kind of assistance that is now rare, we were cleared in for a visual landing, when other traffic was missing doing instrument approaches. We telephoned our thanks on landing, for the controller had deflated a potential problem with his quick thinking. The second call was to Grant to tell him how unimpressed we were and that we would be here for the night. Catch me once, OK; catch me twice, no way.

The variety of the work was its attraction, even as far as the 'cheque run' to Muskoka each Friday. The base there was owned by Grant and he paid the people each Friday. Delivering the cheques was therefore vital to the employees. If they were not delivered Grant got more interest on the money, and so the history of the Friday deliveries was not good. We saw it as a challenge to our low-level abilities and so it was – in the depth of winter in a poorly heated aircraft, VFR, finding a safe way to Muskoka. There was a ridge of higher ground to the north of Oshawa with one low spot in it over a swampy area. The first challenge was to find it and an angle to pass through it safely. Up the power line until the road, and then a planned turn onto the runway. They knew that if we could not make it, it was impossible.

Bill L was leading the Rothmans aerobatic display team; the last time we had met he had replaced me on the Red Arrows, which he went on to lead. They were based locally and practiced from Oshawa periodically, so it was inevitable that Pete and I joined in for a few fly-pasts in the AA trainers of the school.

I was far from secure in the job, for its finances were delicate to say the least. It was not uncommon to arrive at work to find aircraft shackled as Grant had not made some payment or other. The cash was certainly coming in, but the 'to Office' column seemed to be removing it all. Grant did not have the trappings of a high liver, but it was all very unstable. We took on a contract to survey the water temperature of the Great Lakes. This required an aircraft with at least 5.5 hrs endurance. When he said that he was going to do it in the Commander 520, we were all dumbstruck. I guess the 'you know that they know' style was so much a part of the aviation business, that it was necessary for survival. Trying to fly specified tracks of over 150 miles over water without any nav aids is nigh on impossible, but we did it with few failures and witnessed unbelievable temperature changes with the I/R sensor. At 500 feet over Lake Ontario, we saw 15 degrees C change in less than 500 yards.

These flights were to find a possible sea lane through the lakes in winter. I took a survey flight to the 'Rock', as Newfie is affectionately known. The charter was by a large exploration company and we were to meet a helicopter in the centre of the island. When it did not turn up, I suggested that we might be able to view the site from the air and at least complete some of their task. The Cessna 337, Donald Duck as I called it, looks like a duck, flies like a duck, is not an ideal slow-flying unit, but he was more than satisfied with the investigation of the geology at ten feet.

In an effort to break out of the bind that I was in, I investigated scores of business ideas, not least of which was the parcel freight-by-air concept. Emery Air Freight were well ahead of Fedex at this time and a meeting with Emery showed that a Canadian-based freighter would have lots of work. He hated DC-3s, the backbone of Canadian aviation at that time, demanding a square fuselage and one that could be loaded without special equipment.

A Short Skyvan was the ideal, but the price was well beyond my modest means to supply or obtain. I went to the Exploration outfit that I had flown in Newfie and discussed the deal. They would back me with the financing, but not Grant and he had the necessary licence. No matter which way you cut it, it was not possible, and for me a lost opportunity.

I applied for several jobs, and was accepted for the post of a Transport Canada inspector, a fairly secure job, but it came at a time when there was much boiling at JV Aviation. Grant persuaded me to wait a while and Pete, Bill and I left on the first venture of International Air Ferries, a joint business deal between Grant, Pete and I. We were to pick up three DHC-3 Otters from West Africa and Germany, and deliver them to Oshawa. It was an epic trip, for when we all assembled at Biggin Hill, we really had only one aircraft between us, such was the state of all of them. My long-range tanks, 50-gallon drums strapped in the fuselage, were installed at Biggin.

We had made arrangements to borrow survival suits from RAF Valley, through the good auspices of my ex-boss, John L, and so Pete and I flew there whilst Bill went on to Prestwick, where we were all to link up. I had never even been in an Otter, but its characteristics resembled those of the Single Pioneer of long ago.

My aircraft was restricted in speed because of a fault in the tail and as we were to fly in formation this was to become very important later. We certainly gave them something to talk about on our first formation take-off at Valley, for the gusting winds put Pete on his ear almost before we started to move. We met at Prestwick to consider our options and identify the aircraft problems. Pete had the good radio, I had the ADF, Bill had no attitude indicator and my altimeter was intermittent with the T/S being unserviceable.

We set off for the Faeroe Islands with a reasonable weather forecast. Good radio contact from Pete's aircraft told us that all was OK at Vagar. As we neared the islands, the black volcanic rock could be seen protruding through the sea fog, not at all as forecast. We enquired again as to the landing field weather and were reassured. The approach is tricky, down a mountain and up a curving valley, and it was not until the last minute that we could see what was happening. All around was covered in fog, the only clear bit being the runway. If the controller had walked around the corner of his building, he would have seen the reality of the situation.

Kept in the tower is a record of all the aircraft that transit through Vagar. The photographs are witness to the large number of 'adventurers' who were never seen again, for the North Atlantic is very unforgiving to the ill-prepared. Many were doctors and dentists, families who must have looked upon the 'northern route' as just another trip.

We continued to Reykjavik in Iceland and confirmed the high oil consumption of my Otter. I had thirteen hours fuel and seven hours oil. Iceland has a weather system all its own, and so the arrival of the sea fog indicated a stopover of at least a few days. I attempted to solve the oil problem by drilling a hole in the oil filler cap positioned just below the door. Using the 'pee' tube and routing it through the door to a connector in the filler cap, I proposed to top up the oil during flight. My trusty Swiss Army knife did all the work, still a treasured possession from its Indonesian exposure. Pete did a weather check, as his aircraft was more suited to an IFR return. He took off and promptly went into a fog bank. All we could see was the wing of an Otter as it carved around the airfield below the level of the runway. No departure today.

When we finally had weather at the destination of Kulusuk on the eastern shores of Greenland, there was still some fog around. We were convinced that it was thin and local and so took off for the 'tough stage'. Once on top of the thin fog it was about four hours to the coast. They were capable of some 20 kts faster than me and so catching up in formation was a trial. This was to be the first test of the oil replenishment system, and from the oil cans scattered on the floor I set about opening a can and pouring it into the small tube. The aircraft would only assist by staying level for a few seconds, and flying by the 'knees' method was not successful. I managed to pour in one can and was on the second when certain laws came into being. The oil system operates under positive crankcase pressure and having filled up the line, it blew all the oil back into the cockpit. It was dripping from the roof; the instrument panel and the floor was almost too slippery to stand. I radioed my predicament and set about doing some house cleaning. The coast heaved into view, and stayed there for what seemed a decade.

With a ground speed of less than 100 kts it is easy to see why. All the activity had stimulated my bladder to bursting point, and I realised that rather than explode, I would have to let go into my immersion suit. KK is an uninviting spot, with a runway that rises above the terrain, such that going off the edge could have long-term implications. My tail wheel would not unlock, and so turning around at the end off the landing took me to the very edge of the hard pack. The refueller was amazed to see these three ancients, particularly as one covered in oil got out, took of his suit, and poured out a considerable amount of water.

The next leg required an altitude of more than 10,000 ft, which is the height of the Greenland ice cap. It was supposed to be good at Sondrestrom, but the weather for the first part was solid cloud. We climbed to 13,000 ft, with Bill fighting to stay in contact as he was flying having to look across the cockpit to stay in formation. A call to the USN base (Sob Story) in the middle of the ice field showed that we had a ground speed of 65 kts. We were icing up and needed to descend to drier air. A slow descent was performed and we broke out into clear air 'close' to the ice field.

We stopped in the fine airport hotel, recharged our personal batteries and set off for Frobisher. Sea ice made any form of coastal recognition impossible, and the lowering cloud seemed to indicate that it would be prudent to stop in Cape Dyer. This is a DEW line base, Distant Early Warning being part of the radar fence that was erected in the north at the height of the Cold War. We were low over the sea ice when Cape Dyer was identified, and such is the climb rate of the Otter that we had to turn away in order to climb up to the rocky outcrop that served as an airfield. Although unannounced, we were made very welcome for the night.

The trip to Frobisher was still not straightforward, but I did manage to purchase a stirrup pump, in the hope that I would be able to pump in oil. The weather was still dogging our route, and so again we stopped the night, ready for Fort Chimo the next day. The 'hotel' doubled as a Chinese restaurant and laundry, and it was not obvious where one bit ended and the other began.

It began uneventfully, but slowly deteriorated as we were forced lower and lower, down the shores of Ungava Bay, dodging large lumps of rock, hoping to find and fly down the river to Chimo. Just before the river, the weather closed in forcing us to climb and try for an instrument approach into Chimo. In thick cloud, with Bill at a distinct disadvantage, we struggled up to a safe altitude. Sharing the information, we let down for a joint VOR/ADF approach. Bill lost us in very thick cloud and slid back to follow our headings which we could relay to him as long as he was close enough for his weak radio to receive. His compass only allowed him to bracket our headings, and things got fairly tense for a while. We broke out of the murk, to funnel our way to the field, following the river. Bill, now out of radio contact, appeared a short while later.

Another night stop was necessary, and with help from the CAF, a temporary fix was made to my tail wheel. The weather was still looking ominous the following day, but an attempt to get through was reasonable and so we flew for about an hour until the cloud settled on the ground, back to Chimo for another night.

Believing that this was the easy part of the trip made for a more relaxed departure. I got airborne and started to cross the river at a narrow angle. The weeds were thick on each bank, which became significant as the engine stopped. I had the briefest of moments to try to encourage it to restart, and then channelled all my attention to the inevitable 'ditching' that must surely follow. I could not reach either bank, nor make out the edge of the river. Although a slow speed ditching should be survivable, I did have to concern myself with the four 50-gallon drums of fuel strapped behind me. I determined to hold off and then put one wing into the water and spin the Otter, minimising the horizontal acceleration. In the act of holding off, just prior to impact, the engine fired again. Now I had to straighten everything out once more, and try and stay out of the weeds until the power kicked in. My companions said, 'What the hell are you doing', and we assumed a fuel problem and continued on our way to the north shore of the St Lawrence.

I dropped my aircraft in Saint John, New Brunswick and continued on with Pete in his Otter. We were thoroughly fatigued by the time we reached the eastern townships of Quebec and decided not to press on to Oshawa. Grant had set up an import position with customs and needed us to be in Oshawa before midnight, or else. So it was back to the airport for another three hours to Oshawa.

We landed to be met with champagne at the end of a very long ferry flight, some eighty hours from UK. We made little money and my Amex card carried most of the bills until I could squeeze the cash out of Grant. A further run of financial incidents, chained-up aircraft and understanding what 'To Office' really meant, decided me to pursue other jobs.

I was interviewed for the post of Chief Pilot at Browndale Corp, flying an MU-2 and somewhat hastily accepted the job. They had had another MU-2, but wrecked it in two separate accidents. The outgoing pilot was seemingly responsible, and I felt it necessary to iron out a few things before I started.

Firstly, they wanted to retain him in some sort of flying capacity, which I nixed for obvious reasons, and secondly the flying load looked as though it needed two pilots. Pete was the sensible choice and in short order we were in San Angelo, Texas taking the factory course on the Japanese MU-2. Whilst there and walking around the town, we noticed a number of strangely dented cars. There were so many in this condition that it had to be something local. It was a good introduction to 'Tornado Alley', for if hailstones could do this to a stationary car, just imagine what they could do to an aircraft.

We completed our training in Toronto, and relished this new, well-equipped performer. It was not a 'boys' aeroplane', but had immense potential if treated with respect. It was at the top of the corporate list at that time, and the accidents did not start to increase until it slid down the scale to less experienced operators. The owner, John B, had an organisation that supplied a service to states and provinces for emotionally disturbed children. His attitudes were accepted by UNESCO, and Browndale blossomed very quickly. He owned houses and camps to provide care and attention for these children, and employed a multitude of psychologists and social workers. He himself had had some flying training at the end of the War, but there was not much 'Right Brain' activity in Browndale.

Pete and I quickly divided up the workload and set about coping with the very heavy flight schedule. We shared transport to work and many times were forced to stay at the airport in view of the brief period between flights. John was a 'cat napper', sleeping on the late-night arrivals that were the norm. We would depart for a 2-3 hour flight, arriving back in Toronto in the early hours of the morning, to find that there was another flight scheduled to take off at 0600. A 45-minute drive home was not on the cards, and so the work schedule built up rather too quickly for us to get a handle on it.

As is often the case, responsibilities for certain aspects of business fall to the least qualified – one of the secretaries looked after flight schedules, and was completely out of her depth. She would schedule fourteen hours of flying with no breaks for anything, food, sleep, refuelling, delays etc. John would be capable of landing back in Toronto and departing on the next trip 4-5 hours later.

Needless to say it took some time before we could get things under control. My attitude has always been to perform first, and then negotiate from a position of strength. Browndale expanded rapidly and the flying developed accordingly. We spent time in Arizona, including some at forgettable airstrips on Indian reservations. Michigan was an oft-visited state and winter ops there were testing to say the least. We landed one night at a small airport in heavy snow. The runway had not been swept, and with the snow banks on either side of the runway it was rather like landing in the bath. The MU-2 was perfectly at home in these conditions, with a high wing, props well clear of the ground and a strong, rough-field under-carriage.

Pete had planned to return to UK for his holiday and I was faced with using another pilot in his absence. John B suggested the former Chief Pilot, who was working as a computer expert for the company at that time. I stepped around the problem, but John eventually asked me to give him some training and write an evaluation. I did a standard CFS check ride and wrote it up accordingly. Ron had the appearances of a capable pilot, but there were many holes in his attitudes and preparation. I could see why he had amazed everybody and crashed the first MU-2. He had supposedly tried to start an engine by taxiing down the runway at high speed, and at some point had tried to take-off on one engine.

I gave John the report and when Pete left I called in Bill L who was unemployed after a stint with Grant at JV Aviation. John asked why I had not used Ron Y, and I tried to explain that this solution was in my view better all round. I did not recognise that John was not used to having his gentle persuasion ignored. When Pete returned, it was time for our agreed period of probation to end and an automatic increase in salary. John said that he wanted a Chief Pilot and that Pete was to fix my salary. We both attempted to explain that it was unnecessary, for we shared the workload, but I realised that the Ron Y incident was firmly in his mind. Pete could have stood, for we had a contract as to the terms following the probationary period. It was not a happy moment for me, but I think I know what I would have done in the circumstances. A job at McCains in New Brunswick was advertised and I applied instantly, believing that Browndale could never recover from its dishonesty.

It is interesting that John B eventually went to jail in a large fraud case involving his methods and his company. He had become such a large land and property owner, courtesy of the governments, that the numbers were just too large to ignore. I think he was forced to take responsibility for it all, and maybe it was the same dishonesty that I had glimpsed.

Many of the children he cared for returned to work in the system.

At first sight this is not to be unexpected. However when you really examined it, a social/psychological umbrella had been created. It seemed to work from afar, but from my perspective you produced dependent subjects who could only really function within the system. It certainly coloured my attitudes to the world of psychology and the many strange people who inhabit it.

The McCain job entailed living in a tiny kingdom in the depths of New Brunswick. They asked that I bring up my family to view the place, for there was no doubt that a village of 600 souls was going to be a challenge. The main reason for taking the job was the expectation of a jet aircraft within two years. I borrowed the Browndale MU-2, and took my wife, daughter and Linda L, wife of my former boss from Syerston days who was holidaying with us, on the trip to view Florenceville. McCains had their own small airstrip on the banks of the Saint John river. An instrument let-down was not possible in the conditions and so I planned to descend at Houlton and fly underneath to Flo-ville.

We popped out to a snow-covered landscape, quite a change from the May in Ontario. It was not wise to continue underneath and so I continued to Presque Isle, also over the border in Maine, for another let-down. Once below in better weather, I turned for Flo-ville over a flooded landscape. Doug was trying to reach me on an aircraft radio, but I could only hear him intermittently. The weather forced us to make many detours and map-reading was very difficult in view of the flooded ground.

I saw a cleared runway right by a river, with a small aircraft parked there, and did a quick turn-in for a landing on a very short runway. I was far from sure that it was Flo-ville, but at least we could enquire. I landed at Fort Fairfield in Maine on an 1,850-ft runway. I should have cleared customs but that would have taken hours, and so now for a very short take-off and on to Flo-ville. Doug was perplexed as to where we had been, but I put it down to the weather, and hoped that nobody reported it to the customs people. Not a flight that I was proud of, but there were too many other pressures for clear thinking.

It seemed like a good choice for myself and the family, and bringing up children in such an environment away from the perils of a city could not be all bad. The boys had slipped into a love affair with motorcycles, the off-road variety, and I encouraged them all that I could. We began racing as a family, weekend trips all over Eastern Canada and Quebec, and it changed so many ideas and attitudes. I would offer that anyone who has problems with male offspring, recognise it at an early age and get them an off-road motorcycle. My eldest son was not a stellar scholar, preferring the position of class clown. When his class mates came to him for help with mechanical problems, he shouldered this new-found status and never looked back. In fact, motorcycles were to feature in all our lives, for it started a business venture that survived for over twenty years.

The initial intro to corporate flying in the Maritimes, especially for a family dynasty, was more than just interesting. The runway and its ten dollars worth of lights was a challenge. They had grown up needing aircraft and in some ways were unable to function without them. The Navajo Chieftain was fairly new, but still a Piper product and all that that means. The MU-2 was a 'G' model, short ranged and underpowered. Their area of coverage was the Maritimes and Quebec, Ontario (Toronto) and as far west as Chicago. Because of their developing overseas interests they were often dropped in Montreal or Halifax to catch overseas flights. I needed to understand what kind of demand they would place upon their pilots and this is always a gentle chess game. Conditions at Flo-ville could be extreme, and even a short flight to catch Air Canada at Fredericton had all the ingredients for upset if some ground rules were not clearly understood. I attempted to prove my worth and hope that it would all be self-evident. I was partially successful in that, but there were several incidents that are worth relating.

On one very turbulent day, Wallace asked to be taken to Fredericton to catch a flight. Timing was such that if we delayed, I would be held whilst the Air Canada flight landed. By the time I had completed my full approach, it was possible to miss the connection entirely. They were never the best timekeepers, lack of punctuality seems to be a tool of senior business people, and so I was faced with a dilemma. We could try and get into Fredericton underneath and suffer a very bumpy ride, which I knew his constitution did not like, or go IFR (Instrument Flight Rules) and almost certainly miss the connection. I spoke clearly of the implications, that he would quit well before I did, but if he felt it was so important, then I would try and make up for lost time.

It was certainly the roughest flight I had experienced up till then, and we did beat the AC flight by a scant few minutes with the co-operation of the Air Traffic people who knew us well. He was ashen when we landed, but did accept that he had been the cause of his own misfortune.

Forever after with him, I could ask him straight out, how important is this trip, and we would be speaking the same language. The switch from military flying to the civil mode sometimes called for one to revert to first principles. I was on an instrument approach to Fredericton in poor weather, and I broke out of the murk too far up the runway to be able to land straight ahead. A missed approach was the order of the day, but I reverted to former discipline and without thinking, sucked it around for a low-level circuit and landing. Air Traffic were too surprised to say anything, although they did offer that it was a unique solution.

Being new to the McCain manner of operation I was lured into a near catastrophe one day, and only the little things that you have learned along the way saved the situation. It was a weekend flight, one of my early ones on the Navajo. I was dumbstruck by all the children, bags and helpers that appeared for the flight. I had made up a weight and balance using the plastic aid that is supplied by Piper. Knowing that we were to be full, I had used the extreme case to check the loading, I packed all the bags, only to find that another load had appeared. Rather than guess, I emptied the already packed stuff and placed the heaviest items, from the spread-out baggage, in the nose lockers. There were so many people around and Wallace was trying to organise them with some sort of urgency. As the door is at the back it was prudent to be on board whilst the seating was being sorted out. It was only a few yards to the runway, and I was into the take-off before all the noise died down. I rotated normally and the aircraft reared up into a near vertical climb. Power off, ease forward, roll out and gently put the power back on. Not an auspicious start, but the lack of a body in the front seat with me put us right on the rearward C of G. Catch me once OK; catch me twice, no way.

Winter operations in Flo-ville were a continual battle. At that time the runway was short, with a poor quality Non-Directional Beacon (NDB) approach. Returning in the early hours was a test, and sleep did not come easily after an adrenalin-rich landing. They had their own fuel system, but no mechanic at that time, and so each flight had an hour or so added to it to cope with the fuelling and hangar problems.

Being a Japanese aircraft, it was memorable to look back and see nine very white pairs of eyes belonging to the Japanese visitors, as we took off from Grand Falls airstrip, a very muddy potato field. I am probably one of the few pilots who look kindly on the MU-2, but I felt it performed well, was capable of much, and would bite the ill-prepared. In a short period of time, I suffered engine failures in both aircraft, and they have something to contribute to aviation knowledge.

The Chieftain was en route to Toronto, and I had noticed fuel seeping from the wing filler cap. The evaporation was causing ice to form downstream of the cap, but I believed that the loss was small and we were not fuel limited on this trip. I watched the fuel gauges and tried to break any potential syphon effect by switching tanks continually. The affected side showed a slightly higher fuel consumption such that all seemed reasonable. Entering the Toronto area the engine stopped, and I settled to analyse the situation. The landing was not a problem, but I rushed to check the fuel cap as soon as we shut down. The bag-type tank was sucked up tight against the filler, showing that the vent system was not functioning. When we finally examined the system, Piper had placed the flexible vent pipe in such a position that any hint of a syphon would kink the vent pipe and prevent any corrective action. The strange thing was that as the tank deformed, the fuel gauge showed reasonable indications, keeping pace with the other tank.

The MU-2 failure also occurred on a Toronto trip. Passengers tend to slam their chairs around, maybe because they are unfamiliar with the mechanism as they try to adjust the seat. To the pilot, this manifests itself as a thump that could be all manner of things. Usually a check backwards would show someone struggling with a seat mechanism. In this case, I looked back to see a wall of newspapers, but I could have missed it. The smell of burning paper heightened my alertness, for we had suffered such an event once before. Still, all was calm back in the cabin. The engine note changed, and I saw rising oil pressure. Along with an increase in oil temperature, I knew that something was amiss. The options were clear: a very bumpy night with Toronto the best airfield should problems develop. When the oil readings reached their limits, I could throttle back and try to keep them within limits, or just shut down the engine. The Garrett engine can give you more drag in a low-power situation and therefore a shut-down was the only real option. When I shut it down, it stopped instantly indicating something serious.

The turbulence in the lower altitudes did not make it easy to assess speed and altitude requirements. I requested ever lower altitudes and eventually settled at 3,000 ft. We wobbled around the ILS pattern and I prepared for a single-engined approach. The MU-2 is a quasi-STOL aircraft, I say quasi for its handling in the very low speed regimes brings all sorts of potential problems. Single engine, it is wise to have plenty of speed for the unforeseen. I had settled on 140-150 kts, and seemed to have power to spare. I tried the first flap setting and immediately lost 10 kts. The aircraft was yawing badly in the turbulence, and my speed/power reserve was getting low. On lowering the gear late on the ILS, I was pulling almost 99 per cent out of the operating engine. No time for more flap, but a constant reminder that sometimes the practice version does not match the real thing. The bang that I had felt was the main bearing letting go causing the rotating assembly to drop and wear itself away on the case. That failure adjusted my annual rate to about one per year and was to continue throughout my time in the Maritimes.

My sons would often meet the aircraft and help with the fuelling and on one occasion we found a dog, half frozen, sheltering in the snow plough. It had been –35°C for two weeks, rising to –25°C in the daytime. We brought him into the hangar for a drink, but he would not eat. It was inevitable that we took him home, but I did advertise that a dog had been found. He was wild and marginally friendly, but provided we did not intrude on his space, he tolerated us. It took two years to turn him into a loyal protector, a true Disney dog and companion.

Being single-pilot operations, the Chief Pilot and I only flew together on rare occasions. We visited Cuba several times in the

1970s, and took two pilots on those trips. The workload was constant, but I was aware that nothing got done unless you did it yourself. That is fine for you can modify your behaviour accordingly. I therefore began a career of communication by memo, which always included the item 'unless I hear from you further, I will assume that this has your agreement'. The US military call this 'UNODIR', unless otherwise directed.

Whilst the CP was on holiday, the decision was taken to purchase a jet aircraft from a short list of several. I flew them all, and stood my grounds on the Westwind 1123. They needed to get into the Chicago area non-stop, and it was not possible in that beast most of the time. Despite some very sharp numbers on the demo flight to North Carolina, the sales pilot was most put out by my notes and comments, for he had flown the aircraft well outside its published criteria.

They settled on the newer version, the Westwind 1124 built in Israel. A runway extension was required from the 2,800 ft we had, and there was much discussion as to the necessary length. The McCain engineers would have loved 4,000 ft, for that would have eased their problems immensely. I stuck at 5,000 ft for the kind of operation I knew that they required. In the end we got 5,200ft, albeit with a 3 per cent slope. The CP and I really disagreed over the new lights needed, for I was insistent on VASIs, as a minimum. His suggestion of a trial with one light left me flabbergasted. You cannot use one light when the differential between two is how the system works. A flurry of memos followed, with the point that only moths respond to one light.

We left on the 1124 course in Delaware and were half through it when I was told of my mother's near death hospitalisation. I flew to UK in time to bury her, and was back on course in time to finish with the CP. She was a great loss to the family as a whole, a rare bird in the world of so many dysfunctional families.

The new aircraft brought about the need for another pilot and Jim was hired. He inserted a change of pace and I was glad of the company. He was most leery of the CP, whose drinking habits were now beginning to intrude. I rationalised it thus: he would bounce off all the limits ever found in aviation, but in reality was capable enough that he would not kill us. He was the laziest man in the world, and intensely frustrating at times, but an alteration in one's manner of dealing with him generally allowed for an acceptable working relationship.

Loring AFB had radar that covered the border area, and one night at 3 a.m. I was called to ask if I would get airborne and search for an aircraft that appeared to be flying radar triangles, an international distress signal. Up to the hangar, pull out the MU-2 and get airborne rapidly. Never did make contact, but we believed it was poachers or druggies right over the border, just seven miles to the west of us.

When the new strip was finished, it became a focal point for locals as a drag strip. I could see and often hear these early morning incursions, which had to be stopped in view of the risk to a landing aircraft. They would scarper quickly when we drove up to the strip, especially as 'Bomber' was very protective of his terrain. The final incursion took a car at very high speed straight off the end, a 20-foot drop, with the obvious results. They crawled for help and were lucky to find it.

A common trip was to fly visitors to the Grand Falls operation, and then return them to Montreal. In very bad weather, they were flown to Flo-ville in the MU-2, to be taken later to Grand Falls. I doubted that I could get into Grand Falls, but would review at the time of departure. With no approach aids, it was a case of under or around, but even up the river was not possible.

I had filed both flight plans, just in case, so that a switch to Montreal was easy. They indicated that they would accept Montreal and I climbed out of the river to pick up my clearance for the flight. I had just copied it all when I lost all radio and navigation aids. A return to anywhere was not an option and therefore rules dictated that you continue with your flight plan and the system should recognise your dilemma.

I climbed to my flight plan altitude and settled to do all I could to find the problem. It should have been possible to contact Quebec on the VOR frequency, and I alerted them by selecting 7600 on the transponder, which appeared to be now working. I had one VOR, which should at least allow me to arrive in the Montreal area. If contact could not be established by the edge of the terminal area, I would fly radar triangles and then let down to the flat land to the SW of Montreal and hope to break out of the cloud. One of the passengers came to the front to help with the books and data I needed to see as we approached the decision point. For the first time in my career I was entering the radar triangle pattern and committed to some precise flying.

Suddenly Quebec came up on the VOR, and we initiated communication using the transponder to let them know that I was able to hear them. I completed one pattern for I needed to know where I was in case further comm was lost. A landing at Montreal was not too much of a problem as they guided me in and I acknowledged everything on the transponder.

The one unknown common point in the avionics package was at the plug-in for the headset. A fault had shorted out all but the one VOR and the transponder. My passengers were most impressed to be safely on the ground, and I guess that is all that is required in such circumstances.

One night the boys went up to the airfield to begin refuelling for me, but had not been gone long when they called from the hangar to say that there had been an accident. The CP in his usual lazy style had left out the Navajo, parked in a most unusual place. They drove around the corner in their van, straight into the radome of the Navajo. I had tried to always keep my side of the employment situation clean and tidy – no slip-ups to keep the emotional books straight. The McCains were very charitable about it, but I always felt that even if you win, you lose.

Doing anything from Flo-ville, had to involve a drive, and in order not to feel suffocated in such a small village we would drive almost anywhere to see 'newness'. I had a Saab at the time, but servicing was not available in New Brunswick. We would therefore set off for Toronto on Friday evening, to arrive in Toronto Saturday morning, service the car and complete the social stuff. Back Sunday night to check in for work by 7 a.m. Such is the bureaucratic mindset that the only real road in New Brunswick is the Trans-Canada Highway, which at that time was heavily patrolled by the Queen's Cowboys. Eastern Canada, therefore, had to swing through Fredericton and all the way up to the south shore of the St Lawrence in order to get to Montreal. The landowners of Maine had roads going right to the Quebec fence, but we were unable to use them and save 200 miles of driving.

As with any hard-living environment, some pretty heavy drinking comes with the territory. These guys in the main would stay off the main highway, and whiz down the poor secondary roads in company with me as I tried to travel away from big brother. It was only a matter of time before my travel on the safest highway, the Trans-Canada, put me in jeopardy. I was caught speeding three times over a three-week period. I was in good company, for Wallace McCain was caught also, and we both had enough points to lose our licences. Wallace went to a lawyer, and I to the Traffic Board who interviewed all those with too many points. In view of the stupidity of the situation, I determined to be most forthright at the hearing.

The board were most stern as they asked for my explanation. I said that as the TC was almost the only road patrolled, and that for fiscal rather than safety reasons, and that I lived on it and was forced to use it when leaving the province, pure exposure was bound to put up your ticket rate. I did not drink, smoke or even talk much whilst driving. Driving was an art to me, and my car was an extension of that passion. I was a professional driver, having been paid for my skills, and that a radar trap was just that, a trap. The president of the board was most courteous and agreed that in the old days one could know where the 'Feds' were all the time. He said that the Board had the extraordinary powers to grant the return of licences instantly, and he thought that, in this case, they should do that forthwith. Thus I got my licence back clean, there and then, and Wallace lost his case and his licence for three months.

NB was not a rich province, but I came into contact with some of the parochial thinking fairly quickly, and it was an indicator of the troubles to come in Canadian politics. My Saab was purchased in Ontario, as it was not available in NB. When I went to register it in NB, they demanded that I pay the sales tax again. No amount of explanation would deter them, in that double taxation could not be reasonable in any jurisdiction. I therefore jointly registered in my wife/son's name in Ontario, and they got nothing.

The continual rumblings of bi-lingualism and multiculturalism were getting louder, and as ever the core issues never seemed to be discussed, anything but. We lived in a quasi-democratic society, with a strong 'not invented here' base. It seemed to me that all the rumblings were from minorities distressed that they did not have a majority voice. Surely all those rumblings could have been quieted by the simple fact that in a majority system, many choices will not be yours, but you must acquiesce, because a majority wants it.

The new Westwind allowed a much farther ranging flight department. We started trips to Europe, and in the main the WW 1124 was adequate for the task. We routed through Iceland and could get deep into Europe from there. The Garrett engine was the engine of choice, there being little else available. It suffered an inordinate number of failures in its early years of service, such that it became known as the Garrett grenade. We had our first failure in New England just after take-off from Hartford. The bearing failure was one of many that plagued the TFE 31. They introduced 'oil analysis' so that some data could be collected to give an early warning of an impending failure. All our failures were not of the type being endured by other operators, which meant that you were still vulnerable to the more common failures whilst still suffering the rare ones. After the first failure, our oil sample indicated that something was amiss, and so back to the factory for another engine change. This proved false, but Garrett did have 101 loaner engines out in the field to cope with unscheduled removals.

The second failure occurred in Winnipeg the day after the engine on the MU-2 failed. The McCains were duly infuriated and a high-level mission came from Phoenix to placate the owners. As a feature of Canada's myopia, even though the engine was destroyed and that Garrett wished to replace it, for they were intent on bearing most of the costs, warranty would have cost McCain's Tax and Duty on a new engine. Only the data plate remained from the old engine, and I guess it was transferred to the 'new' engine, although on paper it was a rebuild of the old one. Don't you just love bureaucracy.

The final failure of the series happened on a night-flight from Paris to Amsterdam. The flash lit up the sky and the vibration was severe. We slowed, and were carrying far more power than was usual on the operating engine. The manual does not cover the case where the front fan is scarcely rotating, and therefore causing much more drag and vibration. We were on our way home, facing a trans-Atlantic flight and so the implications of a failure over the water did not escape them. I worked until the early hours comparing other alternate aircraft, for they were intent on getting rid of it. We finally obtained an engine from Israel and flew home long after they had left.

The alternates were all too costly, and so after everyone had calmed down it was forgotten. Flying in Europe is (was) quite different to North America. NATO considerations have produced a different environment, without some of the slickness that could be available in North America.

We were in Toulouse, overnight, when HH relayed that we would be departing for Antwerp or Leeds or Geneva. I tried to file all those flight plans, but the Air Traffic would not accept three flight plans to different countries all at the same time. I suggested that he change the times slightly, or even the aircraft registration by one letter. The overabundance of French humour failed him, and in any event we went to Amsterdam.

There followed a string of incidents which probably rest firmer in my mind than in others. A night recovery to Flo-ville sometimes indicated a let-down elsewhere, usually Houlton from where you could fly up the road and river to base.

With the ADF being out, I let down to Houlton and proceeded on towards Flo-ville. It was turbulent and snowing and HH came up front to offer assistance. With a full load and pressure to get back, this was a period of intense concentration. The MU-2 in severe turbulence does not have the roll authority to make maintaining level flight easy. Using 'spoilers', can cause movements in all three axes, as you fight to retain control. I was unable to land straight in, being forced to reverse down the river and suffer the extreme turbulence over the high ground. At times like this, you are using rudder and asymmetric engine to pick up a downgoing wing. The crosswind was on the limit for landing and I determined to land diagonally across the runway to reduce it. With a good coating of snow, all arrivals tend to be soft, but having put it down, I was now faced with the problem of keeping it on the runway. Full reverse and differential wobbled us to a safe conclusion.

The opposite take-off dilemma was another matter. After saying that the wind was well outside limits, but if it was important enough I would take a look, we taxied for an uphill departure.

The wind was over 45 kts at Houlton, and well across at Flo-ville. Again I settled for a diagonal run, and waited for the windsock to swing in my favour. Full spoiler was used to keep the wing down and I needed differential power to keep straight. At about 80 kts, it appeared do-able, and so I cut the power and retraced my steps for a real try. We waited for quite a while for the wind to swing and then we were off. To give me nose-wheel steering I had the stick well forward. At about 80 kts the acceleration slowed, and I realised that my forward pressure was preventing the aircraft from accelerating further. A gentle attempt to ease back caused the MU-2 to leap into the air at a lower than ideal airspeed. We were clawing for altitude and heading sideways for the hangar. I determined that take-off limits were real and that interpolation was not a good idea.

The de-icer gear in the MU-2 was quite primitive, being a small tank of fluid up in the nose for windscreen de-icing. The CP knew that there was a problem in the tank, but it was always winter before we looked at such things. When it refused to function in very heavy ice, I was forced to change seats in order to land using a small clear area on the right-hand screen. Not a very confidence-building manoeuvre for the passengers.

Canadian winters can be brutal, and there was a deal of learning for a transplanted Brit. Bagotville is not on any holiday brochure, and in the depths of winter I was forced to stay with the MU-2 and run the engines every two hours, just to give the batteries a chance. The local facilities were primitive, consisting of a tank holding hot de-ice fluid with a bucket to allow you to throw the fluid over the aircraft.

They were expected to be gone a few hours, and if we were ever to get out of there, I could not let the aircraft get too cold. When they finally appeared, we were deep in snow, but able to start. After starting the first engine, it is usual to charge up the batteries for the second start, and this I did. However, I could not move the power levers from the stops, for being up high in the wing structure, they were frozen. Full heat and high power still took a long time to free them. Taxiing in deep snow in the MU-2 is easy as the props are high mounted and well out of the way, and the low belly is very boat-like.

If we were not going to be here in spring, it was now or never. The take-off was normal until I looked down to check the airspeed. A 'continue' decision was easy, as any thought of remaining at Bagotville was mentally outvoted. As long as everything else worked, flying without an airspeed indicator should not be too much of a problem. The landing in Quebec City was uneventful, but interesting, The 'Pitot' line was depressed allowing moisture to settle and freeze, so that the usual heaters could not possibly do anything.

When the Westwind arrived, there was obviously a need for an adjusted salary base. This had been discussed, but not formalised. They obtained some comparative figures, and took a moment to inform me of the new salary. My look of disbelief made it obvious that all was not well. The analogy I used was that they had a trained surgeon who was employed as a GP. When the skills of a surgeon were required, it was not reasonable to expect the same base salary to apply. I felt uncomfortable discussing money, a hang-back to the Air Force, but I must say that they agreed to take another look and get back to me. This they did, and a fair compromise was reached.

In all my dealings they were fair, although mindset issues were almost impossible to update. After a long period of continuous work, I was either flying or on call for 34 weekends, and so some alteration was needed. I made a suggestion to W, but after consideration, he thought that no matter what we agreed, the problem would keep appearing. In that, he seriously misjudged me, for I would bleed to death rather than fail to uphold my end of an agreement. All these things conspired to undermine my attitude to staying in Flo-ville for a long time. The CP was drinking again, although I must say that it never made him unsafe, only difficult and the scheduling was never going to be benign.

Chapter XI

A<small>N OPPORTUNITY MATERIALISED</small> to move back to Toronto at a substantially higher salary and I accepted a post at INCO, a large mining corporation. The move was very hectic, with a rapid course on the Gulfstream 11, the best of the 'big iron' at that time. Inco had an enviable Flight Department, good equipment and a task that needed little explanation. The mining ventures in the north were not well served with scheduled air services, and a corporate aircraft made eminent financial sense. We would leave with a full load at 0600 and drop them in Sudbury, the nickel centre of north Ontario, load again with engineers for the Thompson mine in Manitoba, and arrive there for a full day's work. We returned at 1800, a 2,500-mile trip, moving 64 pax. This was the bread and butter for the G2 and very satisfying for the crews. The CP was ex-military who had spent some time in the RAF on the DFLS course. As reported earlier the Day Fighter Leader's Course was reckoned to be a significant hurdle for any pilot to pass and he had my vote, although nobody else knew the status it inferred.

We also had a Westwind 1121, the early forerunner of the 1124, known unaffectionately as the Lead Sled. The fuel consumption could get very high and it was not an aircraft to get casual with, especially in the north country.

The CP liked to bring on his pilots, and encouraged responsibility. He, like so many others, just had real difficulty keeping his hands off when he was flying as co-pilot.

With the Chief Engineer, we were en route to New York, and I was flying left seat. The CP was fiddling with the inertials, and as we approached a turning point on the Standard Terminal Approach Route (STAR), which required a large change in heading, the aircraft commenced a turn in the wrong direction under autopilot authority. His mercurial attitudes erupted and he blamed me for the error before I could begin to ascertain the reason for the problem. Rather than get embroiled in a who-does-what conflict, I raised my hands and said, 'You have it.' He took full control, still muttering about my mistake, until the CE pointed out that he had re-programmed the INSs and caused the problem. He said, 'I rather like Terry's response, in that he left you to sort it out.'

The CP had never embraced CRM, but he did under his breath admit to no one in particular that it was finger trouble on his part. He may have learnt from that with regard to me, for on a subsequent flight, we were faced with the flaps stuck in the take-off position. We could complete the schedule at a lower altitude and speed but the bad weather at Sudbury was a complication for landing. They were snow covered, with an approach only possible on the ILS runway, which incurred a tailwind of 12 kts. Heavy, with less than full flap available on a slippery runway, was not a circumstance I would readily accept. The CP said it was OK, for the G2 has magnificent thrust reversers. I tried to check the accurate numbers for the landing, but they were outside the normal data we carried in the cockpit. The V ref for the approach was over 160 kts in view of our limited flap, and it was going to be T/Rs well deployed in the air. Approach limits were hit at 200 kts as I tried to steadily decelerate the G2. Full reverse on a virgin snow-covered runway, and he reached over to confirm that I had full reverse. A sigh of relief that it was all over left little to indicate what had transpired.

Never having been a 'rules' person, I had always tried to create enough room for myself to manoeuvre, by gaining the confidence and trust of those above me. This trust is delicately balanced in that you appear to be successful and that your challenges to the system are rare, but always critically correct and logical.

We dispatched in the 1121 for a complicated series of flights involving both aircraft. I had no part in the planning, and we were due to meet up with the G2 in Minneapolis the following morning after positioning for our pick-ups in Waco, Texas. We were heading for Colorado Springs for the last pick-up, when I checked the runway data for our arrival and departure. It was 'hot' and 'high'. So much so that it was well off the page of performance data for the 1121. When I pointed this out to my co-captain, a discussion was necessary as to how we would handle it. An engine failure on take-off would not allow the aircraft to survive on the remaining engine and I saw no reason to compromise safety without a much better reason than 'we would be late'.

With a light fuel load we departed for Minneapolis, expecting to need a fuel stop en route. When we arrived one hour late to meet the G2, the CP was beside himself and no explanation was possible. It would have been possible had more care been taken with the planning, and so I saw no need for any further involvement on my part. When we all met up at base, the CP was gunning for somebody, anybody and my feeble attempts to disassociate myself did not work. Now my cage has been rattled and some response was necessary. I pulled out the 1121 books and photocopied the relevant pages. Interpolation was out of the question, we were not even close to being on the graph, besides which I had had nothing to do with the planning. With bad grace and a quiet statement that he was not going to apologise, the incident was put to rest. Such things define who you are, and they all knew that I would perform if absolutely necessary, but not on flimsy reasoning or bad data.

The rapid change in the fortunes of INCO, from a hugely profitable company to a massive loss-maker, took less than 18 months. The flight department was decimated and the G2 put up for sale. As last in, I expected to be first out. Initially that was embarrassing to me, and I had a hard time as others were faced with being out of work. As it turned out, they were able to find work, work that had dried up in the recession, when finally INCO closed its doors. The attempts to sell the G2 were the cause of much conflict in the department, for control was handed over to the VP Human Resources. He knew diddly about aircraft, or the manner in which they are sold. We flew to LA, Jamaica even Bermuda touting the G2, wasting large sums of money. He even demanded to be on the aircraft when the contracted broker was attempting to sell it.

When it was sold, he arbitrarily decided that the sales commission was too high, and the subsequent lawsuit proved him very wrong. The 1121 was advertised by him, and by this time all the pilots were laid off. Jamie and I flew it to Oklahoma on contract to meet the broker, buyer and customs agent, late at night. The buyer required the radar to be as advertised in the initial ad. That unit was on the

G2. The Mexican stand-off was exasperating me, and so I barged in to resolve it.

I telephoned for prices on second-hand radar units, and suggested an adjustment based on the differential value. This was accepted, but now the bombshell, in that bonehead had forgotten to indicate that the sale was in US dollars. The buyer demanded that it was in the much less valued Canadian dollars, and he was right. What a bad taste this sort of thing causes, when good companies are forced to let go valuable productive workers, and thousands of dollars are seen to be being wasted.

I learned a hard lesson here, in that reliance on one source of income was foolhardy. The severance was good, but soon spent trying to adjust your lifestyle quickly enough. I flew for the buyers on overseas training, and spent time in Europe and the Middle and Far East looking for work.

Bill L, of Red Arrows fame, who had followed me to Oshawa, was now working as a ferry pilot for De Havilland Canada. With his help I was able to get some trips ferrying Twin Otters and even the Buffalo. The contract to retrieve the DHC-5 demonstrator in Cyprus was a godsend to one out of work, and it also allowed me to pick up a Buffalo-type rating as well. We flew to London for a brief layover whilst awaiting the Cyprus flight. I met Bill in the hotel lobby, as he deposited his heavy bags by the door. That action damaged his back enough to put him in severe pain. He insisted on continuing, but was helpless in bed the moment we reached Cyprus. The Engineer and I went to the airport daily to begin the process of returning the Buffalo to flight status. Bill improved, but even to climb in to the aircraft was going to be a problem. He supervised the engine runs and we planned our departure for the next morning. He did the bits he could and talked me through the rest of it. We reached Torino and night-stopped.

The departure is a spiral climb to clear the Alps before proceeding en route. The Buffalo holds several time-to-height records and we shocked ATC with our rapid climb.

Bill took some time off in UK to further heal before crossing the Atlantic. The Keflavik-Goose Bay leg replicated our Air Race experience, in that the ground speed fell alarmingly as we left the Greenland coast. For a while we were not going to make it, but a search for a better altitude and headwind was successful. Certainly not a restful way to spend the afternoon.

The weather in the Great Lakes area was not good, and so we shortened our leg to stop in Trois Rivieres. By now we were sharing the flying and I had well earned my type rating. Toronto was below limits, but strangely the small airport at Buttonville was holding. In very poor visibility, we did a Red Arrows arrival at Buttonville to conclude my contract.

I turned the flight into several more, including a visit to the Farnborough Air Show and a return ferry in the Twin Otter. But all this was not keeping pace with the bills, and I agonised over solutions. Small businesses were the rage, but the success rate was low. I tried a wine importation venture, only to run head on into the Mafia, and even worse the government Mafia. Liquor sales are a cash cow for the provincial governments, and they have been turned into very corrupt corporations, with business practices that do not stand any examination.

I drove a school bus, with the idea of moving into tour buses, but I needed to be out there shaking the bushes for any flying job before my licence became out of date. The financial burden at that point escalates rapidly, if not for you, then for one's potential employer.

My motorcycle business was facing the same difficulties that Ontario businesses in general were facing, and we could not retrench quick enough to ease the debt load. In the end I was the only one with any resources left to pay the bills, and we were within one month of losing the major asset, our house.

I had met an old Syerston mate, one RC, who was now Chief Pilot at Execaire. This prestigious company was really the only major Management/Charter aircraft operator in Canada. The eccentric owner was a Bronfman of Seagrams fame. Despite his eccentricities, he had built an enviable company in Montreal, at that time operating aircraft for many of the major corporations in Canada. I was offered a job on the Bell Canada Falcon 20, at that time the chariot of the president.

All could not be simple, however, as there was a catch. The crew on this excellent French aircraft were the most experienced Falcon pilots in Canada, and probably the world. Each had close to fourteen years on type, but until recently they had rarely flown together. It was pointed out that somebody needed to arbitrate this crew, and it was going to be my job. They were both superb operators, uncompromising and difficult. It was going to be quite a task for any one to negotiate an armistice.

I learnt a lot, and I hope in some way they did too. I made it personal to soften their hard edges, and had a good time doing it. Such was the Execaire way, that the person signing for the Falcon was responsible for the paperwork and also most of the daily decision making. They, individually, would contribute little to the other's tasks, even to the length of walking off the aeroplane after a flight and leaving the other pilot to do everything. I set about over-contributing, doing more, not less and quietly demanding nothing in return. They were not immune to minor embarrassment, and the climate in the aircraft became a very enjoyable place to live and work. As a study in sociology, I look back upon it as a major success story.

The workload could get extremely high, to the tune of 9 or 10 trips a day and over a shift of 7 days I once did 36 trips. The routine of 'seven on-three off-seven on-four off', a 21-day cycle, was at times very tough. I had to return to Toronto from my apartment in Montreal by any means to grab just a few days at home. Sometimes it was possible to catch a ride down the corridor to Toronto in company aircraft, but I tried them all, Air Canada, car and train. I could expect to move to the Toronto base in less than two years, but in the end it took six. That environment was not conducive to a stable home life, and if you were not planning how to get home, you were worrying about how to get back to Montreal. Some guys drove down each weekend, but their schedule allowed that, mine did not. In fact scheduling became the major topic at Execaire. It could happen that your series of flights did not make it back to base for a shift change. To try and deal with that on a continual basis could be stressful. It was not sensible for me to travel back to Toronto just to turn around and fight my way back.

Holiday periods were initially hard to cope with. Many years were spent alone in Montreal, knowing that I was unlikely to fly, especially at Christmas time, but that I had to be available. There was also the question of cost. I had descended to almost the bankruptcy point prior to the Execaire job, and in that light it was hard to justify an Air Canada ticket for twelve hours at home.

I bought a monstrous great Chrysler as my Montreal beater, and it served me well, but rowing that bulk home over 400 miles was not something that one readily committed to.

The boss at Execaire was as notorious as he was eccentric. He had built up the company from nought, on the way, I suppose, using the family name for leverage. He was after all a Bronfman, and the Seagrams dynasty featured heavily in the grand scheme of things. He was a private pilot with aspirations at lecturing the world at large on the intricacies of aviation. He was sometimes amazingly astute and when depth of knowledge was the issue, sometimes amazingly stupid.

I was in good company with Ralph being Chief Pilot, Jim from McCains and Pete. That in itself made it all worthwhile. With over fifty pilots conflicts were inevitable, but as far as my crewing went it was an excellent place to work. The humour was ever present, for without it, aviation would just be another day at the coal face. One day in the company of Blatch, of Inco days, I was introduced to Barry Johnson, an Air Force acquaintance of Blatchford. He was involved in trying to return some fighter aircraft from Sweden. BJ was larger than life, with almost unrestricted thinking as to the possibilities in life. He had a need to prove himself if only to his previous associates who called him a Bullshitter Extraordinaire.

He had stood the first test by taking seven years to extract the Spitfire from the Canadian Fighter Pilots' Association. They were in serious need of cash, and BJ eventually concluded a large deal with the American millionaire David Tallichet. This multi-plane deal with the Swedish government/Museum was supposed to trade the Spitfire for several aircraft, not least of which were three Saab Lansens, A32s, vintage the late 1950s. The brunt of our conversation was my knowledge of military aircraft, and moreover my ability to utilise friends and associates scattered all over the world.

Swedish politics had dictated a defence posture that was self-reliant. They built their own equipment and tried to be beholden to nobody. Saab had kept pace with the US and the NATO allies by manufacturing some excellent fighters. From my NATO days, I knew much about the Lansen. It used a Rolls Royce engine and was roughly equivalent to a mix of the Hunter and the Swift. The opportunity to fly a military fighter again was not to be ignored, but an Atlantic ferry flight in a very short-ranged aircraft needed careful consideration. I mulled over the risk, weighing it against the business opportunities that might be built upon it. The money certainly was not the attraction, for I accepted $60/day, with $200/day on the Atlantic portion.

I had been looking for a business to support the fragility of corporate aviation, and my love and knowledge of aircraft could, in this venture, be a money maker. I made several trips to Sweden to meet the Museum and Test Centre people. The military hierarchy were extremely difficult to deal with, especially when we were negotiating the J35 Draken trades.

Museums generally do not have money, nor the ability to deal in cash arrangements. Our new-found corporation, Tacair Systems, identified a niche whereby we would conclude multiple trades with many nations and items, in the end obtaining an item that we could sell. It was long winded and often very fraught, for it should come as no surprise that governments are devious and downright untrustworthy.

My ex-Royal Air Force status was checkable, as was my service on the Red Arrows. I made no bones about establishing my bona fides on the basis of my past record.

BJ had tried to use an Air Canada friend to do the ferry flight, but as the Swedish Air Force had studied the proposed flight and concluded that it was not possible, they were in no mood to qualify just any pilot.

It was big news for the Test Centre when I arrived for my conversion, quietly praying that I had not lost my touch. The test pilot, Rolf was gruff and efficient. The afterburning system was similar to the Swift and the weight about the same. The catch was that all was in Swedish and metric. A large portion of the world still operates using the metric system, but I was faced with operating a metric aircraft in a nautical Western environment. A quick hour with the tape machine, labelling all of the switches, and we were off for the check flight.

The power control system was unique, but with manual reversion, a safe, get-you-home design. I was instantly at home in the big Swedish fighter, constantly remembering facts and figures about early swept-winged aircraft. It had much better runway performance than either the Swift or the Hunter, being able to operate without the afterburner if necessary. Like the Swift, it was something of a log at altitude, but well harmonized with insufficient tail authority to break it. Rolf wanted tight circuits in the fighter mode and I was happy to oblige. He was fishing for the gentle wing drop that occurred when the approach speed nudges the edges of a stall. I understand that he had come up with a solution to the idiosyncrasies of A32s, by sticking a narrow piece of tape along the leading edge to more readily harmonise the stalling characteristics of both wings. However, he liked my response to the gentle wing drop a moment before touch-down.

Memories of the catastrophic wing drop in the Hunter years before, made my response orderly and effective. I was sent solo the next trip and sort of blotted my copybook by forgetting to 'switch' on the fuel cock in the start cycle. An electric switch for the fuel cock is most unBritish, the lever-type LP and HP fuel cocks being a feature of Brit jet aircraft since the War.

I wandered into the far north of Sweden and made a few approaches at the Saab factory airfield before returning to Malmslatt. The intended route for the flight was of much concern to the Swedes, for they had turned it down flat. I had studied the range/route options very carefully and knew that all would have to be spot on for the flight to be possible. I left for a short flight to Malmo, routing this way to minimise the sea legs, for I could arrive in UK with a very short sea-crossing inbound to Stansted. I needed time to organise the cockpit for civil flying and make sure the charts and conversion tables were always available. The radio fit had been purchased in California and ably installed by the Test Centre. It replaced the gunsight and was well placed for use.

Less so was the Loran C, which was too bulky to be fixed anywhere. It was placed down by my right side, using the ELT antenna. Very difficult to read in sunlight, and even more of a contortion with a survival suit and oxygen mask on. The VOR/DME worked well but the fixed card ADF would hopefully never be used in earnest.

At cruising speeds the drift angle would not be severe, but for an approach I would be using all my mental acuity. It should be noted that analogue instrument interpretation in part is not only the numbers, but the rate of movement and the portion of the dial used. Thus a rate of descent of 500 ft/min is displayed logarithmically in that it uncovers a bigger portion of the dial than the next 1,500 ft/min. The metric equivalent of 500 ft/min uncovers a much smaller portion of the dial, quite a trap for the instrument pilot.

Apart from a compass error, which was quite disturbing until I found out the reason, the A32 performed well. The load was physical in that I had to refuel the 'AVPIN' tank at every turnaround. This volatile fluid was carried, in my aircraft, in jerrycans stored in the ammunition bay. It required one to perform some labour-intensive work with great care.

Isopropyl-nitrate is a mono-fuel used for starting, rather like a small rocket motor that spins up the starter and makes the A32 independent of ground facilities. I could only carry a limited amount, and therefore all starts, even to move the aircraft on the ground, needed to be calculated. Obtaining a supply outside the military system was not an option, for as Class C stores it was heavily regulated and also very expensive.

I flew to Stornaway for a long sea leg to Keflavik in Iceland. By now I had a handle on the range characteristics of the Lansen, and knew it was critically important to climb correctly, and thereafter cruise climb as the weight reduced. This practice is usually unavailable in the civil air traffic system, and so a step climb had to be carefully worked out, as attempting it too early would negate all the benefits of increased range at higher altitude.

I was now about to enter the Oceanic system, even though I would be generally well north of the bulk of the transatlantic traffic. The refuelling platform at Stornaway was separate from the parking area, and although I tried to prevent a further ground start, I was made to move for the refuel. The ATC officer unfortunately was uncaring and indifferent, and this was to be the first of our clashes over the next few years. Having told me that I could stay there whilst I completed the unending paperwork, he now insisted that I move again for an inbound aircraft that possibly wanted to refuel. I said that I could not move until departure, due to the limited supply of starter fluid. A Mexican stand-off ensued, and the refueller finally towed me forward using rope tied around the main wheels. I wanted to route direct to the Icelandic entry point, but this was refused, mainly I believe because he would not make the special case that the Lansen required. The difference was significant, cutting into my margins.

I left and ran into the first of my problems. The DME gives a ground speed readout, but such was the climb rate of the Lansen, that it broke lock just before I levelled off. I needed to see what my speed over the ground was to check that the wind effect was as notified, and that I had the range to make Iceland. The radar (civil) does not cover this area, and so I was left with my intuition. More to the point I was held down at a lower altitude than planned, another slice of my reserves slid away with that restriction. I coasted into Iceland and knew that I was on schedule and with adequate fuel reserves.

The US military were quite interested in this funny, unknown aeroplane, and I obtained excellent assistance from them and Icelandic Air. The Loran C was only marginally useful, and I could not count on it for the next crucial leg to Sonderstrom in Greenland. The weather looked grim for the next few days, and I could see that I might be forced to leave the A32 in Kef, as I had to be back at work in Montreal.

Such was the case, as a weather system sat over Greenland and did not seem likely to move. I stuck plastic over the vital areas, for we were close to the sea and the salt air was not to be ignored. Moving the A32 was again a problem, but we towed it with the rope method and a bar to turn the nosewheel, to a secluded location. My haunting the weather office in the early hours of the morning did nothing to persuade the stationary system to move, and so back to New York and Montreal.

My next few days off were a month away, and I knew that I would have to do any maintenance myself on my return. There had been signs of a small hydraulic leak, such that I felt it necessary to try and top up the system. All the Swedish fittings were unique, rather than the standard NATO that I was used to. In the end, with fear and trepidation and assistance from a friendly Icelandic mechanic by the monika of 'Lilly', I removed the emergency valve, so that we could top off the system by pouring the fluid in directly. Most unorthodox, but it worked.

Around this time Execaire was moving into the 'big iron'

operation. The first was a Falcon 50 for Seagrams, followed by a Challenger 601 for Bell Canada. This meant that the Falcon 20 would be disposed of and after a certain amount of two-stepping, its crew would translate to the Challenger. The boss was intimately involved in the outfitting of both aircraft and also the certification, for neither were exactly standard.

The process took over 240 hrs on the Challenger, but it meant many sorties validating pieces of equipment and trips to the North Pole and even Egypt. I liked the new aircraft, but its flying characteristics were somewhat unusual. It was very short coupled with a strong nose-down attitude for landing. The new Collins EFIS was state of the art, well in advance of many airliners. It took much getting used to, so much so that several of the older pilots could not adapt and became immensely frustrated.

Leo, a solid, competent operator, resisted the new technology, for it had little to do with 'hands and feet' skills. There was so much data displayed that a mental priority system was needed. There is no doubt that it is the way of the future, but the engineers and the aviation authorities missed the fact that although the overall result is a gain, there is a downside. In times of trouble it can take significant time to resolve displayed data, sometimes enough to precipitate an accident.

The Airbus autopilot logic is a case in point. We programmed our individual instrument displays differently, removing unneeded data. This however begs the question, 'what is the other pilot looking at?'

The boss drove Collins to distraction and we finished up with three LaserRefs and two AHARS. The Lasers were inertial nav systems driven by non-mechanical gyros. The AHARS were 'attitude heading and reference' installations that supplied the normal gyro data of heading and attitude from one central source.

The boss wanted ultimate redundancy in that failure of any two systems would not inhibit the flight. Trying to wire up essentially five systems was not possible, bear in mind that the LaserRef system was supposed to do it all, he just wanted another layer of security. What we finished up with was the AHARS driving the autopilot and the Lasers driving the attitude system. In theory the two could have tried to diverge, but they never did.

As with any new aircraft, there is a period of trust and

complacency that remains until things go wrong. The 601 was very serviceable, but the civil aviation system in any country is very regulation driven. Avoidance of the can of worms sends people into all kinds of protective modes, where the truth has a hard time surviving.

We were returning from New York to Toronto and in the cruise phase, when I noticed that we had a 'green' undercarriage light. This light signifies that the indicated gear leg is down. This could not be the case, as the supporting evidence was just not there, no noise or trim indication. We slowed and discussed our options. If it was not down, how could we fully ensure that it was down when we finally selected it down. The fly past the tower method is OK, but not foolproof and on a busy Friday afternoon, not easy.

We selected the gear down early and both looked at each other in consternation, as the noise of the down-going gear was not right. I said that the nose wheel was not down, for I believed that it had just dropped onto the gear door. After several other system tries we flew past the tower for a visual inspection. The emergency system leaves the nose doors open, thereby restricting the tower's ability to see the wheel clearly. As such the handle has to be pulled, then retracted, then pulled again for the eventual landing.

All was uneventful, until the later inquisition. The boss was going to be hard to placate in this instance, and he assembled the Canadair engineers, including the designer of this part of the 601, to review the incident. He could not get past the notion that a 'green' indication is always a 'safe' indication. The forces marshalled themselves, and strangely, Jamie, who had been a test pilot at Canadair, was quite ready to dismiss the incident as a quirk. The boss and I were being 'snowed', and this feeling caused several unknown facts to appear.

This was the second such incident, the first resulting in a two-wheeled landing. Of course the pilot was held to blame in that he could not have checked the indication properly, for to compound the issue, the shock of falling on the nose had turned the indicator to the unsafe position. He had no evidence to support his contention that the indication was always green.

The system uses 'Proximity' switches, non-mechanical devices that have replaced the more common solenoid type. Intro to the 601 always belaboured the technicalities of prox switches. If the system was as they described, then such a failure was impossible. In the end we were both right, for hidden away, unmentioned, was a mechanical switch. This had failed, and in a complicated way produced the result we had suffered. As I often said, everything I have ever been told about 'electrics' subsequently turned out to be false. This produces a wariness that is good for your health.

We suffered an ignominious failure in Ottawa whilst on a training flight, when the thrust reservers were in translation after landing. We switched to the auxiliary power unit during the translation of the T/Rs from open to closed. This locked them in their present position and ensured that we could only taxi backwards, a definite no-no. It also prevented the engines from starting again until they were in the closed position.

On a much later return flight from Europe, we were coasting into NE Canada, when a massive electrical fluctuation occurred. All the EFIS screens went haywire, and the generator indicators were almost unreadable. A test of the dual indicators was called to identify one possible area of trouble. The Constant Speed Units were a likely candidate, but finding which one was a guess. We had to turn one off, but if you turned off the wrong one and initiated a double 'gen' failure, then the Ram Air Turbine (RAT) would pop out giving rise to another series of less than desirable circumstances. We chose correctly, for the CSU had suffered a major oil leak causing it to fluctuate wildly before finally failing. This was, I believe, the first major failure for the system and it would put a serious dent in the statistics on which evolving certification of the Challenger depended.

This incident, along with an engine failure as the 601 descended into UK, was carefully handled so that there was no adverse publicity. The engine failure was termed a precautionary shutdown, for as the stoppage was imminent, good airmanship says to shut it down and not wait for the bang. Economy with the truth never bothers bureaucrats.

Along with long-range flying came a Trojan Horse – women. Execaire had never had female pilots or flight attendants, and this very male bastion did not know what had hit it. We were very lucky in the addition to our crew, and in fact it brought a totally new dimension to trips. In the way of aviation, humour is a great leveller. Anne would take so much shit, then start throwing things. I have seen the interior dripping with the contents of a soda syphon, well aimed, and the resolution was for us to pick up all the ice cubes she had thrown.

On a day off in Cairo, we were given camels for our sortie around the Pyramids of Giza, and the boy belted them to urge them on their way. The pounding on Anne's pubic bone was evidently not to her liking, but she nearly fell off when I told her to make sure that she did not split her difference.

The macho state of young European taxi drivers was unknown to Anne, but it was easy for us to ensure that she was put in the front seat for the trip from the airport to downtown Brussels. Not being a good passenger and showing too much leg, the set-up was complete. He went faster and she slid lower, finally outdoing himself by speeding down a narrow street and clipping two parked cars.

She was bi-lingual, having been raised in Montreal. Aviators are generally a cosmopolitan lot, well educated and travelled. Shrill causes are normally put to rest with wit and sarcasm. Nationalism and other calls for special treatment are not well taken. The rudeness of the French, especially in the service industries is legion. We had had a bellyful of minorities decrying the democratic process, in that if you are a minority, you have to acquiesce to the wishes of the majority, that's how it works. Well now, our Annie, speaking excellent Quebecois, was having a hard time with Pierre, the *cochon* behind the desk at our Nice hotel. We could see the missile attack gathering, and rescued him by removing her.

Our other long-suffering crew member was a lady schooled by nuns and formerly married to an Australian. What a mixture that was, even though she was most gracious and worldly.

We were trapped nose in to the parking area at Luton airport. With slot times to make, it was necessary to get out of their, pronto. She came up front to witness our recovery, and then left as we started the blind back-up out of the parking area. The 'outflow valves' are up front in a 601, and all of a sudden we were overpowered by a dreadful smell. Jim's loud comment was to the effect that we must have backed into a manure pile. It became obvious that our F/A had gone back to relieve herself of the gaseous effects of last night's Indian curry. She carried it off with grace when it became known that we knew.

With my history of Atlantic flying, at high, medium and very low altitudes, the sale of our old Falcon 20 and its delivery to Paris was dropped on my plate. It came at a time when I was deeply into the A32 flights and also starting the F5 and F104 work with the Royal Norwegian Air Force. The aircraft was not equipped for trans-Atlantic work, and so the long northern route was necessary. The boss was explicit in demanding that I do the trip, but I had to be back in time to turn around and pick up another A32 in Sweden.

We were routed through UK, to deliver some documentation to Flight Refuelling, who had purchased the Falcon. Arriving in Paris after two days of hard going, we were met with a huge strike in Paris. Hotels were full, airlines not flying, rental cars unavailable. The nearest rooms were 200 kms away, with the impression that it would take a few days to resolve. We tried to get return flights to Canada from everywhere – Amsterdam, Munich, London even as far away as Madrid. Each attempt brought its own set of problems, and so we were consoling ourselves in the coffee shop, when I heard English voices discussing their return to UK. Quick as a flash I was inquiring if there was the possibility of a ride to anywhere in the UK. It turned out to be an Aztec, owner flown, accompanied by an instructor. They were grateful to have two qualified pilots on board, especially as the owner had availed himself of a French business lunch and was in no shape to fly.

We set off at low altitude for the less than two-hour flight to Biggin Hill. At that altitude he was working hard to navigate and making it unnecessarily difficult for himself. I offered my assistance, which he refused, but we did climb to a more acceptable altitude. As we neared the coast I saw that the groundspeed readout was less than 100 kts, meaning that we were encountering strong headwinds. He seemed unaware, and so I started to discuss temperature and altitude effects on the Aztec. He had not realised that I knew the aircraft, for in fact my small company, Tacair Systems, was in the process of purchasing one. He handed over control, a little too readily I thought, and I quickly found a better altitude, where the G/S picked up to 130 kts. We could now make closing time at Biggin Hill, and we greeted the customs inspector at 2100 precisely.

The effects of the strike had reached London and so all the hotels that we tried were full. They entreated us to stay with them for the night, but I really wanted to be close to Heathrow to take advantage of any flights that came available. We took a taxi to the airport and found one of those walk-in rooms that hotels hang on to till the last minute.

We were back in Montreal three days after departure, to an astounded boss, for he was sure that we would extend the trip as much as possible, Paris in the spring and all that.

I returned to Iceland and set about checking over the A32 for the 'difficult' leg to Sonderstrom in Greenland. I needed to be over 'KK', a radio beacon known as 'big gun', on the east coast of Greenland in no less than one hour and three minutes. This may seem rather theatrical, but the fuel constraints were that tight. In the worst case I would have about five minutes remaining on landing. In reality five is as good as forty-five for I could not go anywhere else but Sondy.

I waited until I could get a weather scenario from Sondy, and that the headwind component was light enough for the one hour and three bit. The Loran C worked fine on climb-out, and as expected I lost my DME groundspeed readout just before the top of climb. Another few minutes and I would have a cruise figure and with it the knowledge that I could make it.

The Loran C quit, but not before it gave me the data I needed. KK should be crossed in slightly less than one hour and all looked well. I spoke to the USN radar stations in the middle of the ice pack, and they confirmed my speed. They even vectored a Phantom onto me, much to my consternation, for I was cruise climbing the A32 at that time, to give me more padding for my arrival at Sondy. Even though I nipped back down to my metric altitude, they never found me. I popped out of cloud about 8,000 ft still not picking up the DME which is buried in the fjord and therefore very short ranged.

The Danes were knowledgeable about the Lansen, but they all came out to look at it, including several ex-Danish AF pilots who had flown this type in their AF career. They were amazed to think that I had come from Iceland, knowing as they did, the range of the aircraft.

Because of my late start waiting for the weather, I elected to stay the night in the airport hotel. The trip into Canada was short but fraught, for the Davis Strait is a forbidding body of water. Map-reading is impossible, for the sea ice and snow alter the landscape beyond all recognition. I saw the VOR needle twitch at an estimated range of 190 miles and knew that I had not made any silly mistakes. The ILS landing was to put up my heart rate for although I asked for the weather, the radio station spoke of conditions not even remotely like the ones I could see out of the front windscreen. He of course was looking in a direction that was in the clear, and my instrument approach was in dense sea fog. I found it very hard work doing a metric conversion, checking continually that my mental arithmetic was accurate.

There were several ways to cover the remaining distance to Montreal, but the one with the most options was to stop at Schefferville, a once busy mining town. The moon landscape that surrounds the area is not conducive to mistakes, and I was very careful to have as much as possible going for me as I descended for a landing. The weather ahead was awful, and so another night stop was called for. Arriving in Montreal, it was parked to await my next few days off.

To deliver it to Mojave, California was a test of ingenuity, for I only had a very limited supply of Avpin, and the 'Hot/High' performance of the A32 was unknown. It was agreed that I would display it at one of the owner's restaurants in Columbus, Ohio, which was conveniently placed alongside a taxiway at the airport. I was able to fly there and take the A32 to a position opposite his restaurant. There was an old exit road right in front of his place that looked like it might stand the weight of the Lansen. With much trepidation I eased the aircraft off the taxiway. The Lansen sank into the surface and even the application of full power showed that we were within an inch of being stuck. I lit the afterburner, which must have been an interesting addition to lunch for the watching throng, and lurched back onto firm ground.

The best route was stops in Pueblo and Scotsdale, leaving an easy run to Mojave. Pueblo is off any Lansen chart, but I believed that we had sufficient performance for their 8,800-ft runway. It was hot as I started the take-off and acceleration was geriatric, but I had that so important feeling of knowing that it was OK, and we were off with not much to spare. Phoenix were not impressed with my M.90 descent speed, but the flight plan did specify such options.

Mojave was somewhat of a disappointment, for it had taken such a long time to complete the delivery, that the feeling of success was just not there. I was met by Burt Rutan's people, then in the early stages of building highly imaginative aircraft, for which they have become famous. On to Los Angeles and back to the humdrum life of a corporate pilot.

The second A32 ferry was easier to organise, and the Swedes were much more comfortable with idea of the flight, now that they had seen that it could be done. I flew straight from Malmslatt to Lossiemouth, feeling more secure using a NATO airfield. I should have known that this was going to be a difficult trip when I was forced onto the short runway for landing. That night a Buccaneer had crashed in the middle of the field, from, it turned out an unusual technical failure.

I paid my fuel bill in US dollars, much to the consternation of the Accounts Section, who made a major error in their calculations. They caught it just as I was starting up, causing another shutdown and inroads into my precious Avpin supply. It was significantly further from Lossie to Keflavik, and the danger of a beam wind turning into a head wind happened. I felt most uncomfortable as I levelled off and the groundspeed check with Scottish radar confirmed my gut feelings. I turned back for Stornaway, to begin the business of conflicting with the civil requirements yet again. I refuelled and with a more northerly track was happy with the flight plan times.

At that time the Oceanic control area made for the payment of fees from 10°W. if they were going to force me to follow a longer route, then I would avoid their expensive fees. I filed 09.59°W, and saved a bundle.

Keflavik seemed like home after all the energy I had expended there. The en route weather was fair, with Iceland being suspect. I took off and carefully monitored the climb, noticing that the NDB was not working after a few minutes. By the top of climb it was beyond my powers to fix it and so back to KF. The radio man lived in Reykjavik, a thirty-mile drive, and so nothing could be done until tomorrow. He found a fuse blown in a very inaccessible place, and I was happy with that.

The second attempt resulted in the same decision, turn back. This may seem like a fairly innocuous process, but it is in fact very weighty. This leg was bad enough from weather considerations alone, that to have equipment problems was very tiring. Two days of investigation resulted in little satisfaction, although it did work on the ground. The weather and winds were the best that I had seen, but my ability to find 'KK' accurately was not there without the NDB. I took off and climbed in a high mental state. The NDB failed on the climb, followed by the loss of the DME and Loran C as usual. Decision time. I believed that my careful planning would get me into a forty-mile window of Sondy. Using the one-in-sixty rule, I would need to be off track by less than 3 degrees. That was the range of the DME and also the GCA radar at Sondy. I was on track at the top of climb, had one hour and thirty minutes to landing at the most, and I had the sun. Remembering Francis Chichester's epic flights, I marked the position of the sun on the canopy with my chinagraph pencil, and kept the two together for the next hour or so.

The coast of Greenland was obscured by a large band of cloud, covering 'KK'. I could see the coast to the north and south and would have to make a guesstimate of my time over 'K'. I was well inside the magic 63 minutes, for sure, but it was unnerving.

The icecap and cloud melted into one and I established radio contact before letting down. In my many trips to this part of the world, I had never seen the coast from high altitude. To break out of cloud and see the fjords was a heart-stopping moment. I was still over 80 miles out and could ill afford to pick the wrong one. Stick with the plan, and slowly one inlet seemed to be more on the nose than others. At forty miles I picked up the DME, and watched it carefully for the descent.

A quick turnaround and I was off to Frobisher, my entry point into Canada. This was an easy leg in theory, but there was a very strong wind at altitude at 90 degrees to my track. I usually flew magnetic track, but with such a strong wind I could ill afford to be outside the range of the meagre nav aids of my destination. The weather was good for the first part and I used the ADF which had now decided to work, to backbeam up the fjord.

There was a beacon at the top end of the fjord, right on the coast, which was slightly left of my route. Something up ahead is more comfortable than an aid behind you and so I switched to that frequency. Nothing. Back to Sondy, nothing. If there was any casualness, it rapidly disappeared.

A review of my options said that I had less than an hour to go, a VOR/DME ahead of me, and all I had to do was arrive within 150 miles of Frobisher to pick up the navaids. I was trying to receive the coastal NDBs, and finally Cape Dyer came in strong, only on the wrong side of the nose. Should I switch back to magnetic track or accept this new data?

All I had ever learned about ADF/NDB errors was now crucial. They are at their maximum at these latitudes and in coastal sea ice conditions. I plotted my position and times, and decided to revert to a condition that would for surely put me to the south of Frobisher, under the effect of the wind. In this way I would know that my search would have to be to the north.

Radio contact was established very late, first with a BA aircraft who relayed my predicament to Frobisher. The VOR did not twitch at anywhere near 200 miles, and so now it was time to be counted. I turned north-west over some of the roughest country on earth, and waited. By my estimation I was over 100 miles to the south, an indication of the strength of the wind, but the principles were good and a restorer of my faith in myself.

I was totally knackered after these adrenalin efforts, the up/down into the cockpit for the refuel flops and the sweaty confines of the full immersion suit. Even the business of extracting the Avpin jerrycan and climbing up onto the spine to top up the tank was getting to me. Running your motor at high rpm for a long time has that effect, I guess.

The next legs were a blur and I arrived in Toronto ready to sleep for a long time. I followed a different route to Scotsdale this time, for this aircraft had a very rudimentary set of dual controls. David T wished to fly with me on at least the last the leg to Mojave. His experience was almost all Second World War stuff, he owned innumerable types at that time, but he took to the Lansen without wavering. I would have liked to do more for him, but time was against us and we parked this, his second purchase, next to the first delivery. He was impressed with our abilities, so much so that he took on my partner in Tacair Systems to run his aviation empire.

BJ spent the next six months inventorying his widely scattered collection. David had given Jeff Hawke almost a million dollars to obtain the military aircraft on disposal from Morocco. This wily individual had made a name for himself as a pilot and securer of rare equipment. He also managed to stay just ahead of the authorities wherever he went. He obtained several B-25's, but left them scattered around the globe when they had mechanical troubles. BJ found one in Spain at Marbella and another in Paris. The French seized that one for non-payment of parking fees, and it now resides in the Le Bourget Museum. There was a noticeable lack of due process, legal or otherwise, but it was well known that the government was predatory in such matters.

David had a most bizarre attitude to his possessions, not affording them any care or attention. The continual lawsuit route was a way of life for him. I guess that if you show willing to sue and spend $100,000 chasing $20,000, then the less well-heeled individual will cave in most of the time. He obviously thought so.

We used the Spanish aircraft to resolve the Swedish trade and I found, quite by accident, one of his Swedish DC-3s languishing at Reykjavik airport. It was badly damaged by a snowplough, and somewhat vandalised inside. There was over $3,000 owing for parking, and an insurance settlement for the damage. He collected over $45,000 for the insurance and sold off the bits for a handsome sum. His JU-52 was being used by Hawke on the airshow circuit in Europe. Their business deal had by now broken down into open legal warfare. His eccentricity seemed to alienate all around him, but then he was a multi-millionaire, so by that standard we had no right to criticise. I begged him to take the most rudimentary steps to protect the Lansens, but he considered that items like fuel in the tanks to be a waste of cash. Jet aircraft are not like round-engined Second World War fighters; they rapidly revert to scrap if left unprotected, and this was the sad case for all the Lansens.

The second ferry had BJ tracking my flight, and he knew that the Sondy leg was crucial. At that time the USN had the only telephone line into Sondy. BJ tried to call but could not break into the military system. By carefully listening to the operators, he managed to bluff his way in. When I had a call from Major Johnson on the parking area at Sonderstrom, I knew that he had beaten the system.

The last Lansen was significant in that it was the test vehicle for the Air Force Flight Test Centre. The aerodynamic model for all aircraft is a combination of mathematic revision and wind tunnel analysis. There is always some error in wind tunnel data because of interaction with the tunnel walls and also scale effect. Generally models are used in tunnel tests and until the computer simulation reached a certain level of sophistication, there were very few research tunnels that could handle whole aircraft.

The Swedes had attempted to skirt these problems by drilling many small holes in the aircraft and attaching hundreds of tiny pressure gauges to these holes. The wing surface had heat-sensitive film applied to it and a tank of visual fluid installed in the wing tip. The standard pitot boom was replaced by a nose-mounted installation so that a tiny video camera could be mounted on the old wing-tip boom.

All this was controlled from the back seat using a multi-channel tape recorder. In some ways it was crude, but a whole aircraft plot had not been done before. They had funded most of the research, but this was the last aircraft of the trade package and there was still a final series of analytical runs required. It was agreed that I would finish off these tests on the way to California, and that they would pay for part of the ferry cost. The A32 was to be taken to a NASA field where the test equipment would be removed, before the Lansen was taken to Mojave.

The aerodynamicist was Arild Bertilrud, who followed the A32 to NASA to complete his work. All the equipment was either copied or placed in a B 737 which NASA used to validate Arild's work. Along the way I met Anders Hellberg, a flight test engineer at the centre. We had become friends on my many Swedish trips, and he accepted the task of operating the equipment on the ferry to North America. Remember this was a very risky venture by their standard even though I had already done it twice.

We were limited by having to avoid rain/moisture on the trip, to protect the sensitive film. We knew that it would take much more time for the ferry, and we could not complete the trip in winter. As it was we were too late and parked the A32 at Cranfield, UK ready for an Apr/May transatlantic crossing.

A team would be sent to inhibit the Lansen and also prepare it for

One of the last three on route to NASA.

flight in spring. The epic is well documented in Swedish Air Force and Museum history. It was the easiest trip of all, with the tape record being shipped back from each landing point and new tape and film being installed. Even the sun's angle had to be calculated so that the solar heating component could be taken out of the equation.

We entered the Canadair Flight Test area north of Montreal to complete the last tests, with Anders releasing the fluid under specific speed and flight load conditions. The camera worked well and the spiral dive at M.95 and three 'g' certainly woke up the Montreal Air Traffic.

Anders returned home and I took my last flight by delivering the A32 to the Norfolk Test centre.

As a consequence of the work with the Lansens, Tacair Systems discovered a niche: trading ex-military aircraft. Museums, as has already been stated, do not have cash to purchase exhibits, and must rely on their ability to trade to obtain representative material. With my worldwide connections in many military organisations and my partner's record of obtaining the Canadian Spitfire for Sweden, we surged into a far-reaching business.

There was good money to be made if you could complete some multiple trades and end up with a saleable item, from which to obtain your profit. The major market was, of course, the US, where there were many exciting aircraft collections. Britain and Australia were also excellent markets, but the US allowed for the establishment of private museums, which could be run as tax-free businesses. Therefore if the exhibits inflated in value and they could be displayed at air shows as well, it was potentially an attractive venture.

Until the early 1980s only Second World War types had been the focus, but then jet aircraft started to reach private collectors. Governments, through there aviation authorities, had little or no stated policy to serious war material coming into private hands, and their reaction was mostly illogical and unpredictable, but showed the heavy hand of bureaucracy that is caught by its own rules. Where it became an issue they simply changed the rules, and in many cases retroactively.

Canada's position is a case in point, for they had allowed disposal of F-86 Sabres to a dealer in the Maritimes. The disposal was conditional on the aircraft being unfit for flight, with very loose wording as to what constitutes 'unfit'. Most of these Sabres finished up as target drones for the US military, but the odd one went to private hands where it had the 'ice cream parlour accident'. Flown by a very inexperienced pilot, it over-rotated and finished up killing a large number of unfortunates in an ice cream parlour off the end of the runway. As ever the political decision was made to ban the sale of ex-military items when the rules in place were quite able to control this situation, if properly implemented.

Canada suffers today from this silly predicament and is forever having to resort to subterfuge to skirt its own rules. The jet aircraft was no more advanced in its day than the P-51 was in its day, technological advances keep pace with social change and vice-versa. More to the point, jet aircraft are considerably more reliable than piston engines, but those statistics were politically inconvenient.

We were directed to Norway which had strong Second World War history and a large German inventory. At the end of the War, there were 350,000 German troops in Norway, along with their equipment. Their museum was somewhat in advance of the rest, being willing to trade this well-cared-for German stuff for desirable aircraft. They also had F-104 and F-5 jets ready for scrapping.

We found a civilianised Lodestar in Finland, but it was sold to the UK before we could seal the deal. When we eventually agreed on the trade, we had to obtain it from its UK owner, a slippery individual, who would have put the price up if he had known what we were doing. We concocted a cover of using it in Canada for survey work, and quietly flew it to Norway using a contract pilot. Our trade item was an F-5 which was destined for Oklahoma and a wealthy collector. It was the first of a series and it had an interesting impact on the US mindset.

The first thing we discovered was that banks in Canada have little or no understanding of international business. The idea of an exotic multi-nation trade was beyond them. The excuses went something like this, 'This in an old aircraft, correct, so how can we establish its value? It is not in our jurisdiction, and we would not be comfortable with an asset so far from our reasonable control.' When I responded with comments about old pictures or old furniture, they were unmoved.

We therefore had to round up the cash ourselves. This first venture sat cleanly on the equity in my house, and is not something I am particularly proud of. But then without risk there is no reward. Even with the payola that is a necessary part of this, we made a fair profit and moved on to the next deal.

The F-5 was the focus of our attention, because it was twin-engined allowing wealthy collectors to obtain insurance, and more to the point, it was US-made. Although there were better, cheaper items available, there was a mindset that has to be understood. NIH, not invented here, is not peculiar to the US, but it is certainly a major force when solutions are being sought.

As an extension of our F-5 studies, it was obvious that the two-seater would be the prize. Most air forces had a limited number of trainer versions, and so there were very few likely to be put up for disposal. Holland began to dispose of its F-5 fleet, mostly to Turkey which, at that time, was attracting attention for its human rights violations. It became a political hot potato, but did free up one specimen to the Dutch Museum.

We discussed trade options and settled on the Hawker Sea Hawk as a desirable item for the Naval Museum. They had been searching for an acceptable aircraft for ten years, and we found one in UK and delivered it in five weeks. We had no reason to suspect the integrity of the Dutch system, but were about to be dealt a powerful lesson.

The deal was signed with the Director of the well-recognised Museum, in his office with all the trappings that go with such a position. We were comfortable knowing that they were very happy with their Sea Hawk, and sat at Eindhoven to await delivery of the F-5B. The wings were placed in our storage hangar, and the fuselage was unloaded. Consternation, and the military team picked up the wings and fuselage and departed. No explanation was offered, and so it started.

We engaged the services of a prestigious Amsterdam law firm, who usually represent the military. Pressure was applied but we got there first. What followed was incredible, but they tried to say that the Director of the Museum did not have the authority to sign the deal. When the clock starts running on legal procedure, them with the most cash win. We did however have several things going for us, not least of which was the Sea Hawk which the Navy had no intention of relinquishing.

We had photographed the F-5 in storage and had impeccable paperwork to support our case. It finally came down to sheer bloody mindedness on the part of the senior officer in charge. To be at my stage of life and still have dreams of Fair and Reasonable, Honour and Integrity may seem naive, but I had found that disciplined systems usually perform unless the corruption comes from the top.

The Dutch experience was not easily forgotten. There was a scandal on-going involving the head of the Air Force and a certain lady friend. She had been given an F-104 for some artistic reason, but the press got hold of it. We tried to avoid going public with our situation, but it was not until we announced that it would be released to the media as a full exposée did they agree to settle. Even then they stole vital parts from the aircraft just before we collected it.

To travel from Canada to meet with a bureaucrat to discuss semantics was unbelievable but true. I ended up moving through a sentence, word by word, backed up by the Oxford dictionary, as he fought a rearguard action to deny what was written. The air force base gave us a plaque to commemorate our victory over a system that was downright dishonest.

Our first CF-104D was delivered to Jim Robinson in Texas, who at that time was amassing a superb collection of jet warbirds. He eventually gave his collection to the EAA at Oshkosh, fed up with the petty-minded bureaucrats whose mandate is ever remembered with those epic words, 'We're from the FAA, we are here to help you.' Yeah, right.

The next trade was another F-104 destined for Northern Lights, a newly funded outfit that was chasing military contracts requiring high-performance targets. All these aircraft were delivered by C-130 Hercules, courtesy of the RNoAF, apart from the very first aircraft that was flown over by Jerry Westphal, an ex-Canadair test pilot.

Flight International was an embryonic corporation, heavily into military contracts, and they needed an F-5 type to tow an instrumented target. The only one we could get was in pieces, many pieces. In fact there were over 2,000 parts missing, but it was decided to complete a rebuild at Newport News, and we began the long task of obtaining all these parts from Norway and other sources.

Toronto to Newport is an unattractive airline route, and so we purchased an Aztec E to enable us to be there quickly, and to deliver parts and expertise on request. The Az-truck performed well under the circumstances, but it did precipitate us into another round of legal disease. We were ecstatic when the F-5 flew, to begin an interesting episode in its civilian career.

The DHC-4 Otter is a uniquely Canadian aircraft, but it did sterling service for the RNoAF, and consequently was a desired item. We found a specimen in Newfoundland and had it flown to Oshawa for inspection and possible purchase. It arrived in true Newfie fashion having landed at the wrong airport right in the bad ground that was identified as such. We dismantled it and it was flown out on a C-130 from nearby Trenton. The owners had a disagreement over the sale between each other, and sought to get it back, but we knew a good deal when we saw one and spirited it away as fast as possible.

There were several water bombers mouldering away north of Toronto, and it was believed that we could obtain one at a useable price as the company was in receivership. Norway did not have a trade item readily available and so we took a flier on the supposition that a deal could be made, if not now then later.

The owner of the PBY-5A was a lawyer, and we took incredible steps to protect our interests, for his business practices were well known. We assembled a crew to ferry the aircraft and demanded a flight test and flight to Oshawa to see if the PBY was acceptable. This meant that the actual transfer of funds resembled a drug deal. As it was the PBY had a hydraulic failure and assorted other iniquities before it was ready for the Atlantic. We had obtained a spares package valued as high as possible, in order to have some leverage with the seller, in the event of problems. Whilst it did not pay for our out-of-pocket expenses, it did go some way to balancing the books, for we sold the package to cover some of the costs.

Bart, an Air Canada friend, took part in the ferry, for his rating was needed as was his European knowledge. They even took it straight across to Shannon, and parked it at Eindhoven to await developments in Norway. Norway at that time was melting down Second World War equipment, rather than sell it and obtain some return for the expense of storing and cataloguing it all these years.

We focused on the antique pistols, Lugers and P-38s, for they were collector items well worth accepting in trade for the PBY. The problem was to convince the timid Norwegians that such a deal was sensible. Only the US could accept such numbers, and after continual battles with US, Norway and Canada, we set about contracting a buyer.

A well-known dealer and collector was eventually sorted from the incredible variety of personalities that appear at times like this, and we concluded a very reasonable deal. Norway were happy with this test case, even though successive governments got cold feet and refused to sell any more. They made our tenuous position worse by insisting that the last replacement batch stayed in Canada. Our buyer was going to sue instantly when we relayed the news, but I wrote an award-winning letter to explain our situation. Such communication is not the norm, but then Tacair was not a normal company.

We paid our bills, rewarded our helpers and did most of our dealings without massive legal protection. We were on the edge of the 'arms dealer' business, insistent that we were museum traders, but there are none so deaf as those who do not want to hear.

I had spent years as a hobby studying military armaments, and I knew who had what and where. This led us all over the world making deals and connections, and inevitably to two of the sensitive areas. Sensitive that is to Uncle Sam. For in his efforts to be the world policeman, he faces frustration in numerous places where his views are not shared. Under their Trading with the Enemy Act, anybody who dealt with countries on their shit list could be hit hard.

Our first ventures into Vietnam were tentative and discreet. We used the services of a Canadian/Filipino who was known to me from my days at the London Poly studying for my civil pilot's licence. He had gone on to bigger and better things, finally being a pilot for Ferdinand Marcos and also his bagman.

The US arsenal that remained in Vietnam was well documented and of intense discomfort to the US authorities. By any standard it was the spoils of war, but as we all know, when asked where a 400 lb gorilla wants to sit, the answer is always, anywhere he damn well pleases, and the State Department acted always as if gross weight wins.

We identified several aircraft that were good sellers in the US, namely the A-37 and the F-5, even to F-5Es at that time. Rey A was interested in the helicopter engines, many of which were still in their original packing. We concluded a deal on the idea of bringing in an exploratory A-37 and a helicopter engine. Rey could come and go as he pleased in Vietnam, by virtue of past services to the regime. He had affected the transfer of a large amount of Aid in the form of US currency. Whilst this enraged the US, it is worth remembering that Russian troops stationed in Vietnam were paid in US dollars.

Rey finally decided to deliver an A-37 as proof of his ability. He had brought out some intriguing evidence as to his status with the Vietnamese authorities, and we as a group decided to enlist the services of ASTI, a Phoenix-based company, who were well known for their expertise in this area. We met in our office in Toronto, and Rey recorded the meeting. We typed up a resolution of our intentions and everyone signed the copies. It gave thirty days for all to review, and it was to die if no further commitment was made.

We had investigated all the angles with the US State Department, and also External Affairs in Canada. Provided the material did not enter the US, it was not likely to meet with hostility. ASTI was a partnership, and the two major participants were at the meeting. We had, after much persistence, obtained a letter from State signed by the Deputy, stating that the US had no interest in the material left in Vietnam.

We were alerted by the police to a break-in at our office some months later, where a window air conditioner was stolen. Nothing else was apparently taken, although there were several more valuable items easily accessible. We checked very carefully, for we had been warned that the letter from State had gone to only five companies, ours being the only foreign one. It had been obvious that the letter was significant and we had taken the precaution of placing it in a bank safety deposit box.

Rey was arrested at Buffalo as he returned from Florida with the buyer of his A-37. The buyer was known to us and almost everyone else as a very successful drug dealer. He had run a racing team in Florida on the proceeds, and we would never have dealt with him. Rey, however, though wary, thought he could handle it, and to a point he did. For although he returned to Canada with the buyer, the 100K deposit was not found.

In a set-piece sting, the Feds had used our ex-druggies to get Rey and make an example of people trading with their enemies. He was incarcerated in Buffalo jail for 14 months and charged with many crimes, the most important of which were the loss of their 100K and the fact that the A-37 still had its mini-gun pod attached.

At the hearing, the discussion in our office was quoted almost word for word. ASTI was in a panic, for they were sure their notes had not been used, although after years of friendship they were forced to take a close look at their relationship. It became apparent that the break-in was the source of the information, although the local police data on the incident disappeared from the computer.

Rey had been the subject of a sting that cost the US taxpayer over $2 million, started at the behest of a lowly Customs official. Rey won nine of his ten counts at the first round and finally all. But when I last checked the US Customs were still hanging on to his A-37, now legally in the country. Being right is just one thing, it is not the only thing.

There were fifty-nine Lycoming helicopter engines unused, sitting in Vietnam, which we all believed could be extracted at an economic cost. Overtures were made to US authorities to see what the implication would be to bringing them out into the Western world. To be fair there was enough equipment there to destabilise any fragile geo-political area. The answer was not in the least ambiguous, 'not on your life'. In fact a threat was made that the ship would be sunk if any attempt was made.

We contacted Bell Helicopters, now manufacturing in Canada, and asked for their views, for at least the equipment would not be hidden, and in use where it made most sense. They were told by the US government that as a major US contractor, they should think clearly on the repercussions of such a move. Lycoming was only building twelve engines a month, to keep the price up, so fifty-nine on the market would certainly register 'tilt' in the beautifully titled military/industrial club.

The Australians had no such qualms about business, and commenced a lucrative trade in items sensitive to US policy. It, on the surface, looked as if it was designed to limit Vietnamese access to US currency. But large US corporations were already installed in Vietnam whilst all this was going on.

Rey returned to the Far East and began a successful career as an entrepreneur, pulling out many exciting finds, not least of which was a Bearcat, from the French Indo-China period.

We were fully committed to our museum deals, spending much time in Eastern Europe and Israel. I managed to dovetail much of this into my work as a corporate pilot, which as will be explained later, was at a new phase. We were looking for an A-4, of which Israel had a surplus. Using our contacts we visited Tel Aviv and tried to deal for one of their disposals.

This area was also highly active as we tried to free up some of the Saudi F-5Bs. These were low-time trainer aircraft, no longer needed in view of the Ali-Yamamah deal with the UK. I had trained most of the Saudi royal family as they passed through Valley on RAF flight training. To say that I knew them was a gross overstatement, but I did have an avenue of contact that was used to the full. Also the head of the UK/RAF mission to Saudi was an old squadron mate. We made plans to ferry them to Cyprus, and then drip-feed them onto the US market.

The total package was going to need considerable resources and our search for funding continued. We approached the Royal Bank in Toronto, and with a potential profit of $7-8 million they were interested. We concluded the framework of a working relationship, but then choked on the requirement for a percentage of the profits. I had never known or expected such a response from a bank. Surely they made their profit on the costs of the deal, the not-so-cheap fees and expenses charged. As against our earlier experience of the lack of interest in overseas business by Canadian banks, here was a very predatory interest.

The re-arming potential of the area by the US, UK and Europe, knocked aside our small beans approach. Saudi refuses to deal with corporations, insisting on government to government contracts. As such the UK formed a very successful partnership with BAe, to project a pseudo-government organisation. The Saudis were only interested in off-set arrangements, so that some of the expertise would flow through to their country. We put forward all sorts of ideas to the UK, managed at that time by an old squadron boss of mine. We were premature, for long after the ideas had been rejected, we were asked to resubmit our proposals. The opportunity had dissolved, along with the financing.

Tacair found a Daimler-Benz DB605 engine in a museum exhibit in Rome, and were able to trade it if it could be overhauled. It was a great find, as was the deal, for freeing anything from the Italians was nigh on impossible. When it was lowered from the roof, it was found to be useless due to internal damage.

Around this time we were suffering a cash-flow situation that rested heavily on the PBY sitting at Eindhoven. The Norwegians were unable to locate a decision on the Lugers, and so we took a calculated risk with the new Director of the Museum. He was Army through and through, not used to lateral thinking, and so the appearance of the PBY at Gardemoen airport was something of an affront. We said that it had to be parked somewhere for the winter, and that the civil side of the airport was happy to have the PBY. He talked about pressure, but we knew that the sight of the excellent

PBY would start tongues wagging, and so it was. The only gun deal ever with the Defence Ministry, and we could move on to better things.

The Sea Hawk/F-5B deal had left us without the Canadian version of the J-85 engines powering it. They were available from a very few sources, not least of which were Canadian government disposals. We approached Orenda as the overhaul agency and identified a batch coming up for disposal. The Crown Assets system of disposal serves no real purpose, other than to employ bureaucrats with little or no knowledge of the material, or the validity of purpose of potential purchasers. We had the acceptance of all the agencies, US and Canadian, for the user was well recognised as a bona fide contractor. It all looked good until it spun out of control. In losing the bid, we knew that the accepted buyer was intending to ship the engines to Iran, now starving for military parts. The engines could easily be identified as CJ 610s, the civil equivalent, and they would be gone without trace. Some rapid work with External Affairs and they were stopped en route, only to end up with a previous customer of ours, although in this case somewhat a competitor. We were beginning to need these engines as our only hope of concluding the deal. All other sources seemed to close up as we got there.

The CAF had given away several engines to schools and universities, and although we were able to offer better items for their use, the rules were quickly rewritten to prevent any such trades. We were able to set in motion a very significant deal with Norway that produced two spare engines, J-85s but the wrong type. It might be possible to swap these for the J-85-15s that we had to have. This was done but not before the most momentous gut-wrenching period of my life.

As part of our search for a suitable aircraft for trade with Sweden, we had found a Mosquito and the desired Hurricane. This deal had been impossible to cement, but we did retain the information for later use. Norway had an air force anniversary coming up and they were salivating at the thought of a Mosquito for their display. We had settled on an F-5B, in pristine condition as a reasonable trade. The Mosquito was in UK and part of a series of aircraft coming up for disposal. The Royal Air Force Museum changed strategies and got rid of duplication in order to save space and cost. What we needed was a proposal that would ensure we obtained the Mosquito.

We discovered that the UK had taken many exhibits from Norway, but returned little. In fact it is recorded that an Able Seaman's uniform was the sole extent of their largesse. We proposed giving the Mosquito to Norway as a sign of the indebtedness and at the same time providing money for the RAF Museum to purchase a collection that would be lost to them, unless they bought it. This rare collection was part of an estate that was now in settlement.

Several points had to be considered in that any money paid to the Museum would normally go straight into the public purse. It required really an Act of Parliament to change such things, but there were other ways. We met with a very senior officer who happened to be an old squadron associate of mine. The deal was put before him in such a way that the benefits to all parties were evident. The Norwegian debt of honour was settled, the rare collection retained, and a very acceptable home would be found for the Mosquito. Also it would not fly again, which was a major concern because of liability and adverse publicity should it ever crash. We had to have the Mossie out of the Museum on a specific date as part of a huge move around at Hendon.

Colin Allen's very able movers at Downbird completed the disassembly and it began its journey to Norway. We had paid a huge dollar advance for it and fell into a financial nightmare when one of our debtors withheld payment. I flew to UK in an effort to fund the deal in the City, but all possibles were rejected as either unreasonable or too late. Arthur Gibson finally came up with a loan to me and we had the cash, just. Sitting under that debt load was something I had said I would never do, and the mental anguish was frequently not worth the return.

I watched in Oslo harbour as the ship failed to dock, for they could not open the loading door. With such a tight schedule, every hour counted, but it was to be the beginning of a long series of misfortunes that lasted almost two years.

The Mossie was installed at the Gardemoen Museum, and it was really the only representative of the type that was readily capable of flight. This may have enraged the purists, but we took a more pragmatic view in that keeping these ancient aircraft flying opened the door to the risk of losing them in the not-that-infrequent warbird accident.

Norway now had a display second to none and we were proud to have achieved so much in so short a time. Retrieving our asset was not as easy, for although the F-5B was ready for delivery in mid-year, the US did one of its about-turns that have characterised the muddled thinking of its successive administrations. With many aircraft either en route to the US, or at least in contract, they placed a moratorium on the import of ex-military aircraft. A simple cessation of imports after a given date would have been fair business practice, but the unstated policy raised a not unreasonable uproar in the community.

Because our deal had had the acceptance of the US authorities for some considerable time, we believed that as three governments were involved, sense would prevail. It did not. We spent long hours on the telephone going over the issue, the big issue, and our small part in it. It is of course impossible to speak to everyone of influence, and just when you think that 'your' piece of the State Department understands, someone else appears who needs convincing all over again.

We were using up resources fast, and informed Norway that if the F-5B was not released soon, we would have to sell the Mosquito to survive. The Brits then responded by trying to tie our hands further, in that they wanted to approve the sale 'and' take a share of the sale price. No regard to our costs, just pay a percentage, please. The deal reached the ears of Parliament and I believe is recorded in Hansard.

It was satisfactory to Norway, UK and the US in that it had been overseen all the way, and the end user was approved. This document was supposed to prevent abuse of the system, but it just became a stalling tactic for an administration in turmoil.

We started out with an immensely saleable item, but it had to be on US soil to satisfy any US buyer. With all the power that we could muster, nobody would authorise the importation. Part of the problem was an undefined attitude to all that material in Vietnam, potentially destabilising if it went anywhere but the US, and of course it would tilt the market for military parts if it ever reached US suppliers. I do not wish to minimise the dilemma that they faced, but the various arms of US policy were often in serious conflict. With much manoeuvring behind the scenes, the F-5B was finally released just before the floodgates burst and overwhelmed us.

It was flown to El Toro in California by C-130, to be viewed by another customer. We had lost an awful lot of our expected return, but it would set in motion several other deals that we hoped would return some of our 'limbo' finances. We concluded a deal with the Marines in El Toro to allow us to use a hangar for the week-long inspection of the disassembled F-5. There was not enough room on the C-130 for our engines, and they arrived in Las Vegas aboard another C-130 at Nellis AFB a few days later. With a rented truck we met the C-130 and loaded the two J-85-13s for delivery to our customer in Van Nuys. After an inspection he gave us our J-85-15s and we departed for the run to Oklahoma – non-stop in order to dovetail all these pieces together, and also to collect a large chunk of change from the buyer of these engines.

Eighteen hundred miles at 60 mph in a rented truck seemed like a fitting conclusion to the deal of the century. BJ returned to California and I to Toronto where I could settle the outstanding debt load as fast as possible. The F-5B now resides with Microsoft in the name of Charles A, who had at one stage needed it for some research purpose. It was the last aircraft we traded, consuming all our energies and resources for too long a period. The market had gone away, as recession hit and the Wall came down. Exotica of all kinds crashed in value and it has still not recovered, if indeed it ever will.

We were involved in many other projects, not least of which was the attempt to obtain a Mig-29 or an Su-27 from Russia. Contact had been made with some very interesting people in Eastern Europe, searching for Second World War equipment, not least of which were the 'hungry Bulgars'. There was a large land deal involving a resort there, which never flew because title to the lands could not be established, of course as a consequence of the turmoil of the Second World War and the Russian occupation. Through our US contacts it was thought that if a purchase could be arranged for modern Russian aircraft, large dollars would be forthcoming for such a purchase. We investigated thoroughly and decided that it was worth the risk. I was at the time flying into Moscow with Olympia & York as a captain on their Gulfstream 3. During these trips I became more comfortable with the idea that a deal was possible.

We were invited to several seminars/missions at which ex-military equipment was to be displayed. I flew to Moscow just before Gorbachev fell, and it was evident that something was in the air. I was arrested at the airport and only released to the care of my 'hungry Bulgars'. A series of meetings took place to try and establish the validity of the equipment and the sellers. I met 'Greenshirt' and 'Brownshirt' in some dingy offices in the back streets of Moscow. They were cordial but guarded, one pretending not to speak English whilst the other conducted the meeting. I was not comforted by the Semtex logo on the Bulgarian car that took us to the meeting, nor by the obvious concern that the Bulgars had for the Russian authorities. In a police state, it is usually thought that there is less opportunity to operate outside the law. It was quite obvious that for most people it was necessary to operate outside the law just to survive.

I had obtained a briefing as to the specifics of the two Russian aircraft from an old air force associate who was now head of Intelligence. We met in UK and discussed the changing situation in the USSR. The release of military equipment was just a dream at that time, and so if we were to pay millions for this stuff it had better be the real thing. I was told that I could pull any aircraft off a line by the Russians, but they were fond of hybrids disguised as front-line items. Russian developmental policy was to produce many experimental versions until they got it right, thus the display aircraft often seen at air shows were usually far from representative. The production number was in the nosewheel well and vital for ident purposes.

Knowing that many other attempts to purchase items were likely to be ongoing at the same time, I was careful to keep very recent my level of communication. We started out at $3-4M and in conference with the 'Shirts', it rapidly went to $20M. This, however, was for a fully armed and equipped aircraft.

Derek left me and skedaddled out of Moscow as fast as he could, for there was an atmosphere that you could taste, most uncomfortable. Our contact led to the Defence Minister, who was ousted in the Gorbachev affair. It was obviously a bust and I left with an immense feeling of relief to be out of there.

Several other projects followed from this, including an opportunity to fly a 'Bear' bomber to Wright-Patterson Museum in

Ohio. They could not find room for it at that time, or it might have worked.

We had a customer for German Tiger tanks and I knew that there were supposed to be a number still in Hungary. My Gulfstream travels took me to Budapest and inquiries did support the belief that there were still tanks in the marshes, scenes of great tank battles in the latter days of the Second World War. The route to them looked like being expensive for East Europeans had little or no idea of relative values and so they just started with the biggest number they could conceive.

Once on the trail of Tigers, we were contacted by an ex-naval officer with a long family history in the RN. His grandfather, a submariner, had sunk a supply ship just off the North African coast carrying tanks to Rommel. By good detective work the ident of the ship and its cargo was established. It carried with a fair degree of certainty some of the earliest Tigers bound for Rommel. He produced some excellent data at our meeting in London, narrowing it down to one of three charted wrecks, all very close together. We funded his trip to Algeria to do the preliminary research. A French vessel was arrested in these waters, for exceeding the limits of its permit. That along with some very volatile politics, stopped any further efforts to recover the Tigers.

We burrowed into the murky world of major arms deals by being given data on the Nigerian Jaguar Internationals. These aircraft were sold to Nigeria by British Aerospace, with some very complicated financing to grease the deal. Nigeria could no more operate these aircraft than they could afford them. They sat, disused, along with all the support equipment, rotting in dreadful conditions. An RAF team was sent under some secrecy to evaluate their condition, for with all the massive corruption in Nigeria, it was likely that they could be spirited away somehow.

Whilst they were eminently saleable, they were just too difficult to move. Our communication with BAe must have startled them, for they made it known that the UK had a strong financial affection for them.

After six years of commuting from Montreal to Toronto, I finally found a slot on a Falcon 50. It should have led to some stability in my home life, but Execaire politics intruded. I found myself working shifts, again out of Montreal. Noranda's offer of the O & Y Gulfstream job was to my liking, for in all the chaos, I had already taken the refresher course on the G3. In fact during that period, I was trained on or flew the CL601, the Falcon 50, the G3 and the F5 and F-104.

A visit by the UK half of my family, resulted in my falling on the stairs over my grandson's toys. Both feet suffered broken bones and I faced the Ministry of Transport flight check two days later. To start a new job requires some commitment and with the help of the CP, I got into the Captain's seat before the check pilot arrived. The engine failure bit was excruciatingly painful, but the CP in the co-pilot's seat was trying to take some of the load on the rudder pedal without it being obvious to the check pilot. There is little that you can do with broken bones in the foot, for they are already in splints, called 'feet'. As advice to readers, I would not advocate copying my response, for the long-term result is damage that will be a reminder always.

My time with O & Y of Canary Wharf fame was both challenging and demanding. They are not the best timekeepers, and the intensity of their religion was a new wrinkle to the problems of aviation. We had to be on the ground by sunset on each Friday, no matter where we were.

We often travelled with a Rabbi on board, particularly when they were deeply into their Russian charitable work. We brought out the last 'Refusnik', a hold-out against religious oppression, and flew him direct to Tel Aviv. I routed due south to Israel, and was cleared for that route, even though the skies were full of Russian transports en route to stamp out rebellion in the Armenian area.

We were met with full security at Ben Gurion airport and parked in a secure area. Our usual hotel was the Sheraton or the Hilton atop the cliffs in Tel Aviv. We even spent a rainy Christmas there.

This area became the target of the Arab terrorists who made an attack from the sea. Our many days on that sea front had shown clearly that there was a picket boat parked all the time just offshore and also daily helicopter flights up the beach. Unless they knew something that was not obvious, such an attack from the sea was almost certain to fail, and it did.

Because we were away so much some of the servicing had to be completed away from North America. On a random service at

Cambridge, it was discovered that there was a bullet hole in the fuselage high up near the tail. The readily identifiable AK-47 round had punctured the skin and was lying in the head lining of the cabin. When and where were never answered, for there were too many occasions where we were at risk, and motives were never hard to find.

Our trips to Switzerland were memorable in that we took the G3 into Bern and Samedan. The latter airport was the highest in Europe, serving St Moritz. Arrivals were VFR only and a valley route in and out was necessary. To explain the intricacies of such a flight to the passengers was never easy, for basically we would go and have a look. The mountains were generally cloud covered and so some ingenuity was needed. We were talking to Samedan ATC and knew that it would be possible if we could get underneath the cloud deck. A reversal to some 80 nms out allowed us to approach the mountains underneath, but now we had to funnel our way in sandwiched between the mountain tops and the cloud. Although the valleys looked enticing, the risk of cables and the rocky confines for manoeuvring, kept us pinned to the higher elevations. Mr P asked how close we were to the rock faces and so he knew what was at issue here.

A three-day stopover allowed time to visit friends in Geneva, where we were treated royally and I renewed my association with the SF 260. It was as if I had never left it. This and the floatplane flying we all did was to provide a memorable interlude.

A snowy departure from Samedan is recalled for the stress it can bring. We arrived at the airport very early and de-iced the G3. Snow showers were coming down the valley limiting our take-off options. We needed to see a bend in the valley protected by a large chunk of rock. Our passengers were due at 0700 and it was obviously going to be an opportunistic departure in between the showers.

With the APU running we were ready for that opportunity. Switzerland is a noise-conscious country, if you discount all the noise those damn bells make every Sunday, and so ATC demanded that we shut down our APU whilst awaiting clearance. We neither could nor would comply with that instruction, for we needed to be able to keep the G3 warm, talk to Zurich and have our nav equipment up and running.

They were obviously not used to having their rules challenged, and the R/T interchange would make an interesting record. The snow showers continued until a small gap appeared, it was a brief window and we were ready. Full power in the G3 is very noisy, especially in the confines of a valley, but 15,000 ft was needed as soon as possible, and so it was max speed down the valley with steep climb to clear the rocky bits now hidden in snow and cloud. You do not win popularity contests that way, but it was a safe, if unorthodox, exit.

Our long-range trips often ended in Toronto, at that time going through its dreadful period as far as the airport goes. When I arrived in Canada, Toronto was a pleasure to operate from, but it degenerated under political and union mismanagement to be one of the worst airports that we had the misfortune to use. Its operating efficiency fell to new levels of bureaucratic confusion, and trillions of gallons were and are still wasted by aircraft waiting to take-off or land. They introduced a 'slot-system' to restrict aircraft movements, but even the telephone part took months to be anything more than added confusion.

On one return from Europe, I was informed as I coasted into Labrador that there were delays of at least 45 mins going into Toronto. We used every inquiry method available to try and find out what the delays were. The G3 is not known for its miserly fuel burn, and this was a max range flight. Even as we approached the Toronto ATC area, nobody would give a reason for the possible delays. It was of course government in-fighting with the ATC union, such that several of the control positions were not manned. Shortage of staff would have been the correct answer, but that was never going to be released over the air. As one airliner said as he fled Toronto, 'thanks to the second-best ATC system in the world'. ATC questioned who was the best. The answer was 'everybody else'.

It is a sad reflection on Canada that in the areas like the Ministry of Transport, they can just no longer cope. They do not have the resources to be all things to all men. Trying to make believe that they have a viewpoint that rivals the FAA, or even the CAA, is a pipe dream. When Mr Trudeau had control of the finances, he wasted it with illusions of grandeur, not anticipating a time when the level of bureaucracy we could afford would make us a 'Banana Republic', without the bananas. Nationalism is a ghostly, ill-defined shape, oft misused by the snake oil salesmen. As we struggle to compete, it is surely self-evident that many of these bastions must go, as they certainly do not protect Canadians and are expenses we can no longer afford.

The demise of O & Y left me out of a job but struggling to resolve the F-5 issue. I survived by flying, often for free or just the upkeep of my licence. The recession really hit the corporate industry and there was no end in sight. By the time it ended, I had seen many old friends bite the dust. It was obviously about time for me to consider ending a most enjoyable career. I had seen too many hang on when their skills had gone, and most of my era from the Air Force were finished in aviation. Timing is everything, but as I have said to so many, 'You cannot see the view until you get there.'

The Falcon 10 is the corporate aircraft sportscar. It was a rewarding aircraft to fly and I believed that it would see me out of my career. It nearly did, for in all my years flying, I had rarely run to the edge of a take-off performance problem.

Hot and high take-offs are a feature of all simulator training. The sim is an excellent teacher in this respect.

Elko is some 5,400 ft up the high desert of Nevada. We were faced with an hour-long flight to Colorado Springs, also in the mountains with many thunder showers en route. Weight, altitude and temperature are the necessary factors in computing the take-off criteria. I worked out the fuel load knowing that we had a full load of passengers. Refuelling took place in US gallons and in the hot sun it expanded enough for me to have to start the engines and burn off the excess poundage right down to the computed figure. I checked and rechecked the figures, hoping that the temperature would fall before the pax arrived in order to give us an added margin. When you are very close to the book limits, other everyday assumptions can start to have an impact – brake condition, engine computer performance at the limits, and more to the point the actual temperature. The hot desert wind was swinging as we taxied for take off. I had worked out some fallback numbers just in case we did not make the book numbers. With no help from the wind we began the take-off roll, and I realised that the dark-coloured runway would have absorbed far more heat than the temperature readout showed.

My mind recalled the *Reader's Digest* story of an F-104 that took off in similar conditions, and crashed because the temperature had risen after he was forced into a minor delay. The runway had marker boards, not commonly used in civil aviation. I was well aware of them from Air Force days. At 4,000 ft we were not accelerating very quickly and I knew that it was going to be close. My co-captain was alerted by my 'oh shit' and we were beyond our refusal speed, at which point the Falcon stopped accelerating. I knew that it would fly at 126 kts, but whether it had enough power to fly away was another matter. There is a small mound of rock just off the end of the runway, such that a minor avoidance is required. I used all the runway and eased past the rock, holding down over the rail yards and saying that we would land there if flight became impossible. Once clear of the hot runway, the added performance allowed us to retract the gear and slowly climb away.

That was a max performance take-off, something that the big jets do everyday. For us to use all the runway and have such a low rate of climb was not in my library of experiences.

It is hard and maybe mindless to look at aviation with any thought to the past. In communication with pilots of my era, it is common to relate that flying is an art masquerading as a science. There are very few artists being produced by the system at the moment. Perhaps that is progress and my views are extinct, but as aircraft get more and more expensive, both civil and military, virtuosity with a computer, while necessary, may not save the day. As one First Officer was heard to say, 'I cannot fly worth a shit, but I can type fifty words a minute.'

With close to 20,000 hrs in the air, and if I really scratch 150-plus types flown and qualified on, aviation has been good to me. I often ponder the difference between life and death, that small nugget of information that keeps you out of the scenery. Why, in seemingly identical situations, you lived and others died. I guess, in the end, your library of experiences may give you a millisecond of advantage, and that is all it takes. It is interesting to examine that if skills need to be practised repeatedly to maintain a high level, how is it that those who have lived on the ragged edge accept that knowledge once gained remains useful for ever? An unsolvable paradox perhaps.

For one who has lived quite close to the edge for much of his life, some understanding of my attitudes to managing risk may be useful.

I learned very early on about the pilot's creed of not concerning yourself with death, but only caring that your demise, and maybe that of others, was not through stupidity. Some of the equations that you base your decisions on may be flawed, even long-held truths proving quite fallacious, but the control circuit for your behaviour is ego driven in that you do not wish to be remembered as an object lesson for your profession.

As I approach the last hours in the air, can I be more careful, is there another solution available that has previously been discarded? If there were, would I not have included it before now? I think the conclusion is that you must stick to what you are good at, and that includes approaching life in exactly the same way that you always have.

We shall see, for with the Panama-Alaska Rally just months away, will the same flair be there, or will I find that the juice has gone away?

Chapter XII

THE 1993 LONDON-SYDNEY MARATHON was a magnet to me, and Derek shared my hopes. We thought that with Arthur's help and our rallying history, we would be able to secure adequate support and a car. It was not a time for business to be venturesome, and 'sponsorship' was a dirty word. The Red Arrows were aligned with British Aerospace, who owned Rover cars at that time, and also the RA foundation was a now commercial enterprise. All these connections lead nowhere, and we had to face the idea of funding it ourselves.

The initial choice of an Austin 1800 was quickly quashed as research showed that parts availability was unacceptable. Volvo was seen as a reliable choice, as the features of a late-1960s model were sound and advanced. We applied to Volvo to find that there was a short list for a team and a support package. They agreed to support three cars with parts and assistance, and we were chosen along with two Amazons.

The car of our choice was a 1968 144S, sound with some 150,000 miles on the clock. Pretty's Garage was selected as being local and interested in the production of a historic rally car. Here we met Andrew, who was to join me on the London-Mexico in 1995, but then he was just an amazingly knowledgeable Volvo nut, whose family ran a Volvo distributorship.

Having tried several other avenues, including a run in an 'Alec Poole Mini', the Volvo was definitely much more sedate. Motor cars have come a long way in twenty-five years. Alec even gave us a spare Volvo that was cluttering up his lot, and it turned into an excellent source of spares.

Derek and Andrew worked on the car for eighteen months, and we set about securing financial support. In the end it was little assistance from many that eased the burden, but there were many choices taken on a budgetary basis that on reflection should have been reversed. We needed to get the fuel tank up over the back axle, but it was too expensive and complicated in view of the refuel/vent restrictions. The underbody protection (sumpguard) was very heavy and in need of several mods before it was acceptable. Having used the 'Kangaroo' bar in the original events, much time was allocated to this item. It did, however, put the weight well forward.

The rules were followed stringently; I say that for in some respects we followed the letter rather than the intent of the rule. The gearbox was four speed and the choice of final drive ratio a difficult one. There was a large hole between second and third gear, such that you were screaming in second at our limit of 6,000 rpm, or off the cam trying to hang on to 3,000. It would do 100 mph at 5,500 and we believed that this cruising potential would serve us well.

The Volvo seats were retained as rally-style ones were too expensive. Much weight remains in wheels, but Minilites were unavailable and the rest an unknown quality, so it was good old steel standard that at least could be hammered straight. With a sponsored paint job, it looked very smart and Andrew was so knowledgeable about Volvo in general, that we felt confident.

Some testing was done, but destructive testing was not in the budget. Twin fuel lines and hydraulics in the car, plus some new SU carbs, gave us a feeling that we had done the best we could under the circumstances. I chose the tyres carefully with regard to the excellent service I was getting out of my Swedish 'Gislaveds', used on my Canadian car in winter. The distributor in Oxfordshire gave us as many as we wanted, and it proved to be a superb choice. In fact we drove all the way to Sydney on the original four, changing one as a preventative measure some 100 miles from the finish as the wheel was bent. It had been twenty-five years since we had rallied competitively, and there were a few wrinkles that we needed to iron out in our communications. Derek was an excellent pupil of Andrew, the bulk of the maintenance falling squarely to him. I was just a 'mate', trying to have the right tools available. It was quickly apparent that we were slow, but then our strategy was to drive at eight-tenths, make no mistakes and rely on Volvo integrity. On dry surfaces the car handled well, but the polar moment got very exciting if you allowed too much oversteer to develop. I played with the tyres and pressures, believing that we would run out of tyres if the high-wear tarmac stages continued.

Initially it was all European hill-climb sections where horsepower ruled the day. Downhill we were OK, but again the sheer bulk was very evident. We were carrying all our spares and the comparison between those who were not and those who were, was obvious.

The car that seemed to be always behind us was the Mercedes of Igor. It was trimmed so nose up that in the rear-view mirror it looked like a shark. We named it 'Jaws'. He eventually moved all his weight forward and then the vehicle really began to move.

Derek got a trifle excited at the end of a stage in Belgium, which finished through a farmyard. We were lucky to clout the bank lightly; several others were not so.

The Rolls had set fire to his brakes and finally gave up with this problem recurring continually with this very heavy car. The tulip-style road book caught us after a slow special section. Timing starts at the beginning of the special, such that you try to gain the fastest time you can on that closed road piece. However, the section allows a stated time for the stage, which includes the special. If you are slowed in the special, you finish up struggling to make the stage time allocation, and this is on public roads.

We lost much time early on the hill climb and ended up needing to average 100 mph on the Autostrada section at the end of the day. Arriving at the start of a hilly road section, we found the road closed by the 'gendarmes', as a very large truck was approaching. Wasting thirty minutes at the head of the queue, it was evident that all the rally cars were impatient to be off, as they could be seen scouring the town for a way past the 'gendarmes'. Our six minutes lateness cost us six seconds overall. At sixty minutes lateness, instead of being penalised sixty seconds, it switches to a one-hour penalty.

The Rally started to show its characteristics, for the fast guys were breaking their cars during the day and fixing them at night. It seemed that there were no compensations for driving at a speed where the damage risk was minimised. As an original entrant we had a low number at the start, but renumbering took place nightly, and so we slid back to our correct place.

We did not have the power to make any catch-up in our position, and could only expect attrition to move us upwards.

Europe was crossed without serious trouble. An oil leak from the top of the gearbox drove us mad, for it could most easily be reached when the car was on a hoist, so that the sumpguard could be dropped. We had to keep checking it just in case, and it sometimes extended the day by many hours.

The Cyrillic countries were crossed as fast as possible, Romania being difficult and very run down. Turkey was a nightmare of traffic and the beginning of the alterations in the route.

It had been intended to route via Turkey, Iran and into the new states of the Russian Union, ending in Tashkent by way of Samarkand. Iran had embraced the idea of a major sporting event, but words do not always translate into actions. They closed the border and prevented Uzbekistan from enjoying a Western sporting event. The route therefore became a long drive to Erzurum in Eastern Turkey, almost 1,000 kms over a very broken road. It was into the snow and mountains with heavy truck traffic. Erzurum was a small town, high up with few facilities. A special stage started early next day, with a muddy climb that the Volvo barely made. Now was the endless run back to Ankara. One competitor broke a crankshaft on that muddy start, hired a car, drove back to Ankara to collect a new one, retraced his steps to Erzurum and rebuilt his car in time to be on the start line the next morning in Ankara – 4,000 kms says a lot for determination.

The extra section to the north of the city was mountainous and unknown. Here the first rally casualty occurred. An Australian entry had a head-on with a bus, killing the driver. Such was the design of pre-1970 cars that the safety feature of split steering columns was not incorporated, and the head-on drove the steering column into the driver. It put a damper on things, but such is the sport that all know the consequences.

The Volvo was moving up the field as mistakes caused loss of time, and we boarded the Antonov 124 for the flight to Delhi. Three aircraft were used, two freighters to carry almost 100 cars, and the Il 86 for the crews.

I had a fine time in the cockpit, becoming acquainted with Russian technology and flying it for some time. It was heavy, in some respects like a B707 with a long-range nav system that the crew could not explain to me. The instrumentation was remarkably advanced, not at all like the generation I had viewed at Paris in the 1970s. We stopped in Tashkent for fuel in the early hours, to be told that the food supply was not available. The cabin staff, whose manner and build could readily be compared to the front row on any rugby league team, stated that 'booze' would be free. The ever-vital Aussies bought all the sandwiches in the 'terminal', and auctioned them off with the proceeds going to a children's home. They made over 4,000 USD. With such a good cause and ingenuity it is remarkable how daft you can become, twenty bucks for a tired sandwich seemed like a deal. I made a return to the Ashoka hotel, remembered from those far-off days on the Ferry Sqn, for it was the rally hotel for our two stops in Delhi. We spent all day chasing a new radiator cap, as ours was discovered to be far too low a pressure for the anticipated very high temperatures of the Indian plains.

A small convoy snaked all over Delhi, as a group of us tried to find 100-octane fuel to offset the terrible standard stuff sold as 90-octane everywhere.

It was forecast to be very hot as we left for Simla in the foothills of the Himalayas. It was in fact the hottest place on the planet with a temperature of over 50°C. One of the cars had a thermometer installed and it read over 65°C.

All were boiling at every stop and keeping cool was the major priority for everybody and everything. Our fuel line ran close to the engine block, such that the fuel was boiling at each stop. This vapour lock made for some very inelegant starts at the beginnings of the specials. Clean water and a non-risky food supply took planning and diligence. Raiding the breakfast table became an art, for we had plenty of 'bully beef' to go with anything that could be extracted in the morning rush.

We used wet towels on our heads, soon copied by everyone. The head lining of the Volvo was removed and placed on the floor. Soaked in water, it dropped the temperature of the car considerably.

The next casualty was the co-driver of an associate of ours, who succumbed to heatstroke. He did not seem able to improvise in the heat, treating it as a minor inconvenience. Despite all efforts, he died in a Delhi hospital.

The major feature of India was the traffic density: camels, elephants, cows, bullock carts, bikes with a death wish and trucks, endless trucks. As the traffic speed seemed to hover around 10 mph, even our low required average was startlingly fast to them. We made acquaintance with many villages called 'Urine', and tried not to be involved in the multitude of accidents that were commonplace. On one long leg, we calculated that there was one accident per mile. Many were breakdowns occasioned by overloaded machinery, which had the habit of placing rocks around the truck to signify a breakdown, and then working inside this perimeter. At 10 mph, avoidance was not a problem, but at rally speeds it could get quite exciting.

One of the Volvo team cars was making time, to be confronted by a truck and rocks taking up 60 per cent of the road. The rest was full of oncoming traffic. He headed for the ditch to find it full of sleeping truck passengers. Masterful driving and he was through, having injected some powerful sensory material into their dreams.

The long climb to Simla lowered the temperature a little, but we only had to retrace our steps and fight all those trucks yet again.

The lone Kenyan entrant had serious trouble with pedestrians. A small child ran under his wheels, and the fee requested was 20,000 USD. When all this settled down, he paid $2,000 just to get out of there. He was doomed to repeat the process, when on a closed section, one of the watchers ran across the road. Avoiding action by both led to him leaving the road and taking the local with him. The fatality closed the section for the rest of us bringing a sense of futility to this period, in a land where life is cheap, really cheap.

On the lowland section, the road was usually one lane of tarmac or concrete. This meant a game of chicken with all oncoming traffic, as leaving the hard surface at speed could be disastrous. The edges were invariably very broken and holed. Most of the traffic was unsettled by our speed, but after a few Kamikaze attacks, they got pissed off; and it showed. It did not do to be too far behind in the pack.

The long run down the coast to Bombay was a nightmare for some, with frantic diversions to bypass stalled traffic. The 'Yellow Submarine', an Aussie vehicle, was trying to get past a bus. The bus took avoiding action from a head-on attack by a truck, and rolled into a ditch upside down. The Aussies finished up on top of the bus, also upside down. Nobody was hurt, but when questioned they said that they would grease and check the car, now that the whole of the underside was in view, and that they would be on the start tomorrow. They were.

The departure for Australia was paramount in everyone's mind. We had had enough of the Indian sub-continent, thank you very much. Australia has very strict rules concerning the import of anything from India, and so the cars needed to be washed and cleaned very thoroughly. It was set up that the washing facility would service each car at a pre-arranged time. Four washing bays were not enough to get all cars clear by the planned ETD of the Antonov freighter. The pumps and water supply kept breaking down all night, so that nobody got any sleep.

The aircraft must have miscalculated, for a take-off at 1000 in the heat of the day was unlikely in our opinion. The departure was brought forward to 0600, causing 'Jaws' and other late arrivals to miss it. After fighting the traffic and mechanical problems, it must have been an enormous let-down to arrive within the specified time, only to find that it had all been changed.

Back on the Iluysin for the trip to Perth via Kuala Lumpur in Malaysia. The roar of approval was loud as we lifted off, signifying our gratitude to be out of India.

Perth was a huge relief for all the competitors, if not the Aussies. Superb rally country and food you could eat. Andrew appeared and gave the car the once over, not that it needed any mods. We dined at a Barbecue House that night, and by early morning were suffering the dreaded 'runs'. Ironic to traverse India and be laid low in Australia. My medical kit suppressed it to 24 hrs of sickness, but it would remain with me until the rally doctor prescribed a magic bullet in Sydney.

We had powerful memories of Perth and Youanmi from the 1968 event, but the new route did not follow the original. It was still tough, with miles of fast dusty stages, many with the damaging tree roots that we recalled. We felt ready to make a move forward and steadily increased our position.

The Ford Escort of 'Hugh Janus', or that was the name of the prize they gave him at the end, came barrelling through, intent on risk-taking extraordinaire. He would whizz by well into the bushes and then be stopped later on with numerous punctures. I think he turned it over two or three times in the process. The number of roll-overs was a surprise to me, for I cannot recall ever seeing so many vehicles with that kind of damage still fighting for a place.

We were on the old Nullarbor road, now by-passed by a tarmac version, heading for the most difficult section. A ticking noise rapidly developed, followed by a lurch from the front of the car. Inspection showed that the shock absorber had punched a hole through the bottom of the wishbone. Welding was required, but we still had the coil spring to enable us to drive. If the spring broke, the front suspension would collapse onto the wheel. There were no facilities possible until the end of the upcoming stage, which was known to be severe and very rough.

In deep dust and sand we set out to nurse the Volvo through the stage. There were many 'offs' into the trees, and several cars grounded on the high spots. The Volvo never faltered, having excellent traction. We offered assistance to many, but had not the power to tow anyone. Sight of the damage at the end of the stage showed that we were not the only ones in need of welding facilities.

The night stop was to be a tent city but we, like most, did not expect to sleep. Welding was available as we waited in turn for use of the equipment. The collar around the shock absorber was still in place, making a fix possible. However, we found that the Aussie Volvos were heavily strengthened in this area. Whatever we did would leave the suspension suspect, and the other side started making the same noise almost immediately. Our mandate was to finish and there is little doubt that the Turkish pounding had stressed the front suspension beyond our ability to fix it. It turned out that the wishbones were not competition items and the 'R Sport' shocks were too much for the standard ones.

We could avoid the stressful stages and take maximum penalty points, but at least we would finish. Rational thought is not always evident in the heat of competition, but we both knew that there was no chance of finishing with a collapsed front suspension.

Kalgoorlie had closed the town for us, to include a race around the city streets that evening. Our alternator was playing up, and needed to be fixed, particularly in view of the wet sections up ahead. The mining vehicles were supported locally, such that they could fix just about anything. A mechanic made up a new alternator by cutting one in half and borrowing the internals from several types. Two hours work and he had to be forced to take some money for his efforts.

Being light on clothes, it was necessary to wash them each night. Apart from jokes about changing clothes every night by trading with each other, the system worked well. Derek would work on the car whilst I tended to the domestics. This usually entailed putting everything in the shower and stamping on it for the requisite time. On one such stop the shower was set into the room. With much dusty clothing to wash, there was quite a pile in the shower. When I emerged the room was awash from the overflow. I tried to squeegee it all back towards the shower area and prevent it from soaking the rest of the room. Derek appeared as I was stark naked on hands and knees mopping up. Not a pretty sight he said.

With an early snowfall in the mountains, the Rally was forced to use 'chains' for the run over the top, by the local cops. We avoided this and really had a quiet run to Canberra and the finish in Sydney. The Opera House is a magnificent place to hold any venue, and there was much elation from family and friends at the finish. Not a sterling effort from us and I cannot claim advancing years as a reason, for there were several entrants in our over-60 class.

A well-deserved holiday with our wives took us on a 2,000-km jaunt up the coast in an attempt to see something of the beauty of SE Australia. The car was dispatched to UK, but somehow went via South Africa, where the owner of a Porsche was most surprised to find his prize possession had turned into a 1968 Volvo.

The intro to the 1995 London-Mexico was less traumatic for me than the 1993 L-S, and, I believe for my associates the fact that the Volvo was a known entity helped enormously. Being in Canada meant that many of the decisions immediately required were taken and became a fait accompli. Derek and Andrew did a fantastic job and the knowledge and experience gained from the L-S certainly improved the car 100 per cent.

Firstly, the Australian Volvo rally data was the basis of our 1995 car. We incorporated all the mods and included a few from Andrew's knowledge of Volvos. The high-altitude carburation problems were tackled in a number of ways. It was impossible to plan for a full in-

1993 London-Sydney, press photo.

Departure for 'Oz'.

car system, but we did incorporate the BLMH mod from 1970, in the hope that it would do the trick. I believe that it would have performed satisfactorily, but calibration was not possible before the event, and too time-consuming on the event. We therefore fell back on Plan B, which was for Andrew to change and adjust all the components. Apart from one minor inconvenience at the end of a stage, we were able to plan ahead and carry out the adjustments in good time.

The car would not run at all much above 8,000 ft, and we had just made it to the head of the queue on the exit from a very dusty stage, when the overly rich mixture choked the engine to a stop. Andrew's quick fix on the side of a mountain recovered all the power and we quickly caught up with others, now struggling with mixture problems.

A major concern after the 1993 event was suspension and weight. The AUS mods appeared to handle the suspension requirements and the weight was reduced by removing all but the front glass and also the rear door panels. We could not justify the cost of bonnet/boot lid replacement and so whilst the target was a 500-lb reduction, we did not approach that figure. We did, however, significantly increase the power output to close to 100 bhp at the wheels. The new seats and belts were a must, and returned far more than their cost would suggest.

The sump guard was retained, but its design lost too much ground clearance. From other examples we realised that a Volvo needs more clearance at the front. Andrew's rear engine mounting mods were brilliant and effective, being double Range Rover mounts.

The departure plan, therefore, was to drive at 80 per cent in a very strong vehicle and hope that attrition moved us up in the standings. We carried an inordinate amount of parts determined by Andrew's ability to fix almost anything. It would be a delicate balancing act to decide that at 80 per cent, with a strong, well-built car, you should not take so many parts. We intended to finish, and it would have been senseless to be sidelined by a minor part.

The car sat down at the rear, in spite of the AUS mods, when fully loaded and so Andrew put in spacers at the last minute. The front springs were standard, which conspired against us later in the event, not because of springing, but because it reduced the ride height and

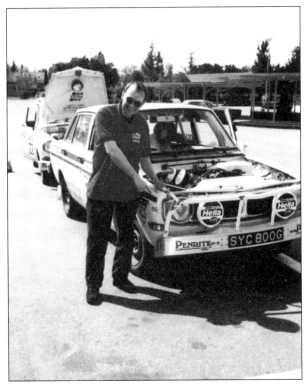

Andrew's 'off' and the damaged 'roo' bar.

loaded up the sump guard. The altered brakes with ventilated discs were a noticeable change from 1993.

Driving at 80 per cent is a demanding task, for the rewards of not using up so much of the car are not readily noticeable. Clutch and gearbox can be consumed quickly if you do not have an eye on the immense distance at competition speeds that you are expecting out of a 27-year-old car. The tyre plan was based on our L-S experience: Gislaveds, four spares, two on rims.

Andrew left the Heathrow start and the trip to Salisbury was a good intro to the daily discipline of a long-distance event. The stages were wet and muddy and our 80 per cent target was reflected in our times.

Portsmouth entertained us royally before we embarked for the night ferry to Le Havre. An easy run across rural France put us in Biarritz for the first night stop over the Channel. The Spanish stages

Ant-124 – tramp steamer of the skies.

were tarmac in the mountains and in the rain. Andrew entered a series of tight slippy bends that placed him on the wrong line at the exit. The collision with the Armco was at slow speed, but inevitable. We reversed and raced to the finish as the damage was thought to be cosmetic.

Repairs in Salamanca were needed to restore the crash bar and the bumper. Andrew was beside himself for such a mistake, as it had also altered the looks of his prized possession. We utilised the hotel fence to hydraulic the bumper back to shape, and apart from a broken indicator light, little sign of the damage could be seen.

I had asked to drive the Arganil stage to see if I could remember it from 1970. It was very tough and demanding, an eye opener of what the car was going to be subjected to. We had power and traction, but the front-rear balance was causing the car to pitch, potentially putting severe stress on the sump guard. We needed to bring everything from the boot forward of the rear wheels. In comparison with the other 140 series Volvos, we were far too heavy with too little ground clearance. However the strength versus lightness argument was not going to be resolved for some time.

363

In Lisbon, we had checked in to the hotel and then left to find the Volvo dealership. En route we met the Russians who were hopelessly lost. Having no English it was impossible to explain to them that we were not going to the hotel. Their gearbox was making horrible noises as we found a taxi to lead them there.

The Antonov 124s, as before, took all the cars to South America, whilst we enjoyed a regular Varig flight.

Brazil, in the form of Sao Paulo was an interesting start to South America. Our original destination had been Rio de Janiero, but it was by-passed because of martial law in the city. The airport buses did not arrive, and so we were put into taxis for the drive to the hotel and the cargo airport where the cars were.

The traffic and pollution made all wish to vacate the city as soon as possible. Deciding if the police are with you or just treating you as everyday traffic is a delicate choice. The road book is written for an individual vehicle which can expect no special treatment. But sixty rally cars can demand very special treatment by the police. To know when this is the case is very difficult. The road book spoke of radar traps but the unknown speed limit was not adhered to by the locals, and so when we were stopped for speeding it looked like a local tax trick. We could not communicate very well, but the twenty dollars went swiftly into his pocket with a 'thank you' in clear English.

The turning point in the rally, I believe, was the first stage in South America. The fast guys were going to get going, and we were bent on no mistakes. The road book spoke of 'pothole, keep left, very wet', some 800 m from the start. We left on the fast sugar cane plantation road and could see an Escort stuck in a hole about where the hazard was supposed to be. He was on the left and obviously blocking the intended route through. All eyes were on the Escort, when I caught sight of another path cut through the cane on the left. We made an awkward slide left down the real route, being slow enough to do so.

A short distance ahead we came upon Roger Clarke's Escort off the road with a front wheel off. One down I said. Next was the Rover looking like the rear suspension had collapsed. The Austin Healey had broken a wheel, tearing out the hub. A Datsun was facing the wrong way and also stopped. Finally we were slowed by what had to be a major 'off'. The car could not be seen, but turned out to be

Lorimer's Escort. Our strategy looked very effective at that stage. Human psychology being what it is convinced people that this kind of attrition could not be sustained, and so I think everybody slowed for quite a few stages.

The next days were a blur of long days and heavy traffic. We, at 33rd, needed to press on relentlessly on the road sections to produce a buffer in case of problems. We therefore generally were running in the front ten cars, helped by the O/D gear in the 144, which allowed 155 kph at 4,000 rpm. This, coupled with a range on the highway of 700 kms, meant that we had to refuel less than others on the transport stages. We had made all the adjustments possible to the car, but the rough stages were pounding the sump guard.

Andrew worked continuously fixing the damage there. Our times were consistent, putting us in the field where a Volvo driven at 80 per cent should be. The attrition continued, but not nearly at the pace seen earlier.

Volvo dealers everywhere offered their facilities, and it became almost a ritual for six Volvos to be camped at the end of the day in some dealer's yard. The PV544 was always being welded as a result of David's spirited driving, and Andrew was a fount of knowledge for all, including the odd Mercedes and MG. He insisted on checking everything, for although the locals were eager workers, they could not be trusted to finish anything. One dealer had an electronic engine analyser, which Andrew used to check our car. He dismissed it as being out of calibration, and amazed the owner by recalibrating it so that others could use it.

Tony Fall was watching one local put oil in his gearbox. A bag of oil was used to pump the oil up into the filler. He watched as the willing worker pumped away, then stuck his finger in the hole to announce that it was full. Tony checked to find no oil on his finger. He examined the bag to find that it was not even opened.

We were slowly working up the field, and were comfortable with our capabilities compared to those around us. The Rover was immediately ahead and rapidly caught on the dusty stages. Getting by was another story. We finally had a clear two minutes behind him with the non-arrival of the 'cool dudes' Porsche. This meant that we could gain a minute without being in his dust. The road was rough and very dangerous, a minor slip would be very costly. We closed but could not penetrate the dust safely. Andrew noticed a series of river crossings coming up, and so I closed to be ready to pass when the dust subsided. We smashed through the crossings and pulled away from the Rover to be some thirty seconds ahead of him at the stage end. When the results were posted at the end of the day our times indicated only a one minute thirty second advantage, not two minutes thirty that had to be the case. An inquiry was duly filled in, with the Rover crew stating that we had passed them. We were not happy with the resolution that no mistake had been made, for the times must have been crossed. We should have paid more attention to the time entered in our book.

The car suffered briefly as we climbed to over 8,000 ft again. At this point we had to change the needles and timing. Thereafter we had power and a smooth-running engine, more than can be said for some.

At 15,000 ft, for the first time I saw signs of hypoxia. The stage was cancelled for safety reasons, but there would have been many mistakes made, if it had been run. By now all the Escorts were known to be suffering from a design problem. Only two were up front, and they obviously were suspect. We found by chance, a dynamometer, the only one in Bolivia, at a dealership. Here the 144 was fine-tuned for the altitude.

The Lima loop was going to be a severe test, six stages in a day and many believed that this was their moment to advance. We had bent our rims on the very rough roads and tyres were now going to be a problem. The first Lima stage had several surprises with unmarked hazards. We were moving up steadily, running about twelve minutes ahead of our schedule. One enormous bombhole at the start of the first stage cost time for many; we probably bent our rims there.

Stage two was a beach dash, and a short sprint around a cliff road. The beach crossing was difficult to follow as no clear route could be seen. The second trip across the beach caused us to mount a hidden sewer inspection structure and flip onto two wheels. Remy Julienne I am not, but I did a quick turn right to put the wheels back on the ground, hard left to avoid the sea and up the cliff road to the finish and a round of applause from the crowd and marshals.

The third stage was long and dusty, crossing a very sandy area. Many bogged there, but we had little trouble other than punctures.

One occurred just seconds from the stage start, our sixth in two days. Andrew fixed it in record time just three seconds from a penalty. We now had no spare tyre and faced the final sand stage for the second time. A loud noise announced the failure of the shock, and inspection showed that the strap, limiting the travel of the trailing arm, was broken. There was no time to fix the problem, we had to hope that we could cross the deep sand without causing the rear spring to fail. The surface was now broken and rough, and the axle tramp caused the spring to pop out and jam in the bodywork. To remove it needs two jacks, but Andrew somehow used them to get the spring free. Time lost, approx nine minutes. We made the finish and needed to really hustle to not lose more time on the road section to the final halt for the day.

The seventh puncture was at speed on the road, and I stopped quickly to minimise the damage to the tyre carcass. Out came Mr Halfords' foam puncture can and something that I have carried for years was utilised. No time to check the pressure, just go. I must write and tell him that they should add a one in front of the speed limit advised on the can of '45 kph'.

At the end of the day, we had survived seven punctures in three days, and five in two days as a result of bent rims.

The shock failure was a feature for all the Volvo 144s, and maybe to be expected in Tony Fall's case, as he was obviously driving much harder than us. He was snapping the ends of shocks almost daily, and these were the best competition Bilsteins. We had one start to fail on a stage and I believe that it overheated. Once cooled down, they are known to recover. Tony had one very discoloured by heat, but we think that as all our rear suspension bushing was new and the fact that Andrew had taken inordinate care in rear alignment, we did not suffer the shock failure rate that Tony suffered.

After the Lima Loop, the Rally became a profit and loss argument. We could risk much to gain a place, maybe, or drive for no mistakes and know that the car behind us could not catch us unless we made a mistake. We had only gathered six seconds penalty on the road stages, and lost out severely when at least half the field was late because of traffic conditions at the end of the day. In both cases the time allowed was cancelled, much to our chagrin. Up to fifty-nine minutes late is penalised at one second per minute, after which it becomes an hour.

New tyres had been found, but they did not wear like the Gislaveds. Without a doubt we would have made it on our planned tyre load, had not the rims been bent.

With no mistakes in mind we approached some of the stages cautiously. A steep climb in mist and rain on a tarmac section was enjoyed, not because of the abundance of power, but because our lack of speed reduced the risk. However, the rapid change to downhill was attention getting, as the surface was impossibly slippy. Our weight and tyre combination required the utmost concentration. One road section was 400 kms over the mountains with dense truck traffic. To maintain momentum was very difficult as the trucks were travelling as slow as 4 kph.

A landslide had almost closed the road, with water cascading down the slide. The water runoff was cutting deep into the mud, and the locals were throwing rocks into the water to prevent it from eroding a deep channel that would be uncrossable. We charged to the head of the queue behind the Austrian P1800, crossed the slide to be stopped by a truck broken down 100 m from the mud. Another truck was head on to us passing the stalled vehicle. The P1800 went right and I went left in a pincer movement. My exit cleared first and I darted ahead of the Volvo. That move put us ahead on the road for some 200 kms before the fast guys caught us up.

A feature of South America is 'speed bumps'. We think that there is a design award each year for the cleverest idea. They can be Harrier launching ramps, pointed sharp-edged mounts, doubles, triples, even corrugated ones. They are called 'Topes' and only 90 per cent are marked. Everyone must have hit at least one, and Clay Reggazoni retired because of his high-speed launch. His 6.3 Mercedes needed parts and so after a long saga he purchased the only 6.3 Mercedes in the country. Even with that effort, he took out the sump on another 'Tope' a short while later to end the Rally for him.

We tried to cross them one wheel at a time, a BLMH technique, that reduces the pitching moment but frightens the oncoming traffic.

South American roads can have the deepest potholes that man can devise, and they are cut even deeper prior to them being filled in. We were following a Honda Accord that was joining in the spirit of the event. He suddenly locked up all four and slid into a hole that had room for us as well. Thanks, that at least allowed us to miss it.

The final run in to Acapulco along the coast road had me in a high state of awareness. A donkey strolled out from the bushes alongside the road and Andrew locked up all the wheels. We were doing 145 kph, and a strike was inevitable as leaving the road was not an option. At the last moment the donkey turned his head away, and we drifted by under his neck. I had visions of a 'Godfather' head in my lap.

A magnificent event, long and hard. We planned to finish and throughout organised ourselves accordingly. The car was too heavy, but superbly prepared. Driven at 80 per cent we finished exactly where such effort should finish. My fourth event and a new beginning for Andrew.

Rumours of an interim event from Panama to Alaska surfaced at the final dinner in Acapulco. Whilst it had little attraction for most of the Europeans, it certainly had interest from my side of the water. As 1997 approached we were well on the way to yet another entry in the redoubtable Volvo, introducing historic rallying to North America.

With preparation of the Volvo being continued in England, there was a certain loss of continuity for me. I had seen the car in 1996 and of course was in continuous contact with Andrew, as he again completed the rebuild. We set several goals, not least of which was a serious weight reduction programme. The sump shield was replaced and the bonnet traded for a fibreglass version. These and other measures, coupled with a reduction in spares in the car, for we could not begin to match Andrew's mechanical ability, yielded a substantial decrease in weight, an increased ride height, and a more responsive feel to the Volvo.

I discovered a radically new fuel system in Wisconsin, where modification to the SUs was expected to give an increase of 10-13 per cent in power and a corresponding reduction in fuel consumption. Although I found some SUs in Toronto, they were not exactly to Andrew's liking, and lack of time forced me to abandon that idea. It would be a feature for the next event.

Little to show for the month-long event.

Looking for advertising revenue from the car was a lengthy business, but Falconbridge came good with a small package, as did Volvo Canada, who supplied a used set of wheels and tyres to be positioned in Las Vegas. The tyres of choice were still the trusty Gislaveds from Sweden, excellent in the mud and sand, but in need of care when the tarmac was wet.

I knew that selling an alien idea in the North American market was going to be difficult, for rallying is not understood in the real sense, and even more I felt that the event was in for a hard time with small town law interpreters in their tiny fiefdoms. Nick as ever was far from brilliant in marketing the rally, but then I did not have his problems. The last three have, in my view, been superb concepts that never achieved their PR potential.

It is important to recall the rule changes that were a feature of this event, and I for one put my own spin on things, which subsequently turned out not to be the case. There was a touring category which at first reading was to include all the service vehicles. Indeed, I understood that the service side was to be restricted to the touring rules. As such, the support vehicles would have to leave after the last rally car had entered a stage and in this way they would be able to save a car from exclusion, but give it only a limited advantage. As it was, the service vehicles ignored any pretext of 'touring', and were there to rebuild some very badly damaged cars. This strategic change altered the rally beyond all recognition. It put modern high-performance sports utilities on the road at the same time as the rally cars, very often as traffic that had to be circumvented every day. They had paid their dues and had every right to be there, including at-the-border delays when time was a concern for everyone. There were some harsh words until the message was understood, but for me the touring idea is a bust, as is the service vehicle, for it provides a bias that the historic rallyist in his thirty-year-old car, self-supporting, cannot overcome. The tourists soon learned that leaving the hotel after all the rally cars had departed was a guarantee of very late arrival at the next night stop. There were also too many accidents involving touring/service vehicles, but I will not ponder the reason for that, as it could be a difficult statistic to produce.

I arrived in Panama in late May to find the usual confusion regarding importation and Customs. In the end I had to go to Colon some 70 kms away to collect the Volvo. I was the last to arrive and found my car in a container with an inch of fuel swimming around in it. The Volvo had either vented or leaked, or perhaps it was the other car, a Peugeot. The Customs lady had to come with me to Panama City, which must have been an experience for her, sitting in the left-hand seat of a right-hand-drive noisy motor car in Panama traffic.

On the way to the hotel, traffic in the opposing lane slid into me, damaging the Falconbridge logo and removing some trim. Resolution was impossible, what with the traffic and the language problem. Shortly thereafter, a parked car turned into the traffic stream and I was clipped again.

It was evident that the tools had been stolen in UK, and so I could do little to work on the car until that was solved, but a look around the car park showed that there were some seriously fast vehicles present. The two South African derived Ford Capris were carrying highly potent V8 engines, reportedly in the 380-420 bhp range.

A Canadian Datsun 240Z, looking distinctly tatty, was the centre of much crashing and banging as an almost impossible rebuild was completed in the hotel car park. The pile of discarded parts grew by the minute, but some crafty local saw opportunity and they disappeared 'rapido'.

Pete arrived and we set about finding the misfiring problems and obtaining tools. The engine trouble turned out to be water in the fuel, through condensation on the voyage, and it took much alcohol/methanol to finally clear the system. Several things probably evolved from that initial problem and our attempts to fix. The SU needles were changed as were the points which showed signs of pitting. The float chamber gaskets were damaged from numerous removals, and all these problems lumped together to provide a level of stressful anticipation we could do without.

It had been planned to run a prologue in the Canal area, of two stages to get the uninitiated into the swing of things. At the last minute the military commander (US) found a small clause in the Canal Zone Treaty that prohibited the closing of any road. This kind of myopia seems to be a feature of US military thinking, and so all was cancelled. The local motor club managed to find an alternate area and so we commenced the Panama-Alaska in a massive housing development. The roads were partially completed, even to dual carriageways and a lovely clubhouse, but the houses were still a dream.

The stage had some gravel and bush, and navigation was difficult amongst the ambiguous road markings. Many experienced rallyists made mistakes leading to an unusual starting order for the following day. We made several errors, mostly compounded by cars coming the opposite way. Bob Almond's Datsun was confronted head on at a junction in a dance that could have been metallic.

The return run was slightly different and again there were many mistakes. Over the hill for a sharp right turn onto gravel, and we met the noisy Porsche of Dr Rolfe completing a reversal that put him head on to us. We were unable to safely make the turn and slid past the junction, knowing that we had missed it. I started my reversal not expecting him to come by yet again, and he was going like a bat out of hell as he just avoided us, going off in the wrong direction once more.

It took a while for us to get settled, for it had been 1970 since we last rallied together. The plan, as always, was to create a buffer on the road sections, such that the untoward could possibly be coped with.

We pressed on when others stopped for coffee, always running in the top 10-15 cars. Fuelling for minimum delay meant careful planning to never take the last fuel stop indicated, or the one where everybody would be topping up. The Volvo has a range of close to 800 kms, but needed to be much lighter than that on all those hill climb stages, of which there were many. We said it was anti-Volvo, for even the starts were uphill. Downhill we could at least feature, having good brakes and reasonable cornering power. It was a horsepower rally for most of the early stages, and our times showed that. The strategy was still: no mistakes, drive at 80 per cent and save the car. We also had to manage fatigue, being the oldest crew, and did so very effectively.

The first stage in Costa Rica was known to me, being a road through a national park. The surface was tarmac, broken and wet in places. The other Volvo of John and Igor had holed its radiator right at the stage start. They made a temporary fix, but needed water for the top up. A mountain stream lay just below and it needed a rope for the person filling the container. I held the rope for Igor as he struggled to fill up, but the jiggling around finally pulled me in for a precarious jump into mud and rocks.

We were going well when one of the V8 Capris appeared in the mirror. Being right-hand-drive, I hugged the right-hand side of the road, leaving him at least two thirds to pass. The tulip notes spoke of hazards ahead, but then he could read just as we could. He was oversteering badly as he passed us. The rear left was off the road, and Pete and I discussed his fate as we backed off to avoid a possible collision. He lost it and careered across the front of us to thump into the bank on our side of the road. The impact was damaging but not terminal, it stalled his engine and he drifted across in front of us. Round the back of him and we were off once more. With a short distance left to the end of the stage, he appeared once again. This time Pete said there was a narrow bridge ahead with a double caution. Same scenario, right hander, and he was oversteering wildly. The car started to swap from side to side and at one point we expected him to roll it, for we could see much of the underside of the Capri. He slipped into the ditch on the right, seemed to recover some control, and then dived off to the left fully in the vertical when last we saw him. There was heavily treed jungle there, and a big drop. Onlookers rushed to the scene and we pressed to the end of the stage which was almost in sight. There the stage could be stopped and help organised. We were far from sure that they were safe, but when it was known, we were able to laugh at the cartoon that they had provided.

Ahead was a night transport section that was probably the worst I knew. Climbing to over 10,000 ft, wet, in the clouds, potholed with much truck and bus traffic all moving very slowly on the steep winding road. We planned to complete as much as possible in daylight, fuelling just once. The fuel stop was slow and about twelve rally cars went by as we exited the gas station. We caught them as they were almost stopped behind a large truck grinding up the hill. They had lost their momentum but we still had a head of steam. Pete said 'go for it', and this most important overtake was completed taking the lot of them. The time we gained, stress that was avoided and punishment on the car, all add up on a 25-day event such as this. As it was, we only just made it out of the mountains for a night run in to the hotel.

The next stages were a blur of long days and careful planning. We realised that working on the car after a long day can be counter-productive, in that mistakes are made and poor decisions are accepted when you are tired. We arose early, worked on the car and hoped that nothing terminal was found. There was a strong belief that we should be able to get it to Las Vegas where Andrew could fix it. We were partly correct, only the Baja interfered. The tyre consumption looked fine on the tarmac stages, and attrition amongst the competitors was becoming a factor. Several of the leading pack went off on a fast stage; strangely the stage was closed to get them out. There was no injury or blockage of the stage and this occurrence led to other similar decisions, which were questioned by most of the drivers. It certainly favoured the fast guys up ahead, and destroyed much of my rationale. Once maybe, but the bias was too much to ignore.

The mountain roads and traffic took their toll, the German Opel falling 600 ft and the Discovery a like distance. All were OK, but not before the Mercedes troup showed its mettle (metal). Clay Regazzoni in his 6.9 rocket ship, flew off the road so far we never saw him. He recovered to try the cliff side next time, with an impact that put him

Alaska – the end of an era?

out of the Rally as a competitor. I recalled that in the early days of this big Merc, it could never finish a race, as no tyres could be found to stand the weight and torque. He says that tyre failure was the culprit both times. The Pan Americana Mercedes went down the mountainside in a more convincing fashion, injuring both when the roll cage failed. It is believed that sub-standard material was used for the cage tubing. The other Merc was again on a transport stage following a Porsche, when it entered a dust cloud and smacked into the cliff face. It was repaired, but like Regazzoni, continued as a non-competitor. Only Pat Cole's trusty 280 Merc finished in fine style, and he was fighting the Porsche club all the way.

We spent some time in the close proximity of Phil Hooper and his beautifully prepared Datsun 240Z. He had all the experience and knew what to put into a long-distance rally car. It appeared to handle superbly, but those unplanned events put him behind us, when he really outclassed us in all but the downhill stages.

Pete and I were commenting on the big buzzards seen on the road and it was said that like crows, you never hit them. Phil proved us wrong by hitting a large specimen and demolishing his windscreen in the process. It was many miles later before he could solve that problem.

Volvo did its usual show in El Salvador and Guatemala, providing a service tent and many eager mechanics. They even organised aviation fuel in Guatemala City to make up for the poor quality of the local stuff. Punctures and bent rims seemed to plague us, but in reality we suffered no more, no less than others. The problems of altitude found on the London-Mexico were never evident, and the power loss we had expected never really intruded. Most border crossings were painless, except the Mexican which we knew would be a problem. The masses of pointless paper had been reduced, but not eradicated. Running hard for the border had put us there early and ahead of the delays that compounded later.

We even arrived in Mazatlan at the hotel before the desk opened to check us in. One Volvo amongst the batch of Porsches, and I had to demand to check in first, just for the record.

We flew to La Paz whilst the cars went by sea, but were off to a quick start in what was to be the decider for us, the Baja. I had studied the Baja, watching all the TV Baja 1000 events. It was obviously going to be a car breaker, with tyre consumption a major factor. Dust and sand were catered for, but not in the fashion in which they appeared. The first two stages were along a shale road on the east coast of the Baja – fast, dusty with just a few dangerous drop-offs.

We passed the Nascar-style Ford Falcon upside down on the first serious bend, and he recovered to finish after many hours of penalties. The stage retraced its steps for a rerun and we caught the Skoda on the flat and passed him when his electrics gave out. At the turn around, everyone tried to find shade at the beach. When the restart commenced, our little parking place turned into a 'gotcha', when we broke through the surface and bogged in the soft sand. Luckily there were enough cars still around to push us out. Not a confidence builder when I believed that the Volvo had good traction in sand. The Rainsford Capri, a much-favoured car, had a head-on with a Mexican pick-up truck. It was a serious accident, but an indicator of how careful you have to be in taking nothing for granted. I believe that the truck just turned in front of the Capri, not acknowledging how fast it was moving. As part of our everyday humour, Pete and I had a never-ending joke, the punchline of which is 'Mexicans in pick-up trucks'.

It is a true story and whilst not politically correct, bears telling. A close friend was stopped late one night for speeding, in the deep south. As a Canadian, he was hauled off to night court. The judge's house was the venue, and he came downstairs in his dressing gown and slippers. His opener was as follows, 'There's three things we hate around here: niggers, spics and Mexicans in pick-up trucks, which are you?' Bill managed a flustered 'none', and was rewarded with a case dismissed. So you see . . .

I had expected to be in the rough bush country with many rocky outcrops, but the stage that set everyone back on their heels was quite short, requiring very accurate nav in difficult terrain. Starting around 28th, we were presented with numerous tracks, and cars going in all directions. There was sand specifically marked on the notes and therefore it was unexpected when we popped into a sand bowl to find five cars pointing in all over the place, stuck in sand. Pete yelled to keep going, anywhere was better than being stuck. I crashed through the bush trying to find hard ground, and having to circle when I could not find any. He jumped out to look for the road whilst I continued to circle. With much tree clearing I made it to the 'road', any chance of accurate nav now gone with the extra distance I had completed. We turned at a possible intersection, where the stones were more freshly turned than others, and found ourselves at the beach along with many other cars. Phil Hooper was directed off the cliff top by his navigator, and declined, only to get stuck in the sand. We followed the dust clouds after a fashion and reached the sand trap marked in the notes. There were several Porsches surrounded by grey and white beings digging frantically, so they must have been there for some time. Full power with a clutch groaning under the load and we made it through. This was early in the day, with another tough stage up ahead. All we could hope for was that the car would get us through.

The stage to San Felipe was really the Rally for us – a west to east crossing of the peninsula, terrible roads, dust and heat. Probably the roughest roads so far were completed without the belief that we had done too much damage. However, there was at least 200 kms of further rough stuff to get us to the coast road and the hotel. A metallic clunking noise told me that we had broken a shock absorber. From memories of the London-Mexico I knew the noise and the implications. The Volvo had been specifically strengthened to take care of this problem and it was therefore a gamble as to whether we could take it very easy and limp out. Rather than stop, we pressed on in dust and a strong desert wind. The sequence of events seemed to be a tyre failure at high speed that destroys the rim before you detect the problem. This loads up the suspension and wrecks the damper. After only a short distance, the other damper let go. With the extra strapping on the back axle, it was possible that we could make it out of there. The rear springs were putting a noisy load on the strap, and if they broke we would be left with springs that would certainly separate from their housing. Choosing a place to stop was difficult enough. The mountainside provided little room for passing and we needed a flat area to work. Perched on the only spot that appeared to give us room, we began to try and remove the broken bits and replace with the three spares we carried.

The wind was so strong that it blew Pete's travel bag off the car and over the cliff. Also it upended the toolkit given to us by Igor and John as they stopped to help. All the sockets fell in to dust and gravel which took a considerable time to find. The car was rocking badly in the swirling wind and the unstable base was a cause for concern even with two jacks for security. Laying under the car and being sandblasted in an estimated 50-kt wind was much more of a limitation than one would think. We removed the broken pieces, but the Volvo 'R' Sport replacement shocks were slightly different from the installed Bilsteins. In any event they would not slip into the upper mounting. We could not remove the sleeve without tooling, and trying to co-ordinate placing the gas shock was beyond us. The gas shock is held under pressure by a simple strap, which, when cut slowly extends hopefully allowing you to insert the bolt. Trying to compress the shock now partially mounted was impossible for us. We used all our spares, but missed every time.

After such a long time with most of the rally cars having gone through, we decided that our only choice was to limp through very slowly. The road deteriorated even more such that we were barely making 20 kph. The bouncing could be limited by careful braking, and each thump of the straps registered as a failure for me. By now it was dark and the road seemingly endless. It was with no feeling of success that we checked into the hotel with a large time penalty. We had to find local help and were told that there was one garage still open, especially for rally traffic.

It was really a tyre place but they at least had equipment that would ease the problem. They, under our watchful eye, began to replace the dampers. They seemed to be very conscientious, but finally got into a muttered Spanish situation with the damper nut. I followed him around as he worked on the nut, which looked like he had damaged it. When they announced that all was finished, there was one wheel nut missing which he said was for shop. No chance, I said, a rally car needs them all.

There was much communication between the two of them, until finally another wheel nut appeared. I was suspicious that all was not what it seemed, but at least we were a lot further ahead than had seemed possible a few hours before. A clanking noise a few metres up the road told us that our suspicions were well founded. At the hotel I checked and found that our wheel nut had been used in place of the proper nut that he had stripped. Of course a wheel nut is blind and so could not possibly be tightened enough to hold the shock in place. We had another proper nut, which was quickly used, but we were far from happy with the 'fix'. The sump guard was vibrating badly against the exhaust, and any hard acceleration created a terrible racket.

There was a transport run up to the border and the Yuma stage before Las Vegas. Could we keep it together until then? The bottom bushing of both dampers was checked at every stop and looked to be holding, but the vibration was getting worse. Bending the sump guard helped a little, reinforcing the idea that the guard was bent. As it turned out, we had broken two engine mountings, which Andrew discovered in Las Vegas.

The Yuma stage through the military training area was a long, fast stage on good gravel. We drove very steadily and lost a lot of time, but we at least made it through and looked set for Las Vegas.

The fast, good roads into Nevada made up for the earlier punishment and we arrived at the Monte Carlo Hotel to be greeted by family and friends. Andrew was there to eye his prized possession and comment that we did not appear to have damaged it 'too' much.

Concern for the repair work made for little small talk, but he was confident that all could be fixed the next morning at Jim Marsh Volvo, the main agent. My son John stepped in to help Andrew, whilst I ferreted around for parts we did not possess. He was surprised to find both engine mountings broken and looked with disdain at the Mexican repair work. I had sent him a fax reporting that we had found one bolt loose, of course as a joke, for Andrew never has anything come loose. The rear damper mount was bent but useable. It had to be as we did not possess another one. Phil Hooper threw us his newish rally tyres and so they were installed at the rear, to supplement our Volvo-supplied cache of four. The Gislaveds compared very favourably with the Michelins, lacking only the side wall protectors. We used all-new tyres for the muddy mountain stage in Dawson City, and they performed flawlessly, confirmation that they are the equal of any rally tyre, lacking grip only on damp tarmac.

The US route took us through fantastic country, well known to me from earlier trips. For many it was a disappointment as several stages were cancelled through conflict with the 'law', or the non-arrival of the emergency services. Our position varied but little from the mid-twenties, and there was pressure from several fast cars behind. The other Volvo was quicker uphill (we had different carbs), and slowly reducing the gap. It was entertaining to guess at the stage strategy, whilst we tried to maintain our 80 per cent plan. Overtaking was all but impossible on several dusty runs, and I maintained that I would do everything short of stopping to allow faster cars through.

Some very rough stages were cancelled, and I was unsure whether they were to our benefit or not. We met the Sheriff's pick-up coming towards the stage finish and knew that he would meet rally traffic that was using all the road. His head-on with the Inglebys' Mustang was remarkably gentle.

Some of the stage cancellations were mindless in that the 'law' had decided to restrict closed-road stages and it would be too time-consuming to resolve the issue.

We were able to run up front and now started to find garage services before checking in to the hotel. The car felt as though it would last, but an ominous noise from the exhaust told us that the Mexican vibration had done a number on the system under the floor. Checking well ahead showed that the only chance to find a 'Midas' shop would be in a major town. Once into Canada we would be too late arriving each evening to plan on service. Northern Montana with its 'unknown' speed limits was traversed at speed with the last target town of Kalispel.

We stopped for a tyre repair after picking up a large screw and drove quickly through the stage which ended on a narrow track down a mountainside. Around the corner was the Tuthill support vehicle, trapped and trying to back up. There was almost no room to pass and they were locked into reversing the trailer. After all our planning this was almost too much, for every minute was valuable. We finally squeaked through leaving a helluva mess behind. Full bore to Kalispel and we found our hoped-for repair shop. Only in America, you say. Washed and fed, we were out of there in forty-five minutes. Apart from having the whole of the carb assembly come loose, found at our nightly checkover, we had a plug lead fall off during a stage, but it was downhill and gross weight made up for it.

The Dawson City stage was very muddy and driven very carefully by all. Along the old creek dredgings, it was hard not to be taken back in time by the immensity of it all.

Alaska was a piece of America that does not quite conform in my estimation. Nothing works quite as advertised, and the USA slickness is just not there. The usual blatherings from the police were broadcast on local radio, about an unauthorised road race. North Pole, Alaska, you deserve each other. One smart highway patrol car assembled as many cars as possible into a convoy and led us at high speed through his jurisdiction.

The final stage was rough and luckily shortened. The other Volvo was suffering terminal problems and at our guess would not make it to the end if driven quickly. He had to go fast to just stay ahead of us and was stopped after the stage with head gasket problems. It was very tight on the final run into Anchorage and so there was no time for us to assist. We made it with a few minutes to spare and asked pointedly whether the final time would count. The Clerk of the Course replied that they would stand and we knew that we must therefore beat the Volvo of Igor and John. What we did not know was that even with a tow, they were not going to make it. John, in a rather surprising move, jumped into a passing tourer and checked in without his car or co-driver. In the turmoil at the shopping centre finish, this went unnoticed. Neither Pete nor I would have done that, but then sportsmanship has many faces. To top it all the final check-in was cancelled and so they appeared to have finished ahead of us. It would have been sour grapes to have protested at that stage, and beneath us. However, for the record, we did finish twenty-fifth, ahead of the other Volvo.

Yet again we had maintained our strategy and not gone off or seriously damaged the car. It had sustained damage in the Baja, which under other circumstances would have been fixable by a good mechanic. Andrew would have done that without a qualm.

With the tight running at the front, the attrition that was to be expected did not take place because of the immense difference that organised service vehicles make. To be able to run very light, without most spares or tyres, to check into the hotel and make the most of the rest period with little of the gut-wrenching worry, makes too much of a bias to be catered for. Of course, without the service support, the leaders would have conducted themselves differently. In my view there would have been fewer of them at the finish, but the general result would not change.

Secret support, always a feature of other rallies, is hard to detect, and those that hanker after it will find a way. My perception is that you do not put too much of your energy into chasing those who would bend the rules; there is no prize other than one's self esteem, and in the end we all know.

The invitation to compete in the Targa Tasmania caused a re-evaluation as to the priorities for 1999 and the year 2000. We had intended to enter the Trans World London-Sydney 2000, a forerunner to the Sydney Olympics. However, I was feeling distinctly mortal with the death of two Red Arrows leaders, both good friends. Do it now seemed like a more reasoned response, and 2000 was too far off for comfort.

It was also incredibly expensive and all my early attempts at finding sponsorship were met with very luke-warm reactions. Andrew had decided that 2000 was going to be his year no matter

what, and so Derek and I consigned the Volvo, as it were, to him for
the event. He actually bought another Volvo 142S, hoping to make a
better rally car out of the two.

If Betti and I were to take full advantage of an Australia trip, it
would have to be the trip of a lifetime and include as much as
possible, for another long flight to 'Oz' was not on the cards.

Phil and Lina had asked us to visit many times, and he indicated
that he was considering entering the Targa himself. He offered me
the loan of his Datsun 240Z, already quite a famous car, and
although I was honoured, it was a gesture that weighed heavily on
me. You just do not borrow someone's beautifully prepared rally car
without some thought as to the risk.

He intended to enter his 1970 TVR Tuscan with its potent Ford
BDA twin-cam engine. This would have been an excellent entry, for
the Targa has unusual rules which favour older, high-powered, re-
engined vehicles.

Preparations had to be cemented early and as an International
Entrant you are treated very well by the excellent Targa organisation.
The Island comes alive for the event which is so important for the
economy as it brings about $5M to the government coffers.
Although it is an unusually bureaucratic event, overall it works
extremely well.

We flew via Hong Kong, arriving in Perth in good time to prepare
the car and get it to Tasmania. Phil by now had given up on the idea
of entering the TVR, as it could not be finished in time and so we
had amalgamated our entries into his Datsun. The car was being
prepared about 50 km away, necessitating much commuting to get
all the last-minute details completed. Phil's busy schedule left much
of this to Betti and I, and we finally put the 240Z on the train for
transhipment to Adelaide, a three-day train ride. Not what we would
have chosen, but it turned out to be immensely enjoyable, in fact
getting the car to Tasmania was a feature of our holiday.

Western Australia will always be remembered for its colourful birds
and distinctive trees. Phil's incredible hospitality included use of his
lovely stable of motorcars. A 1969 E-type V12, a concours XK120 and
a re-engined Jaguar 3.8 with a 300ZX engine and transmission.

Because we had intended to do some flying in his Piper Malibu,
getting that sorted out took much planning. Running into the

Australian equivalent of the FAA/MOT was an experience. They go under the title of CASA, but could be better known as the campaign against aviation. I presented my documents for inspection, a current Air Transport Licence and medical, plus a recent Flight Safety Falcon training validation, all of which seemed to mean nothing. As a tourist, one does not carry log books, which are almost an anachronism anyway, by virtue of their ability to be wildly inaccurate and fraudulent. My employer scarcely acknowledges them, for sharp pencilling has got too many unqualified pilots jobs for which they were not trained. My offer to have the company telefax my details was answered by the statement that they did not use telefaxes. I guess that being an island removes the interface with other bureaucracies and cements the belief that your attitudes are shared by others. They are nationally detested in Australia, held, it would seem in contempt, and bringing about day-to-day choices for general aviation that to an outsider seem idiotic. In fact they have frightened the GenAv community by their adversarial attitudes, the end result being choices that are far from safe.

Most GA traffic neither talks to Air Traffic Control, nor files a flight plan, preferring to rely upon notification at the home base. There is an intensity of radio communication that shows a fear of using anything but the Australian version of good R/T. It seems that the idea of ATC being there to help and assist the orderly flow of traffic has long vanished. I assume IFR traffic is orderly and little different from the rest of the ICAO community. I could not check this as I was not allowed to even contemplate an IFR flight until my log book had been inspected. Needless to say, the internal strife within CASA is well known, and it shows.

We disembarked in Adelaide and drove the coast road to Melbourne, a chance to see a part of Australia that is not on most tourists' itinerary.

Overnight on the car ferry to Devonport was also enjoyable, but just to be in Launceston with the assembly of 260 Rally cars is an unforgettable memory.

We assembled in the Silverdome, a 'Velodrome' built and maintained as a banked circuit for cycle racing. A superb start to the event and the night stop for the first few days. All those interesting vehicles under one roof is a rarity indeed. Little was needed to prepare the Datsun, but I had noticed some play in the steering. The rack has a large nut adjustment and we took out what play we could. When Phil left for the start outside, the steering was locked solid. An ignominious start, being on the roadside just feet from the 'off'. With help from an old co-driver of Phil's, we made it to the stage start on time.

We took little notice of the competition, just trying to drive steadily without making any real mistakes. It was apparent that the competition in our division was powerful, two other Datsun 240s and a Porsche 911. A real 911 of our vintage would be around 160-180 bhp, but the later 911S would of course be well into the 200-plus bhp. The Targa rules allow much modification, so that our age bracket 1965-1971 is then broken into three groups of SS-standard, LMS-limited modified and M-modified. Our mods of plastic lightening panels placed us in the LMS category, but a major engine upgrade could also result in a LMS category as well.

Phil had chosen a new Dunlop tyre, rather than racing rubber used by most of the competition. It would give more uniform characteristics in wet and dry conditions. We also chose not to use pace notes, as they would have been prepared by others. I have found that pace notes not produced by yourself rarely give any degree of confidence. I believe I was proven right, if nightly conversation with other drivers is to be accepted.

We took in very easy on the prologue, for this determines the start order and, unusually, the event is run with the slowest cars starting first.

The first full day of stages showed that the Datsun is not a 'boy's' car, needing to be muscled around continually. My forearms were pumped up to solidity at the end of the day. Phil had indicated that the ceramic brakes worked better if punished, there was little feel at low loads, but tread on them and they were absolutely fantastic. Phil, quite rightly, is either on the gas or in a cloud of blue smoke, for he did build the car and knows its characteristics. I prefer to try and flow, using the excellent gearbox. Trying to change your spots in mid-rally was not going to be successful and so I stayed with what I knew. The road holding is stupendous but brutal, and after some major changes to the rebound settings on the rear shocks, and large alterations to the brake bias, all done from inside the car, we could both settle down to some steady rallying. Because the seats are bolted to the floor, I had to use foam cushions to compensate for the almost ten inches difference in stature between Phil and I. This meant that I was a loose object when in the navigator's seat, and not utilising the security of the Recaros when driving.

I know that our Volvo has a strong drive line, but the racing 300ZX bits in the 240Z were supposed to be bullet proof. Apart from incredible noises from the limited slip differential, which sounded like the back axle was separating, we competed without mechanical problems. The tyres needed to be rebalanced a couple of times to make up for the 'flat spots'. We both enjoyed the event, our concerns being similar. Neither of us like doing 200 k.p.h. down narrow roads, preferring to exercise some skill and judgement on the twisty bits.

The use of racing rubber by most competitors – you are only allowed six tyres – only once was to our advantage. A Porsche 356 was depositing oil on the racing line, high up in the mountains. Here we were in cloud and the surface was 'wet'. Only once did I utter an 'oh shit', when we slid off line and used all the available flat-ish stuff. I gather that the high-speed merchants were more embarrassed!

Neither of us was a professional navigator, Phil never having 'naved' before. We finished 7th in class out of 42, and 61st out of 260 for the overall. Right where I usually finish. Thank you Phil.

We fled immediately after the event ended, for a night dash to catch the overnight ferry, the only one that would allow us to make Townsville in Queensland the following day.

The ferry had some major failure during the night, that slowed us to two hours late in Melbourne. The plan to organise a truck pick-up for the car did not happen, nor was the rental car waiting for us as expected. Leaving the car in the shipping company car park seemed like a very poor idea to me, and with the petty crime that seems to be endemic in Oz, Phil had the Weber carbs, steering wheel and spare wheel stolen. Who carries those tools around just in case? you might well ask. Most of these crimes are not crimes of 'need' that arguably are the case in N America. Rather of 'envy': you can afford it, therefore it is OK to take it. This I see as a social virus that in some way characterises Australia.

Townsville on the NE coast is experiencing a population boom. Apart from being a major military base, it is attracting a new wave of job-seekers. The Malibu had been there for several months, getting yet another engine tear-down. The Teledyne Continental engine, used in many other installations, seems to suffer harmonic problems that have plagued an otherwise fine aircraft. Phil and I discussed the use of a new composite four-bladed prop as a means to reducing the vibration that is an issue with all the ancient designs that power most of the GenAv fleet. The German prop was supposed to offer improvements all round. Having not flown the Malibu before, I took extra care with the preparation, being left to do my thing whilst Phil was away on business.

The running-in process requires a strict procedure for the first hour, and was slightly complicated by the changes of a new prop. Not least of the complications was that we faced a 6-7 hour flight over some very inhospitable terrain, en route to Uluru or Alice Springs.

I bought new charts and was very careful with the Australian ATC, wanting no comebacks on Phil or myself.

We left on a VFR flight heading south to Ayr where I intended to check out all the systems before committing to the desert crossing. The engine numbers were carefully noted and all the systems exercised satisfactorily. At 180 kts we had ample fuel and a chance to enjoy the geography. The wind dictated a lower altitude than usual at 8,500 ft and all was fine until I noticed that each minor bump seemed to bring back the prop rpm, just a touch. The lever was fully forward, although it seemed to be locked some distance back from the maximum gate position. I could have exercised the lever, but thought about that before doing anything. We were almost at full power, temperatures and pressures all good, as it were in fifth gear, but without the ability to change down. Further reductions in prop rpm convinced me to leave well alone. A quick calculation, a guesstimate, showed that even if we had to set off downhill, with three hours to go and a slight rate of descent, we would make Alice Springs.

The rpm continued to ease back and I planned a Supermarine Swift approach, with bags of altitude in hand for the final landing. We hoped to get some technical assistance at Alice, for the prop was jammed fully coarse and the problem was almost certainly in the prop itself. The old prop took three days to arrive and be fitted before we could continue to Perth. On arrival at Murrayfield, we were grounded yet again by another crankshaft anomaly of the TCM TSIO 520 series engines.

Betti and I made our way to Sydney and straight onward to Norfolk Island for a few days R & R. Norfolk Island has always been a dream of mine since schooldays, when I was the only boy to know where it was. Being there was déjà vu, a dream that I recalled well.

Auckland was very brief, and Hong Kong a pleasant interlude, before the long trek home. So much to take in and somehow it was not the end of an era, as I had presumed.

Almost thirty years have passed since the first escapade, and the dry mouth that goes with trying to perform and yet make no mistakes is still with me – the test, forever the test, knowing that you cannot continue to run on the edge without a teeny weeny mistake. I love it – risk in an arguable fashion cleanses the soul. Knowing the everyday risks of just being on this planet, it somehow confers control in that amongst all the others, you have chosen to accept these.